The Cambridge Companion to
Victorian Culture

The Victorian era produced artistic achievements, technological
inventions and social developments that continue to shape how we live
today. This Companion offers authoritative coverage of that period's
culture and its contexts in a group of specially commissioned essays
reflecting the current state of research in each particular field. Covering
topics from music to politics, art to technology, war to domestic arts,
journalism to science, the essays address multiple aspects of the
Victorian world. The book explores what 'Victorian' has come to mean
and how an idea of the 'Victorian' might now be useful to historians of
culture. It explores too the many different meanings of 'culture' itself in
the nineteenth century and in contemporary scholarship. An invaluable
resource for students of literature, history and interdisciplinary studies,
this Companion analyses the nature of nineteenth-century British
cultural life and offers searching perspectives on their culture as seen
from ours.

Cambridge Companions to Culture

The Cambridge Companion to Modern American Culture
Edited by CHRISTOPHER BIGSBY

The Cambridge Companion to Modern Irish Culture
Edited by JOE CLEARY *and* CLAIRE CONNOLLY

The Cambridge Companion to Modern Latin American Culture
Edited by JOHN KING

The Cambridge Companion to Modern French Culture
Edited by NICHOLAS HEWITT

The Cambridge Companion to Modern Italian Culture
Edited by ZYGMUNT G. BARAŃSKI *and* REBECCA J. WEST

The Cambridge Companion to Modern German Culture
Edited by EVA KOLINSKY *and* WILFRIED VAN DER WILL

The Cambridge Companion to Modern Russian Culture
Edited by NICHOLAS RZHEVSKY

The Cambridge Companion to Modern Spanish Culture
Edited by DAVID GIES

The Cambridge Companion to Victorian Culture
Edited by FRANCIS O'GORMAN

The Cambridge Companion to
Victorian Culture

Edited by
FRANCIS O'GORMAN

CAMBRIDGE UNIVERSITY PRESS
Cambridge, New York, Melbourne, Madrid, Cape Town, Singapore,
São Paulo, Delhi, Dubai, Tokyo

Cambridge University Press
The Edinburgh Building, Cambridge CB2 8RU, UK

Published in the United States of America by Cambridge University Press, New York

www.cambridge.org
Information on this title: www.cambridge.org/9780521715065

First published 2010

Printed in the United Kingdom at the University Press, Cambridge

A catalogue record for this publication is available from the British Library

Library of Congress Cataloguing in Publication data
The Cambridge companion to Victorian culture / edited by Francis O'Gorman.
    p.   cm. – (Cambridge companions to culture)
Includes index.
ISBN 978-0-521-88699-4 (hardback)
1. Great Britain – Intellectual life – 19th century.   2. Great Britain – History – Victoria,
1837–1901.   3. Great Britain – Social life and customs – 19th century.   4. Great Britain –
Civilization – 19th century.   I. O'Gorman, Francis.   II. Title.   III. Series.
DA533.C36   2009
941.081 – dc22   2009037746

ISBN 978-0-521-88699-4 Hardback
ISBN 978-0-521-71506-5 Paperback

Contents

Illustrations

Notes on contributors

TIMOTHY ALBORN is Associate Professor and Chair of the History Department at Lehman College, City University of New York. He is the author of *Conceiving Companies: Joint-Stock Politics in Victorian England* (1998) and *Regulated Lives: Life Insurance and British Society, 1820–1920* (forthcoming). He has published widely on Victorian business and finance in journals including *Victorian Studies, Journal of Victorian Culture, Business History Review, Romanticism and Victorianism on the Net* and *Journal of Modern History*.

NICHOLAS DALY is Chair of Modern English and American Literature at University College Dublin, and he has also taught at Trinity College Dublin, Wesleyan University and Dartmouth College. He is the author of *Modernism, Romance, and the Fin de Siècle* (1999) and *Literature, Technology and Modernity* (2004), and is currently completing a study of high and low culture in the years before the 1867 Reform Act.

DENNIS DENISOFF is Research Chair in the English Department at Ryerson University, Toronto. His most recent books are the monograph *Sexual Visuality from Literature to Film (1850–1950)* (2004) and the essay collection *The Nineteenth-Century Child and Consumer Culture* (2008). He is currently writing a monograph on the eco-paganism of Victorian decadence.

NICOLA HUMBLE is Professor in the Centre for Research in Modern Literature and Culture at Roehampton University. Her books include *The Feminine Middlebrow Novel 1920s to 1950s: Class, Domesticity and Bohemianism* (2001) and *Culinary Pleasures: Cookbooks and the Transformation of British Food* (2005).

ANNA MARIA JONES is Associate Professor of English at the University of Central Florida, where she teaches Victorian literature and critical theory. She is the author of *Problem Novels: Victorian Fiction Theorizes the Sensational Self* (2007), as well as articles on Wilkie Collins, George Meredith and Sarah Grand. Her current book project is a study of Victorian revenge.

BERNARD LIGHTMAN is Professor of Humanities at York University, Toronto. Currently the editor of the journal *Isis*, he has published extensively on the cultural history of Victorian science, including his books *The Origins of Agnosticism: Victorian Unbelief and the Limits of Knowledge* (1987) and *Victorian Popularizers of Science: Designing Nature for New Audiences* (2007).

SAMANTHA MATTHEWS is Lecturer in Victorian literature at the University of Sheffield. She is the author of *Poetical Remains: Poets' Graves, Bodies, and Books in the Nineteenth Century* (2004), and has wide-ranging interests in the literature, culture and book history of the Romantic and Victorian periods. Her current project is a cultural history of manuscript and printed albums and album verse in the 'long' nineteenth century.

KATHERINE NEWEY is Professor of Drama and Theatre Arts at the University of Birmingham. She has published widely on women's writing and popular theatre of the nineteenth century, including *Women's Theatre Writing in Victorian Britain* (2005) and *John Ruskin and the Victorian Theatre* (2009). She is co-editor of the journal *Nineteenth Century Theatre and Film*.

FRANCIS O'GORMAN is Professor of Victorian Literature at the University of Leeds.

ELIZABETH PRETTEJOHN is Professor of History of Art at the University of Bristol. Her books include *Art for Art's Sake: Aestheticism in Victorian Painting* (2007), *Beauty and Art 1750–2000* (2005), *The Art of the Pre-Raphaelites* (2000) and *Interpreting Sargent* (1998). She co-curated the exhibitions *Imagining Rome: British Artists and Rome in the Nineteenth Century* (1996), *Sir Lawrence Alma-Tadema* (1996–7), *Dante Gabriel Rossetti* (2003–4) and *John William Waterhouse: The Modern Pre-Raphaelite* (2008–10).

MATTHEW RUBERY is Lecturer in Victorian Literature at Queen Mary, University of London. His book *The Novelty of Newspapers: Victorian Fiction after the Invention of the News* was published by Oxford University Press in 2009. His work on nineteenth-century print culture has appeared in *English Literary History*, *Nineteenth-Century Literature*, the *Henry James Review* and the *Journal of Victorian Culture*. He is currently working on a project about Victorian sound technology.

RUTH A. SOLIE is Sophia Smith Professor of Music at Smith College in Massachusetts. She is a former president of the American Musicological Society and is the author of *Music in Other Words: Victorian Conversations* (2004).

EDWARD M. SPIERS is the Professor of Strategic Studies at Leeds University. He has written several works on military history, including *The Late Victorian Army, 1868–1902* (1992), *The Victorian Soldier in Africa* (2004) and *The Scottish Soldier and Empire, 1854–1902* (2006). He edited *The Sudan: Reconquest Reappraised* (1998) and is currently co-editor of *A Military History of Scotland*.

JOHN STRACHAN is Professor of English at the University of Sunderland. His books include *Parodies of the Romantic Age* (1999), *British Satire 1785–1840* (2003) and *Advertising and Satirical Culture in the Romantic Period* (2007).

Acknowledgements

Thanks to Dr Linda Bree at Cambridge University Press for her prompt and professional advice through the course of this book. Thanks also to Professor Dinah Birch, Professor John Gooch, Dr Katy Mullin, Professor Edward S. Spiers and Professor Andrew Thompson. It is perhaps worth stating the obvious that the views of the contributors are their own and are not necessarily the editor's.

Victorian culture chronology

1815	Battle of Waterloo and final defeat of Napoleon
1823	Monroe doctrine formulated in US to protect American interests relative to Europe
1825	Stockton and Darlington Railway, first public railway, opens
1830	Accession of William IV on the death of George IV; French rioting sees Louis Philippe accede to throne
1831	Reform crisis in Great Britain: serious danger of rebellion; voyage of HMS *Beagle* (–1836)
1832	First Reform Act increases electorate to c. 700,000 men; abolishes rotten boroughs and increases representation of cities
1833	John Keble's 'Assize Sermon' in St Mary the Virgin, Oxford, launches the Oxford Movement; formal end of slavery in British colonies
1834	'New Poor Law'; Tolpuddle martyrs
1835	Henry Fox Talbot begins to perfect photographic techniques
1836	First train in London (between London Bridge and Greenwich)
1837	Death of William IV; accession of Victoria
1838	Founding of the Anti Corn-Law League; People's Charter (foundational document of Chartism issued)
1839	First commercial telegraph in UK; opening of West Cemetery at Highgate
1840	Penny Post introduced
1841	First paperbacks published; British occupation of Hong Kong; Thomas Carlyle, *On Heroes, Hero-Worship, and the Heroic in History*

1842	Chartist riots after the rejection of the first Chartist petition; Mudie's Lending Library opened
1843	Wordsworth becomes Poet Laureate
1844	Factory Act shortens working day, increases minimum hours of schooling
1845	Irish Great Famine period begins (–1852)
1846	Repeal of Corn Laws, a major achievement for free trade
1847	10 hours' factory act; success in use of chloroform as anaesthetic announced
1848	European revolutions; second Chartist petition; formation of Pre-Raphaelite Brotherhood; Marx and Engels, *Manifesto of the Communist Party*
1850	Tennyson becomes Laureate; restoration of Catholic ecclesiastical hierarchy; Public Libraries Act allows towns and cities to open libraries funded by local taxes
1851	Great Exhibition; John Ruskin, *The Stones of Venice* (–1853)
1852	Opening of new Palace of Westminster (Barry, Pugin and others)
1853	Crimean War (–1856)
1854	Opening of the Crystal Palace with material from the Great Exhibition
1855	Abolition of final newspaper tax; Langham Place Group founded (feminist group)
1857	Indian Uprising; Matrimonial Causes Act permits women's access to divorce under conditions
1858	Jewish Disabilities Act allows Jews to take seats in the Houses of Parliament; abolition of property qualification for MPs
1859	Charles Darwin, *The Origin of Species*; J. S. Mill, *On Liberty*
1860	Wilberforce–Huxley debate on evolution (which Huxley is generally thought to have won)
1861	American Civil War (–1865); death of Prince Albert and the Queen's withdrawal from public life; Morris, Marshall, Faulkner and Co. founded (partly by William Morris) and becomes important outlet for Arts and Crafts designs
1862	London Exposition; Lincoln's Emancipation proclamation
1864	Ruskin delivers *Sesame and Lilies* lectures at Manchester; Contagious Diseases Act (controversial in its handling of prostitution)
1865	Abolition of slavery in N. America; birth of W. B. Yeats

1866   Success with commercial transatlantic cable; Second
        Contagious Diseases Act; first petition to parliament for
        female suffrage

1867   Second Reform Act raises electorate to c. 2 million; Queen
        Victoria lays the first foundation stone for the Royal Albert
        Hall

1868   Trades Union Congress formed

1869   Suez Canal opened; first issue of *Nature*; Girton College
        Cambridge for women founded; Arnold, *Culture and Anarchy*;
        Mill, *The Subjection of Women*

1870   Elementary (Forster's) Education Act to improve children's
        schooling and its monitoring; Married Women's Property Act
        permits women rights over property and earnings after
        marriage

1871   Paris Commune; legalization of trade unions

1872   William de Morgan sets up as a potter in Chelsea

1873   Girls' Public Day School Trust established; Pater, *The
        Renaissance*

1873   Financial crisis begins US Long Depression

1874   First Impressionist Exhibition (Paris); Women's Trade Union
        League

1875   Third Republic in France; Theosophical Society founded

1876   Telephone patented; Cruelty to Animals Act

1877   Victoria crowned Empress of India; first public telephone;
        Grosvenor Gallery founded in Bond Street and becomes
        important for Aesthetic Movement art

1878   Exposition Universelle (Paris); Frederic Leighton becomes
        president of the Royal Academy (–1896)

1879   Lady Margaret Hall Oxford founded as a college for women

1880   First Anglo-Boer War (-1881); Henry James, *The Portrait of a
        Lady* (–1881)

1881   Assassination of US President James Garfield

1882   Phoenix Park Murders; Egypt now British protectorate; Leslie
        Stephen begins to edit the *Dictionary of National Biography*;
        birth of his daughter, later Virginia Woolf

1883   Death of Richard Wagner

1884   Third Reform Act, extends franchise to most adult men;
        petrol engine and machine gun invented

1885	Motor car invented; death of General Gordon at Khartoum; Criminal Law Amendment Act 1885 which restored homosexual acts to criminal status; W. T. Stead's 'Maiden Tribute of Modern Babylon' on child prostitution
1886	Gladstone's first Irish Home Rule Bill
1888	Kodak box camera invented; T. S. Eliot born
1889	London Dock Strike
1890	Tennyson records his voice on wax cylinders
1891	US International Copyright Act
1892	Keir Hardie becomes first Independent Labour MP; first automatic telephone exchange
1893	Ford builds his first car; Gandhi's first civil disobedience in India
1894	Armenian massacres (important Liberal cause)
1895	Beginning of radio communication; Oscar Wilde imprisoned for homosexual offences; Thomas Hardy, *Jude the Obscure*; Alfred Dreyfus sentenced to Devil's Island for treason, resulting in a long French political scandal
1896	Founding of *Daily Mirror*
1897	Queen's Diamond Jubilee
1898	Zeppelin builds airship; the Curies discover radium; Émile Zola published 'J'accuse' in support of Dreyfus
1899	Second Anglo-Boer War (–1902)
1900	'Black body' radiation explained by Max Planck
1901	Death of Queen Victoria and accession of Edward VII; Theodore Roosevelt becomes president of the US

1

Introduction

The facts of the past have a habit of confounding intellectual speculation. It is as well never to forget that surprise may wait around a corner to mock the best endeavours, the most serious and learned efforts to analyse history. Why might the Prime Minister William Gladstone have demurred about recommending to Queen Victoria that Alfred Tennyson, her poet laureate, be offered a baronetcy? Perhaps, in 1883, Gladstone might have wondered if literature was really a dignified enough career – if 'career' it was – to deserve such an honour. Could writing poetry really qualify one to speak in the House of Lords? Perhaps he felt that Tennyson's political poems were no ample recommendation for actual involvement in politics. Perhaps the poet's famous religious uncertainty might be too controversial for the Bishops in the upper chamber. None is a poor suggestion. But Hallam Tennyson records in his *Memoir* (1897) of his father the real reason. 'The only difficulty in Gladstone's mind', Hallam remembered, 'was that my father might insist on wearing his wide-awake in the House of Lords.'[1] It is a ludicrous turn, a confounding of serious explanations by the comical practicality of a hat. That hat *was* a difficulty, no doubt. But Hallam's account is awkward all the same, for it is not comfortable to find such trivialities in the heart of sober matters. Tennyson's wide-awake is worth remembering, though. It has a point to make, however unlikely that may seem, which is relevant to a compendious project of the current kind. It might best be recollected as a quirky reminder of how quickly history, the business of trying to understand and analyse the past, can slip out of our hands. It is as well to test the grandest theory against the humblest of facts; to make some space for the sudden and strange and unpredicted; to remember that grave argument and deep thought are hardly the only motivators of human behaviour; and that intellectually coherent analyses of the past are not guaranteed merely because they are intellectually coherent.

Neither yielding to the temptation of over-confidence, nor forgetting the importance of going beyond the expected, historical analysis is always engaged in the curious task of trying to understand the past without all the data to hand. That is always to be running-up against a kind of defeat. It is as well to be frank about this as well as rigorous. But that failure does not mean the historian's efforts are forever fruitless, or that the terms by which we might make attempts to understand the past are always already out of order. It means simply that we must be candid about what the historian – literary or cultural historian included – is doing. We must not claim to know too much; we must retain some scepticism and readiness to change; be doubtful of what look like accepted terms that have not been thought about for a long time; in particular be doubtful about metonymy, about making single events or instances stand without qualification for larger wholes; be doubtful of coherence that persuades only because it *is* coherent; be wary of plausibility that resides only in rhetoric and not in the concepts the rhetoric is struggling to describe. A permanent look-out for evidence that does not fit in with grand narratives, or expected routes, is a great ally. Readiness for surprise, readiness to admit that not everything has been taken into account: these are not the worst attitudes with which to approach the difficult business of understanding the past.

In endeavouring to discuss 'the Victorian period', this collection of essays does not, at least in one headline matter, claim too much. What weight can be put on 'Victorian' as an interpretive category? What is to be gained in looking at *Victorian* as opposed to *nineteenth-century* culture? The period label, of course, is enabling and distracting. Currently, it is attracting renewed attention, not least because our own relationship with the nineteenth century shifted both significantly and subtly with the arrival of the new millennium. Suddenly the nineteenth century became *two* centuries away, and that accidentally created a new opportunity to rethink the Victorian just as anniversaries of individual deaths can sometimes be the starting point for real re-assessments. Richard Price, in the stimulating study published just before the new millennium, *British Society, 1680–1880: Dynamism, Containment and Change* (1999), suggested historians were wrong to think of the Victorian period as a period not least because key matters of government, economics and social organization remained intact from the end of the seventeenth century to the seventh decade of the nineteenth. Martin Hewitt replied with a prize-winning essay in *Victorian Studies* proposing an argument that the Victorian period *did* make sense viewed, at the least, from the perspective of economic history, relations between metropolis and province, cultural geographies, visual regimes, 'dogmatic doubts' and conceptions of time.[2] The *Journal of Victorian Culture* ran intriguing discussions alongside this about when the period began and when it ended.[3] Some authors have rejected the title altogether and some academics prefer to avoid it even to the point of the celebratedly awkward – and probably mythic – job advertisement for a 'Lecturer in Nineteenth-Century British Literature (Not Romantics)'. The problems with 'Victorian' are not hard to find. The adjective is parochial. It is monarchical, too – it suggests an aristocratic history rather than one about all classes and social divisions. It is plainly fortuitous rather than necessary: why should the reign of a single constitutional monarch, albeit a long one, cover a period that was distinctive from what went before and what came after?

For others, there is more to be said on the side of 'Victorian'. It has never lost its champions. Among the literary critics, there have been more than elsewhere. Such scholars have generally been more comfortable with the distinctiveness of some *Victorian* literary forms and practices of writing – the realist novel, the dramatic monologue, the ghost story, naturalism – than some historians are with the idea that historical change occurs in the nineteenth century to a degree sufficient to define a discrete period. But what the literary critic sees is discipline specific. It is not necessarily what the musical historian, or the analyst of the development of electric-powered technology, or the historian of fashion, or the scholar of the development of empire, or even the student of the tumbler pigeon, so suggestive to Charles Darwin, sees. What is important is the object of analysis and what narrative of period it will sustain. And therein is the guiding assumption of this collection of essays, for 'Victorian' is defined as a *post hoc* category, an idea that exists in the critical analysis of critics subsequent to its end. And how one defines the Victorian – whether one finds it useful at all – depends on what story is being told about the period, not the other way around.

The 'Victorian' as a historical category does not exist in any meaningful way prior to the set of knowledges from which it is derived. As a historical category, it is continually being redefined by critics examining different aspects of an exceptionally diverse set of possible knowledges. 'Victorian' has local aptness or inaptness primarily. This *Cambridge Companion to*

Victorian Culture accepts that writing history starts with a set of choices. It is always a matter of paths followed or not. What is 'history', what makes up the contents of a 'historical' account, is the product of after-the-event decisions about the objects of analysis: 'history' as a discourse is created by the act of drawing out a narrative or structuring an argument from particular sets of data, from particular objects of concern. There are always, only, different histories, different ways of conceiving the past – and, accordingly, different 'Victorian' periods or arguments about why there is not a Victorian period. The specially commissioned essays comprising this collection are not to be read as accounts of different aspects of the same 'period'. They are not offered as if somehow they add up into a coherent, organic whole that reveals to the reader a single, consistent and defining idea about what the Victorian age was. There are Victorian *periods*, and there are notions of the nineteenth century that do not find the label 'Victorian' useful at all.

Such mobility does not absolve the historical critic from the requirement for rigour, coherence, exactness. It does not mean that history, or 'the Victorian period', is merely whatever one thinks it is or would like it to be. The idea of the period – or otherwise – must arise from the careful analysis of a set of data. The essays here have different notions of how the nineteenth century might be understood in period terms. But difference does not mutate into indifference. A consciousness of the local and provisional nature of an idea of a historical period does not become a casualness, an off-handedness about the way in which time might be divided into phases, spans, eras. Neither does that consciousness mean casualness towards empirical fidelity, analytical credibility. Implicitly and explicitly, authors here are conscious of the integrity of their notion of a period, through the careful analysis of their particular object of knowledge, but they are also conscious that they are each offering but one way in. John Strachan's conception of part of the history of print culture moves seamlessly from the Regency into the mid-nineteenth century. Implicitly, he finds the 1837–1900 frame less enabling than one that recognizes a marked continuum between the first decades of the nineteenth century into the 1850s and 1860s, particularly in relation to the writing of Charles Dickens. Matthew Rubery finds a more specifically 'Victorian' period visible through the history – the rise, rise and rise – of the national newspaper. Bernard Lightman's investigation of the role of the scientific naturalists defines another way in which a 'Victorian' period can have a specific identity through, here, the struggle for cultural authority of men including Charles Darwin, Thomas Henry Huxley and John Tyndall. Periods are negotiated as they are made: they are the offspring of retrospective tact.

One way in which the 'Victorian' might be understood is, certainly, through the notion of 'culture' itself. The idea of 'Victorian culture', indeed, has a unique aptness because the Victorians designed a powerful meaning *for* 'culture'. And they argued about who had, or should have, access to it. Matthew Arnold's conception of the healing and restorative power of an idea of 'culture' assumed a body of texts, a canon of writing, which, properly possessed, defined as it sustained a civilized mind. That canon was a bulwark against egotism, narrow-mindedness, *parti pris* and ignorance. Around Arnold's vision of a conflict between culture and anarchy – his *Culture and Anarchy* was published in 1869 – was a set of debates about the purposes of literary or humane knowledge and the objectives of education. Anna Maria Jones considers some of them in her analysis of Victorian 'literary theory' (a proleptic category, of course, but a useful one). One conception of the Victorian is, accordingly, of a period pursuing arguments about the identity of culture itself and discussing the continuing development of a division between high and popular culture; the relationship between a literary and a scientific education; the purposes of the ancient Universities of Oxford and Cambridge in relation to new institutions and their educational priorities; how class and sex and 'race' allowed or forbade access to particular forms of culture; the relationship between the ruling landed classes and culture; the claims of the ancient classics to form the texts of culture against modern writing. There were many questions that derived from such considerations and they are present in different chapters of this book. The volume is, in this respect, maintained by arguments about what and where 'Victorian culture' was.

If the Victorians regarded the matter of access to Arnoldian culture as inseparable from the sustainability of a civilized life, we in the twenty-first century still have to make up our mind about the status of such culture. Should we celebrate popular culture and encourage it as a formal part of education or should educators endeavour to make high culture available to all? Are educators in danger of perpetuating oppression by imagining that some sectors of a population can deal only with undemanding versions of popular culture and not with High Art? Arguments about 'culture' may be one way to define the Victorian period as a period. But they also indicate one of the multitudinous ways in which the

Victorian age had not ended. The Victorians in many different ways live on, not least because contemporary liberal societies wrestle with terms, arguments and irresolutions that still look like theirs. What is the relationship between an education based on skills-learning and a humane, liberal education? What are the merits of a scientific versus a literary education? What is the difference between education and training? Is 'high' culture necessarily accessible only to a few and in what ways is popular culture educative? Who should have access to culture – or education – and on what terms? What constitutes success in culture? Beyond these arguments is the panoply of Victorian 'afterlives', too, which are diversely intriguing journalists and critics at present. Do the Victorians still live? They are present in contemporary debates about ethnicity, gender, moral responsibility, the limits of religion, the idea of a city, the expectations of fictional realism, the structure of the British railway system, modern divisions of domestic space, ideas of justice, the romance of the English pub, the censorship of literature and media. The Victorians, or ideas imagined to *be* Victorian are, as Samantha Matthews indicates, everywhere.

But what is called 'culture' has now, in academic writing at least, conspicuously changed. Arnold's sense of a body of valuable literary knowledge is still present if more in private conviction than public, academic discourse. For some, it has been tainted with political anxieties about elitism, and for others, Arnold's canon of culture is a too distant and arduous ideal. But 'culture' has come to serve in contemporary academic discourse far from any Arnoldian sense. Historical critics once spoke about 'the history of x'. The implication was, perhaps, that there were extractable, discrete histories to be disinterred about whatever 'x' was: international relations, Judaism, the periodical press, beer. But human activities, understood through the compound analytical models of Marxism, cultural materialism, New Historicism, Michel Foucault and Pierre Bourdieu, are now perceived – even by those who have come to know this intellectual succession from a distance – as surrounded by, inscribed by and in continual negotiation with a 'culture'. That conception of culture is omnipresent in this *Cambridge Companion* which is, in this sense, about many different nineteenth-century cultures: oral culture, print culture, popular culture, the culture of the street musician, the culture of the dead, nineteenth-century reading culture. 'Culture' now in academic discourse means an irreducible and complex web of social forces and energies. It is necessary to speak of the 'culture of x', not simply its 'history'. 'Culture' means an environment – intellectual, material, economic, social – that creates and negotiates with the individual thing or person or discourse or activity; that surrounds and defines human labour; that inscribes, makes possible and limits all categories of human endeavour. Without this matrix of culture – its limits hardly knowable, its actions and reactions hard to fix – neither individual actions nor human productions now make sense.

Of course, there are difficulties with this near-ubiquitous historical method. How much is the business of cultural history as it is now practised encouraging, accidentally, what Arnold found among the Nonconformists of the mid-nineteenth century: narrowness, one-sidedness, incompleteness? Such a result might seem the least likely outcome of a critical inquiry built on an acceptance of highly complex social networks and energies, the limits of which are barely knowable. But present-day cultural analysis is sometimes in danger of excusing itself from being a really serious attempt to understand the past *because* of that seemingly limitless conception of context or culture. Such analysis is too close to claiming that history is never really knowable because it is *too* multifarious, because context or culture are too vast and unwieldy. The contexts that need to be re-assembled are, it may be, beyond reach, and too provisional for certainty in the limitless polygon of what 'culture' is. The pattern is beyond our grasp. The cultural or literary historian in turn must now explore the interpretive power of a more limited selection of individual contexts and offer new readings of human productions based perhaps on one or two new contextual reconstructions. The sense that such readings are always limited, that they implicitly acknowledge their own narrowness, is always there. The narrowness is understandable and unavoidable. But the persistence of a historical method that recreates individual contexts because the whole web is too great must guard itself against parochialism.

With an intended audience comprising largely literary readers, this volume naturally examines forms of print culture in variety: satirical prints; the history of newspapers and periodicals; the variety of forms of print that comprise popular culture – from the ballad to the new popular daily newspaper and the 'sensation' press. Popular culture more widely defined cannot now be excluded from cultural history by the rubric of an Arnoldian canon that insists on writing that is not ephemeral but permanent. Literary history that remembers primarily those who read high art poetry and forgets the readers of the popular press or visitors to the music hall offers a curious, off-balance account of Victorian aesthetic life. Dennis Denisoff provides a discussion of critical models of popular culture in the nineteenth century and of the models that have emerged in subsequent academic debate. His chapter analyses the dubiety that attended the development of popular-cultural forms at the end of the nineteenth century from, often, representatives of high culture. And popular culture, as Denisoff explains, attracts many myths. There was, for a start, no necessary alignment then (as there is not now) between 'popular culture' and the working classes, and neither was there then (as there is not now) any absolute divide between 'high' culture and popular.

Elizabeth Prettejohn considers the nature of Victorian painting in relation to the shape of culture too, arguing that, properly understood, Victorian art defined its own sense of modernity that was as robust as the modernity of the French schools, so often prized above the achievements of the British. Domestic crafts and arts – food, household decoration, fashion – comprised activities of growing significance for the middle-class woman in the period. Nicola Humble's chapter examines the development of arts of living – and their role in *defining* the new Victorian middle class. Much was at stake in the construction of ideas of home where women proposed an image of leisure even as they laboured to control the demands of domestic space: the middle-class home accrued to itself the expectation of social stability that was placed against a rapidly changing and risky public world. There were national dramas behind closed doors. Katherine Newey's essay offers a survey of some of the most engaging and important actual dramas: those acted on the nineteenth-century stage. Her topic is, in part, the responsiveness of the Victorian theatre – long regarded in critical prose as intellectually and aesthetically impoverished – to contemporary nineteenth-century life. Once again, issues about the nature of what would later be named an Arnoldian culture – access to it and state control of it – emerge in the relations between 'legitimate' and 'illegitimate' theatre. If there is a myth of Victorian Great Britain as without the stage until Oscar Wilde, then there is a similar conviction that it was also a land without music. Ruth A. Solie contemplates this problem and suggests, against that perception, some of the lively forms of musical activity, and some of the ideological work that music undertook in a period in which, in fact, remarkable developments in home and public music-making took place.

In so many ways the Victorian world was becoming smaller. Another way of perceiving a Victorian period is through the changes to an individual's sense of connections with others. If space travel beyond the planet was still possible only imaginatively, the movement of human meanings across huge terrestrial distances became a reality with the development of telegraph technology and the utilization of Samuel Morse's code, patented in 1840. This was a transformation in how an individual might understand himself or herself in relation to a greater web of human life. Darwin's celebrated metaphor of the tangled bank in *The Origin of Species* (1859) – his image of the interrelation of living things – has often been used to exemplify the Victorian period's new sense of the profound connectedness of things. But telegraphy suggested, at first primarily to the commercial and journalists' world, what it meant to communicate and to *live* in a complicated web, in a strange and new network of international relations. '[S]ound it far, from shore to shore,/To vibrate o'er earth evermore', wrote James Breeze of the news Morse could carry in *The Glory of the Age: The Atlantic Cable – A Poem on the Wondrous Achievements of Science* (1866), a poem confident that human progress came from technological invention.[4] Nicholas Daly examines some of the changes to Queen Victoria's world through such innovation and not only in the realm of communications technology. The telephone, electric light, train, camera, cinema, phonograph and the motor car were the products of the nineteenth century, with all their multiple implications and irreversible consequences for lived life and the shape, the *feel*, of Victorian modernity.

If the Victorian world was, through technology, becoming smaller, the Queen's armies knew in a peculiarly literal way how remote some of its borders still were. Conventional histories of the nineteenth century – concerned with politics, economic development and social change – have often omitted the history of the Victorians at war though, as Edward S. Spiers indicates, warfare across the terrain of empire was an almost constant feature of Victorian life. His chapter probes in particular the response of literary and artistic figures to war, as well as its conflicted ideological basis. Technology sustained Great Britain's advanced capitalist society, making the transfer of commercial news faster (including from the war front), the movement of goods quicker, the exploitation of new and remote markets more possible. Timothy Alborn discusses major facets of Victorian business and economics, a topic that has newly found a wider audience, including literary scholars, engaged in nineteenth-century analysis. By the middle of the first decade of the present century capitalism had become a less objectionable subject for many literary scholars of the Victorian period, a large number of them distant from the convictions – though not explanatory models – of Marxist critique. The collapse of the Soviet Union had something do with that alteration in view; generational change, and the prosperity of the 1990s and early in the new millennium were relevant as well. Capitalism's apparent inseparability from democracy emerged morally in its favour, not least as the United States assumed the position of sole super-power. But this book is published in the midst of change. The consequence on the intellectual perception of capitalism following the fracturing of the global economy after the 2008 sub-prime crisis has yet to be seen. The 'New Economic Criticism' in the academy, not least, will need to digest what may be a huge re-orientation of perception about what capitalism can deliver and sustain. Historians of nineteenth-century banking, business and economics – the foundations of the contemporary financial world – have never interested readers more.

The relationship between aesthetic productions and science was a matter of considerable interest to the Victorians themselves. Science, in its full diversity, has now become one of the most revealing topics for cultural analysis in the period. And, of course, the study of science provides another way of defining the 'Victorian' period. The age of the scientific naturalists; the shift of authority in University education from the Anglican establishment to the men of science ('scientist' was not a widely used term in the nineteenth century); the assertion of the experimental method; the professionalization of science and its division into the disciplines and sub-disciplines that are still familiar today comprise some of the issues in Bernard Lightman's chapter, as he examines the breakdown of natural theology as the authoritative mode for reading nature in the nineteenth century. Throughout, connections with literary writing are examined and the place of scientific argument in ideas and practices of writing apparently distant from the world of Darwin, Tyndall and Huxley are drawn out. The history of Victorian science underlines, as many of the chapters here implicitly do, the deeply rooted nature of Christian theology, variously understood, in Victorian life. But that theology was changing and its authority altering. My chapter, on the Victorians and the dead, considers the retreating authority of Christian ideas of eternal life and resurrection, and examines how they were re-imagined and re-created in literary and visual texts and in ideas about how literary texts were, literally, readable.

These essays do not make up various facets of a single, complex but finally unitary claim about what constitutes 'the Victorian period'. They propose different possible avenues into the stretch of historical time between 1830 and 1900 and ways in which that time may or may not be regarded as a period. They are not a single narrative and, indeed, I have deliberately introduced them in this chapter in a slightly different order from how they appear subsequently: it is a small gesture to underline the importance of recognizing the provisional and contingent that lie at the heart of efforts to construct narratives about the past. Offered to the reader as arguments about the nineteenth century arising from particular choices of the object of knowledge, all the essays derive from sustained research. And research, of course, means not only the tracking down of facts or sources in archives or online: it means reading and thinking. Primary material remains at the heart of the literary critical enterprise as at the heart of all historical inquiry. The wealth of material to be read is vast and there is no substitute for it. Perhaps we are approaching in some areas of literary critical inquiry in nineteenth-century studies an overly narrow sense of what constitutes the appropriate knowledge from which generalization is possible. But the opportunities for reading Victorian texts have never been more numerous. There is nothing but sustained growth in the range of nineteenth-century primary material in print or available cheaply from used-booksellers: even buying *nineteenth-century* editions of nineteenth-century works still does not require the bank account of an emperor. Digitization, e-books, online libraries and databases are beginning to make more primary material accessible for those with computer access. But the trick is to read the texts. It may be that the best thing for the reader to do is to set this volume aside at once and turn to a novel, a poem, a play, a diary, a volume of correspondence, a biography from the nineteenth century. It is, at any rate, to facilitate such turns that this *Cambridge Companion* is intended. In the service of a vast and challenging canon, this volume is confident of the exceptional stimulation that readers can obtain from coming to know as much of it as possible for themselves.

Notes

1 *Alfred Lord Tennyson: A Memoir by his Son*, 2 vols. (London: Macmillan, 1897), vol. ii, 299.
2 Martin Hewitt, 'Why the Notion of Victorian Britain *Does* Make Sense', *Victorian Studies*, 48 (2006), 395–438.
3 See *Journal of Victorian Culture*, 11 (2006), 'Round Table on Richard Price *British Society, 1680–1880*', 146–79.
4 James Breeze, 'The March of Science: The Electric Telegraph across Ocean', accessible from http://o-lion.chadwyck.co.uk.wam.leeds.ac.uk/, 28 Aug. 2008.

2
———

Science and culture[1]

In 1882, in the pages of the widely read journal, the *Nineteenth Century*, Matthew Arnold (1822–88), poet, essayist and social and literary critic, took the biologist Thomas Henry Huxley (1825–95) to task for his views on the ingredients of a proper education. Arnold rejected Huxley's proposal 'to make the training in natural science the main part of education, for the great majority of mankind at any rate'. Scientific knowledge, Arnold declared, was unable put us 'into relation with our sense for conduct, our sense for beauty'. The moral and aesthetic impulses were essential to human beings because of our very nature. If science could not fulfil basic human needs, then, Arnold argued, we must turn to another body of learning as the foundation of education: classical language and literature. As befits a graduate of Oxford, Arnold defended the value of 'knowing the Greeks and Romans, and their life and genius, and what they were and did in the world'. He maintained that the 'instinct for beauty' and the 'instinct for conduct' were served by classical literature 'as it is served by no other literature'.[2] From Arnold's perspective, Huxley's science-based conception of education was impoverished.

In the past, Arnold's trenchant criticisms of Huxley have often been read as evidence of a rupture between science and literature continuing into the twentieth century, most poignantly expressed by C. P. Snow in his *The Two Cultures* (1959).[3] But does the debate between Huxley and Arnold in the early 1880s really mark the origins of a cultural divide between scientists and literary intellectuals? Can we read the debate in a different way that will shed light on the deeper relationship between science and culture in the Victorian period? If we examine Huxley's 'Science and Culture' (1880), the essay that elicited Arnold's condemnation, it is clear that the biologist is not attempting to divorce science from literature, or from culture. On the contrary, Huxley's main goal is to redefine the Victorian concept of culture while including a significant role for literature in education.

Huxley valued literature, modern as well as ancient. 'I am the last person to question the importance of genuine literary education', he asserted, 'or to suppose that intellectual culture can be complete without it.' He rejected educational establishments that produced 'lop-sided men'. Huxley believed that 'an exclusively scientific training will bring about a mental twist as surely as an exclusively literary training'. Huxley was not arguing for the elimination of literature from education, rather, he was claiming that modern literature and science should be added to a curriculum overly focused on classical literatures and languages. Moreover, he wanted to broaden the definition of culture to include science. Assenting to Arnold's proposition in his *Essays on Criticism* that 'a criticism of life is the essence of culture', Huxley denied that literature alone was competent to supply knowledge of life's possibilities and limitations. 'After having learnt all that Greek, Roman, and Eastern antiquity have thought and said, and all that modern literatures have to tell us,' Huxley wrote, 'it is not self-evident that we have laid a sufficiently broad and deep foundation for that criticism of life, which constitutes culture.' Huxley rejected the view that culture was obtained only by a liberal education synonymous with instruction in one particular form of literature, that of Greek and Roman antiquity. He objected that those who were learned in other branches of knowledge were perceived as specialists 'not admissible into the cultured caste'.[4]

Huxley's protest against 'the pretensions of our modern Humanists to the possession of the monopoly of culture' (152) was an integral part of his larger campaign to wrest cultural authority from the leading Anglican clergy and put it into the hands of the modern scientist. Like-minded scientists, including the physicist John Tyndall, joined him in this battle. Early in their careers they fought to be considered part of the intellectual elite and they argued that this elite should endorse a scientifically inflected notion of culture appropriate for a modern age born of the industrial revolution. Their wish to reconfigure the concept of 'science' was closely related to their redefinition of what constituted 'culture'. Just as 'culture' had to be pried from the grasp of the Anglican clergy, so did the notion of science as handmaid to religion. Oxford and Cambridge, the same Anglican universities that supported Arnold's emphasis on classical literature and languages, were also the home of the natural theology that Huxley and his allies wanted to eliminate from science.

Many of Huxley's beliefs were shared by key literary figures of the day. Novelists belonging to the literary school known as 'realism', including George Eliot and Thomas Hardy, also recognized the importance of modern science. They incorporated scientific themes into their novels. Both the Victorian novel and the science of Huxley and his allies encouraged the secularizing of nature and society and both explored the consequences of secularization characteristic of mid-Victorian England.[5] The notion, then, that the Huxley–Arnold debate signalled the beginning of a cultural divide between scientists and literary intellectuals, is misleading. During the Victorian period there were at least two groups vying for cultural authority, and both had their science and their literature. In this chapter I will attempt to map out the parallels between science and literature in the larger cultural context of the Victorian period. I will argue that Huxley and his friends joined the literary realists to form a prominent group that promoted a culture shaped by science. Though influential, this group's programme for a redefinition of science, as well as its promotion of a scientific culture, was resisted by a powerful, though informal, coalition that included Scottish scientists, conservative Christians, spiritualists, idealists, feminist anti-vivisectionists and working-class intellectuals.

The culture of scientific naturalism

When Queen Victoria ascended to the throne in 1837, the aristocratic gentlemen of science, largely Oxbridge-educated Anglicans, dominated the scientific scene. Relatively few of the gentlemen of science were actually genteel by birth. They were committed to the serious pursuit of knowledge as a vocation, but not for pay. George Airy, Charles Babbage, John Herschel, George Peacock, Adam Sedgwick and William Whewell, all Cambridge men, were some of the key gentlemen of science. William Buckland from Oxford University, Charles Lyell, his student, and Richard Owen of the Royal College of Surgeons were also important figures in this group. Many of these men were instrumental in the creation of the British Association for the Advancement of Science (BAAS) in 1831, which came to be seen as the public face of science. Embracing natural theology, the gentlemen of science pointed to a divine order behind both nature and society. This was a message tailored for a British nation undergoing the stress of the 1830s and 1840s, turbulent decades when heated debates over reform brought the country to the brink of revolution.

The success of the Great Exhibition of the Works of Industry of All Nations, held in London in 1851, signalled the beginning of a new era for science. The Exhibition was housed in an immense glass and iron building of unique architectural design, earning it the nickname 'Crystal Palace'. Never before had an industrial exhibition drawn such huge crowds. The aspiring young biologist T. H. Huxley wrote to his future wife in 1851 that visitors to the Crystal Palace approached it with awe and reverence, as if they were on a sacred pilgrimage to a holy shrine. 'The great Temple of England at present', Huxley told her, 'is the Crystal Palace – 58,000 people worship there every day. They come up to it as the Jews came to Jerusalem at the time of the Jubilee.'[6] The popularity of the Crystal Palace sparked a deep interest in science, and in museums and galleries of practical science, including the Royal Polytechnic Institution, managed after 1854 by the colourful lecturer John Henry Pepper (Figure 1). In order to compete with the other attractions in London, Pepper began to emphasize entertainment over instruction. Increasingly, he incorporated optical tricks, and, in 1862 created his sensational ghost illusion that drew a few thousand visitors a day to the Polytechnic at its peak. He also presented plays and musical acts, which underscored how much science was a part of general culture.

The natural history crazes of the 1850s were another indicator of a growing interest in science. Two years after the opening of the Crystal Palace, the aquarium became a national rage and members of the British middle class travelled to the coast to comb the beaches for specimens. At the same time fern collecting became a widespread fad. The Victorian fascination with aquaria and ferns was followed by an intense curiosity in dinosaurs. When the Crystal Palace Company relocated the Great Exhibition as a permanent site in Sydenham, just south of London, a new exhibit of extinct reptiles and mammals became one of the most popular attractions. The public was treated to the first life-sized restorations of the *Ichthyosaurus*, the *Plesiosaurus*, pterodactyls, the *Megalosaurus* and the *Iguanodon*, built by the natural history illustrator Benjamin Waterhouse Hawkins in collaboration with the anatomist Richard Owen. Opening on 10 June 1854, over a million people a year for the next fifty years saw these full-scale models. Dinosaurs became part of the popular imagination. Victorians also came into contact with science at social gatherings, known as

INTERIOR OF THE POLYTECHNIC INSTITUTION, SHOWING THE DIVING BELL.

Figure 1. The Great Hall of the Royal Polytechnic Institution, home of the showman of science, John Henry Pepper. From University of Westminster Archive, R Illust 10.

'conversazione', held by learned or art societies. Conversazione usually included an informal meeting, an exhibition and one or more lectures. Here science became part of a culturally sophisticated urban middle-class identity.[7] The Victorians encountered science in countless articles in the periodical press. The latest scientific discoveries and dazzling technological inventions, whether they were Darwin's theory of evolution by natural selection, or the first successful laying of undersea cable across the English channel in 1851, were the hot topics of the day. Science was everywhere – in the news, in the monthly and quarterly periodicals, in literature, in the museums, in exhibitions and even in the theatre. Science became an integral part of Victorian culture after the mid-century. Historians have sometimes referred to the period from 1850 to 1890 as an age of the cult, or worship, of science.

Scientific naturalists rode the wave of this newfound interest in the natural world. When Huxley's generation of scientific practitioners arrived on the scene at the mid-point of the century, a changing of the guard took place within the scientific leadership, though it was not without friction. Many of the middle-class 'Young Turks' of science, including Huxley and John Tyndall (1820–93), came from outside the Oxbridge environment (see Figure 2). Where the gentlemen of science had insisted that knowledge of nature was to be conceived within a religious framework, the aims of this new group included the secularization of nature, the professionalization of their discipline and the promotion of expertise. Huxley (see Figure 3) had a catchy name for this new vision of an emancipated, professionalized science: scientific naturalism. He believed that the development of scientific naturalism had been in the making for centuries. He wrote

> It is important to note that the principle of the scientific Naturalism of the latter half of the nineteenth century, in which the intellectual movement of the Renascence has culminated, and which was first clearly formulated by Descartes, leads not to the denial of the existence of any Supernature; but simply to the denial of the validity of the evidence adduced in favour of this, or that, extant form of Supernaturalism.

Huxley argued that proper science excluded any reference to a divine being – scientists should stick to studying observable causes and effects in nature. Huxley was considered to be one of the leaders of a significant group of intellectuals, many of them scientists, which aggressively

Figure 2. A caricature of John Tyndall, pictured as an eminent man of science and popular lecturer. From *Vanity Fair,* 6 Apr. 1872.

Figure 3. A caricature of Darwin's Bulldog, Thomas Henry Huxley, spoiling for a fight. From *Vanity Fair,* 28 Jan. 1871.

pushed for a redefinition of science in the latter half of the nineteenth century. The ranks of scientific naturalists included Charles Darwin, the philosopher of evolution Herbert Spencer, the physicist John Tyndall, the mathematician William Kingdon Clifford, the founder of eugenics Francis Galton, the statistician Karl Pearson, the anthropologists John Lubbock and Edward Tylor, the biologist E. Ray Lankester, the doctor Henry Maudsley and a group of journalists, editors and writers such as Leslie Stephen, G. H. Lewes, John Morley, Grant Allen and Edward Clodd.[8]

But the scientific naturalists were not just aiming at a reform of scientific theories and institutions. They were also interested in transforming British culture as a whole. They put forward new interpretations of humanity, nature and society derived from the theories, methods and categories of empirical science, especially evolutionary science. Many of the scientific naturalists came out of humble middle-class backgrounds. They chose to challenge the cultural authority of the Anglican, aristocratic establishment by claiming that they provided the best intellectual leadership of a modernized and industrialized Britain. They viewed many of the gentlemen of science, trained at Oxford, Cambridge and other aristocratic institutions, as the scientific representatives of the old establishment. This is why Huxley was so critical of Arnold's conception of education, despite their shared liberalism.[9] Arnold's emphasis on classical literature and languages smacked of his Oxford training. Huxley desired to undermine the power of Anglican and aristocratic institutions as they were obstacles in his goal to reform British culture. In one essay, 'A Liberal Education; and Where to Find It', he declared that 'our university trainings give but a narrow, one-sided, and essentially illiberal education'.[10] In their contest for cultural authority with the Anglican clergy, Huxley and his allies worked towards a redefinition of both British science and culture based on a more secular, liberal and middle-class vision.

To reach their goal of transforming British science and culture, the scientific naturalists adopted three closely related strategies. First, they argued that only science (as they defined it) offered a path to genuine knowledge of nature. Neither the church nor the Bible could be considered as authoritative sources of scientific truth. This was the main significance of the Darwinian controversies. The scientific naturalists seized upon the publication of *The Origin of Species* (1859) as an opportunity to divorce science from religion. Darwin's book, they maintained, should be judged solely on its scientific merits. They argued that rightly conceived science and religion could never come into conflict because religion belonged to the realm of feeling while science was a part of the world of intellect. By dividing science and religion into two spheres, the scientific naturalists essentially broke the bonds between them and, for better or for worse, allowed scientists to pursue their investigations of nature guided by principles that they established independently of religious authorities. Second, scientific naturalists claimed that only they possessed the expertise to speak on behalf of science. Expertise was the result of training that could only be obtained in specific sites, especially the laboratory, and it was only achievable through a discipline of self-renunciation – a surrender to nature – and a willingness to seek out truth regardless of the consequences. In 1854 Tyndall declared that

> the first condition of success is patient industry and honest receptivity, and a willingness to abandon all preconceived notions, however cherished, if they be found to contradict the truth. Believe me, a self-renunciation that has something lofty in it, and of which the world never hears, is often enacted in the private experience of the true votary of science.[11]

The gentlemen of science were doubly condemned, since they mixed up science and religion and they did not possess the necessary expertise to be proper professional scientists.

The scientific naturalists embraced a third tactic as part of their strategy. After arguing that science was the sole path to knowledge of nature, and that they alone had the skill to tread that path, they insisted that scientific knowledge provided a good deal of insight into the human condition, not just the state of nature. Huxley himself was hesitant to erase completely the line between the human and the natural worlds. In his 'Evolution and Ethics' (1893), a lecture delivered near the end of his life, Huxley argued that ethical principles could not be derived from the amoral evolutionary process. But other scientific naturalists were not so reluctant, particularly Herbert Spencer and his disciples, who applied evolutionary theory to understand both nature and the entire spectrum of human thought and activity. In an essay on 'Evolution' in the *Cornhill Magazine* for 1888, Allen, one of Spencer's followers, defended how some scientific naturalists dealt with the application of evolutionary theory to human culture and society, as illustrated in Tylor's and Lubbock's anthropological work. 'Having shown us entirely to their own satisfaction the growth of suns, and systems, and worlds, and continents, and oceans, and plants, and animals, and minds', Allen declared, 'they proceed to show us the exactly analogous and parallel growth of communities and nations, and languages, and religions, and customs, and arts, and institutions, and literatures.'[12] Scientific naturalists often argued that only they could comprehend the full ramifications of new scientific theories like evolution for understanding how human culture had developed over time.

Scientific naturalists not only pointed out that science could account for the growth of human culture, they also maintained that science could provide an alternative to the outmoded Christian culture of the aristocratic, feudal past. Huxley emphasized that science was not just a 'mere provider of physical comforts'. In addition to bestowing 'practical benefits' to humanity, science had 'affected a revolution in their conceptions of the universe and of themselves and their views of right and wrong. I say that natural knowledge, seeking to satisfy natural wants, has found the ideas which can alone still spiritual cravings.' Even religion, Huxley insisted, had been purified as a result of the influence of science, as it had been forced to renounce 'the idols built up of books and traditions and fine-spun ecclesiastical cobwebs'.[13] Scientific naturalists recognized that they could not merely reject the Anglican-aristocratic culture that they opposed. They had to offer a new vision of a scientifically inflected culture to replace it if they aspired to supplant the Anglican clergy as the new cultural authorities.

In their efforts to articulate that new vision, and in the process of explaining their scientific theories to the public, they did not hesitate to draw on literature and literary devices. Doing so allowed them to demonstrate that they too, like their classically trained opponents, were learned and cultured individuals who belonged to the intellectual elite. Instead of looking to Greek and Roman literature, the scientific naturalists often expressed their admiration of the Romantics. Though committed to the realist project of describing the world as it is, the scientific naturalists also shared the Romantics' intense aesthetic response to nature, their love of adventurous exploration, their rebellion against authority and their fascination with transcendence.[14] Both Huxley and Tyndall revered Goethe. For the opening article of the first issue of the important journal *Nature*, Huxley chose to praise Goethe's poetic vision as containing 'a truthful and efficient symbol of the wonder and the mystery of Nature' that would be valid long after the scientific discoveries of the Victorian age were obsolete.[15] In his 'Belfast Address', Tyndall declared that Goethe was not only a great poet, but also an important contributor to natural history.[16] Tyndall quoted from Goethe on several occasions and penned an entire essay on his *Farbenlehre*.[17] Tyndall and Huxley also voiced their debt to Thomas Carlyle on numerous occasions. During the 1840s Carlyle's writings inspired Tyndall and Huxley with a passion for social reform and a disdain for conventional Christianity. Later they acknowledged that Carlyle's conception of nature as a living, organic entity had had a profound influence on them.[18] Tyndall devoted two essays to Carlyle, quoted from him at least twice, and corresponded directly with him.[19]

In addition to Romantic figures including Goethe and Carlyle, Huxley and Tyndall paid tribute to Tennyson as a great literary author in tune with modern science. Huxley spoke highly of Tennyson's insight into scientific method in his poem *In Memoriam* (1850). He believed that Tennyson was the only modern poet 'who has taken the trouble to understand the work and tendency of the men of science'.[20] Huxley ended the lecture 'Evolution and Ethics' with two quotations, one from Browning's '"Childe Roland to the Dark Tower Came"', and the other from Tennyson's 'Ulysses'. Tyndall included Tennyson's poetry in several of his essays.[21] Tennyson, as read by Huxley and Tyndall, shared their scientific worldview and explored its emotional and spiritual dimensions.[22] Literary allusions to Tennyson's poems were also used to denote respectability. Darwin drew from Tennyson's poetry in the *Descent of Man* to distance himself from charges of immorality while Tyndall quoted from Tennyson in his 'Belfast Address' to ward off accusations of materialism.[23] The scientific naturalists demonstrated their familiarity with literature to counter charges that they lacked the credentials needed to be members of the intellectual elite.

Scientific naturalists not only quoted, or alluded to, literary figures, their writings had a literary quality. Some wrote novels depicting the quest for a new worldview or advancing the public understanding of evolution. In Karl Pearson's *The New Werther* (1880) the central character is a young man who wanders Germany seeking a satisfying creed. Grant Allen, who wrote a series of sensational novels in the 1880s and 1890s, used fiction to push forward his scientific naturalist agenda. Though not novelists, other scientific naturalists drew on literary techniques to convey their scientific ideas. In the mid-nineteenth century, scientists still shared a common language with the educated readers and writers of their time. Scientific texts could still be read as literary texts. In his *Origin of Species*, for example, Darwin's use of vivid literary images facilitated the communication of his novel and complex notion of an evolutionary natural world.[24] He likened the relationship between orders, families and genera to the branches of a 'great Tree of Life' and, famously in the concluding paragraph of the book, he compared the interdependence of living beings to a tangled bank.[25] Despite Darwin's admission in his *Autobiography* that he had lost his early love for Shakespeare, Milton, Byron, Wordsworth and Shelley as a consequence of the grind of scientific investigation, his writing has a rich literary quality.[26] In his addresses to the British Association on 'Scientific Limit of the Imagination' (1868) and 'Scientific Use of the Imagination' (1870), Tyndall explained why the scientific naturalists retained a literary dimension to their writings. He insisted that the imagination played an important role in science.[27] In his mind, the scientific imagination surpassed the most fantastic flights of the poetic mind while also providing empirical truths about a wondrous and mysterious natural world.[28] Tyndall believed that Darwin served as an example of the creative operations of the scientific mind. 'In the case of Mr. Darwin', Tyndall asserted, 'observation, imagination and reason combined have run back with wonderful sagacity and success over a certain length of the line of biological succession.'[29]

Victorian siblings: literary realism and scientific naturalism

Just as the scientific naturalists quoted from literature, and aimed to give their writings for the general audience a literary quality, Victorian poets and novelists incorporated scientific imagery, themes and narrative patterns into their work.[30] The new interest in science at mid-century symbolized by the Crystal Palace, then, cut across Victorian culture. It is no accident that a new literary genre was first created in the second half of the nineteenth century that owed much of its inspiration to the worship of science. Emerging from the Gothic romances of science of the early nineteenth century, including Mary Shelley's *Frankenstein* (1818), science fiction became a distinct genre of fiction due to the success of Jules Verne and H. G. Wells.[31] Science fiction really took off in the 1890s due to changes in the world of publishing. Expensive three-decker novels were replaced by affordable one-volume novels and mass-market magazines, which, along with respectable periodicals, began to carry SF short stories.[32] Wells, who was at one time a student of Huxley's, was a beneficiary of this development. Wells wrote four of his best-known science fiction books near the end of the century, including *The Time Machine* (1895), *The Island of Doctor Moreau* (1896), *The Invisible Man* (1897) and *War of the Worlds* (1898). Here he dealt with such themes as degeneration, the struggle for survival between species, vivisection and the dangerous power of scientific knowledge.

But a literary school of this period was connected more directly to scientific naturalism. The project of the realist novel, George Levine has argued, was the 'cultural twin to the project of Victorian science'.[33] Both the scientific naturalists and the realist novelists shared a common scientific perspective. Realist novelists, including George Eliot and Thomas Hardy, attempted to bring out the hitherto unseen complexity and depth of ordinary life. They presented human existence as it was in Great Britain and they did so in ways that parallel the scientists' approach to understanding the natural world. This shared scientific perspective is most evident in the way that Victorian literary figures attempted to know the world. The scientific naturalists and their literary twins both held to an epistemological ideal of self-sacrifice, or self-annihilation, in order to reach a position of objectivity from which to locate truth or describe reality. This epistemology required that the individual begin by putting aside religion as an authority in the quest for knowledge and it demanded a willingness to suffer the consequences of finding out the unpleasant truth that the world was not made for humanity. In many Victorian novels, knowledge seeking and truth telling were at the heart of the story. Plots often turned on the ability of the protagonist to develop the proper temper and objective state of mind to permit a realistic confrontation with the world.[34] Searching for truth in the world with this epistemological approach yielded similar results for scientific naturalists and key characters in realist novels. The science and literature scholar Tess Cosslett sums them up neatly: 'the acceptance of unpleasant Truth and renunciation of "supernatural" consolations; the vision of unifying, all-pervasive Law; the recognition of kinship with Nature; the appreciation of organic interrelatedness and co-operation within Nature; and the admiration for the scientific imagination'. The scientific imagination created an organic unity in what it perceived by penetrating through the surface appearances to an unseen rational order behind them.[35]

The epistemology of self-annihilation was only one way that the scientific perspective entered the Victorian novel. Another concerned the narrative form of the novel and the patterns it exploits and develops.

Many novels prior to the middle of the century adopted narrative conventions consonant with the views of natural theology. Jane Austen's, for example, rely on a narrative that unfolds teleologically, make providential use of coincidence and contain an implicit faith in the coherence, beneficence and intelligibility of the world. Ultimately, Austen's novels move towards closure. Austen's *Mansfield Park* preserves an ordered, designed and essentially closed system.[36] By contrast, novels from the second half of the century adopt a different set of conventions informed by the scientific perspective. George Levine identifies a series of structural conventions tied to Darwinian modes of thought. The third-person narrator, who is detached from the characters in the novel, patiently records their behaviour in the same way that the 'true' scientist endeavours to adopt the role of the disinterested observer. Just as Lyell's geological uniformitarianism undergirds Darwin's views on the evolutionary process, the Victorian novel depended on the notion that all events, even extraordinary ones, can be explained by causes now in operation. Darwin's world of change is echoed in the novels' emphasis on how everything is changing and to be understood in historical context. The parallel to Darwin's erasure of the rigid distinction between species and varieties is the erasing of borders in the novel. Darwin's tangled bank is mirrored in the novels' interweaving of characters in complex webs of relationship and patterns of inheritance. Whereas Darwin depicted nature as bursting with life, the world of the Victorian novel is overpopulated. Darwin's denial of design and teleology corresponds in fiction to the way characters must learn to adapt to their environments and to chance.[37]

The poets Alfred, Lord Tennyson and George Meredith, and the novelists George Eliot, Thomas Hardy, Anthony Trollope and Joseph Conrad, are among the major Victorian literary figures whose works contain significant aspects of the epistemology of self-sacrifice and the narrative conventions associated with science.[38] Although Charles Dickens is the 'great novelist of entanglement' who finds in the urban landscape 'those very conditions of interdependence and genealogy that characterize Darwin's tangled bank', he is actually a transitional figure who is posed halfway between the conventions of the earlier period and those embedded in the realist novels after the mid-century.[39] I will focus on Marian Evans, better known under her pseudonym George Eliot (1819–80), and Thomas Hardy (1840–1920) in order to illustrate in more detail how epistemologies and narrative conventions played out in the work of two key realist writers of the period.

George Eliot's acquaintance with, and sympathy for, Victorian scientific thought is well known. During her life she had close personal relationships with two of the scientific naturalists, Spencer and Lewes, whom she had met in the early fifties when they were all involved with the liberal periodical the *Westminster Review*. In 1854 she and the already married Lewes scandalized London by living together openly. She stayed with Lewes until his death in 1878. Tyndall and Huxley were regular visitors to her home. She owned books and articles by Darwin, Tyndall, Clifford and Huxley.[40] French Positivist August Comte and Lewes had a profound influence on her thinking and on her novels. Like these men, she believed that the growth of the social organism was governed by the operation of the same immutable laws governing physiological life. From her first to her last novel, Eliot was engaged in an active dialogue with contemporary scientific thought that transformed both the social vision and the narrative structure of her novels. In her first novel, *Adam Bede* (1859), she adopted the role of the natural historian, the passive observer, who recorded the tensions between the individual's right to self-fulfilment and the commitment to duty in a somewhat fixed, though harmonious, social order. This clash between the needs of the individual and the demands of social duty formed the central drama of each of Eliot's novels. But by the end of her career, Eliot had worked out a more dynamic model of the social organism, and she had assumed the role of the detached, creative, active experimenter. These changes can be correlated with transformations in contemporary scientific theories of the organic, the rise of the experimental method in the laboratories of scientific naturalists and Eliot's assimilation of Darwinian theory by the late sixties.[41]

Eliot's last two novels, *Middlemarch* (1871–2) and *Daniel Deronda* (1876), reveal her debt to Darwin and Lewes, and indicate that she was wrestling with the problems posed by their scientific perspective. *Middlemarch* is the first novel in which science is dealt with explicitly as a theme. One reviewer complained that '*Middlemarch* is too often an echo of Messrs. Darwin and Huxley.'[42] The major characters attempt to apprehend the underlying organic unity beneath the disorder of appearances. The ambitious Dr Lydgate searches for the one primitive tissue; the pedantic Casaubon hunts for the key to all mythologies; and Dorothea Brooke seeks the hidden unity of the social organism. Gradualism is the pervading principle of the novel. The narrator emphasizes the slow action of ordinary causes and their effect on character and action. The structure of the novel concerns the gradual growth towards moral health and effective living of some characters, including Dorothea, and the gradual decay of others, including Lydgate. Dorothea triumphs because she gradually learns consciously to detach herself, which allows her to perceive her oneness with the unconscious processes of life.[43] But in *Daniel Deronda*, Eliot raised questions about the epistemology of self-effacement. While she desired a rigorous epistemology, she was unwilling to accept one that required the annihilation of the self, or the renunciation of passion and imaginative vision. Levine has persuasively argued that '*Daniel Deronda* implies that one price of realism is a vision of a society emptied of meaning and a fate for its protagonist (in this case, heroine) utterly desolate. Achieving true knowledge of the other, conditional on a stern refusal to make any demands for the self, regularly entails failure or death.'[44]

Like Eliot, Thomas Hardy grappled with the difficulties of the evolutionary worldview, including its epistemology of self-annihilation. Hardy was influenced enormously by his reading of Spencer and Darwin. Incorporating biological theories into his novels seemed to Hardy to offer a route for drawing nearer to the truth and for challenging literary and social conventions.[45] He greatly admired Huxley's fearless determination to confront the unpleasant truths revealed by science. Edward Clodd, Huxley's biographer, as well as a popularizer of anthropology and cosmic evolution, was one of Hardy's acquaintances. Hardy was also a close friend of Leslie Stephen, editor and man of letters, who had the courage to be the first to refer to himself in public as an 'agnostic' in 1876.[46] Hardy is often seen as embracing the darker, pessimistic aspects of Darwinism. In *Jude the Obscure* (1896) the protagonist, a manual labourer who yearns for spiritual truth, encounters tragedy when he attempts to rise above his station. Jude seeks knowledge, but it only leads to his death. The epistemology of self-effacement does not reveal a moral order behind the veil of matter. There is no meaning in nature in a world where natural theology has ceased to be persuasive. Hardy seems to follow out the search for objective truth to its logical and unforgiving conclusion.[47]

But in his earlier *Two on a Tower* (1882), Hardy is less negative. In this novel the struggles of the main characters to find meaning are explored through the science of astronomy. Living through the astrophysics revolution in astronomy initiated by the use of the camera and the spectroscope during the 1860s and 1870s, Hardy viewed the earth's evolution as part of the larger cosmic evolution of the entire universe. *Two on a Tower* entertains a number of cosmological myths by which late Victorian readers could understand their relation to the universe and to each other. Swithin St Cleeve, an astronomer, and Lady Viviette Constantine are confronted by the hazards of scientific objectivity early on in the novel. As they gaze into the night sky, they see thousands of stars. St Cleeve points out that a powerful telescope brings millions of stars within sight, which implies to him that the stars 'were not made to please our eyes. It is just the same in everything, nothing is made for man.' Constantine is appalled. She observes that astronomy is a 'bad study' for St Cleeve since it makes him 'feel human insignificance too plainly'. She is overpowered by what she sees in the telescope. 'It makes me feel that it is not worth while to live', she remarks, 'it quite annihilates me.'[48] But St Cleeve is willing to risk annihilation night after night in his quest to be 'the new Copernicus'. Though star-crossed lovers, St Cleeve and Constantine defy the cosmic meaninglessness revealed by astronomical science by finding happiness in human companionship – at least for a time. Here, and in his other novels, Hardy counters the most negative dimensions of Darwinism and the epistemology of self-sacrifice with an alternative cosmological message. This message is conveyed in his fiction primarily by female characters through whom he expresses an appreciation for morality and sympathy in a godless universe, though the possibility of a harmonious relationship with the universe grows less likely in each subsequent novel.[49]

Contrary voices: contentious scientific theories

Although the scientific naturalists and their literary allies constituted a formidable cadre in the second half of the nineteenth century, their views on science and culture were widely contested by a host of groups, as were their claims to cultural authority. First, there were their opponents within the scientific community. Former allies who had been excommunicated from the Darwinian circle were the co-discoverer of natural selection, Alfred Russel Wallace (for his spiritualism); biologist St George Mivart (for his rejection of natural selection and his Catholicism); medical scientist Charles Bastian (for his materialism) and novelist and popularizer of science Samuel Butler (for his attacks on Darwin and the theory of natural selection). Other members of the scientific elite who challenged the dominance of the scientific naturalists included physicists based in Scotland, among them William Thomson and James Clerk Maxwell, who wanted to retain a religious framework for science, as well as the gentlemen of science who were still active in this period, including the anatomist

Richard Owen. Many of the self-educated popularizers of science, including John George Wood, were keen to perpetuate the natural theology tradition. British intellectual and religious leaders were also opposed to scientific naturalism. This would include representatives of the old aristocratic-Anglican establishment, including Bishop Samuel Wilberforce, and distinguished Tory politician A. J. Balfour. They were joined by leading Catholics, including John Henry Newman, and prominent Nonconformists, including Congregationalist minister Robert William Dale, and Robert Flint, a philosopher and theologian in the Church of Scotland. Idealists, among them Thomas Henry Green, and spiritualists, including Oliver Lodge, and literary figures, for example John Ruskin, were also among those who challenged the scientific worldview championed by the scientific naturalists. Frances Power Cobbe, like other feminists and anti-vivisectionists, clashed with scientific naturalists over their views on women and animal experimentation. Socialist intellectuals, including Henry Mayers Hyndman, dismissed Darwin and Huxley as pro-capitalist due to their emphasis on competition in the evolutionary process.

The critics of scientific naturalism objected to their attempts to professionalize and secularize British science no less than to their claims to cultural authority. Since scientific naturalists often argued that scientific theories, especially evolution, could legitimately be applied to all aspects of human culture, disputes between them and their detractors concerned virtually every area of scientific investigation and raged across the entire spectrum of cultural issues. The debates took place in a multitude of cultural spaces, in the universities, in the pulpits, in the pages of periodicals like *Nineteenth Century*, in the meetings of scientific societies, such as the BAAS and in the British parliament over such issues as the limits of animal experimentation.

Each scientific discipline contained at least one contentious theory, or practice, that became a lightning rod for controversy involving the scientific naturalists and one or more of their critics. Fights often centred on the larger cultural significance of these theories and practices, and on who had the authority to determine what science had to say on matters of such crucial importance. New developments in mathematics in the second half of the century, particularly in geometry, played an integral role in the debates between scientific naturalists and their opponents. Whewell, Herschel and many of the other Cambridge gentlemen of science subscribed to a unitary view of truth based on a Euclidean foundation. Prior to the 1870s, the seemingly transcendental truths of

Euclidean geometry attested to the ability of the human mind to arrive at valid truths about God, humanity and society. But Clifford, the mathematician among the scientific naturalists, argued that the development of non-Euclidean geometry had destroyed the illusion of certainty on which geometry's epistemological claims had rested, which therefore cast grave doubt on the human ability to obtain any knowledge of a transcendental God.[50]

Theories in astronomy and physics were also at the centre of disputes. The nebular hypothesis, formulated by Laplace in the late eighteenth century, was associated for much of the nineteenth century with social and religious radicalism. John Pringle Nichol, Scottish political economist and astronomer, began to support the nebular hypothesis in the 1830s. He argued that telescopic observations of the Orion nebula provided proof that it was composed of the nebulous, or gaseous, material that would be expected if the nebular hypothesis were true. He concluded that this confirmed the idea of the existence of natural laws that exemplified universal progress. In his quest to undermine the nebular hypothesis, William Parsons, the third Earl of Rosse, built a gigantic telescope on his estate at Parsontown. After it was completed in 1844, the 'Leviathan of Parsontown' was the largest telescope in the world for the next six decades. Parsons claimed that the Leviathan provided evidence that the Orion nebula was resolvable into separate stellar objects.[51] But in the mid-sixties William Huggins announced that spectroscopic evidence showed that objects like Orion were gaseous and not stellar. Huggins's findings seemed to lend support to a cosmic evolutionary view. Effective opposition to scientific naturalism from the 'hard sciences' came from a group of scientists who, from the 1850s to the 1870s, constructed the science of energy. Bearing the impress of Scottish presbyterianism, representing Whig and progressive values, and linked to the industrialists of northern Britain, energy physics was founded by a 'North British' group composed of Glasgow Professor of Natural Philosophy William Thomson, Scottish natural philosophers James Clerk Maxwell and Peter Guthrie Tait and the engineers Fleeming Jenkin and Macquorn Rankine. These men found the perceived anti-Christian materialism of the scientific naturalists quite distasteful and they were prepared to enter into an alliance with Cambridge Anglicans to undermine the authority of Huxley and his allies. They promoted a natural philosophy in harmony with, though not subservient to, Christian belief. Whereas Tyndall and his allies interpreted the principle of energy conservation as excluding the possibility of divine intervention, the North British physicists saw it as a law of nature that confirmed the existence of a God, since energy flowed in a definite direction.[52]

Theories from the first half of the century concerning the age of the earth in geology, and the transmutation of species in biology, continued to serve as focal points for controversy. In the early 1860s Thomson attempted to undermine the indefinitely long time-scale maintained by geologists, including Lyell, based on calculations of the rate of the sun's cooling. Thomson's ulterior motive was to challenge the validity of the theory of evolution by natural selection, which led Huxley to intervene on Darwin's behalf.[53] But Thomson was only one of many Victorian intellectual figures who engaged the scientific naturalists in debate on the subject of evolution. Bishop Samuel Wilberforce's encounter with Huxley at the BAAS meeting at Oxford in 1860 has become an almost iconic story about the battle between Anglicans and evolutionists. Traditionally it has been seen as a victory for Huxley and the forces of evolution over a gifted, but nonetheless ill-informed opponent. But it should not be viewed as the triumph of science over religion. The Anglicans had their natural theology, and the scientific naturalists their notion of religion as the realm of feeling and poetry. The fight was over competing notions of science and religion and how they could best be harmonized.[54] Later in 1874, when John Tyndall delivered 'The Belfast Address', he antagonized pretty much all of Christendom with his aggressive assertion that any systems that infringed 'upon the domain of science' must 'submit to its control'. Scientists, Tyndall declared, 'shall wrest from theology, the entire domain of cosmological theory'.[55] But in the ensuing outrage Catholics and Protestants alike denied that Tyndall spoke on behalf of true science. On the contrary, the critics of scientific naturalism used the occasion to attempt to cleanse science of its current materialism and reclaim it for Christianity.[56]

The practice of animal experimentation in the medical sciences became a high-profile issue and ranged the formidable Frances Power Cobbe (1822–1904) and her feminist allies against Darwin, Huxley and the scientific naturalists. Cobbe knew Darwin personally, and initially admired him. But she was critical of Darwin's *Descent of Man* (1871), especially the section where he had argued that women were intellectually inferior to men due to the evolutionary process. In 1875 she became involved in the anti-vivisection movement when she circulated a memorandum urging the Royal Society for the Prevention of Cruelty to Animals to put tight restrictions on experimentation with live animals. This alarmed Huxley and Darwin, who saw the anti-vivisectionists as threats to the progress of the new science of experimental physiology. To Cobbe, her work as a feminist and as an anti-vivisectionist was intimately connected. Both women and animals were subject to the brutal power of doctors, scientists and other males. Cobbe attacked Darwin in *The Times*. She accused scientists of taking sadistic pleasure in animal suffering, which challenged the scientific naturalists' claim that they were the appropriate moral arbiters of important social and cultural questions.[57] Novelists took up Cobbe's depiction of the cruel vivisectionist, particularly Wilkie Collins in *Heart and Science* (1883). A character in the novel, Doctor Benjulia, performs animal vivisections in secret in order to make a grand medical discovery. Ultimately, he cannot bear the suffering of the animals, and commits suicide. Throughout the novel Benjulia, and other scientific characters, are portrayed as egotists who claim to pursue knowledge for the good of humanity, but who care only for fame.

Psychology could also become a battleground for scientific naturalists and their foes. From 1850 to 1880 psychology was a relatively open field since it lacked settled lines of theory or rigid protocols for investigation. Commentary on psychological issues appeared in periodicals, novels, poems and philosophical tracts as debates raged over the best way to study the human mind. During the second half of the century psychologists operated in one of four discourses. First, the discourse of the soul, influenced by natural theology, aimed to guard against materialism by insisting on the mysteriousness of the mind. Second, the discourse of philosophy, an approach to psychology that inherited the concepts of the philosophical traditions of the past – both those who emphasized the innate faculties of the human mind and those who, like John Locke, stressed the role of experience. Among the latter were the associationists including John Stuart Mill. Associationism – the theory that the mind moves from one idea to another because the first is associated with the next – had fallen into discredit in psychology circles by the end of the 1860s, and was superseded in the 1870s by the third discourse, that of physiology in general biology. Two areas of investigation were crucial for physiological research, the study of the sensory-motor arc (which linked mind and brain to the environment through the nervous system) and the examination of the localization of the cerebral functions in the anatomy of the brain. The discourse of medicine, which emphasized the diagnosis and correction of dysfunction, was the last to develop, nearer the end of the century.[58]

The discourse of physiology was especially important to scientific naturalists. Huxley supported the conception of psychology as a part of the science of biology. Both Lewes and Spencer were leaders in the development of evolutionary psychology, which focused on the dynamic link between organism and environment. Spencer's *The Principles of Psychology* (1855) struck a decisive blow against associationism and called for investigation into the intersection between physiological and psychological studies. Though Lewes was not an experimentalist, he disseminated and synthesized new physiological research, developed informed speculation on its significance and nurtured the discipline's emerging reputation in the public domain. In 1870, in the pages of *Nature*, Lewes proclaimed that a general alteration in cultural outlook would occur as a result of the new evolutionary psychology. Eliot's later novels engage powerfully with the theories put forward by Spencer and Lewes. Her accounts of the psychological development of her characters, as well as her shift from natural historian to experimenter, are indebted to the methods and theories of evolutionary psychology. However, liberals including the Unitarian James Martineau, and the idealist T. H. Green, vehemently criticized evolutionary psychology.[59]

In addition to being challenged on the cultural meaning of specific scientific theories in different disciplines, the scientific naturalists could be questioned on the scientific status of their entire agenda. Aristocrats could be effective critics of scientific naturalism in the second half of the century. Lord Salisbury, William Siemens, William Armstrong and Lord Rayleigh built laboratories on their estates in which they created knowledge congruent with their social and religious beliefs. Here they examined gases, spectra, photographs and the ether.[60] Salisbury and Rayleigh were part of an extensive aristocratic family network comprised of the Balfours of Whittinghame, the Gascoyne-Cecils of Hatfield, the Strutts of Terling, the Sidgwicks of Hillside, the Campbells of Inveraray and the Parsons of Birr. From these families came some of the most eminent men and women of science in the second half of the century. In addition to the physicist Lord Rayleigh, the group included among its ranks the zoologist Francis Maitland Balfour, the astronomer William Parsons and the mathematician Eleanor Mildred Sidgwick.[61]

Aristocratic science was informed by a moderate evangelicalism based on the belief that God's providence worked through physical laws that were a manifestation of a permanent, moral law. Members of this network were sympathetic towards spiritualism, champions of amateur practice and sceptical about natural selection. They held to a worldview that reconciled science and religion while offering an alternative to the conception of science championed by scientific naturalism. Their science was embedded in aristocratic and Christian values. In their role as presidents of the BAAS, Rayleigh (1884), Salisbury (1894) and Arthur Balfour (1904) delivered addresses in which they defended theism and criticized scientific naturalism.[62] In his *Foundations of Belief* (1895), Balfour dissected the weaknesses of the secular conception of scientific knowledge, denying that scientific naturalism had any intrinsic connection to, or authority over, science.[63] To Balfour, naturalism was but a 'poor relation' of science that had forced itself into the 'retinue of science' and now claimed to 'represent her authority and to speak with her voice'.[64] Aristocrats continued to play a significant role in the second half of the nineteenth century, challenging the authority of scientific naturalists.

Contrary voices: contentious cultural issues

Just as disputes over scientific theories, practices and the status of scientific naturalism inevitably involved significant cultural issues, scientific concepts were used to resolve contentious matters in areas such as ethics, aesthetics, politics and popular culture. In their writings on ethics, Spencer, Stephen and Clifford all maintained that evolutionary theory provided a touchstone for determining moral principles. Their Christian opponents argued that a godless philosophy built on the concept of 'survival of the fittest' could never become the basis of a system of morals. They attempted to link scientific naturalism with materialism, which had a long association with moral corruption and debauchery. As Gowan Dawson has pointed out, Darwin's critics claimed that by negating the metaphysical criterion for morality – which, according to many, was the very basis of the civic order – the overtly naturalistic science of Darwin and his inner circle of friends and colleagues threatened to unleash a torrent of immorality and corruption that would surpass the scandalous vices of even the pagan world.[65]

From the late 1860s to the mid-1890s the chief strategy for damaging the respectability of scientific naturalism was to link it with the supposed immorality of avant-garde art and literature, in particular, Aestheticism. In their arguments that Darwin's *Descent of Man* had transgressed Victorian standards of respectability, his critics connected him to Algernon Swinburne, for them a notorious poet of the Aesthetic

Movement. Darwin's book became increasingly implicated with Swinburne's political radicalism, aesthetic sensualism and flagrant sexual depravity. Some detractors complained that Darwin's seeming obsession with sex in the *Descent* made it suitable reading material for only the worldliest gentlemen. These attempts to connect Darwin with immorality became significant impediments to establishing the naturalistic worldview as a morally acceptable alternative to the Christian one. Darwin's *Descent* was altered in order to avoid any hint of indecency, and Tyndall and Clifford were also forced to change portions of their writings for similar reasons. The scientific naturalists had no choice but to construct their model of professional scientific authority in line with their opponents' standards of respectability.[66]

Arts and aesthetics was another area of culture where scientific naturalists found themselves assailed by adversaries, in particular the art critic John Ruskin (1819–1900), when they tried to intervene with their evolutionary theories. In his *Descent of Man*, Darwin naturalized the human aesthetic sense by locating its origins in the physical sensations of animals. The notion of beauty, Darwin argued, was an evolutionary inheritance from animals. Similarly, in a number of his botanical books, Darwin naturalized the existence of colour in flowers by demonstrating that it was an evolutionary adaptation for attracting insects to ensure cross-pollination. Instead of seeing beauty as a gift to humanity from God or as a sign of moral and spiritual health, as it was for natural theologians and Ruskin, Darwin conceived of it as a utilitarian trait produced by, and for, evolutionary survival. Darwin's theories were central to a new evolutionary and physiological aesthetics popularized in the 1870s and 1880s by Grant Allen, which became part of serious discussions about art and beauty. Allen was by no means the only scientific naturalist exploring the relationship between science and aesthetics.[67] Ruskin, whose response to empirical science was complicated, certainly mistrusted the scientific naturalists for, as he saw it, their exclusive commitment to materialistic explanations, and for their claim that evolutionary science could account for aesthetics. In *Proserpina* (1875–86), Ruskin critiqued and rejected the utilitarian approach of Darwinian aesthetics as spiritually and morally impoverished.[68]

Opponents also confronted scientific naturalists when they tried to pontificate about the cultural implications of science for political and social issues. T. H. Green, F. H. Bradley, Edward Caird, Henry Jones, John Watson, William Wallace, J. S. Mackenzie, David George Ritchie and

Bernard Bosanquet formed an idealist school which dominated British philosophy in the last three decades of the nineteenth century. Drawing on evolutionary theory to construct a distinctive social philosophy, British idealists nevertheless embedded it in a quasi-Christian metaphysical system.[69] Similarly, representatives of the working class staked their claim to scientific territory. The economic downturn in the 1870s, accompanied by high unemployment and labour unrest, led to an increase in working-class support for socialism and trade unionism. While Huxley was attempting to prevent workers from falling prey to socialism in four essays published in 1890, socialist journals including *Justice* aimed to undermine the Darwinian world of liberal capitalism. During the 1880s *Justice* championed the interpretation of evolution as co-operative presented by the anarchist and scientist Prince Kropotkin. By claiming that bourgeois science missed the final step in evolution, collectivism, *Justice* questioned the association commonly made between struggle, survival and fitness and scientific truth. Such working-class periodicals attempted to establish themselves as scientific sites where their political message had scientific legitimacy.[70]

When the scientific naturalists attempted to bring their agenda to a popular audience, a large cadre of self-educated popularizers of science often frustrated their efforts. Many of them were professional writers and journalists. The overwhelming majority of them were members of the educated middle class. They assumed the role of interpreters of science for the growing mass reading audience in this period. They saw themselves as providing both entertainment and instruction to their readers. Some were extremely successful, producing best sellers that were as widely read as the *Origin of Species* or the other key scientific texts of the day. John George Wood's *Common Objects of the Country* (1858), for example, sold six times as many copies as the *Origin* within the first ten years of publication. For Huxley and his professionalizing colleagues, only the practitioner could interpret the meaning of the natural world and communicate it to a popular audience. The existence of a group of influential and widely read popularizers who wrote authoritatively about science could only confuse the public from Huxley's point of view, especially since their agenda differed so profoundly from that of the scientific naturalist. For many of these popularizers, nature was full of meaning, charged with religious significance. They looked back to the natural theology tradition and in their writings offered new audiences a vivid glimpse of the design they perceived in nature. Wood, an Anglican clergyman turned popularizer who produced over thirty volumes on natural history while lecturing extensively, filled his books with discussions of the goodness and beauty that he found in nature. The popularizers, for the most part, chose not to engage the scientific naturalists in public controversy. But fearing that the Victorian reading audience was being seduced by their religiously charged interpretation of science, Huxley decided in the late sixties to become heavily involved in popularizing projects in order to counter their influence.[71]

Conclusion: science as culture

During the early 1850s the scientific naturalists were outsiders to the Anglican dominated world of science. Taking advantage of the controversies surrounding the publication of Darwin's *Origin of Species*, they were able to redefine British science and promote a notion of scientific culture that furthered their goals. The cultural authority of scientific naturalists reached its highest point of influence during the 1860s and 1870s, when figures including Huxley and Tyndall were in their prime. Despite their many critics during this period, by the 1870s they were prominent members of the scientific establishment who held key positions in the important scientific societies. The 1880s brought a series of social and cultural changes that led to the decline of scientific naturalism. They were perceived as defenders of the *status quo* when working-class support for socialism and trade unionism increased in the final decades of the century. The worship of science inaugurated by the Crystal Palace in 1851 drew to a close by the end of the 1880s. During the 1890s eminent thinkers from around the Western world, including the American William James, Henri Bergson of France, the German Edmund Husserl and James Ward of England, critiqued the naturalistic analysis of nature. Realism ceased to be a powerful force in British novels. Eliot had died in 1880 and Hardy had returned to writing poetry by the end of the 1890s. The scientists who had championed scientific naturalism were dying off. Tyndall was gone in 1892, followed by Huxley in 1895 and Spencer in 1903.

But in their heyday, the scientific naturalists constructed a powerful notion of culture that was based more on scientific than on religious principles. The title of Huxley's article, 'Science and Culture', is actually somewhat misleading. Huxley did not intend to assert that science was somehow separate from culture, as implied in the use of the little word 'and'. He meant in his piece to demonstrate that science and culture were inseparable in a period when evolutionary theory had so profoundly transformed British thinking about literature and the arts. Tyndall referred to science 'as a means of intellectual culture' or an 'agent of culture', since the disciplines of science were 'based upon the natural relations subsisting between Man and the universe of which he forms a part'.[72] He rejected the notion stated 'by its opponents that science divorces itself from literature'. On the contrary, he insisted, 'a glance at the less technical writings of its leaders – of its Helmholtz, its Huxley, and it Du Bois-Reymond – would show what breadth of literary culture they command. Where among modern writers can you find their superiors in clearness and vigour of literary style?'[73] Tyndall and his allies maintained that the scientific perspective provided a unique access point to culture. They argued that this conception of culture was more appropriate for a modern, industrialized society. In effect, they campaigned to promote science as culture.[74] Since they thoroughly understood this new scientific culture, they also claimed to be the group within the intellectual elite that could best provide leadership in the future. They argued that they, not the Anglican clergy, should be considered the true authorities in an age of the worship of science. For a time, despite the chorus of contrary voices, they were widely recognized in Britain as peculiarly modern arbiters of culture.

Notes

1 The author would like to express his gratitude to the following colleagues, who pointed him towards scholarly sources that immeasurably enriched this piece: Ruth Barton, Tina Choi, Lorraine Janzen and James Moore.
2 Matthew Arnold, 'Literature and Science', *Nineteenth Century*, 1 (Aug. 1882), 222, 225, 220, 229.
3 Paul White, *Thomas Huxley: Making the 'Man of Science'* (Cambridge: Cambridge University Press, 2003), 97–9.
4 Thomas Henry Huxley, 'Science and Culture', in *Science and Education: Essays* (New York: Appleton, 1894), 153–4, 142–3.
5 George Levine, *Darwin and the Novelists: Patterns of Science in Victorian Fiction* (Chicago: University of Chicago Press, 1988), vii–viii.
6 Imperial College, Huxley Collection, Huxley/Heathorn Correspondence, Huxley to Heathorn, 23 Sept. 1851, letter no. 165–6.
7 Samuel J. M. M. Alberti, 'Conversaziones and the Experience of Science in Victorian England', *Journal of Victorian Culture*, 8 (2003), 208–30.
8 Thomas Henry Huxley, *Science and Christian Tradition* (New York: Appleton, 1894), 38; Frank Turner, *Between Science and Religion: The Reaction to Scientific Naturalism in Late Victorian*

England (New Haven: Yale University Press, 1974), chapter 2; Theodore Porter, *Karl Pearson: The Scientific Life in a Statistical Age* (Princeton: Princeton University Press, 2004), 288.

9 White, *Thomas Huxley*, 75–94.

10 Huxley, *Science and Education*, 108.

11 John Tyndall, *Fragments of Science*, 2 vols. (New York: Appleton, 1897), vol. I, 291.

12 Grant Allen, 'Evolution', *Cornhill Magazine*, 57 (Jan. 1888), 45–7.

13 Thomas Huxley, 'On the Advisableness of Improving Natural Knowledge', *Fortnightly Review*, 3 (Jan. 1866), 631–2, 636.

14 John Holmes, 'The X Club: Romanticism and Victorian Science', in Amanda Mordavsky Caleb (ed.), *(Re)Creating Science in Nineteenth-Century Britain* (Newcastle: Cambridge Scholars, 2007), 12–31.

15 Thomas Huxley, 'On the Aphorisms of Goethe', *Nature*, 1 (Nov. 1869), 11.

16 Tyndall, *Fragments of Science*, vol. II, 148.

17 Ibid., vol. II, 52, 100; John Tyndall, *New Fragments* (New York: Appleton, 1897), 47–77.

18 Bernard Lightman, *The Origins of Agnosticism: Victorian Unbelief and the Limits of Knowledge* (Baltimore: Johns Hopkins University Press, 1987), 96–7, 99, 147; Frank Turner, 'Victorian Scientific Naturalism and Thomas Carlyle', *Victorian Studies*, 18 (1975), 325–43; James G. Paradis, *T. H. Huxley: Man's Place in Nature* (Lincoln: University of Nebraksa Press, 1978), 47–63.

19 Tyndall, *New Fragments*, 347–97; Tyndall, *Fragments*, vol. II, 53, 74.

20 Leonard Huxley, *Life and Letters of Thomas Henry Huxley*, 2 vols. (New York: Appleton, 1902), vol. II, 359.

21 Tyndall, *Fragments of Science*, vol. II, 91; Tyndall, *New fragments*, 247.

22 Tess Cosslett, *The 'Scientific Movement' and Victorian Literature* (Sussex: Harvester Press; New York: St Martin's Place, 1982), 39.

23 Gowan Dawson, *Darwin, Literature and Victorian Respectability* (Cambridge: Cambridge University Press, 2007), 52–3; Tyndall, *Fragments of Science*, vol. II, 141.

24 Gillian Beer, *Darwin's Plots: Evolutionary Narrative in Darwin, George Eliot and Nineteenth-Century Fiction*, 2nd edn (Cambridge: Cambridge University Press, 2000), 4.

25 Charles Darwin, *The Origin of Species* (Harmondsworth: Penguin, 1985), 172, 459.

26 Francis Darwin (ed.), *The Autobiography of Charles Darwin and Selected Letters* (New York: Dover, 1958), 53–4.

27 White, *Thomas Huxley*, 94–7.

28 Jonathan Smith, *Charles Darwin and Victorian Visual Culture* (Cambridge: Cambridge University Press, 2006), 27, 280.

29 John Tyndall, 'The Scientific Use of the Imagination', in *Fragments*, vol. II, 127.

30 Cosslett, *The 'Scientific Movement'*, 3.

31 Martin Willis, *Mesmerists, Monsters, and Machines: Science Fiction and the Cultures of Science in the Nineteenth Century* (Kent, OH: Kent State University Press, 2006), 2.

32 Paul Fayter, 'Strange New Worlds of Space and Time: Late Victorian Science and Science Fiction', in Bernard Lightman (ed.) *Victorian Science in Context* (Chicago: University of Chicago Press, 1997), 261.

33 Levine, *Darwin and the Novelists*, vii.

34 George Levine, *Dying to Know: Scientific Epistemology and Narrative in Victorian England* (Chicago: University of Chicago Press, 2002), 12, 15, 66, 148–9.

35 Cosslett, *The 'Scientific Movement'*, 13, 26.

36 Levine, *Darwin and the Novelists*, 25, 59.

37 Ibid., 14–19.

38 For Tennyson, see Cosslett, *The 'Scientific Movement'*, pp. 39–73; Meredith: ibid., 101–31; Trollope: Levine, *Dying to Know*, 177–209; Conrad: ibid., 238–72.

39 Levine, *Darwin and the Novelists*, 119, 154.

40 Cosslett, *The 'Scientific Movement'*, 74.

41 Sally Shuttleworth, *George Eliot and Nineteenth-Century Science: The Make-Believe of a Beginning* (Cambridge: Cambridge University Press, 1984), ix–xii; Beer, *Darwin's Plots*, 148.

42 [Henry James], [Unsigned Review], *Galaxy* 15 (Mar. 1873), 424–8, as cited in David Carroll (ed.), *George Eliot: The Critical Heritage* (New York: Barnes and Noble, 1971), 359.

43 Cosslett, *The 'Scientific Movement'*, 75–7, 88, 93–5; Shuttleworth, *George Eliot and Nineteenth-Century Science*, 142–6, 169.

44 Levine, *Dying to Know*, 171, 174–7.

45 Angelique Richardson, 'Hardy and Biology', in Phillip Mallet (ed.), *Thomas Hardy, Texts and Contexts* (Basingstoke: Palgrave, 2002), 158.

46 Cosslett, *The 'Scientific Movement'*, 133.

47 Levine, *Dying to Know*, 201–2, 216.

48 Thomas Hardy, *Two on a Tower* (Harmondsworth: Penguin, 1999), 28–9.

49 Pamela Gossin, *Thomas Hardy's Novel Universe: Astronomy, Cosmology, and Gender in the Post-Darwinian World* (Aldershot and Burlington, VT, Ashgate, 2007), xvii, 107, 121–2, 201.

50 Joan L. Richard, *Mathematical Visions: The Pursuit of Geometry in Victorian England* (Boston: Academic Press, Inc., 1988), 21, 29, 61, 75, 93, 109–12; Daniel J. Cohen, *Equations from God: Pure Mathematics and Victorian Faith* (Baltimore: Johns Hopkins University Press, 2007), 164–6.

51 Simon Schaffer, 'The Nebular Hypothesis and the Science of Progress', in James R. Moore (ed.), *History, Humanity and Evolution: Essays for John C. Greene* (Cambridge: Cambridge University Press, 1989), 131–64.

52 Crosbie Smith, *The Science of Energy: A Cultural History of Energy Physics in Victorian Britain* (Chicago: University of Chicago Press, 1998).

53 Ibid., 172–3; J. D. Burchfield, *Lord Kelvin and the Age of the Earth* (London: Macmillan, 1975).

54 Bernard Lightman, 'Victorian Sciences and Religions: Discordant Harmonies', in John Hedley Brooke, Margaret J. Osler and Jitse van der Meer (eds), *Science in Theistic Contexts: Cognitive Dimensions Osiris,* 16 (2001), 343–66.

55 Tyndall, *Fragments of Science*, vol. II, 197.

56 Bernard Lightman, 'Scientists as Materialists in the Periodical Press: Tyndall's Belfast Address', in Geoffrey Cantor and Sally Shuttleworth (ed.), *Science Serialized: Representations of the Sciences in Nineteenth-Century Periodicals* (Cambridge, MA: MIT Press, 2004), 199–237.

57 Evelleen Richard, 'Redrawing the Boundaries: Darwinian Science and Victorian Women Intellectuals', in Lightman (ed.), *Victorian Science in Context*, 128–35.

58 Rick Rylance, *Victorian Psychology and British Culture 1850–1880* (Oxford: Oxford University Press, 2000), 3, 7, 22–7, 40, 94, 112.

59 Ibid., 71, 78, 205, 212, 204, 209–12.

60 Simon Schaffer, 'Physics Laboratories and the Victorian Country House', in Crosbie Smith and Jon Agar (ed.), *Making Space for Science: Territorial Themes in the Shaping of Knowledge* (New York: St Martin's Press, 1998), 172–7.

61 Donald Luke Opitz, 'Aristocrats and Professionals: Country-House Science in Late-Victorian Britain', Ph.D. Dissertation, University of Minnesota, 2004, 7–10.

62 Ibid., 33, 101, 109, 256–7; Donald L. Opitz, '"This House is a Temple of Research": Country-House Centres for Late Victorian Science', in David Clifford, Elisabeth Wadge,

Alex Warwick and Martin Willis (eds.), *Repositioning Victorian Sciences: Shifting Centres in Nineteenth-Century Scientific Thinking* (London: Anthem, 2006), 143–53.

63 Bernard Lightman, '"Fighting Even with Death": Balfour, Scientific Naturalism, and Thomas Henry Huxley's Final Battle', in Alan Barr (ed.), *Thomas Henry Huxley's Place in Science and Letters: Centenary Essays* (Athens: University of Georgia Press, 1997), 323–50.

64 Arthur James Balfour, *The Foundations of Belief: Being Notes Introductory to the Study of Theology* (London: Longmans, Green, 1895), 135.

65 Dawson, *Darwin, Literature and Victorian Respectability*, 6.

66 Ibid., 4, 8, 12, 15, 28.

67 Peter Allan Dale, *In Pursuit of a Scientific Culture: Science, Art, and Society in the Victorian Age* (Wisconsin: University of Wisconsin Press, 1989).

68 Smith, *Charles Darwin and Victorian Visual Culture*, 2–3, 27–9, 32, 136, 161–6, 170, 176, 243, 280.

69 Sandra Den Otter, *British Idealism and Social Explanation: A Study in Late Victorian Thought* (Oxford: Clarendon, 1996).

70 Erin McLaughlin-Jenkins, 'Common Knowledge: Science and the Late Victorian Working-Class Press', *History of Science*, 39 (2001), 445–65; Erin McLaughlin-Jenkins, 'Henry George and Darwin's Dragon: Thomas Henry Huxley's Response to "Progress and Poverty"', in John Laurent (ed.), *Henry George's Legacy in Economic Thought* (Cheltenham: Edward Elgar, 2005), 31–52.

71 Bernard Lightman, *Victorian Popularizers of Science: Designing Nature for New Audiences* (Chicago: University of Chicago Press, 2007).

72 Tyndall, *Fragments of Science*, vol. I, 293, 302.

73 Ibid., vol. II, 198.

74 White, *Thomas Huxley*, 68.

3

Technology

Few aspects of Victorian life escaped the impact of industrialization. The experience of time and space was transformed in fundamental ways, but so too were the visual, aural, olfactory and tactile environments. To this extent the period saw an intensification of processes already well under way by 1837, as well as the effects of new forces. Industrialization had significantly developed in the previous century, but Victoria's reign was to see steam power reach its full potential. And towards the end of her reign a second phase of industrialization took place, this time based on electricity, the combustion engine, organic chemistry and new ideas about scientific management.

At its most basic, the industrial revolution was a revolution in the nature of manufacture, transport and communications, but shifts in these areas affected almost all aspects of experience. The nature of work was transformed, and the nature of class relations, but so was the link between workplace and home, and the material culture of both; the industrialization of manufacture brought the prices of goods down, beginning the democratization of consumerism, while improvements in glass and lighting created a new consumer environment of arcades and department stores. When transport changed dramatically, the experience of landscape and cityscape altered; new methods of communication brought the regions closer together, creating standard national time in place of the many local times. New technologies directly affected the sphere of culture: steam presses facilitated the mass manufacture of the printed word and image, and steam also carried the latest books and newspapers into every corner of the country. The sounds of the Victorian city changed along with its appearance and smell; nor was the countryside immune to such metamorphoses – the piercing whistle of the railway was heard even in Wordsworth's beloved Lake District. A new tactile world was shaped by mass manufacture, and by new techniques in the creation of textiles. Even the realm of the unconscious felt the impact of industrialization: at the beginning of the Victorian period advertising tightened its grasp on the material imaginary; at its end, film, the 'last machine' as it is sometimes termed, offered a powerful new dreamworld.

Coal-fuelled steam power was the motor of change in the early Victorian period, as it had been for decades before. For the working class this meant a radical re-organization of the nature of work. It meant factory work rather than agricultural work or cottage industry; life ruled by the clock rather than by more traditional diurnal and seasonal patterns; and a strong gravitational pull towards the towns and cities. By the late 1830s this process had created cities like Manchester – Cottonopolis, as it was known to its admirers, Darkchester to those who remained less enthusiastic – a city whose wealth was founded on the mass production of a basic commodity: cloth. Working conditions in the manufactories of the new towns and cities were often abysmal, a source of anger to the workers, as well as to radical commentators like the young Friedrich Engels, whose *Condition of the Working Class in England* (1844) assesses the impact of industrialization on the lives of the 'hands', that telling metonymy.

The working class itself was, of course, one of the most durable things manufactured in the new towns: by the 1830s new forms of affiliation had been brought into being by the experience of factory life and urbanization; the late 1830s sees the appearance of the Chartist movement, with its demands for improved conditions and political recognition for the creators of Great Britain's wealth, or at least the adult male portion of them. Although their demands were peremptorily refused, they could not be refused forever. The 1867 Reform Act for the first time gave the vote to a significant number of adult male working-class voters, and advanced the gradual transfer of power from the country to the towns and cities. These changes did not occur without a good deal of rather phobic anticipation from the enfranchised minority in the years leading up to the 'leap in the dark' of the second Reform Bill. Carlyle's intemperate 'Shooting Niagara – and After' (1867) and Matthew Arnold's *Culture and Anarchy* (1867–8) are among the best-known non-fiction responses. But similar concerns already animate the fiction of the late 1850s: Dickens's *A Tale of Two Cities* (1859), for example, revivifies the spectres of the mob and working-class 'combination' that had haunted the political elite in the late eighteenth and early nineteenth centuries. Indeed, fear of the urban masses, and the desire to control them, underlie some very different Victorian phenomena across the century: the rise of an organized police force, and the surveillant power of the detective police; the museum movement, with its ambitions to assimilate the masses into a national culture; and the new interest in attention and its management that Jonathan Crary identifies after mid-century.[1] At the end of the century, the crowd as an object of interest re-appears in a new form in such books as Gustave Le Bon's *Psychologie des foules* (1895), and by the early twentieth century attention becomes the key topic of modern times for theorist of attention-engineering Gerald Stanley Lee, who in *Crowds* (1913), sees such phenomena as advertising and department stores as machines of attention that shape the behaviour of the masses.[2]

Some saw the workers as a 'dumb class', but working-class writers including Thomas Cooper, Benjamin Brierley and Thomas Preston sought to put the experience of their peers into autobiographies, novels, poetry, plays and journalism.[3] Literary history has tended to pay more attention to the viewpoint of the middle-class commentators, and the term 'industrial novel' is associated with such works as Disraeli's *Sybil* (1845), Elizabeth Gaskell's *Mary Barton* (1848) and *North and South* (1853), Charlotte Brontë's *Shirley* (1849), Charles Kingsley's *Alton Locke* (1850), Charles Dickens's *Hard Times* (1854) and George Eliot's *Felix Holt* (1866). These industrial novels are not always as preoccupied with factory life as the term may suggest. They are, in fact, for the most part domestic novels that seek to negotiate individualist solutions to the social problems created by industrialization. By the 1860s the industrial novel seems to have run out of steam, as it were, though some of its concerns can be found in oblique form in the 'sensation novels' that dominate the 1860s and remain significantly popular in the 1870s.[4] As a keyword of the period, the term 'sensation' marks a perceived shift in the cultural market, a disruption of a cultural sphere stratified by class. The novels themselves, which set out to capture a mass market, remain preoccupied with the issue of just how the wandering attention of the crowd might be held. The working class and the city re-emerge as more obvious focuses of interest at the end of the century in slum novels including Arthur Morrison's *A Child of the Jago* (1896).

Industrialization appeared directly in the industrial novel, but there were other literary outcomes. One consequence of the separation of workplace and home was the high level of emotional investment in the snugness of the hearth, and the elevation of its presiding angel in the house. We see this investment across a wide range of Victorian cultural production, but especially, perhaps, in Dickens, where it amounts to a form of domestic fetishism. Of course there were also darker fantasies that derived from the isolation of domestic space from the outside world, the world of values from the world of facts: the Gothic novels of the eighteenth century prepare the way, but locked-room mysteries, which present the home as a death-trap, appear for the first time in the 1830s (J. S. Le Fanu's 'Passage in the Secret History of an Irish Countess' (1838), Edgar Allan Poe's 'Murders in the Rue Morgue' (1841)); the sensation novels of the 1860s likewise dwell on domestic crimes and household mysteries. Thus one of the most popular literary modes of the last two centuries, the detective story, is inextricably linked to the social geography created by industrialization.

Cultural responses to industrialization were not by any means confined to prose fiction. Plays including John Walker's *The Factory Lad* (1832) vividly staged class conflict, and the mid-Victorian theatre-going public could watch stage versions of the industrial novels, with *Mary Barton* becoming Dion Boucicault's *The Long Strike* (1866), for example. The major Victorian cultural critics also had a good deal to say about the industrialization of work. Thomas Carlyle was not an antagonist of industrialization per se, and was indeed more likely to celebrate the tremendous forces harnessed to human use; but he was unhappy with the superstructural changes that accompanied the age of steam. His *Past and Present* (1843) contrasts the lot of the industrial worker, hard-pressed and left without any sense of his place in the order of things, with the life of the medieval serf, who worked just as hard, but at least had a sense of his place in a hierarchical community (the opposition anticipates that of *Gemeinschaft* and *Gesellschaft*, 'community' and 'society', outlined by Ferdinand Tönnies in 1887). John Ruskin's medievalism was of a different cast: for him industrial production itself was flawed, since it gave no ambit for the expression of individual creativity. In *The Stones of Venice* (1851–3) he argues that the craftsman of the middle ages, who could produce his grotesque carving within the overall scheme of the cathedral, was infinitely better off than the industrial worker, who was rendered a mere cog in the machine, compelled to produce identical, smoothly finished goods for the consumer public. The medievalism that cropped up everywhere from the Eglinton Tournament of 1839 (a re-enacted medieval tournament in Scotland), to the work of the Pre-Raphaelites (championed, if cautiously, by Ruskin), to architecture, owes something to a similar perspective on the Britain of the past as a happier, more stable, more organic nation.

For the middle and upper classes their most significant encounters with mechanization were not in the workplace, but on the railway platform and compartment, as Wolfgang Schivelbusch has shown.[5] More than any other machine, the train became their icon and vehicle of industrial change, introducing them to the same time-discipline that had arrived with the factories, as we see from such pamphlets as Alfred Haviland's *Hurried to Death* (1868), which looks at the pernicious effects of railway-driven time-consciousness. The experience of space was no less transformed by the train: as the transport network spread, the railways shrank the country, bringing remote regions within easy striking distance of London, the ports and the industrial towns. People as well as goods circulated as never before, for pleasure as well as for business, and the railway 'excursionist' becomes a stock figure in the novels, plays and songs of the mid-nineteenth century. The response to mechanized transport was not always a positive one. Ruskin, for example, equated railway travel with being 'a living parcel'.[6] As Schivelbusch illustrates, ambivalence about modernization appeared as symptoms: a constellation of physical and mental disorders were linked to the railway experience, including 'railway spine'.[7]

The telegraph network that accompanied the railways had almost as great an effect as the railways themselves, providing as it did a system that made it possible to send a message over long distances without its incorporation in a physical object. This had obvious ramifications for the military, for business and for journalism, but it also dramatically altered everyday private communication, at least for those who could afford to pay for 'telegraphic messages', or telegrams as they were soon called. When the Atlantic Cable was finally laid successfully in 1865, the speed of communication between Great Britain and the United States was greatly increased (while being far from instantaneous). In the long term, this would help to create an intercontinental, Anglophone media network.[8]

The artistic response to the railways and the transformed landscape that came with them is more obvious in the pre- and early Victorian period, not only in works including Turner's *Rain, Steam, and Speed – the Great Western Railway* (before 1844), but also in the many fine aquatints of railways engraved by Robert Havell, Henry Pyall and others. But for the most part Victorian fine art eschews the direct representation of the industrialized landscape, just as it tends to pass lightly over the industrialized towns and cities. Many artists, as Herbert Sussman has noted, took part in an anti-industrial counter-revolution, confining themselves to the painting of pastoral landscapes and pre-industrial genre scenes.[9] Certainly there is a greater likelihood of seeing sheep (and indeed shepherds) or cows than factory workers, or steam engines, in the average auction of Victorian pictures, which are probably more representative of the bulk of the artistic production of the period than what one sees in galleries; even street scenes are relatively rare. There are, however, some remarkable mid-Victorian exceptions to such pastoralism. Ford Madox Brown's allegorical *Work* (1852–65) is hardly a realistic portrait of the urban scene, but it does attempt to capture the energy of railway times; William Powell Frith's *Railway Station* (1862) deploys Paddington to provide a panorama of urban Victorian life (it can be compared to the very different treatment of railway stations by the French impressionists, notably Monet and Tissot); George Elgar Hicks's *The General Post Office, One Minute to Six* (1860) is a similar image of kaleidoscopic urban bustle.

Transport interiors allowed artists to convey the random and sometimes claustrophobic aspects of urban experience, as with Charles Rossiter's *To Brighton and Back for 3s 6d* (1859) and William Maw Egley's *Omnibus Life in London* (1860). (Alfred Concanen's illustrated cover to Frank Musgrave's *Excursion Train Galop* (c. 1860) provides a comic take on the same theme.) But the romantic potential of the railway compartment is also a topos common to popular and High Art alike, as in Abraham Solomon's *First Class: The Meeting* (1854) and C. H. Mackney's *Kiss in the Railway Train* (1864); when motion pictures came at the end of the century the erotic possibilities of the railway were revisited in such films as *A Kiss in the Tunnel* (1899).[10]

The telegraph system that developed alongside the railway from 1844 did not lend itself so easily to visual treatment, making one curious to know what Charles Allston Collins's unfinished *The Electric Telegraph* would have been like. Popular images of the telegraph do appear in illustrated sheet music of the 1860s (e.g., George Leybourne's *The Telegraph* (c. 1860)), and the laying of the Atlantic Cable offered an opportunity to give visual form to a medium that resisted visual representation: images of the *Great Eastern* proliferated.

Literary and dramatic responses to the new networks are, as one might expect, diverse. Wordsworth's pre-Victorian poem, 'Steamboats, Viaducts, and Railways' shows the poet willing to welcome the new industrial technologies, but by 1844, when the rail network had spread as far as the Lake District, Wordsworth was asking, 'is then no nook of

English ground secure/From rash assault'? ('On the Projected Kendal and Windermere Railway'). Even within the one text, there can be a variety of viewpoints on the impact of industrial technology, as with Dickens's railway novel *Dombey and Son* (1846–8), where the railway is at once the vehicle of progress that turns Staggs's Gardens from a down-at-heel backwater into a thriving commercial area (in chapter 20, where Dickens also pokes fun at Wordsworth's dire warnings), and in chapter 55, a monstrous force that acts as the novel's avenging angel that does not so much kill as annihilate the villainous Mr Carker.

This more Gothic aspect of trains re-appears in Dickens's later work, in the short story 'The Signalman' (1866), part of the railway-themed Mugby Junction Christmas issue of *All the Year Round*. Whether or not Dickens's own experience of the Staplehurst disaster in June of 1865 made him less inclined to celebrate the railway, 'The Signalman' explores the idea that the railway network has not so much speeded up the world as erased the line between present and future. The railway is often used as a synecdoche of grander historical changes: novels as different as Thomas Hughes's *Tom Brown's Schooldays* (1857) and George Eliot's *Middlemarch* (1871–2) use this device to evoke organic societies on the brink of transformation by new forces. Victorian melodrama put the railway to direct and spectacular use, placing a variety of last-minute 'railway rescues' on stage in 'sensation melodramas' including Augustin Daly's *Under the Gaslight* (1867) and Dion Boucicault's *After Dark* (1868), the latter featuring the recently opened London underground railway. The telegraph made a stage appearance in Boucicault's *The Long Strike*, where the testimony that is to save Jem Wilson from the gallows arrives over the wires in the nick of time. The telegraph was not always tied to the railways, and the successful laying in 1866 of the transatlantic telegraph cable between Valentia Island, of the coast of Ireland, and Heart's Content, Newfoundland, after several failed attempts, created a flurry of popular interest; it even provided material for a burlesque of that year by F. C. Burnand, in which the cable appears personified, and takes part in an underwater scene.[11] The music hall found in the railway a rich source of material. Like the London omnibus, the railway compartment features in comic songs as a place where random romantic encounters can occur, often with comically disastrous consequences. Examples include *The Charming Young Widow I Met on the Train* (1863), and *The Underground Railway* (1863): the moral of such songs is that the strangers one meets on the train cannot be trusted – especially if they are young and pretty. At least some of these songs found their way from the music halls to the middle-class parlour, where they provided material for one of the other most important technological developments of the nineteenth century: the piano (the affordability of the more compact, overstrung piano from the 1840s is a significant factor here).

Whatever its representation within Victorian literature and drama, the railway fundamentally transformed the literary marketplace and the theatre as a business. The new transport network facilitated the distribution of books, and thus expanded the national market, but it also created a new transport experience into which reading fitted very neatly. Railway booksellers (notably W. H. Smith) sprang up to meet the needs of bored travellers in search of light reading, and the term 'railway novel' came to denote a particular type of fiction – cheaply printed, colourfully bound, strongly plotted. New literary magazines appealed to the same market, from the *Cornhill* in the 1860s to the *Strand* in the 1890s. Advertisers also realized that bored travellers could be easily captivated, and railway stations were covered in hoardings, as we see in Alfred Concanen's print, *Modern Advertising: A Railway Station* (1874). Flyers could also be used: tens of thousands of these were printed for the launch of Dickens's *All the Year Round*, for example.

The rail network made possible two closely linked theatrical phenomena: the metropolitan long run, and the touring provincial production. Investment in new productions with elaborate props and top-level actors became possible when productions could draw on a large enough population to recoup their costs. Suburban rail networks expanded the reach of the West End theatres so they could attract a commuting middle-class public. Concomitantly, successful West End productions could deploy one or more touring productions, using a different cast, to cash in on metropolitan success by taking the show to the provinces, or indeed overseas. Dion Boucicault's *Colleen Bawn* (1860) is an early example of this pattern. While this new system of extracting more profit from the one play had beneficial effects for the London theatre, it sounded the death-knell of the provincial repertory theatres.

Curiously, the Victorian stage remained a relatively non-mechanized one. Stages were complex, often with elaborate traps and flies, but for the most part these complex systems depended on wood, ropes and human pulling-power. One aspect of the theatre that readily embraced new methods more was lighting. Gaslight replaced candlelight; lime light, or oxy-hydrogen light, allowed for spotlight effects; electric light eventually took over. But change was gradual, and even at the end of the nineteenth century many theatres still depended on gaslight, making them hot, airless and headache-inducing, not least because the house lights were often on during performances.

Gaslight and later electric light transformed the world of the theatre, but it changed the world outside the theatre too, of course. In working-class districts the landscape was altered in direct ways by the appearance of giant gasometers, some of which still survive. But the effects of gas lighting on life in the cities and towns were at once more subtle and profound. As the shadows shrank, people ventured on to the streets at night in greater numbers (the establishment of an organized police force was a factor here too). The twenty-four-hour London of Poe's 'The Man of the Crowd' offers a surreal vision of this gaslit city, while also suggesting that it produced new kinds of obscurity. London shops stayed open until 8pm or later, making the day of the shop-workers a long one, though some concessions, such as a Saturday half-day holiday, were won by the Early Closing Movement. Improved lighting, together with the increasingly widespread use of plate glass, made possible a new kind of immersive experience of the world of goods, first in the shopping arcades and the great exhibitions, later in the department stores: in the Bon Marché in Paris and Whiteleys in London the street moved indoors. In such temples of consumption, glass, light and consumer goods combined to produce the phantasmagoria of commodity fetishism that Walter Benjamin set out to describe in his Arcades project.

The Great Exhibition of 1851, housed in Joseph Paxton's enormous 'Crystal Palace' saw the world on the move to look at merchandise, and it is often seen as a turning point in Victorian culture at which Britain's position as the workshop of the world begins to shade into modern consumer culture. Many of the items on display in 1851 were not, however, consumer goods as we would now understand them, and a great deal of space was devoted to new technologies for businesses, from patent locks to steam engines. The international exhibitions that followed in Dublin, Paris and elsewhere kept to this pattern by reserving space for cutting-edge technologies, from improved sewing machines at the 1865 Dublin Exhibition to the 'trottoir roulant' (moving pavement) shown at the Exposition Universelle in Paris in 1900. Entertainment technologies also found an early outlet at such events: international exhibitions, but also more modest charity bazaars and fairs were where many people had their first glimpse of such novelties as the x-ray and the moving pictures of the cinematograph.

The great exhibitions made looking at goods an end in itself; the department stores provided a similar experience, though one that was meant to culminate in actual purchase. One unexpected side effect of this powerful theatre of shopping, with its temporal disconnection of the shopping experience and purchasing, was the appearance of a new psychopathology: kleptomania. The *Oxford English Dictionary* gives its first citation for this word (spelt 'cleptomania') as 1830; and it is first used in medical discourse is the 1840s; by the 1860s it had entered common parlance, and by 1863 the term was popular enough to be used as the title of a comic music hall song that described the new illness as simply a cover for rich people's thieving ('When rich people prig and steal/They call it Kleptomania').[12] In 1895 it provided the plot of Mark Melford's play, *Kleptomania*, in which a mother's light-fingered compulsion creates comic complications for her daughter's marriage plans.

Plate glass and bright lights created a phantasmagoria of consumption. But they also underpinned one of the literal phantasmagoria of the mid-century, Pepper's Ghost, a stage illusion invented by Henry Dircks and improved by John Henry Pepper for display at the Royal Polytechnic in Regent Street. A large sheet of plate glass was placed between the audience and the actors, and used to create a semi-transparent image of another actor – often clad as a ghost – who remained out of sight of the audience. The special effect was used in a revival of Charles Dickens's *The Haunted Man* (Adelphi, 1863), and other versions appeared at the music halls, inspiring the Harry Clifton song, *Have You Seen the Ghost?* (1863).[13] In this period there is a proliferation of new and often exotically titled technologies of the image, symptomatic, Jonathan Crary has argued, of a new conception of human vision as an embodied, rather than a purely abstract, intellectual activity, and thus inherently unreliable.[14] The zograscope, or diagonal mirror, a mirror-and-lens combination that could add a sense of depth to two-dimensional images, hand-coloured *vues d'optiques*, appeared first in the 1750s. Its more sophisticated successor, the stereoscope (which gave 3-D vision), had first been developed in the 1830s by Sir Charles Wheatstone, but its subsequent popularity derived from improvements made by Sir David Brewster (also inventor of the kaleidoscope), as well as from advances in photography. Brewster's 'lenticular stereoscope' became a common household object, and almost every aspect of Victorian life was photographed for stereoscopic consumption. Other technologies of the image created the sense of movement rather than depth: these included the phenakistoscope (which created the illusion of motion), the thaumatrope (which generated the illusion of a single image out of two separate images) and the zoetrope (another device that gave the illusion of motion to pictures).

Photography was the most important of the new image technologies until the 1890s, when a rival appeared in the moving images of the kineto-scope and cinematograph. Strictly speaking, photography is another pre-Victorian technology, since Nicéphore Niépce had experimented with ways to fix the images projected by the *camera obscura* in the 1810s and 1820 – and there is some evidence to date photographical experimenta-tion to the Renaissance. Louis Daguerre, Niépce's one-time partner, and William Henry Fox Talbot independently arrived at successful methods for fixing images in the 1830s; the daguerrotype emerged for a period as the more successful commercial process from its announcement in 1839, though it was Talbot who pioneered the modern negative/positive process with his calotype. The new image technologies had various limi-tations: daguerrotypes, for example, were very delicate, and could not be reproduced. Nonetheless, photography proved to be enormously popu-lar, as one can discern from the countless 'cartes de visite' portraits that we still have. The relationship of photography to painting is far from being that of a simple rival: some portrait painters may have been put out of work by the new technology, but many painters saw it as an extension of the *camera obscura* that they had used for hundreds of years, and adopted it as an artist's aid: nineteenth-century artists, from William Powell Frith to Gustave Courbet, worked in part from photographs. Nor was this a one-way street: Oscar Rejlander, for example, created a distinctive set of photographic images by combining the conventions of academic paint-ing (including ideas of the nude) and special photographic effects. His best-known photograph, the allegorical *The Two Ways of Life* (1857), uses combination printing to create a single large and complex image out of multiple photographs.

The photograph, then, was not always a simple record of what the eye could see, and indeed, in the popular practice of spirit photography – the alleged capturing of ghosts on photographs – the camera became directly associated with the unseen world. By the end of the century user-friendly cameras like the Kodak 'Box Brownie' made amateur photography a rela-tively cheap and undemanding activity, and the 'photo-fiend' is described as a type of the times. Photo-journalism also proliferated at the end of the century, in journals including the *Strand* and the *Illustrated London News*, radically increasing the circulation of the photographed image. The iconic qualities of the photograph were also harnessed by the state: by the 1850s the police had learned the utility of photography as a way of recording the faces of those in custody.[15] In the 1870s Rejlander's special effects re-appeared in a new guise, when Francis Galton produced composite photographs that were supposed to provide images of 'typical' criminal faces, prominent of jaw and low of brow, in keeping with contemporary discourses of degeneration.

In terms of its literary and dramatic take-up, as early as 1859, the camera was a familiar enough piece of equipment for it to provide a crucial plot device in Boucicault's *Octoroon*, in which the camera of a keen amateur photographer captures the murder of the young black slave, Paul, saving from the mob Wahnotee, the 'red Indian', who has been wrongfully accused. A farce of 1869, Frederic Hay's *A Photographic Fix*, is set in a photographer's studio, and much is made of the potentially deadly effects of photographic chemicals. In a final address to the audience, the photographer, Michelangelo Chrome, hopes that they have 'succeeded in developing a smile and fixing [our] attention'.[16] But in general the photographer is a relatively uncommon character in Victorian literature and drama. This is not to say that the impact of photography was not felt in literature: Nancy Armstrong has argued, for example, that the conventions of photography profoundly affected the ways in which Victorian novelistic realism developed, and that this imbrication of visuality and ideas of the real extended into the modernist period.[17]

As we have seen, there is a long pre-history to the projection of moving pictures to a paying audience by the Lumière brothers at the Salon Indien of the Grand Café on the Boulevard des Capucines in December, 1895. Nor was the Lumière brothers' show the first to deploy moving photographic images, since from 1894 Edison's kinetoscope parlours provided moving, film-based images in a peep-show format. It has often been averred that what the Lumières added was the crucial ingredient of projection, which produced a very different experience of the moving image. Increasingly, however, their primacy in this area has also been cast in doubt, since it is possible that such pioneers as the Lathams in the US and Max Skladanowski in Germany may have preceded them. At any rate, though the cinematograph was to have its greatest effect after Victoria's reign, its importance in late Victorian culture should not be discounted. The end of the Victorian era is brought closer to us by the existence of many actualités of Victorian street scenes, royal occasions and, of course, the Second Boer War, among the first to be captured in this way, notably by William Kennedy-Laurie Dickson, who describes his experiences in *The Biograph in Battle* (1901).

The cinematograph had a rival for the capture of lived experience in the phonograph. First demonstrated in 1877, Thomas Alva Edison's device allowed recordists to preserve the sounds of the Victorian period, using foil-wrapped cylinders as a medium. Engraved wax cylinders appeared with the gramophone, first developed in 1886, and cylinder-based machines survived into the 1920s, although disc-based systems existed from the 1890s. We thus have recordings of Victorian music, but perhaps of even greater interest is the surviving archive of Victorian voices: Tennyson reading 'The Charge of the Light Brigade' in 1890, and Browning's 1889 recording of 'How They Brought the Good News from Ghent to Aix', recorded not long before his death. (The recordings we have of Tennyson, and of a speech by Florence Nightingale, were made in 1890 by Edison's British representative, Colonel Gouraud, to raise money for the survivors of the Crimean War.) The significance of the phonograph, which broke the link between voice and the living person, at once seeming to extend the powers of the subject and undermine them, was not lost on the first generation of writers to encounter it, though they did not always explicitly describe the new technology: as Ivan Kreilkamp has argued, Joseph Conrad's *Heart of Darkness* (1898), written at a time when the phonograph was being widely discussed in Britain, can be read as a meditation on the curious magic of the disembodied voice.[18] George Du Maurier's *Trilby* (1894), which features a tone-deaf laundress-cum-model who is turned into a 'singing-machine', an automaton-like diva, by the mesmerism of the novel's villain, Svengali, may also have been inspired by the new machine: Du Maurier had visited the 1889 Paris Exposition, where Edison's prototype 'Talking Doll' or 'Phonograph Doll' (a doll containing a small phonograph with a recording of a nursery rhyme) provided one of the attractions. Popular culture registered the new phenomenon in other ways too, in such songs as Gus Elen's song of 1896, *The Finest Flow of Langwidge 'Ever 'Eard* ('You ought to see my phonygraff');[19] and in such blackface minstrel farces as *The Demon Phonograph; or, the Battery and the Assault* (c. 1890).

Nor was it only the recording of sound that transformed the aural landscape of late Victorian Britain. The telephone was first patented by Alexander Graham Bell in 1876, and displayed at the Centennial Exhibition in Philadelphia the same year. That it was best suited as a telecommunications technology was not immediately apparent, and as late as the

1890s it was also being used for entertainment, broadcasting concerts and providing distant access to theatrical performances for an exclusive clientele, including Queen Victoria.[20] 'Telephone Concerts' were also a popular attraction at late nineteenth-century exhibitions and fairs. Exclusivity characterized its early use for voice calls, and some early users were appalled at plans to introduce public telephones that would for a small fee allow any Tom, Dick or Harry to call private subscribers. Nonetheless, the public telephone system spread, and by 1888 a city such as Glasgow had seventy-six call boxes; by 1897, some customers were going ex-directory.[21]

One of the simpler, non-electric technologies that transformed late Victorian communications was the typewriter. In practical terms, the typewriter, and the carbon copy, had a dramatic effect on the business world, but as Friedrich Kittler has argued, typewriting also meant a profound alteration in the relationship of the writer to his or her own written words: handwriting is an externalization of thought that still maintains some connection to the personality of the writer; typewriting is something else. Typewriters also created a new form of employment for tens of thousands of middle-class women. Typists – or 'typewriters', as they were called – became an iconic feature of the commercial landscape. Mina Harker, in Bram Stoker's *Dracula*, is an early literary example of the 'typewriter' in action; the story we are reading, she tells us, is in fact assembled by her from diverse sources, and typed up. The vampire is a suitable monster for the age of mechanical reproduction, since he can make carbon copies of himself.[22] Among the less fantastic early accounts is George Gissing's *The Odd Women* (1893), set against the background of the increasing presence of women in the white-collar workplace. As Christopher Keep has argued, the 'typewriter girl' becomes not just an iconic figure of women's entry into the workforce, but a figure who mediates more general social and economic changes including the presence of new possibilities of communication across distances.[23]

The cinematograph, the phonograph and the telephone arrive during what is sometimes referred to as the second industrial revolution of the end of the nineteenth century, ushered in by the internal combustion engine, the use of electricity, new developments in chemistry and new discoveries about the nature of matter, in particular about radioactive substances. Although William Conrad Röntgen is often credited with the invention of the x-ray, or Röntgen ray, a number of scientists had preceded him in experimenting with radiation of this kind, including Tesla, Crookes and others; and Marie and Pierre Curie and Henri Becquerel were also exploring the nature of radioactive substances derived from pitchblende (e.g., radium and polonium) in the 1890s. H. G. Wells's 1908 novel, *Tono Bungay* is probably the first novel to make use of the properties of radioactive materials: the dangerous 'quap' which the protagonist tries to bring back from a murderous raid on the coast of Africa resembles pitchblende; in Wells's symbolic scheme its destructive power suggests a more general *fin de siècle* process of degeneration and collapse.

The car, like the cinematograph, makes its greatest impact after Victoria's era, but again it is worth noting its appearance within the Victorian period as another key product of the second industrial revolution. The first automobiles using internal combustion engines appeared in the 1880s in Germany, and by the 1890s they had become a relatively common sight in Britain, though actual ownership was within the reach of only the very wealthy. Kipling was an early convert to the automobile, after he was taken out for his first drive by Lord Harmsworth in 1899. He soon purchased his own car – actually a steam-powered Locomobile, though he bought a combustion engine Lanchester not long after – and as Sean O'Connell notes he later wrote that 'in three years from our purchase, the railway station had passed out of our lives'.[24] Cars feature in many of his subsequent poems and short stories, most famously perhaps in the post-Victorian 'The Village that Voted the Earth Was Flat' (1913), where he pokes fun at rural hostility to speeding motorists, which he represents as hostility to progress.

One of the most significant effects of the second industrial revolution was economic: the US and Germany outperformed Britain in harnessing new discoveries for commercial ends – the balance of industrial power shifts away from Britain, the one-time workshop of the world, during these years. Some historians have argued that the reasons for Britain's supercession had more to do with cultural than technological factors. Martin Wiener, for example, in *English Culture and the Decline of the Industrial Spirit, 1850–1980* (1981), attributes the shift to the devaluation of entrepreneurial culture in Britain, and the overvaluation of the lifestyle and worldview of the landed gentry.

The second industrial revolution involved a modernization of management as much as production: in particular it was underwritten by a commercial and managerial revolution that saw cartels and syndicates replace the family firm (the financial basis for such developments was put in place as early as the 1850s with legislation to limit liability, including the Joint Stock Companies Act of 1856).[25] As companies became larger and more complex, managers and an ever-expanding number of professionals were needed. But a clerical army was also needed to sustain this corporate world, to write its letters, keep its records, manage its accounts. This army was drawn from the more educated section of the working class, but also comprised a significant number of middle-class women, as we have seen in the case of the typewriter. The fiction of the late nineteenth century gives us abundant examples of these white-collar, lower-middle-class workers. Leonard Bast in *Howards End* (1910) is a post-Victorian example, but he is preceded by the more comic Pooter of George and Weedon Grossmith's *Diary of a Nobody* (1888–9) as well as by a number of H. G. Wells's protagonists.

The end of the nineteenth century saw Britain flex its imperial muscles, and between 1870 and 1900 millions of square miles of new territory in Africa and Asia were added to the empire. One of the factors underlying Britain's military power was, of course, its ability to deploy modern weapons and transport and communications technologies, which gave it a huge advantage in its confrontations with non-industrialized nations. This was already evident in the early nineteenth century, when paddle steamers and artillery gave the British forces an edge in the Anglo-Burmese war of 1823–6, and most of Britain's 'small wars' were marked by similar imbalances between the sides. Of course the industrialization of warfare also affected conflicts where both sides had access to modern weaponry: the American Civil War is a case in point. By the 1880s there were some significant innovations in industrialized killing, notably the machine gun. The Gatling gun had appeared during the American Civil War, and used a hand-operated crank to produce rapid fire. But the first 'proper' machine gun, the Maxim gun, was produced from 1884 by Hiram Maxim, an American inventor living in Britain. With a capacity to fire 600 rounds a minute, it saw use in the First Matabele War, and in the Benin Massacre of 1897.[26] Its most famous appearance, though, was at the Battle of Omdurman, where Kitchener's force destroyed the Mahdist army under Abdullah al-Taashi: Kitchener lost 48 men, al-Taashi lost some 10,000. The same gun, improved and renamed the Vickers gun, was used by the British Army from 1912: in various versions it would inflict devastating losses on all sides during the first World War. It was clear by the end of the century that industrial firepower would win out over manpower on almost every occasion.

Victoria's death in 1901 does not mark any neat end to the machine age any more than her accession to the throne announced a neat beginning.

Many of the most significant Victorian technologies would continue to be significant (e.g., the railway, the telephone). Other technologies created during the nineteenth century would rise to dominance in the twentieth (the automobile, the cinema, electric light, automatic weapons). The discoveries in particle physics that were beginning to be made would have even more dramatic effects. Nor did the cultural modes shaped by the first truly industrial century disappear: melodrama lingered on stage and migrated into the cinema; the domestic novel was outflanked by other literary modes, but it has never gone away; the detective story continues to function as a cultural staple in a dozen baroque variations, from regional crime fiction to the North American television series *CSI: Crime Scene Investigation*. And like the Victorians we continue to see machines as the opposite of ourselves, however much we write of cyborgs; their pastoral fantasies as much as their technological fantasies linger on, even while, for us, the Victorian era has itself come to represent the pastoral past.[27]

Notes

1 Jonathan Crary, *Suspensions of Perception: Attention, Spectacle, and Modern Culture* (Cambridge, MA: MIT Press, 1999).

2 On Lee, see Gregory W. Bush, *Lord of Attention: Gerald Stanley Lee and the Crowd Metaphor in Industrializing America* (Amherst: University of Amherst Press, 1991).

3 See Owen Ashton and Stephen Roberts, *The Victorian Working-Class Writer* (London: Cassell, 1999).

4 For a different view of what happens to the issues of the industrial novel after the 1860s see Catherine Gallagher, *The Industrial Reformation of English Fiction: Social Discourse and Narrative Form, 1832–1867* (Chicago: University of Chicago Press, 1985).

5 Wolfgang Schivelbusch, *The Railway Journey: The Industrialization of Time and Space in the 19th Century* (Berkeley: California University Press, 1986).

6 Cited in ibid., 54 n. 8.

7 See ibid., 135–6.

8 On the power of that media network by the late Victorian period, see, for example, Clare Pettitt, *'Dr. Livingstone, I Presume?' Missionaries, Journalists, Explorers and Empire* (Cambridge: Harvard University Press, 2007).

9 Herbert Sussman, 'Industrial', in Herbert F. Tucker (ed.), *A Companion to Victorian Literature and Culture* (London: Blackwell, 1998), 244–57 (253).

10 On Solomon's painting and railway-compartment erotics, see Christopher Matthews, 'Love at First Sight: The Velocity of Victorian Heterosexuality', *Victorian Studies*, 46 (2004), 425–54.

11 See F. C. Burnand, 'The Very Latest Edition of Black-Eyed Susan', in Richard Schoch (ed.), *Victorian Theatrical Burlesques* (Aldershot: Ashgate, 2003), 97–150.

12 On the history of the use of the term, see Elaine Abelson, *When Ladies Go A-Thieving: Middle-Class Shoplifters in the Victorian Department Store* (New York: Oxford University Press, 1989), 278 n. 88.

13 For more on Dickens and ghosts, see pp. 260–2.

14 See n. 1.

15 See Tom Gunning, 'Tracing the Individual Body: Photography, Detectives, and Early Cinema', in Vanessa R. Schwartz and Leo Charney (eds.), *Cinema and the Invention of Modern Life* (California: University of California Press, 1995), 15–45.

16 Frederic Hay, *A Photographic Fix: An Original Farce in One Act* (London: Lacy (1869)).

17 Nancy Armstrong, *Fiction in the Age of Photography: The Legacy of British Realism* (Cambridge: Harvard University Press, 1999).

18 Ivan Kreilkamp, 'A Voice Without a Body: The Phonographic Logic of Heart of Darkness', *Victorian Studies*, 40 (1997), 211–44.

19 This song was published in London by Francis, Day and Hunter in 1896. 'You ought to see my phonygraff' is the first line, sometimes given as the subtitle.

20 Carolyn Marvin, *When Old Technologies Were New* (New York: Oxford University Press, 1990), 210–11.

21 Ibid., 103–4.

22 Jennifer Wicke, 'Vampiric Typewriting: Dracula and its Media, *English Literary History*, 59 (1992), 467–93.

23 Christopher Keep, 'The Cultural Work of the Type-Writer Girl', *Victorian Studies*, 40 (1997), 401–26.

24 Sean O'Connell, *The Car in British Society: Class, Gender and Motoring, 1896–1939* (Manchester: Manchester University Press, 1998), 194.

25 For discussion of this, see pp. 61–79.

26 On the Benin Massacre and other colonial policing operations, see Ian Hernon, *Britain's Forgotten Wars: Colonial Campaigns of the 19th Century* (Stroud: Sutton, 2003).

27 For more on the Victorians, machines and personality, see pp. 266–7.

4

Economics and business

For the first three decades of the Victorian age, economic writing and economic development proceeded along paths that joined at every opportunity.[1] Not only did much economic writing directly inform policies that altered the relations between land, labour and capital, it also shaped economic behaviour by alternately generating perceptions of stability and uncertainty. Although some of this writing found its way into textbooks or specialist monographs, equally sophisticated and/or influential analyses of economic activity were as likely to appear in tracts, sermons, speeches or periodicals intended for the lay public. This situation started to change in the 1870s, and by the 1890s an avowedly less 'political' discipline of economics had begun to distinguish itself from genres of 'literary' economics, which persisted in the lay press. This new writing, which would mature in the twentieth century as neoclassical economics, appeared in new professional journals and in textbooks designed for mathematically trained specialists. Broadly speaking, it accompanied a maturing economy, for which much of the political framework had been set by earlier debates.

The early Victorian economy

By the 1830s, Great Britain's industrial revolution was reaching its peak. Its core products were consumer goods including textiles, pottery and tools, but early Victorians devoted comparable levels of enterprise and capital to transporting, financing and insuring their rising volume of commodities and people. Major iron and coal mining industries also emerged to contribute to the construction and running of the new factories and railways. These industries, along with railways, employed larger workforces than most textile mills, which usually focused on a single process (spinning, weaving or finishing) and retained the workshop model that had developed in the eighteenth century. The exception to this rule in textile production was cotton, which combined several processes in a single factory. As they switched to mechanical spinning jennies and power looms, most textile trades traded skilled, mostly male, workers for unskilled women and children. According to the 1841 census, only 44 per cent of the 781,000 textile workers in Britain were adult males, and just one third of cotton and silk operatives. Although 1.3 million Britons in 1841 toiled on farms and another million were domestic servants (together comprising 34 per cent of the workforce), most economic writers at the time paid most of their attention to the changing nature of work in the manufacturing sector.

All this economic activity both generated and required new forms of finance capital. Although factory owners met most of their fixed-capital needs by tapping stored-up profits, they relied on banks to provide short-term credit for trade. In Scotland, large banking companies had performed this role since the 1760s; south of the Tweed, these were forbidden by the Bank of England's charter until 1825, when a wave of failed small banking partnerships prompted parliament to legalize joint-stock banking in England. Until the 1840s, banks mainly made loans by issuing their own notes, which circulated alongside Bank of England paper. After that, as banks began paying interest for deposits, more of their loans came in the form of bills of exchange (transacted through, and often backed by, third-party brokers) or cheques, and the Bank of England increasingly took over sole note-issuing powers – a process that was finalized in 1908. Total British bank deposits passed £1 billion by 1914, while the Post Office Savings Bank and its voluntary-sector counterparts attracted an additional £256 million.

Besides contributing deposits and share capital to banks, Victorian investors also poured money into the developing railway network, which absorbed nearly £300 million in new capital between 1845 and 1847 alone. It was mainly to accommodate this huge new demand that the London Stock Exchange evolved beyond its original function of trading shares in the national debt and a handful of chartered companies; in 1836 new stock exchanges also appeared Manchester and Liverpool, closer to where many railways were being built. A final major player in the capital market was insurance, which expanded from an eighteenth-century focus on marine and fire coverage to cover life, accidents, fidelity and livestock by 1900. Life insurers evolved into major institutional investors by the late Victorian period, attracting £300 million in funds by 1900, and further diffused the investing habit by sharing most of their profits with policyholders. Friendly societies (which paid sick benefits to working-class members), building societies and retail co-operatives held an additional £140 million in funds in 1900.

Underlying these new developments in production and finance was a new focus on foreign trade. If rising consumer spending within Great Britain's borders provided the initial impulse to the industrial revolution in the eighteenth century, Great Britain became aggressively open for business with the rest of the world in the decades after Waterloo. Some of these new trading partners, including American planters and Russian farmers, were happy to supply Great Britain's voracious appetite for cotton and food. Elsewhere, British merchants forced their way into new markets. Following a change in policy in 1813, the East India Company promoted the rapid demise of Bengal textile production, to the benefit of Manchester cotton bosses; and wielding its steam-powered navy, Britain went from smuggling drugs into China to trading freely through Hong Kong and fifteen other ports following the Opium Wars of 1839–42 and 1856. Since the price of British exports typically exceeded the cost of imported raw materials, gold flowed into London to balance this account. This enabled Britain to return to the gold standard in 1821 (it had temporarily gone off the standard in order to pay for the war), and the resulting strong currency made imports even cheaper.

Great Britain's rapidly expanding export economy joined forces with its capital-hungry stock market to create major commercial swings between 1825 and 1870. Its increasing integration with world markets rendered it vulnerable to downturns abroad – most notably between 1836 and 1843, when a trade deficit deprived Americans of sufficient money to buy British-produced textiles; and in 1857, when shocks in the American financial system had an immediate impact on the British money market. Home-grown crises hit Britain in 1847, following a 'railway mania' in which investment far outstripped the capacity to build new lines, and in 1866, following the crash of Overend, Gurney, a brokerage firm that had specialized in finding credit outlets for bank deposits. Behind this second crash was a second railway bubble, this time involving smaller bond-financed 'contractors' lines'.

Economic debate and economic policy

The first decade of Victoria's reign was dominated by overlapping economic debates concerning free trade, factory production and monetary policy, each of which indirectly addressed the instability wrought by new forms of trade and credit.[2] These debates played out across nearly every imaginable genre, and writers often shifted from one genre to another when industry or finance was the topic. This flourish of discourse was a tribute to the contentious and confusing place of new economic ideas and institutions in people's lives, and marked an effort, from a number of different moral perspectives, to bestow order through utopian visions or didactic lessons.

A dramatic rise in industrial output led many to question the policy of agricultural protection that had been in place since 1815, when a new Corn Law prohibited grain imports once their price fell below 10 shillings per bushel. This law (which liberal Tories softened with a less severe sliding scale in 1828) maintained the high rents that landlords had been able to charge during the Napoleonic Wars, when disruptions to trade insulated British farmers from foreign competition. During the 1830s, support grew for abolishing the law: first among London foreign merchants and later among Lancashire factory owners. By the end of the decade, the latter group dominated the free trade movement, with the establishment in 1839 of the Manchester Anti-Corn Law League. In parliament as well, the two leading defenders of free trade, Richard Cobden and John Bright, were factory owners from the north of England.

Cheap grain imports, argued free traders, were vital for feeding the growing ranks of industrial workers, and also for giving foreign consumers more opportunity to exchange their goods for British exports. Their arguments built on Adam Smith's earlier defence of an international division of trade based on comparative advantage, and on David Ricardo's 'law of diminishing returns', which held that it was more cost-effective for Britain to feed factory workers with imported grain than to pay them to till unproductive soil. A failure to take the cost-effective option, Ricardo warned, would lead to a 'stationary state', which might be good for landlords but was injurious to the economy as a whole. As he concluded in his *Principles of Political Economy and Taxation* (1817): 'Rent increases most rapidly, as the disposable land decreases in its productive powers. Wealth increases most rapidly... where the disposable land is most fertile [and] where importation is least restricted.'[3] The same logic informed Ricardo's theory of wages: without the saving grace of free trade, too much capital would be absorbed by what later writers would call the 'wages fund' to allow for adequate profits to keep the economy growing.[4]

In practice, Ricardo was unusual in his application of careful deductive logic to issues of economic policy. A more typical collection of free trade arguments, both in substance and chaotic form, was Thomas Perronet Thompson's *Catechism on the Corn Laws*, which went through nineteen editions between 1827 and 1839. Among many other claims, Thompson urged that the Irish would be better off working in English factories than growing protected grain for absentee landlords; that free trade would 'bind nations mutually to keep the peace'; and that landlords were 'drones' who 'never go to work at all'.[5] As the hectic 1830s gave way to the 'Hungry Forties', free trade advocates moved away from stridently attacking landlords and instead focused on the stability and prosperity that free trade would allegedly bring. A leading architect of this approach was James Wilson, who used evidence of major swings in grain prices since 1815 to argue that the Corn Law confused farmers into mistaking high prices for high demand, hence recurrently planting more than the market could bear – leading to, among other things, overpopulation, unemployment and financial panics.[6]

Against such arguments, protectionists condemned the moral implications of unfettered industrial growth; worried that lower rents would prevent landlords from playing their historic role as Britain's big spenders; and scoffed that lower grain prices would not, as some free traders insisted, enable workers to buy more manufactured goods, but rather would simply result in lower wages. Thomas Malthus fired an important opening shot shortly after the passage of the Corn Law, opposing free trade on the grounds that 'the addition of wealth and population so acquired would subject the society to . . . greater unhealthiness and immorality'.[7] Appealing to statistics that revealed an excess of domestic over foreign demand for British goods, the Tory historian Archibald Alison added in 1840 that it was 'surely an unwise thing . . . to seek to extend a distant market of half the dimensions, by crippling a nearer one of double'.[8] Finally, to counter the support that some workers were lending to the slogan of 'cheap bread', protectionists accused free traders (in the words of one broadside) of 'a more ignoble interest – mere mercantile gain – *the profit of the mills*'.[9]

After getting nowhere with Whig ministries in the 1830s, free traders formed a fragile alliance with the Conservative Prime Minster Robert

Peel, who in 1842 reduced the sliding scale on corn, abolished tariffs on wheat from British colonies and lowered duties on many other imports. In 1846, following a prolonged commercial depression and a year into the Irish famine, Peel abolished the Corn Law, leading to a major split in his party. Within another decade so-called 'Peelite' Conservatives would join with pro-free trade Radicals and Whigs to form the Liberal Party under Lord Palmerston. Although Cobden and Bright refused to join his cabinet, they negotiated an important trade treaty with France in 1860. Other countries did not return Britain's favour of unilateral free trade: Prussia and the Rhineland remained hunkered behind their *Zollverein* (or customs union), which expanded upon German unification in 1870, while the United States pursued consistently high tariffs from 1861 through to the end of the century.

If one tenet of classical political economy declared that free trade in grain was vital for economic prosperity, another loudly proclaimed that an unbridled factory system was the best way to postpone the Ricardian stationary state. It was mainly to advance this proposition that Ricardo developed his famous labour theory of value, which would loom large over economic writing for half a century. What mattered for Ricardo was how much labour went into the production of different types of goods. Assisted by machinery and living on an infertile island, he claimed, British workers would produce more wealth as factory operatives than as farmers. He also held out hope that moving workers from the farm to the factory might prevent Malthus's spectre of overpopulation – where the number of human beings exceeded the resources and opportunities for work available to keep them. Contrasting industrial England with agricultural Ireland, he urged that factory labour would give Irish workers the same 'taste for the comforts and enjoyments which habit has made essential to the English labourer', which (as Malthus himself suggested towards the end of his life) was the best incentive to postpone marriage.[10]

A second plank of this argument, which came to be known as Say's Law after the French economist Jean-Baptiste Say, held that a permanent and general glut of factory-produced goods was impossible. James Mill was the first British economist to articulate this theory when he argued in *Commerce Defended* (1808) that '[t]he production of commodities . . . is the one and universal cause which creates a market for the commodities produced'. This was another way of saying that manufacturers automatically created sufficient demand for their products through the simple act of bringing these products to the market, and that a free market would always eventually steer producers from sectors with an excess supply of goods into those in which demand exceeded the supply. 'Whenever this balance is properly preserved', concluded Mill, 'there can be no superfluity of commodities.'[11] The same reasoning applied to labour as a commodity, and economists employed it to deny that converting to new technologies would produce long-term unemployment.

This defence of the factory system carried with it a danger, from the perspective of capitalist apologists, of proving too much. So-called 'Ricardian socialists' soon emerged who were willing to concede that Britain's factories produced more wealth than its farms, but who demanded a greater share of that wealth for the workers whose labour was said to create its value. Typical was Thomas Hodgskin, who argued that 'the best means of securing the progressive improvement, both of individuals and of nations, is to do justice, and allow labour to possess and enjoy the whole of its produce'.[12] In *Labour's Wrongs and Labour's Remedy*, John Bray offered a practical application of this idea by proposing large-scale co-operative factories. Under his profit-sharing plan, he urged, 'machinery would no longer be an antagonist of the producer' (i.e., worker), but 'a universal friend and assistant'.[13] Revealingly, neither Hodgskin nor Bray opposed free trade, which they saw as adding to the wealth of a transformed factory system.

From the other end of the political spectrum, the Scottish evangelist Thomas Chalmers provided an influential Malthusian argument against Say's Law. Far from postponing the stationary state, he argued, unhindered factory production would accelerate it, by encouraging overpopulation and further taxing a nation's food supply. The way for a country to stave off a stationary state was 'not by the multiplication of its products, but by a wholesome and moral restraint on the multiplication of its people'.[14] A final set of critics stressed factories' deleterious impact on family values and social order. Among the most influential of these were novelists including Charles Dickens and Elizabeth Gaskell, whose plots suggested the virtues of domesticity as a necessary supplement, if not alternative, to what Thomas Carlyle famously derided as the 'dismal science' of political economy.[15]

The leading policy implication of the factory debate concerned the long hours that workers (and in particular children) spent tending machinery. In England, this aspect of factory reform effectively began in 1819, when the Cotton Mills Act restricted child labour in that sector to twelve hours a day. With strong aristocratic support, the Tory MP

Michael Sadler introduced a ten-hour bill for children in 1832; this accompanied loud calls by 'short time committees' to extend the ten-hour limit to all workers. A key context for this debate was the abolition of West Indian slavery, which was working its way through parliament at the same time. The Tory factory reformer Richard Oastler attacked mill owners for 'requiring that the innocent children of the poor should . . . be subjected to a period of labour more excessive and more extensive than that which the law of England allows to an adult Negro slave'.[16] More generally, factory reformers exposed the negative influence of long hours on the education, health and morals of working-class children.

Economists defended the *status quo* by arguing that high fixed-capital costs forced factory owners to keep their machines running twelve hours a day in order to make any profit at all, and by insisting that the machines did most of the work in any case. By doing this mathematics most explicitly (and insistently), William Nassau Senior earned himself a special place on Karl Marx's list of capital's 'hired prize-fighters'.[17] Senior started with the premises that 'the great proportion of fixed to circulating capital . . . makes long hours of [factory] work desirable' and that 'the extraordinary lightness of the labour, if labour it can be called, . . . renders them practicable'. He then calculated how much money the typical factory owner invested and earned if he kept his machinery running twelve hours on weekdays and nine hours on Saturdays, and famously concluded that 'in a mill so worked, the whole net profit is derived *from the last hour*'.[18]

Defenders of the existing factory system supplemented these arguments by telling scare stories about competition from foreign factories (where conditions were even worse), and by insisting that most British factory owners extended moral and educational benefits to their workers that would otherwise be unavailable to them. These efforts were enough to water down the original bill: the Factory Act that passed in 1833 imposed a nine-hour day for children under twelve, but kept the twelve-hour day for teenagers. Even with these less stringent provisions, overworked factory inspectors had difficulty enforcing them. Looking back on this era in *Capital*, Marx wryly recounted Leonard Horner's beleaguered efforts to expose evasion and to persuade local magistrates (many of whom were factory owners themselves) to prosecute offenders.[19]

A final major Victorian economic debate concerned Great Britain's supply of paper money. A 'free banking' school led by joint-stock bankers argued that competition among banks would be enough to keep credit under control. A 'banking school', including many Bank of England

directors as well as Thomas Tooke and James Wilson, called for the Bank
to wield discretionary power as a lender of last resort. The 'currency
school', finally, which attracted most mainstream economists, sought
tougher restrictions on the amount of paper money that the Bank of
England could allow to pass into circulation. A leading proponent of this
position was the banker Samuel Jones Loyd (later Lord Overstone), who
extended a Malthusian and evangelical perspective on human frailty to
the financial community. Only the 'natural' check of the Bank's limited
gold reserves, he argued, would be enough to contain people's impulse
to borrow more than they could repay.

To judge from the attention given to this currency debate, the bank
note might appear to have been the only important form of paper that
circulated in the early Victorian money market. In fact, the financial sector generated endless varieties of paper, each of which pulled credit one
way or another: including bills, bonds, shares (paying ordinary, prefer-
ence and guaranteed dividends) and 'scrip' (signifying a subscription to
shares). Other forms of paper altered the money market as it simultaneously professed to describe it, by shaping public opinion. Company
promoters issued prospectuses that painted rosy visions of future prosperity; novelists including Dickens and William Makepeace Thackeray
lampooned unrealistic joint-stock promises in fictions of their own; and
a vibrant financial press reported investor meetings and tracked rising
and falling share prices.

In the realm of monetary policy, the currency school won the battle but
lost the war. They convinced parliament in 1844 to pass the Bank Restriction Act, which capped Bank issues at £14 million beyond the value of its
gold reserves. Similar ideas lay behind William Gladstone's Joint Stock
Companies Act in the same year, which newly enshrined the privilege
to form a company without special legislation, but paired that privilege
with unlimited shareholder liability for corporate debt. In the long run,
neither of these laws had much impact, either in slowing down Victorian investment or in teaching investors personal responsibility. Nature
bit back, when a huge influx of gold from California and Australia after
1848 made a mockery of the Bank Restriction Act, which in any case
had little reference to new forms of credit that were starting to replace
bank notes; and in 1856 Robert Lowe, a new Chancellor of the Exche-
quer with a less moralistic definition of liberalism than Gladstone's,
devised a new Companies Act that relieved shareholders of unlimited
liability.

Political economy as a science

Although the vast bulk of early Victorian economic writing took sides in policy debates, many Victorians aspired to shape behaviour more generally by undertaking a more systematic approach to the subject of political economy. As Harriet Martineau put it in a preface to one of her popular *Illustrations of Political Economy* (1832–4), her object was 'less to offer my opinion on the temporary questions . . . which are now occupying the public mind, than, by exhibiting a few plain, permanent principles, to furnish others with the requisites to an opinion'.[20] Martineau accomplished this by translating economic theories into narrative fiction; others offered more standard elementary textbooks, as when James Mill published in 1821 'a schoolbook of Political Economy', which detached 'the essential principles of the science from all extraneous topics'.[21]

Besides teaching people how to appreciate, and thereby abide by, the principles of political economy, early Victorians also strenuously tried to turn their subject into a science. Dozens of full-scale treatises on political economy appeared in Britain between 1815 and 1850, authored by college professors, lawyers, landowners, bankers, clergymen, geologists, actuaries and accountants; and scarcely a year went by in the first half of the nineteenth century without a new edition of Smith's *Wealth of Nations*. Until John Stuart Mill published his *Principles of Political Economy* in 1848, the leading expositor of the science in the wake of Ricardo was John Ramsay McCulloch, whose *Principles* went through four editions between 1825 and 1849, and who also influenced economic opinion in the *Encyclopaedia Britannica* and the *Edinburgh Review*. Another key figure was James Wilson, who went from writing anti-Corn Law pamphlets to founding *The Economist*, which from 1843 combined financial news with sophisticated economic analysis.

The fact that writers from so many walks of life felt compelled to add to the pile of treatises attests to how seriously the genre was taken. In 1811, before he achieved fame as an opium eater, Thomas De Quincey rebuked economists as 'fungus heads' whose 'dregs and rinsings' made for easy sport; three decades later, he published a book-length *Logic of Political Economy* (1844) that fully supported political economy's premises if not its clarity of thought.[22] Most such treatises followed a rigid formula that seldom deviated too far from Ricardo's discussion of value, rent, prices, wages, profit, trade, taxes and money, usually in that order. Many of these writers parted company with Ricardo only on his labour theory of value, in order to distance themselves from the socialist spin on that theory. Most of them fully shared his assumption of static equilibrium, with 'market prices' forever oscillating around 'natural prices' set by supply and demand. Readers comparing each year's new crop of political economy treatises with Adam Smith would have noticed almost none of Smith's complex account of historical change; this gave way to an insistence (inspired by Ricardo) that the laws of the new science could be deduced from a series of timeless axioms.

Along with inflecting the nuances of Ricardian economics with increasing fineness, early Victorians devoted volume upon volume to describing the internal workings and social consequences of the new factory system. Writers including Charles Babbage and Andrew Ure provided detailed descriptions of machinery and suggestions for improving their efficiency. In forums including the Manchester Statistical Society, social reformers including James Kay Shuttleworth and Peter Gaskell inquired into the impact of the factory system on rapidly growing towns and cities. Although these self-described statisticians did generate numbers, they mostly produced what we would now call ethnographies; and the same could be said for the voluminous reports that issued forth from parliamentary inquiries. The point in nearly all such studies was to discover how to improve conditions by changing workers' behaviour, instead of changing the structures that organized capital and labour. This perspective, which typified what passed at the time as a 'liberal' stance on social reform, would persist into the early twentieth century, when it began to give way to a 'new liberal' approach that assumed a universal entitlement to minimum levels of social welfare.

Not all Victorians shared in the assumptions or aspirations of classical political economy. In *Past and Present* (1843), Thomas Carlyle accused the 'lawless anarchy of supply-and-demand' of eroding Britain's traditional hierarchies, and looked instead to a pre-capitalist golden age for guidance.[23] In *Hard Times* (1854), Charles Dickens famously personified political economy in the schoolmaster Thomas Gradgrind – 'a man of facts and calculations . . . ready to measure any parcel of human nature, and tell you exactly what it comes to'.[24] Neither did the statistical societies monopolize the 'condition of England' question. Henry Mayhew wavered between middle-class moralism and a deeper empathy in his popular *London Labour and the London Poor* (1851); after visiting Manchester from his native Germany, Friedrich Engels more stridently catalogued the wrongs suffered at the hands of capital in his *Condition of the Working Class in England* (1844).

Classical political economy reached its apogee, but also began to fray around the edges, with the publication of John Stuart Mill's *Principles* (1848). In many ways, Mill offered a lively and closely reasoned defence of Ricardian economics, including the wages fund theory and Say's Law. In other ways, however, Mill expressed important reservations about the relevance of these dicta to social welfare. This evolution in thinking paralleled his journey (inspired by Coleridge and Carlyle) away from the narrow utilitarianism of Jeremy Bentham and James Mill. To this end he welcomed the prospect of a stationary state, which previous economists had regarded with 'unaffected aversion', as an occasion for people to stop 'trampling, crushing, elbowing, and treading on each other's heels' and to focus instead on 'improving and elevating the universal lot'.[25] In such a state, he urged, certain forms of co-operation between labour and capital would be well worth pursuing – a perspective in line with that of a briefly influential mid-century circle of Christian socialists whose ranks included the theologian Frederick Denison Maurice and the novelist Charles Kingsley.

After Mill, political economy settled into two decades of complacency that accompanied unprecedented prosperity and an absence of pressing policy debates. Into this anaemic stream of thought, John Ruskin injected *'Unto this Last'* (1860), a jeremiad against the 'first principles' of the science. His study of art had led him to conclude that the medieval age had been the last to produce true beauty; from this premise, he concluded that political economy was misguided to celebrate the present as the pinnacle of progress. Instead of conceiving man as a 'covetous machine', Ruskin re-envisioned capitalism as a system in which fair wages enabled respect between master and servant, and in which everyone in society aspired to 'the possession of the valuable by the valiant'.[26] Although the four essays that comprised *'Unto This Last'* were poorly received when they first appeared in the *Cornhill Magazine* in 1860, Ruskin's blend of ethics and economics would inspire a later generation of cranky luminaries (like William Morris) and luminous cranks (like Frederick Rolfe) – not to mention most of the founders of the Labour Party.

An even more enduring critique of classical political economy erupted from the pen of Karl Marx, whose *Capital* appeared in three volumes between 1867 and 1894 (Engels completed and published the second two after Marx's death). Marx rested his critique on an inverted version of Adam Smith's history of the free market, filling capitalism's 'rosy dawn' with tales of 'extirpation, enslavement and entombment in mines ... conquest and looting of the East Indies, [and] the turning of Africa into a warren for the commercial hunting of black-skins'. After modern machinery subsequently turned factories into 'productive mechanism[s] whose parts are human beings', he argued, human agency (by capitalists, workers or political reformers) came to an end: competition, spurred onward by ever-increasing productive capacity, was impelling the system to an inevitable explosion. Marx also inverted the typical organization of the treatises he had pored over in the British Library. Instead of ending with a discussion of money, his first order of business was to expose its role in concealing from workers the fact that their labour was entirely responsible for 'surplus value'. Once they had realized this, he famously predicted, the world's workers would shed their chains and take full part in the 'social value' of what they produced.[27]

The mature economy, 1870–1900

Great Britain entered the final third of the nineteenth century with rising standards of living, but also with the nervous sense that other nations were beginning to challenge its economic dominance. German unification in 1870 and westward expansion in the United States created huge domestic markets that fuelled a 'second industrial revolution' in these countries, which relied on new or improved manufacturing processes and energy sources. The twin titans of US Steel and Standard Oil signified a widening gap between American and British business in the decade after 1900: what Alfred Chandler later distinguished as 'managerial' versus 'personal' capitalism.[28] British manufacturers had sunk too much capital into outmoded processes and infrastructures to allow for an easy adjustment to the new competition, while a world grain glut drove down rents after 1870 and confronted landlords with the unpleasant prospect of selling off their wide acres.

British merchants and financiers made up for much of the ground they were losing to the US and Germany in the late nineteenth century by turning to their expanding empire in Asia and Africa, as well as an 'informal empire' in Latin America. British merchants consistently shipped around half of their exports to places other than Europe and North

America after 1860; and by 1914, Asia, Africa, Latin America and Australia absorbed nearly 60 per cent of the £4 billion that British investors held in overseas assets. By shifting their sights to what would become known as the third world, British capitalists avoided much of the risk that had once accompanied foreign trade. When the American Civil War threatened to disrupt cotton imports, textile mills tempted Indian farmers to switch to cotton as a cash crop; when the end of the war led to a cotton glut, the resulting depression in India fuelled a famine that killed millions. When Baring Bros., a leading London investment bank, lent Argentina more capital than its money market could bear in 1890, Argentine citizens paid for the ensuing crash with higher taxes and spiralling inflation – while a Bank of England bailout left London financial markets undisturbed.

Under these circumstances, the financial services emerged by 1880 as Britain's only lasting bastion of economic might. Most banks converted to limited liability to maintain stable share prices following the failure of two major banks in 1878, and individual banks amassed enormous revenues by aggressively acquiring smaller competitors. By 1900, five joint-stock banks – Barclays, Lloyds, Midland, London and Westminster and National Provincial – dominated the financial scene, and worked closely with investment bankers to channel their deposits abroad. British fire insurance companies converted their strong financial position into a successful export strategy, surviving major fires in Boston, Chicago and San Francisco to emerge as market leaders in North America. Life insurers, finally, diversified into pensions after 1900 to build on their strong Victorian foundations.

In the realm of economic policy, apostates emerged by 1880 to question the once-holy trinity of free trade, *laissez-faire* and the gold standard. Protectionism, once the domain of landowners, emerged as a manufacturer's issue as factory owners tried to keep 'cheap and nasty' goods from invading British shores. In the 1880s, the National Fair Trade League tried (without much luck) to convince newly enfranchised workers that protected markets would save jobs and improve wages. Joseph Chamberlain's Tariff Reform League (1903–10) included grain on its list of products it hoped to protect, which attracted the support of farmers and landlords, but alienated workers by conjuring the prospect of higher food prices. While these tensions kept free trade as Britain's official policy until 1932, *laissez-faire* was less durable. Labour unions began to chip away at the ideal of minimum government intervention, first by securing basic safety and workmen's compensation laws, and then by securing the right to strike with the Trades Disputes Act of 1906.

The gold standard, long a symbol of British economic might, also came under fire after 1880. As more countries converted to gold as a basis of their currency, and with new discoveries of silver in Nevada, regions still on the silver standard (including India and Japan) took advantage of the cheapness of their currency to export goods at bargain prices into Britain. 'Bimetallists' emerged, both in America and Britain, who argued for a sliding scale between gold and silver that would prevent such aberrancies. They never achieved much traction, partly because Britain forcibly raised the value of the Indian rupee in 1893 (which contributed to a trade depression there, followed by a catastrophic famine), and partly because new gold discoveries in South Africa after 1880 brought silver and gold prices back in line. If late Victorians' faith in gold wavered, their regulation of the financial sector also shifted from the days of currency school dominance. The increasing irrelevance of the Bank Restriction Act meant that the banking school's preferred policy of discretionary central banking came into its own during the final third of the nineteenth century. This usually worked, mainly because the increasingly powerful joint-stock banks quietly stood behind the Bank of England's decisions to raise or lower interest rates.

From political economy to economics

Looking back in 1876 on the century since the publication of *The Wealth of Nations*, Walter Bagehot concluded that the teachings of political economy had 'settled down into the common sense of the nation'.[29] Assuming the truth of this assertion (which critics including Ruskin would have hotly disputed), this apparent victory of political economy begged a still-unsettled question about the proper role of economic writing in the 1870s. One response, first mooted by Stanley Jevons and seconded by Alfred Marshall, was to find aspects of economic theory that could be tested using mathematics, and jettison the rest as someone else's problem. Another, which Bagehot perfected on taking over from his father-in-law James Wilson as editor of *The Economist*, was to mould a more dynamic view of the economy by borrowing from evolutionary thinking.

Like Mill, Jevons extended to economics a new way of thinking about utilitarianism; but the key to his rethinking was calculus, not Coleridge.

He presented *The Theory of Political Economy* (1871) as an attempt to treat the economy as 'a Calculus of Pleasure and Pain', presenting 'a close analogy to the science of Statical Mechanics'.[30] The result was his theory of marginal utility, which converted consumer choices into mathematical functions that could be mapped against marginal changes in supply. By wholly equating value with consumer satisfaction (reflected in price), Jevons accomplished a complete break with the Ricardian focus on production as a measure of value, and enabled future economists to plug measurable quantities into curves depicting incremental changes in price (or rent, or wages) as a function of demand. Although many earlier economists had flirted with this idea, usually in an effort to avoid recourse to Ricardo's labour theory of value, Jevons succeeded in locating it at the centre of what economics would become in the twentieth century.

Alfred Marshall emerged as the leading British economist on his appointment as Professor of Political Economy at Cambridge in 1885. His baggy *Principles of Economics*, which went through eight editions between 1890 and 1920, included a full exposition of static equilibrium theory, the beginnings of neoclassical labour economics (which would be developed by his student Arthur Pigou) and a lengthy section on industrial organization, and sprouted calculus in its appendices. While paving the way for neoclassical economics, Marshall also looked fondly backwards to John Stuart Mill and to Adam Smith, whom he admired for heeding the 'many incidental evils' of capitalism.[31]

Although Marshall aspired to develop a theory of dynamic equilibrium that would enable economics to ascend to the level of evolutionary biology, the closest any late Victorian writer came to successfully combining evolution and economics was probably Walter Bagehot. Bagehot made a name for himself in the 1860s by developing a conservative take on social evolution that appealed to his readership of stodgy but generally liberal professional and business elites. He cynically concluded that a 'cake of custom' performed the good work of holding society together while its dynamic elements (entrepreneurs, speculators and ambitious politicians) kept it moving forward. This general perspective informed his writing in *The Economist*, which he took over from his father-in-law James Wilson in 1860 and edited until his death in 1877. He applied it to the money market in *Lombard Street* (1873), which explained that the City of London was 'often very dull, and sometimes very excited' owing to the time-sensitive, 'singularly varying' nature of credit in an economy that had become as thoroughly integrated as Britain's.[32] His solution, which paralleled his defence of the monarchy in *The English Constitution*, was to promote the Bank of England's traditional role as a lender of last resort while teaching a class of professional financiers how to minimize the damage during a crisis.

More generally, halting professionalization was the common denominator of British finance and economics after 1880. London's increasingly powerful financiers formed the Institute of Bankers in 1879 as a forum for discussing management and lobbying parliament. The financial press, meanwhile, spent less time teaching businessmen how to think and more time supplying their readers with increasingly sophisticated economic indicators. The British Economics Association formed in 1890, although only a fifth of its original members actually taught economics; the rest came from business, law and journalism. The new society's main function was to publish the *Economic Journal*, which cast a broad net: its first issue featured articles by Leonard Courtney and Sidney Webb on 'The Difficulties of Socialism' and 'The Difficulties of Individualism', respectively.

This pairing roughly summed up the perspectives on economics available to the British student at the beginning of the twentieth century. Under Marshall, Cambridge offered rigorous training in mathematical economics but little attention to what would now be called macroeconomics. Its leading competitor was the London School of Economics, which Webb and other Fabian Socialists founded in 1895 as a research arm of their programme to reform society by scientifically studying its history and structure. Whether in Cambridge or London, few practitioners of the new economics (newly bereft of the adjective *political*) possessed the same levels of moral engagement or political influence that had marked prior economic writers. For better or worse, Ricardo's earlier generation of 'prize fighters' often achieved striking success in their battle to transform society, and always occasioned lively and wide-reaching debates over the merits of the dynamic Victorian economy.

Notes

1 Victoria's reign (1837–1901) lands the historian in the middle of debates that date back at least to Adam Smith's *Wealth of Nations* (1776) and comprises at least two very distinct periods of both discourse ('classical' and 'neoclassical' economics) and economic activity (the end of the first and the beginning of the second industrial revolution). To make sense of the earlier pair of these periods it has been necessary at times to look back before 1837.

2 A fourth central economic policy debate, concerning the Poor Laws, had largely played out by 1837, after the passage of the Malthusian-inspired New Poor Law of 1834.

3 David Ricardo, *On the Principles of Political Economy and Taxation* (London: John Murray, 1817), 66.

4 The term 'wages fund' first appeared in Harriet Martineau's *Cousin Marshall*, an anti-Poor Law tale: see Martineau, *Illustrations of Political Economy*, 9 vols. (London: Fox, 1834), vol. III, no. 8, 111.

5 Thomas Perronet Thompson, *An Abridgement of the Catechism on the Corn Laws* (Bungay: Manchester Anti-Corn Law Association, 1839), 3, 4, 6.

6 James Wilson, *Influence of the Corn Laws as Affecting All Classes of the Community and Particularly the Landed Interests* (London: Longman, Orme, Brown, Green, and Longmans, 1839), 10; see also his *Fluctuations of Currency, Commerce, and Manufactures, Referable to the Corn Laws* (London: Longman, Orme, Brown, Green, and Longmans, 1840).

7 T. R. Malthus, *An Essay on the Principle of Population*, 3 vols. (London: Murray, 1817), vol. II, 495.

8 Archibald Alison, *The Principles of Population, and their Connection with Human Happiness*, 2 vols. (Edinburgh: Blackwood, 1840), vol. II, 431.

9 *League Hypocrisy! Or, The 'Friends of the Poor' Unmasked* (London: n.p., c. 1843), 1.

10 Ricardo, *Principles of Political Economy*, 101.

11 James Mill, *Commerce Defended* (London: Baldwin, 1808), 81, 85.

12 Thomas Hodgskin, *Labour Defended against the Claims of Capital* (London: Knight and Lacey, 1825), 33.

13 John Bray, *Labour's Wrongs and Labour's Remedy* (Leeds: Green, 1839), 186.

14 Thomas Chalmers, *On Political Economy, in Connexion with the Moral State and Moral Prospects of Society* (Glasgow: W. Collins, 1832), 159.

15 Carlyle coined the phrase 'dismal science' in his 'Occasional Discourse on the Negro Question', *Fraser's Magazine*, 40 (1849), 677.

16 Richard Oastler, *Report of a Speech Delivered in Favour of the Ten Hours' Bill* (Preston: Livesey and Walker, 1833), 3.

17 Karl Marx, *Capital: A Critique of Political Economy*, 3 vols. (New York: Modern Library, 1906), vol. I, 21 (from the preface to the 1873 edition).

18 William Nassau Senior, *Letters on the Factory Act, as it Affects the Cotton Manufacturer* (London: Fellowes, 1837), 11–12.

19 Marx, *Capital*, I, 312–17.

20 Martineau, *Illustrations of Political Economy*, v, 148 (preface to *Berkeley the Banker*).

21 James Mill, *Elements of Political Economy* (London, n.p., 1821), iii.

22 Cited in A. W. Coats, 'The Role of Authority in the Development of British Economics', *Journal of Law and Economics*, 7 (1964), 92.

23 Thomas Carlyle, *Past and Present* (London: Chapman and Hall, 1843), 355.

24 Charles Dickens, *Hard Times: A Novel* (New York: Harper, 1854), 14.

25 John Stuart Mill, *Principles of Political Economy*, 2 vols. (London: Parker, 1848), vol. II, 308, 312.

26 John Ruskin, *'Unto This Last': Four Essays on the First Principles of Political Economy* (2nd edn, Orpington: Allen, 1877), 2, 125.

27 Marx, *Capital*, I, 823, 371, 348.

28 Alfred Chandler, *Scale and Scope: The Dynamics of Industrial Capitalism* (Cambridge, MA: Belknap, 1990).

29 Walter Bagehot, *The Postulates of English Political Economy* (London: Longmans, Green, 1885), 1 (originally published 1876).

30 W. Stanley Jevons, *The Theory of Political Economy* (2nd edn, London: Macmillan, 1879), vii (from the preface to the first edition).

31 Alfred Marshall, *Principles of Economics* (8th edn, London: Macmillan, 1920), 205.

32 Walter Bagehot, *Lombard Street: A Description of the Money Market* (New York: Scribner, 1877), 129.

5

War

Examining 'war' in the Victorian era may seem at odds with classical Whig and Marxist interpretations of the nineteenth century with their focus upon political reform, urbanization, free trade, technological development, religious activism and intermittent class conflict. In dubbing the Victorian era as the 'Liberal Age',[1] Colin Matthew reviewed an era dominated by domestic issues and one spared major military challenges such as the wars with revolutionary and Napoleonic France and the two world wars of the twentieth century. Yet the Victorians engaged in numerous wars. Byron Farwell aptly took the popular phrase, *Queen Victoria's Little Wars* as the title of his 1972 study, and it was these conflicts that precipitated intense debate about the impact of war on Victorian values and culture. Whereas some imperial, military and cultural scholars contend that imperial wars aroused strong feelings within Victorian Britain, even if these feelings like the wars themselves were often short-lived,[2] Bernard Porter disputes that Victorians were 'imperially minded' before the onset of the 'new' imperialism towards the end of the century. Great Britain's 'cultural record', he claims, reflected 'the major concerns and priorities of most British men and women in the greater part of the nineteenth century', namely their interest in 'the problems attendant on Britain's *progress*, the unprecedented domestic changes she was undergoing in this period, for ill as well as for good'.[3] While not disputing the predominance of domestic issues, this chapter will argue that war retained a fascination for many Victorians, even dominating the political agenda at times, and that the cult of the heroic-warrior evolved over the course of the century.

When Victoria came to the throne in 1837, more than two decades had passed since the Battle of Waterloo (18 June 1815). But memories of the

French wars, often intermingled with myths, were sustained through a profusion of biographies, portraits, histories, statues and literary works. In writing *On Heroes, Hero-Worship, and the Heroic in History* (1841), Thomas Carlyle synthesized his ideas about the role of the great man in history, and in popular terms, the two great heroes of the age remained Lord Nelson and the Duke of Wellington, who died only in 1852. Although Nelson had already been the subject of numerous biographies and monuments, it was not until the late 1830s that a committee began raising funds for an iconic memorial in the newly laid-out Trafalgar Square. By November 1843 when Nelson's statue, seventeen-foot high and weighing eighteen tons, was placed on view in Charing Cross it attracted a hundred thousand visitors in two days. Later in the same month it was erected on top of the column, with the lions at the base by Edwin Landseer only finished in 1867. The design was copied from Augustus's Temple of Mars Ultor in the Roman imperial forum, a temple that linked a dead hero – Julius Caesar – with the god of war and an empire that was supposed to last forever. 'The parallel', writes Andrew Lambert, 'was clear . . . Built at the height of enthusiasm for Roman architecture, Nelson's column was the ultimate expression of British power'.[4]

Complementing the column was the completion of a seven-volume edition, *The Dispatches and Letters of Lord Nelson* (1844–6) by Sir Nicholas Harris Nicolas, an invaluable work of reference even if it omits some passages showing Nelson's weaknesses. Colonel John Gurwood's publication of a thirteen-volume edition of *The Despatches of Field Marshal the Duke of Wellington during his Various Campaigns, 1799–1815* (1833–9) also revealed much about the personality and character of the other great hero. If controversies had coloured the reputations of both men, memories of Nelson's private life had faded over forty years, unlike those of the duke's role as a Tory prime minister, staunchly opposed to political reform in 1831–2. Less identified with party politics after his caretaker premiership in 1834, and willing to support the repeal of the Corn Laws, Wellington saw his military and diplomatic reputation enhanced by the publication of the *Dispatches*. Even political opponents confirmed that the duke's own words had done much to rehabilitate his reputation[5] before he returned to his military duties as commander-in-chief in 1842.

During the last decade of the 'Iron Duke's' life, comparisons were repeatedly made between Napoleon and Wellington. The egotism, cruelty and self-aggrandizement of Napoleon were contrasted with Wellington's loyalty, duty, stolid application, common sense and gentlemanly civility. In *Vanity Fair* (1848), William Makepeace Thackeray, who visited the battlefield at Waterloo and read G. R. Gleig's *Story of the Battle of Waterloo* (1847) as soon as it appeared, described how children 'never tired of hearing and recounting the history of that famous action'. Disparaging the 'Corsican upstart', he extolled the achievements of the duke, who 'had but twenty thousand British troops on whom he could rely' (the allies were discounted as 'raw militia' or 'disaffected'), facing 150,000 French. Thackeray wrote of the 'glorious victory of Waterloo'.[6]

That victory had a meaning for Victorians beyond the defeat of Napoleonic tyranny, not least in its capacity to forge a more distinctive British identity. Apart from the equestrian statue of the duke raised opposite Apsley House in London (1846), the two main statues raised in Wellington's honour at this time were in Glasgow (1844) and Edinburgh (18 June 1852, just a few months before his death). Although Wellington had never visited Scotland nor had any connection with Scotland, Scottish Tories saw the opportunity to commemorate his achievements and promote 'the idea of Wellington as the personification of a British nation'.[7] In launching their fund-raising campaigns in 1840, seeking about £10,000 for each statue (an easier task in Glasgow than Edinburgh, where the fund-raising had to assume a national dimension under the direction of the Duke of Buccleuch), the committees wished to celebrate Scotland's role in liberating Europe from the Napoleonic yoke. At the unveiling of the Glaswegian statue in a space where barely 4,000 could gather, 20,000 spectators appeared and the Royal Scots Greys and 92nd (Gordon) Highlanders, regiments that had fought at Waterloo, waited to parade past. Sheriff Archibald Alison reminded them that they had come to pay homage to 'the greatest hero and the first man of the age'. Wellington's career, he added, 'from Assaye to Waterloo . . . was one of continued triumph, unchequered by defeat, unstained by cruelty'.[8] After Wellington's death, nearly a quarter of a million people filed before his coffin, many of them brought to London in 'funeral trains', and a million and a half lined the route to St Paul's on 18 November 1852. In Tennyson's 'Ode on the Death of the Duke of Wellington' (1852), he captured the 'mourning of a mighty nation', referring to the many qualities of the 'Great Duke' and particularly his sense of duty: 'The long self-sacrifice of life is o'er.'[9]

Conspicuous in a spectacular funeral was the abundance of heraldic images – pennons, guidons, banners, trophies and banderols – all testifying to the pervasive Victorian interest in chivalry.[10] Derived in large part from the popular historical novels of Sir Walter Scott, notably *Ivanhoe* (1820) and *Quentin Durwood* (1823), this fascination with matters medieval and the Arthurian legends underpinned the Romantic Movement whose legacies lasted well into the middle of the nineteenth century. It found reflection in attitudes to war, particularly the spirit in which war should be waged. Chivalry, as Mark Girouard argued, softened the 'potential barbarity' of war by 'putting it into the hands of men committed to high standards of behaviour' and noble ideals.[11] The Victorian officer, perceived as a latter-day version of the medieval knight, was assumed to be a gentleman imbued with the qualities of bravery, loyalty and courtesy, and endowed with a sense of honour, duty, mercy and *noblesse oblige* towards women and social inferiors. Ultimately he was thought willing to face a noble death and place death before dishonour (as evidenced in at least three poems about the wreck of the troopship, *Birkenhead* (1852) and the painting 'The Wreck of the Birkenhead' by Thomas M. M. Hemy, where officers and men were depicted calmly awaiting death by drowning as they helped women and children into the few serviceable boats).[12]

Upholding chivalrous ideals was made easier by the restricted base of officer recruitment (predominantly from the sons of aristocracy, gentry and military families) and by the durability of the officer-gentleman tradition. Army officers could not live on their pay, the rates of which were unaltered between 1806 and 1914, and officers in the guards, cavalry and infantry had to purchase their commissions until 1871. Meeting all the expenses of regimental service, field sports, mess hospitality and the social role captured in five of Jane Austen's novels[13] preserved both the social cohesiveness and shared values of the regimental officers.[14] In popular discourse, army and naval officers described themselves as serving queen and county, a devotion reciprocated by the monarch and her military-minded prince consort. Queen Victoria and Albert (until his death on 14 December 1861) took their military duties extremely seriously, conducting innumerable reviews of the fleet, and army units often in the wake of colonial wars, and visiting the wounded in hospitals. They also promoted the armed services by commissioning works of military art, including the paintings of Lady Butler and the immense works commemorating Waterloo and Trafalgar for the Royal Gallery at Westminster. They enhanced the cult of the Highland soldier through many visits to Balmoral, and recognized military bravery through the institution of the Victoria Cross. With her cousin, the Duke of Cambridge, serving as commander-in-chief (1856–95), and two sons, the Duke of Edinburgh and Duke of Connaught, in the navy and army respectively, the royal patronage of the armed services was all too conspicuous, not least in the celebrations marking the Golden and Diamond Jubilees (1887 and 1897).[15]

Victorians realized, nonetheless, that war irrespective of its mode of conduct served distinct purposes, pursued, as Michael Paris observes, in 'foreign fields'.[16] Lacking any experience of war in the United Kingdom since 1746, Victorians relied upon the mastery of the seas to defend the British Isles and a small volunteer army to maintain order at home, garrison the empire and fight overseas, often supported by the navy. Unlike their continental neighbours, the Victorians avoided the burdens of conscription and a large standing army. After Waterloo they also enjoyed nearly forty years of peace in Europe and so conducted wars primarily in an imperial context. If these wars were sometimes triggered by officials 'on the spot', and met with varying degrees of success, the opening of Chinese ports to British commerce or the annexation of Sind province, and later the Punjab, would be interpreted as bringing the benefits of civilization and the Christian mission to the unenlightened.[17] None of these wars may have excited the passions of later conflicts, even if they inspired some memorable paintings (notably *Remnants of an Army* by Lady Butler on the disastrous retreat from Kabul, 1842), but commentators exaggerate when they claim that the early Victorians were bereft of imperialist sentiment.[18] Quite apart from the imperialism implicit in the tales of naval heroism by Captain Frederick Marryat, forerunners of the juvenile fiction that burgeoned in the latter half of the century,[19] the imperial legacies of Wellington were recognized and appreciated in Tory circles. While Sheriff Alison spoke in Glasgow of the empire as a monument worthy of the duke, leaving 'the world overshadowed by its mighty dominion', Sheriff Gordon, after the Edinburgh inauguration, claimed that Britain was 'the first nation of the world', whose

> colonies are as vast as continents; her manufactures travel beyond the Chinese wall; her commerce circulates with the ocean round the habitable globe; and her language is ... known wherever enterprise can pierce, or valour tread, or dauntless heroism carry the Divine message of Christian truth ... How much of this do we owe to the crowning victory of that man who pacified the whole world since 1815?[20]

Such an interpretation was diametrically opposed to that of the peace movement and its utilitarian allies in the Anti-Corn Law League. The first Peace Society, founded by a Quaker, William Allen, in London in 1816, was dedicated to the promotion of permanent and universal peace. By the 1830s it had evolved from a body that distributed moral tracts and pamphlets into a political pressure group. In advocating the total abolition of war, and the use of arbitration to resolve international disputes, the society embraced the widely circulated writings of Jonathan Dymond, who had died prematurely in 1828 aged thirty-one. War, argued Dymond, derived from an indifference to human suffering, the pursuit of national prestige, glory and sinister interests either of governments seeking an illusory balance of power or the upper classes who controlled governments and sought outlets for their sons in the trade of war. A just war of defence might be conceivable in theory but not in practice as the consequences of war were wholly negative: loss of life, high taxation, the moral depravity of all who were involved, whether as soldiers or civilians, and the loss of civil liberty.[21]

Yet the London Society was not an exclusively absolutist body; it welcomed more pragmatic or 'conditionalist' advocates of peace and worked with utilitarians promoting free trade. By the late 1840s, the society comprised part of a more broadly based peace movement led by the Anti-Corn Law politicians, Richard Cobden and John Bright. Embracing both the moral and utilitarian wings of the movement, Cobden wrote in 1846 that 'brute force' was 'as much worshipped now, in the statues to Wellington and the peerage to Gough, as . . . two thousand years ago'. He feared, too, that the present system of international relations 'corrupts society, exhausts its wealth, [and] raises up false gods for hero-worship'. Nevertheless, he affirmed that 'If we can keep the world from actual war, and I trust railroads, steamboats, cheap postage and our own example in Free Trade will do that, a great impulse will from this time be given to social reforms.'[22]

Underpinning this optimism was the assumption that only the ruling classes wanted war, and that 'the people' would rally in support of peace. Slowly but steadily this assumption unravelled, and with it the confidence and cohesion of the peace movement. In the wake of Louis Napoleon's coup in France of 2 December 1851 an invasion scare erupted, and when Lord Palmerston proposed reviving the militia, Cobden was shocked by the lack of protest: the petitions to parliament, he acknowledged, 'were not so numerous as I expected & they did not come from all parts of the country'.[23] A few months later when Wellington died, an event still overshadowed by the ascent to power of Napoleon III, Bright was perplexed by the public response: 'That the Crown & Aristocracy should weep is perhaps not unreasonable, but why the people should look upon themselves as lost, I cannot understand.'[24] After Russophobia gripped much of the nation in 1854, and the peace movement tried to intercede by sending a deputation to meet the Tsar in St Petersburg, the public response was incandescent. While Mancunian crowds burned Cobden and Bright in effigy, the veteran peace activist, Joseph Sturge conceded: 'that the Government was far less to blame than the people of England'.[25] By the outbreak of the Indian Mutiny in 1857, neither Cobden nor Bright was willing to champion the cause of peace. As Cobden informed Sturge, 'The only possible course for our authorities to pursue is to put down by any means in their power the murderous rebels who have cut the throats of every white woman & child that has fallen into their hands.'[26] Bright wrote that 'the success of the Indian revolt would lead to anarchy in India, and I conceive that it is mercy to India to suppress it'.[27]

If the Crimean War (1854–6) confounded the peace movement, it absorbed the attention of the newspaper-reading public. Both the telegraph and railway connections between London and provinces enhanced the volume of news coverage and the rate of its circulation, particularly in the provinces, as the price of newspapers fell after the repeal of the advertisement tax in 1853 and the abolition of the stamp tax in 1855. War could now be followed through the medium of war correspondents, particularly the writings of William Howard Russell of *The Times*. He provided memorable descriptions of battlefield scenes, immortalizing the 93rd (Sutherland) Highlanders at Balaclava as the 'thin red streak topped with a line of steel' (later misquoted as the 'thin red line'), chronicled the sufferings of the ordinary soldier during the first winter in the Crimea and provided a trenchant critique of the failings of Lord Raglan's command, his staff and the support services.[28] After reading that 'someone had blundered' in the charge of the Light Brigade, Tennyson seized upon the metre and drafted 'The Charge of the Light Brigade' (1854) in a matter of minutes. A hugely popular, if controversial, poem, a thousand copies were printed in the summer of 1855 and distributed to the soldiers before Sevastopol. Even more contentious was the justification of war by Tennyson's hero in *Maud* (1855), where he claimed that war embodied

> . . . higher aims
> Of a land that has lost for a little her lust of gold,
> And love of a peace that was full of wrongs and shames,
> Horrible, hateful, monstrous, not to be told;
> And hail once more to the banner of battle unrolled![29]

Moral justifications for war might incur literary criticisms as *Maud* did, but the drama of battle captured the popular imagination. As *The Times* leader of 27 October 1854 observed, the British public had become 'engrossed' in the spectacle of war.[30] During 1854 and 1855 at least twenty-five plays, dealing with some aspect of the war, were produced at, or licensed for, ten London theatres. Military spectacles, staging versions of *The Battle of the Alma* were performed at theatres in Edinburgh and Glasgow, and pyrodramas (evening plays illuminated by fireworks and cannon fire) held in the summer months at the Belle Vue Gardens, Manchester, dramatized *The Siege of Sebastopol* and *The Storming of the Malakoff and the Redan*.[31] This intense preoccupation with war found reflection in Charles Kingsley's *magnum opus*, *Westward Ho!* 'The martial atmosphere of the novel', writes Brenda Colloms, 'neatly coincided with the military mood of the nation, and the Elizabethan battlescenes were strangely appropriate.'[32]

If the Crimean War aroused mixed feelings about the conduct of the war, and provoked demands for army reform, domestic opinion was far less divided over the sepoy revolt in Meerut (10 May 1857). The rebellion spread rapidly across provinces in northern and central India in an orgy of looting, arson and the murder of Europeans, and climaxed with the treacherous massacre of 73 women and 124 children at Cawnpore. By posing an unprecedented challenge to what Britain regarded as its civilizing mission and the promotion of the Christian message, the mutiny caused immense shock and outrage. If 'I were Commander-in-Chief in India', wrote Charles Dickens, 'I should do my utmost to exterminate the Race upon whom the stain of the late cruelties rested.'[33] However extreme, his views reflected the widespread indignation, fully shared by the soldiers in India: 'They will never get any mercy', promised a soldier of the 93rd, 'for we must be revenged for the barbarous way they used the women and children.'[34]

War in this context became an act of retributive punishment, and one that riveted attention on India and the empire as never before. The mutiny not only absorbed public attention in 1857–8 but also had long-lasting consequences beyond the replacement of the East India Company by direct Crown rule: these included 'painting, sculpture, public monuments in both India and Britain, journalism, popular biography, memoirs, books of heroes, as well as the Anglo-Indian literature of the late nineteenth century'.[35] In the brutal suppression of the revolt, Victorians found many new heroes, not least Major-General Sir Henry Havelock, a sixty-two-year-old career officer and a practising Baptist, who proselytized among the rank-and-file of the Indian Army. The remarkable exploits of his small column that fought its way into the besieged residency at Lucknow, and Havelock's subsequent death, captured the public imagination. Dubbed a 'soldier-saint' in the then popular image of the Puritan soldier, Havelock attracted innumerable eulogies, pamphlets and hagiographies, not to mention the renaming of many streets and public houses. His 'pantheonization', argues Olive Anderson, helped to establish the cult of the Christian soldier, encouraged a sense of Christian mission within the army (in the form of Soldiers' Homes, institutes, reading rooms and Temperance Societies) and ensured that the army by the mid-1860s was 'more obtrusively Christian than it had ever been since the Restoration'.[36] The popularization of the army and its wartime mission led to the para-militarism of later years – the formation of the Salvation Army, Church Army and Boys' Brigade between 1878 and 1883 – and the popularity of hymns such as 'Onward Christian Soldiers', 'Fight the Good Fight' and 'Stand Up, Stand Up for Jesus'.

This responsiveness to war or the threat of war received a further boost in the wake of another French invasion scare in 1859. While the government responded with a naval building programme and fortifications along the southern coast, *The Times* championed the revival of the Volunteer Force, formerly raised during the Napoleonic Wars, for the purposes of home defence. After the aristocratic blunders of the Crimean War, *The Times* was expressing the martial aspirations of members of the professional and business middle class. Faced with the scepticism of the government and military establishment, *The Times* published Tennyson's poem, *Rifleman Form* on 9 May 1859, with its famous warning and invocation:

> There is a sound of thunder afar
> Storm in the South that darkens the day!
> Storm of battle and thunder of war!
> Well if it do not roll our way.
> Storm, Storm, Riflemen form![37]

Within three days the government authorized the enrolment of Volunteers, and by October 1860, that enrolment numbered 119,146. It soon doubled as the Force attracted an increasing proportion of men from the urban working class, and the Volunteers remained in being for the remainder of the century. Although the enrolments fluctuated, they tended to rise during crises and anxieties such as those aroused by the Prussian victories in France (1870–1). When George Chesney wrote his account of a successful German invasion of England, 'The Battle of Dorking', *Blackwood's Edinburgh Magazine* (1871), he pioneered a highly popular genre of invasion fiction. By the 1890s many racy invasion narratives, exploiting the themes of shortsighted politicians, inadequate defences and devious enemies exploiting modern technology, appeared as serials in the large-circulation newspapers and magazines, and were later reprinted as lavish books.[38]

In the last forty years of the century, there were only two years (1869 and 1883) in which Britain was not engaged in real wars or colonial campaigning. In exotic locations, facing a variety of foes – Chinese, Abyssinians, Maoris, Fenians, Asante, Xhosa, Zulus, Afghans, Boers, Mahdists, Pathans and other tribes on the north-west frontier – British forces undertook punitive expeditions on foreign territory usually to avenge a wrong, wipe out an insult or overthrow a dangerous enemy. There were also campaigns to suppress an insurrection or lawlessness within existing colonies, and subsequently campaigns of conquest when Britain participated in the 'Scramble for Africa'. All these wars, as Colonel Charles Callwell observed in his authoritative treatise, *Small Wars* (1896), were first and foremost 'campaigns against nature',[39] and accounts or depictions of the landscapes added to the appeal of Victorian wars. They involved representations of daunting terrain (mountains, deserts, rivers, tropical rain forest and the veld), extreme climatic conditions and sometimes immense distances. If the battle paintings, prints, photographs and sketches concentrated upon action sequences, many included real or imagined landscapes. They replicated the formidable heights stormed by the Gordon Highlanders at Dargai (Allan Stewart's painting, 1898), or depicted the isolated plight of the 44th at Gandamak (William Barnes Wollen's painting, 1898), where the soldiers made their last stand amidst a 'litter of bodies in the surrounding rocks, set against the inhospitable, snow-covered landscape beyond'.[40]

Despite the overwhelming, if not universal, support for the brutal suppression of the Indian Mutiny, the ferocity of military methods could still prove divisive. A *cause célèbre* erupted when the Jamaican authorities crushed a black rebellion (October 1865), killing 500 people, injuring many hundreds and burning 1,000 homes. After a Royal Commission condemned aspects of the suppression, a Jamaica Committee, chaired by Charles Buxton MP, formed to denounce Governor Eyre and the authorities in Jamaica. It involved Radical Members of Parliament, including Bright and John Stuart Mill, middle-class businessmen, representatives of the dissenting churches and supporters of emancipation and universal suffrage. With Mill pressing for the trial of Eyre, he split the intelligentsia; whereas the men of science rallied in support, notably Charles Darwin, Thomas Henry Huxley and the geologist, Charles Lyell, the men of letters (apart from Tom Hughes) joined the Governor Eyre Defence Committee. The literati included Carlyle, author of an 'Occasional Discourse on the Nigger Question', *Fraser's Magazine* (1849), Dickens, Kingsley, Tennyson and John Ruskin alongside representatives of the landed society, 400 clergymen (mainly from the Church of England), 20 MPs, 40 generals, 26 admirals and another 30,000 individuals. While the intellectuals debated such issues as the liberties of Englishmen, colonial authority, race and the theory of evolution, Eyre resisted all attempts to prosecute him through the courts. Eventually the Liberal government moved to defray his legal expenses in 1872, and two years later, the Conservatives voted him a pension.[41]

Even more contentious were the origins of certain wars, especially when triggered by the 'forward' or provocative policies of the 'men on the spot', including the Anglo-Afghan War (1878–81) and the Anglo-Zulu War (1879). In his Midlothian speeches of November 1879 and March 1880 William Ewart Gladstone denounced 'needless and mischievous engagements' and extolled 'the rights of the savage . . . the happiness of his humble home [and] the sanctity of life in the hill villages of Afghanistan, among the winter snows'. This attack upon the 'high-spirited and warlike people' of Afghanistan, he asserted, risked making Britain 'odious and detested'.[42] Anthony Trollope expressed similar scepticism about the origins of the Zulu War in his travelogue on *South Africa* (1879), possibly the most widely read book on the continent since David Livingstone's *Missionary Travels and Researches* (1857). Unconvinced by the reasoning of Sir Bartle Frere, the governor-general of Cape Colony, whose ultimatum started the war, Trollope doubted that the Zulus posed any threat to Natal. Confident that the British forces after their initial disaster at Isandlwana (22 January 1879) would prevail, as they did, Trollope feared that the outcome would add 'another country to what is already our own – as we always have done'. The war, he suspected, would involve 'unnecessary expense' (a fear vindicated by the costly transport arrangements), and worried that 'Any question of abstract justice in such matters seems to have been thrown altogether to the winds. We are powerful, we are energetic, we are tenacious; but may it not be possible that we shall attempt to clutch more than we can hold?'[43]

Only some Liberals, like John Bright, were non-interventionist in principle. When Bright resigned from Gladstone's cabinet in 1882 following the bombardment of Alexandria (11 July), he was in a distinct minority within the party. That minority may have overlooked the fine print of the Midlothian speeches (about avoiding *only* 'needless and mischievous' engagements) and the premier's bellicose record (every cabinet in which he had served since 1843 had authorized a military expedition). So although Gladstone sympathized with the cause of 'Egypt for the Egyptians' (just as he would later describe the Mahdists in the Sudan as 'a people struggling to be free, and struggling rightly to be free'), he reacted to reports of riots and the 'massacre' of Europeans in Alexandria. Fearing for Britain's financial interests in Egypt and the Suez Canal, he approved an intervention and a 'temporary' occupation to restore 'order'.[44] From a Liberal perspective, the war proved mercifully short and overwhelmingly decisive, without any of the disasters that had scarred recent campaigns, notably Isandlwana, Maiwand (27 July 1880) and Majuba (27 February 1881). On the contrary, it climaxed with one of the great military triumphs of the Victorian age, the storming of the fortifications at Tel-el-Kebir (13 September 1882). Both the metropolitan and provincial press revelled in accounts of the daring night march across the desert and the pre-dawn assault, with sketches of the Highlanders carrying the trenches at the point of the bayonet. Memorable paintings followed, notably *Tel-el-Kebir* (1883) by Alphonse de Neuville.[45]

After this victory Sir Garnet Wolseley entered Cairo two days later. It was the apogee of a career that had so far been marked by gallantry in the field (he lost an eye in the Crimea), a commitment to army reform and success in small, logistically demanding campaigns: the Red River campaign in Canada (1870) and the Asante War (1873–4). The phrase 'all Sir Garnet' became a synonym for efficiency, and W. S. Gilbert caricatured him as the 'modern major-general' in *The Pirates of Penzance* (1879). Although Wolseley regarded war correspondents as 'newly invented curses to armies', he knew how to assist and co-opt them to promote favourable coverage of his own and the army's exploits. He also ensured that his own dispatches reached London first. After Tel-el-Kebir he lavished praise upon the Irish, who were somewhat behind the Highlanders in storming the ramparts, and the guards, who were held safely in reserve, to mollify Gladstone, then embroiled with the Irish at home, and the Queen whose son, the Duke of Connaught, had commanded the guards. Desperately wanting a peerage and a pension, Wolseley received both from a grateful government.[46]

Wolseley was by no means the only commander who recognized that he could influence the press, and hence the ways in which wars were interpreted in Victorian Britain. After the Crimean experience, Sir Colin Campbell and his staff went out of their way to accommodate Russell during the Indian Mutiny, and Major-General Frederick Roberts, VC, after enduring withering criticism at the outset of the Afghan War from Hector Macpherson of the *Standard*, had him replaced first with a military *aide de camp* and then by the compliant Howard Hensman of the *Daily News*. Hensman not only extolled the achievements of Roberts's column, including its epic 320-mile march from Kabul to Kandahar, but also dedicated a book about the war to the 72nd and 92nd Highlanders on account of their wartime hospitality.[47]

Of all the wartime commanders, though, none compared with Major-General Charles 'Chinese' Gordon as a personality that resonated with the Victorian public. A deeply religious man, he earned accolades as a Christian soldier after confronting the Taiping rebellion in China and the slavers in the Sudan. In 1884 he dominated the debate over Britain's response to the Mahdist revolt. Public outcry, fanned by the influential *Pall Mall Gazette*, prompted Gladstone's cabinet to send Gordon up the Nile, and after further Mahdist massacres, inflammatory dispatches from Gordon and the tightening of the siege of Khartoum, press and public pressure again drove the government to send a relief force. When the latter failed to arrive in time, with Khartoum falling and Gordon killed (26 January 1885), obloquy rained down on Gladstone. His nickname GOM (Grand Old Man) was changed to MOG (Murderer of Gordon), and Robert Louis Stevenson was far from alone in writing about 'these dark days of public dishonour'.[48] Gordon became venerated as a Christian martyr, the subject of hundreds of biographies, tracts and poems and a hero commemorated in all manner of imperialist iconography, sculpture and George William Joy's imaginative painting, *The Death of General Gordon, Khartoum, 26th January 1885* (1894).[49]

The Gordon cult reflected many of the martial values that Victorians had come to revere. These included Christian discipline, promoted within the burgeoning Boys' Brigade movement (by 1899, there were 276 companies in Scotland, 470 in England and 66 in Ireland) and replicated within the Anglican Church Lads' Brigade (1891), the Jewish Lads'

Brigade (1895) and the Catholic Boys' Brigade (1896).[50] Complementing
these religious formations was drilling in schools (cadet corps in public
schools and military-style drill in state schools), and the promotion of
'manliness' involving physical prowess, courage, fortitude, nerve, loyalty, patriotism, unselfishness and self-control. All these qualities were
propagated in boys' papers, notably the *Boy's Own Paper* launched by the
Religious Tract Society in 1879, and later *Chums* (1892) and *The Captain*
(1899).[51] Another crucial medium, well developed in the public schools,
was the playing of games, and 'playing the game', thought to instil moral
values as well as manliness, character, team spirit and a sense of duty, all
values that could be transferred into wartime service. Ultimately public
schools, as Geoffrey Best asserts, sought to inculcate loyalty, which 'began
with loyalty to your house . . . and rose through loyalty to your school (a
paradigm of the nation) to loyalty to your country, faith and leaders'.[52]
Juvenile literature spread these ideas more widely with the publication
of over 900 new books annually by the 1880s. Many of these adventure
yarns, set in an imperial context, carried an aggressive militaristic message, if not in the writings of W. H. G. Kingston and R. M. Ballantyne,
then emphatically in the stories of Dr Gordon Stables and of G. A. Henty,
the doyen of this genre.[53]

Even if the juvenile literature served primarily as 'escapist' reading,
and never prompted any rush to the colours,[54] it perpetuated the heroic-
warrior ideal expressed in the theatre, popular music, a myriad of images
and popular literature. Martial values recurred in melodrama with its
strong passions, vigorous action and moral themes: the Zulu War in *Youth*
(1881), the Sudan campaign in *Human Nature* (1885), the Burmese war in
A Life of Pleasure (1893), the Matabele rising in *Cheer, Boys, Cheer* (1895) and
the South African War in *The Best of Friends* (1902), all performed at Drury
Lane. In a poster for *One of the Best* (Adelphi Theatre, 1895), a Highland
soldier proclaims, 'You may take my life/But you cannot take from me
my Victoria Cross.'[55] Popular music and the music halls both reflected
and constructed views on imperial war, sometimes employing writers
from the stage (Charles Godfrey) and usually sharing preoccupations
about hero-worship, manliness and patriotism. There were songs about
contemporary heroes (*Sir Garnet Will Show Them the Way* and Gordon's
death in G. H. MacDermott's *Too Late, Too Late*), and, by the 1890s, the halls
celebrated the heroics of individual soldiers, with Leo Dryden becoming
known as the 'Kipling of the halls'. Ever since the Russo-Turkish War
(1877–8) when 'MacDermott's Warsong', written by G. W. Hunt, put

'jingoism' into the language, the music halls had embraced a bellicose patriotism, bouts of Germanophobia and, by the 1890s, the theme of 'Motherland' underscored during the South African War (1899–1902) by the rallying of imperial forces (George Lashwood's *Motherland, or Australia Will be There*) and Irish loyalty (Dryden's *Bravo Dublin Fusiliers*).[56]

These songs, like the many other images of war in the late Victorian years, confirmed wartime stereotypes, particularly that of the Highland warrior. Just as the stoicism, loyalty and martial prowess of the Highland soldier had been lauded since Waterloo in paintings, prints and in the novels of James Grant, so the later wartime exploits found representation in art (Robert Gibb's *The Thin Red Line*, 1882), on the stage, in jubilee productions (*Victoria and Merrie England*, 1887, and *Under One Flag*, 1897) and in songs and marches (Gerald F. Cobb's *The Gay Gordons*, 1897, and *The Charge at Dargai*, 1898). In an era of drab, khaki-clad soldiers, the picturesque Scots advertised products as disparate as Bovril, cocoa, biscuits and whisky; they appeared on court cards, postcards, cigarette cards and scraps for children's albums. After the failure of the Gurkhas and English soldiers to storm the heights at Dargai, Sir Edwin Arnold, the poet laureate, composed an eleven-stanza tribute, concluding with 'The Colonel's simple word did make it/ "The Gordon Highlanders will take it!"'[57]

If Highland ferocity was often depicted in racial terms as demonstrating a peculiar propensity for war, it was widely understood that the Highland regiments depended upon recruits from the urban communities of central Scotland with a substantial influx of English (often known as 'Whitechapel Highlanders') and Irish soldiers. As Heather Street argues, since 'any Briton could potentially "become" a Highlander, the language of race functioned in this context as an inspirational tool', demonstrating that Britons possessed all the intrinsic qualities to confront their enemies.[58] Ultimately such analysis reflected a form of social Darwinism whereby war became the ultimate moral test of a nation and victory a reflection of its racial superiority. Writing in 1899, Sidney Lowe asserted that 'there is scarcely a nation in the world – certainly not in our high-strung, masterful, Caucasian world – that does not value itself chiefly for its martial achievements'. Crushing the dervishes, he asserted, was a 'righteous and necessary war' that would bring 'the benefits of civilised rule'.[59] War had become a test of character and will as exemplified at the Battle of Atbara (8 April 1898), where George Warrington Steevens (*Daily Mail*) described how soldiers advanced through a hail of bullets, which 'whispered to raw youngsters in one breath the secret of all the glories of the British Army'. Destroying a dervish army in two hours of fighting, he observed, had 'sobered them from boys to men'.[60]

Of all the writers, none was more influential than Rudyard Kipling. Having spent seven formative years in India (1882–9), he forged some military contacts when based at Lahore but much of his writing was derived from secondary sources – his father's knowledge of India and his library, as well as the files and reference works of *The Civil and Military Gazette*. Despite never seeing a shot fired in anger until 1900, Kipling wrote evocatively about the realities of frontier fighting. In *Arithmetic on the Frontier*, he depicts the risks, hardships and the possibility of an unheroic death that faced a young subaltern:

> A scrimmage in a Border station –
>> A canter down some dark defile –
> Two thousand pounds of education
>> Drops to a ten-rupee jezail –
> The Crammer's boast, the Squadron's pride,
>> Shot like a rabbit in a ride![61]

Even more original was his writing about the private soldier, including two hugely popular collections of verse, *Soldiers Three* (1890) and *Barrack-Room Ballads* (1892). No one had written so extensively about the private soldier before nor, in the age of Yeats, Conrad and Wilde, had anyone done so 'in the language of the people and with the rhythm of the music hall'.[62] By using local dialect, and by stripping away pretence, Kipling portrays the grim life of *The Young British Soldier* in India, dominated by the climate – 'the worst o' your foes is the sun over'ead' and the risk of cholera – with release sought through drinking, whoring and barrack-room brawling. War, as in *Oonts*, becomes part of a soldier's routine:

> Wot makes a soldier's 'eart to penk, wot makes 'im to perspire?
> It isn't standin' up to charge nor lyin' down to fire;
> But it's everlastin' waitin' on a everlastin' road
> For the commissariat camel an' 'is commissariat load.

Kipling captures, too, the profound paradox about Victorian attitudes towards 'Tommy Atkins', a man of lowly status shunned by respectable society in peace but lauded as a potential hero in war:

> I went into a theatre as sober as could be,
> They gave a drunk civilian room, but 'adn't none for me;
> They sent me to the gallery or round the music-'alls,
> But when it comes to fightin', Lord! They'll shove me in the stalls![63]

Although Kipling's work provoked criticism as well as plaudits, it was immensely popular not least among the soldiers themselves. When he visited the troops during the South African War (1899–1902), Kipling received cordial receptions wherever he went. Whether rankers had always spoken in the manner described by Kipling may be moot but they adopted terms like 'Fuzzy Wuzzy' and came to express themselves, as Sir George Younghusband recalls, 'exactly like Rudyard Kipling had taught them in his stories!'[64] More significantly, by focusing upon the individual like so many late Victorian commentators, and by doing so primarily in an Indian context, Kipling reinforced the perception that war was a remote activity undertaken in exotic locations where qualities of character, valour and will prevailed. The military agreed. In colonial warfare, wrote Colonel Callwell, small British forces had to seize the strategic initiative, sustain the offensive, bring the enemy to battle and beat him thoroughly (as at Omdurman, 2 September 1898). The aim was to undermine the enemy's will to resist and compel him to recognize the dominant 'forces of civilization'.[65]

None of these assumptions prepared the army or the country for the test that would occur in October 1899 when the Boers delivered an ultimatum and invaded Cape Colony and Natal. For the first time British forces faced a highly mobile enemy, adept at the use of cover and armed with German field guns and smokeless magazine rifles. Character, valour and will were all too evident in response but not always sufficient as British and imperial forces struggled to engage an enemy they could not see and to cross fire zones swept by magazine rifle fire. Admittedly the sieges of Ladysmith, Kimberley and Mafeking were raised, and the humiliating defeats of Stormberg, Magersfontein and Colenso, the so-called 'Black Week' (10–15 December 1899) avenged, but even after the capture of the Boer capitals of Bloemfontein and Pretoria, it would take nearly two years and an expenditure of over £201 million and the deployment of 448,435 British and imperial troops to suppress the Boers. The war was a massive shock to British self-confidence, arousing demands for army reform, compulsory service in peacetime and inquiries into the physical quality of British manhood prompted by the large numbers of men rejected as unfit for military service.[66] Kipling, though, was not dismayed; in *The Lesson*, published in *The Times* (29 July 1901) he urged his readers:

> Let us admit it fairly, as a business people should,
> We have had no end of a lesson; it will do us no end of good.[67]

Notes

1 H. C. G. Matthew, 'The Liberal Age (1851–1914)', in K. O. Morgan (ed.), *The Oxford Illustrated History of Britain* (Oxford: Oxford University Press, 1984), 463–522.

2 G. M. MacKenzie (ed.), *Popular Imperialism and the Military 1850–1950* (Manchester: Manchester University Press, 1992); M. Paris, *Warrior Nation: Images of War in British Popular Culture, 1850–1920* (London: Reaktion, 2000); E. M. Spiers, *The Scottish Soldier and Empire, 1854–1902* (Edinburgh: Edinburgh University Press, 2006).

3 B. Porter, *The Absent-Minded Imperialists: Empire, Society, and Culture in Britain* (Oxford: Oxford University Press, 2004), 163.

4 A. Lambert, *Nelson: Britannia's God of War* (London: Faber, 2004), 328–9; 'The Nelson Statue', *Illustrated London News*, 4 Nov. 1843, 289.

5 C. M. Woolgar, 'Wellington's Dispatches and their Editor, Colonel Gurwood', in Woolgar (ed.), *Wellington Studies 1* (Southampton: Hartley Institute, 1996), 189–210.

6 W. M. Thackeray, *Vanity Fair*, ed. G. and K. Tillotson (London: Methuen, 1964), xxix–xxxii, 167, 311, 314, 342; I. Pears, 'The Gentleman and the Hero: Wellington and Napoleon in the Nineteenth Century', in R. Porter (ed.), *Myths of the English* (Cambridge: Polity, 1992), 216–36.

7 J. E. Cookson, 'The Edinburgh and Glasgow Duke of Wellington Statues: Early Nineteenth-Century Unionist Nationalism as a Tory Project', *Scottish Historical Review*, 83 (2004), 23–40, at 34.

8 'Inauguration of the Equestrian Statue of the Duke of Wellington', *Glasgow Herald*, 11 Oct. 1844, 1; 'The Wellington Statue at Glasgow', *Times*, 11 Oct. 1844, 5.

9 C. Ricks (ed.), *The Poems of Tennyson* (London: Longmans, 1969), 1007–9; Pears, 'Gentleman and Hero', 232; E. Longford, *Wellington: Pillar of the State* (London: Weidenfeld and Nicolson, 1972), 493–5.

10 M. Greenhalgh, 'The Funeral of the Duke of Wellington', *Apollo*, 98 (1973), 220–6.

11 M. Girouard, *The Return to Camelot: Chivalry and the English Gentleman* (New Haven: Yale University Press, 1981), 16.

12 Ibid., 13–14.

13 D. F. Bittner, 'Jane Austen and her Officers: A Portrayal of the Army in English Literature', *Journal of the Society for Army Historical Research*, 72 (1994), 76–91.

14 Officers, possessing more modest means, either required a patron to advance their careers in the purchase army or sought service in India, E. M. Spiers, *The Army and Society, 1815–1914* (London: Longman, 1980), 14–23.

15 C. Erickson, *Her Little Majesty: The Life of Queen Victoria* (London: Robson, 2004); J. W. M. Hichberger, *Images of the Army: The Military in British Art, 1815–1914* (Manchester: Manchester University Press, 1988), 77, 82, 107; Spiers, *Scottish Soldier*, 4–5, 35, 81, 112, 121; Lambert, *Nelson*, 332–3.

16 Paris, *Warrior Nation*, 25.

17 Ibid., 20–1; D. French, *The British Way in Warfare 1688–2000* (London: Unwin Hyman, 1990), 120–7.

18 Cookson, 'Edinburgh and Glasgow Duke of Wellington Statues', 35; W. J. Reader, *At Duty's Call: A Study in Obsolete Patriotism* (Manchester: Manchester University Press, 1988), 44.

19 P. Brantlinger, *Rule of Darkness: British Literature and Imperialism, 1830–1914* (Ithaca: Cornell University Press, 1988), chapter 2.

20 'Public Meeting in the Music Hall', *Scotsman*, 19 June 1852, 3; see also 'Inauguration of the Equestrian Statue', 1.

21 P. Brock, *Pacifism in Europe to 1914* (Princeton: Princeton University Press, 1972), 339–41, and *Varieties of Pacifism* (Syracuse: Syracuse University Press, 1998), chapter 7.

22 J. Morley, *The Life of Richard Cobden* (London: Fisher Unwin, 1903), 410–11. Sir Hugh Gough received a baronetcy after the First Sikh War (1845) and a viscountcy after the second (1848–9).

23 British Library (BL), Add. MSS 43,656, fol. 267, Cobden MSS, Cobden to Sturge, 31 Mar. 1852; see also M. E. Howard, *War and the Liberal Conscience* (London: Temple Smith, 1978), 45–6.

24 BL, Add. MSS 43,383, fol. 253, Bright MSS, Bright to Cobden, 15 Oct. 1852.

25 'The Peace Society', *British Banner*, 24 May 1854, 375.

26 BL, Add. MSS 43,722, fol. 249, Sturge MSS, Cobden to Bright, 1 July 1857.

27 G. M. Trevelyan, *The Life of John Bright* (London: Constable, 1913), 261.

28 L. Brown, *Victorian News and Newspapers* (Oxford: Clarendon, 1985), 27, 31–2; A. Hankinson, *Man of Wars: William Howard Russell of The Times* (London: Heinemann, 1982).

29 Ricks (ed.), *Poems of Tennyson*, 1092; see also J. Richardson, 'The Most English of Englishmen: An Impression of Tennyson', *History Today*, 23 (1973), 776–84.

30 *Times*, 27 Oct. 1854, 6.

31 J. S. Bratton, 'Theatre of War: The Crimea on the London Stage 1854–5', in D. Bradby, L. James, B. Sharratt (eds.), *Performance and Politics in Popular Drama* (Cambridge: Cambridge University Press, 1980), 119–37; B. Findlay (ed.), *A History of Scottish Theatre* (Edinburgh: Polygon, 1998), 172, 188–9; D. Mayer, 'The World on Fire . . . Pyrodramas at Belle Vue Gardens, Manchester, c. 1850–1950', in MacKenzie (ed.), *Popular Imperialism*, 179–97.

32 B. Colloms, *Charles Kingsley: The Lion of Eversley* (London: Constable, 1975), 186, 193.

33 C. Dickens to Miss Burdett Coutts, 4 Oct. 1857, in G. Storey and K. Tillotson (eds.), *The Letters of Charles Dickens*, 10 vols. (Oxford: Clarendon, 1965–2002), vol. VIII, 459.

34 'Letter from a Soldier in the 93rd Regt', *Glasgow Herald*, 12 Apr. 1858, 5.

35 J. M. MacKenzie, 'Heroic myths of empire', in MacKenzie (ed.), *Popular Imperialism*, 116.

36 O. Anderson, 'The Growth of Christian Militarism in Mid-Victorian Britain', *English Historical Review*, 84 (1971), 46–72.

37 Ricks (ed.), *Poems of Tennyson*, 1110–11.

38 H. Cunningham, *The Volunteer Force: A Social and Political History, 1859–1908* (London: Croom Helm, 1975), 11–12, 15, 50; I. F. Clarke, *Voices Prophesying War* (2nd edn, Oxford: Oxford University Press, 1992), chapter 2.

39 Colonel C. E. Callwell, *Small Wars* (London: HMSO, 1896; reprinted by Greenhill Books, 1990), 44.

40 P. Harrington, *British Artists and War: The Face of Battle in Paintings and Prints, 1700–1914* (London: Greenhill Books, 1993), 256–7; P. Usherwood and J. Spencer-Smith, *Lady Butler: Battle Artist 1846–1933* (Gloucester: Alan Sutton, 1987), 175.

41 G. Heuman, *'The Killing Time': The Morant Bay Rebellion in Jamaica* (Knoxville: University of Tennessee Press, 1994), xiii–xiv, 165–74; B. Semmel, *The Governor Eyre Controversy* (London: MacGibbon and Kee, 1962), 62–5, 116–19.

42 'Mr Gladstone's Visit to Mid-Lothian', *Scotsman*, 27 Nov. 1879, 5; 'The General Election', *Scotsman*, 18 Mar. 1880, 5; R. Kelly, 'Midlothian: A Study in Politics and Ideas', *Victorian Studies*, 4 (1960), 119–40.

43 A. Trollope, *South Africa*, a reprint of the 1878 edition with an introduction and notes by J. H. Davidson (Cape Town: Balkema, 1973), 18, appendix A, 465, 470–1; D. Morris, *The Washing of the Spears* (London: Cape, 1966), 587.

44 H. C. G. Matthew, *Gladstone 1875–1898* (Oxford: Clarendon, 1995), 123, 131–5; *Parliamentary Debates*, third series, 288 (12 May 1884), col. 55; A. Schölch, 'The "Men on the Spot" and the English Occupation of Egypt in 1882', *Historical Journal*, 19 (1976), 773–85.

45 'The Battle of Tel-el-Kebir: First in the Fray', *Illustrated London News*, 7 Oct. 1882, 1; Spiers, *Scottish Soldier*, chapter 4.

46 Spiers, *Scottish Soldier*, 74–5; G. J. Wolseley, *The Soldier's Pocket Book for Field Service* (London: Macmillan, 1886), 170.

47 Spiers, *Scottish Soldier*, 13, 52–3; H. Streets, *Martial Races: The Military, Race and Masculinity in British Imperial Culture, 1857–1914* (Manchester: Manchester University Press, 2004), 121–32; H. Hensman, *The Afghan War of 1879–80* (London: Allen, 1881).

48 R. L. Stevenson to J. Addington Symonds, 30 Feb. 1885, in B. A. Booth and E. Mehew (eds.), *The Letters of Robert Louis Stevenson*, 8 vols. (New Haven: Yale University Press, 1995), vol. v, 79–80.

49 D. Johnson, 'The Death of Gordon: A Victorian Myth', *Journal of Imperial and Commonwealth History*, 10 (1982), 285–310; R. Hill, 'The Gordon Literature', *Durham University Journal*, 47 (1955), 97–103.

50 J. O. Springhall, *Youth, Empire and Society: British Youth Movements, 1883–1940* (London: Croom Helm, 1977), 27, 37.

51 J. Springhall, 'Building Character in the British Boy: The Attempt to Extend Christian Manliness to Working-Class Adolescents, 1880–1914', in J. A. Mangan and J. Walvin (eds.), *Manliness and Morality: Middle-Class Masculinity in Britain and America 1800–1940* (Manchester: Manchester University Press, 1987), 66; P. A. Dunae, 'Boys' Literature and the Idea of Empire, 1870–1914', *Victorian Studies*, 24 (1980), 105–22.

52 G. Best, 'Militarism and the Victorian Public School', in B. Simon and I. Bradley (eds.), *The Victorian Public School* (London: Gill and Macmillan, 1975), 128–46, at 143; J. A. Mangan, *The Games Ethic and Imperialism: Aspects of the Diffusion of an Ideal* (Harmondsworth: Viking, 1986), 69–70.

53 Dunae, 'Boys' Literature', 110–11; J. Richards (ed.), *Imperialism and Juvenile Literature* (Manchester: Manchester University Press, 1989).

54 J. McAleer, *Popular Reading and Publishing in Britain 1914–1950* (Oxford: Clarendon, 1992), 29; on army recruiting problems, A. R. Skelley, *The Victorian Army at Home* (London: Croom Helm, 1977), chapter 5.

55 G. Rowell, *Theatre in the Age of Irving* (Oxford: Blackwell, 1981), 138–9, 144–5.

56 D. Russell, *Popular Music in England, 1840–1914: A Social History* (Manchester: Manchester University Press, 1997), chapter 7; J. Richards, *Imperialism and Music: Britain 1876–1953* (Manchester: Manchester University Press, 2001), 328–34; L. Senelick, 'Politics as Entertainment: Victorian Music-Hall Songs', *Victorian Studies*, 19 (1975), 149–80.

57 'At Dargai', *Daily Telegraph*, 26 Oct. 1897, 9; Spiers, *Scottish Soldier*, 116–22; D. Russell, '"We Carved our Way to Glory": The British Soldier in Music Hall Song and Sketch, c. 1880–1914', in MacKenzie (ed.), *Popular Imperialism*, 50–79.

58 Streets, *Martial Races*, 9–10.

59 S. Lowe, 'The Hypocrisies of the Peace Conference', *Nineteenth Century*, 45 (1899), 689–98.

60 G. W. Steevens, *With Kitchener to Khartum* (London: Blackwood, 1898), 146–7, 152; R. T. Stearn, 'G. W. Steevens and the Message of Empire', *Journal of Imperial and Commonwealth History*, 17 (1989), 210–31.

61 *Rudyard Kipling's Verse, Definitive Edition* (London: Hodder and Stoughton, 1946), 45; see also C. Carrington, *Rudyard Kipling: His Life and Work* (London: Macmillan, 1978), 142–4.

62 P. Mason, *Kipling: The Glass, The Shadow and The Fire* (London: Cape, 1975), 73.

63 *Rudyard Kipling's Verse*, 398, 408, 416–17.

64 'Amusing Letter from a Cameron Highlander', *Edinburgh Evening News*, 22 Mar. 1898, 4; Sir G. T. Younghusband, *Soldier's Memories in War and Peace* (London: Jenkins, 1917), 187.

65 Callwell, *Small Wars*, 75–6, 85, 91, 151–71.

66 Parliamentary Papers, *Report of the Inter-Departmental Committee on Physical Deterioration*, Cd 2175 (1904) XXXII; A. Summers, 'Militarism in Britain before the Great War', *History Workshop*, 2 (1976), 104–23.

67 *Rudyard Kipling's Verse*, 299.

6

Music

British musicality

Victorian musical life was shadowed by a troubling constant: soul-searching about musicality. Britain suffered an extraordinarily vivid, widespread and long-lived reputation as a nation without musical sensibility or talent. Nietzsche complained that 'what . . . offends us about the most human Englishman is his lack of music', and Emerson bluntly pronounced that 'England has no music.' Frederick Crowest's 1881 history *Phases of Musical England* – despite the bravado of its title – conceded that 'we are not essentially a musical people', although he countered in characteristic Victorian fashion that 'we probably spend upon the Art and its Artists more money than any two or three other nationalities combined'. By 1914, when German sociologist Oscar Schmitz was looking for a book title that would instantly identify England in the minds of his continental readers, he chose the obvious: *Das Land ohne Musik*.[1]

Scholars today understand that the fixation arose largely from Britain's failure in the early part of the century to produce an 'English Beethoven' – a frequently voiced lament – or to provide home-grown products for the wildly popular opera stage. Anxiety was heightened by Victorian confidence, mounting throughout the entire century, of Britain's superiority in virtually every other realm, whether military, industrial, imperial or literary. In retrospect, the situation was only compounded by the disciplinary practices of both history and musicology, obsessed as they have been until recently with 'great men'.

In fact, Britain's dismal composerly reputation obscures two contrary aspects of its musical life: that the Victorian public created the most welcoming and the most lucrative market that continental musicians found anywhere, and that in terms of interest and participation there was no more vital musical culture in Europe.

The first of these phenomena was called by some 'xenophilia' and by others 'foreign domination', giving us an idea of the range of attitudes towards what is perhaps the most salient feature of the Victorian relationship to the art music tradition. The mixed feelings reflected mixed ideas about whether the 'parade' (another favorite epithet) of foreigners was cause or effect of the famed dearth of home-grown musical talent. Many contemporary commentators argued that it prepared the ground for the later enormous expansion of British musical life, since it accustomed listeners to very high standards of composition and performance, and helped to generate well-informed demand. In any event, it remained a constant topic of debate throughout the century.

As far as performers were concerned, it was widely acknowledged that sooner or later everyone worth hearing could be heard in London; many international stars made repeated visits and long stays, playing to enthusiastic and growing audiences, so that it might even be called the metropolitan epicentre of musical activity for most of the century. Largely, of course, this came about because Britain's long lead in industrial development meant that for several decades its cultured middle classes had more leisure time and more disposable income than other Europeans. A regularly appearing theme of Victorian novels, however, was the social awkwardness generated by these musicianly visits: touring virtuosi were lionized, but were never really respectable, nor was it clear to what social class they belonged.

The fondness of the British for foreign composers was even more striking. It was, of course, an already settled tradition, since one of the acknowledged greats of the eighteenth century – George Frideric Handel – came to live in England permanently; he is listed in the *Oxford Dictionary of National Biography* and is called by many reference books 'an English composer of German birth'. Handel lived and worked in London from around 1713 until his death in 1759, and changed certain aspects of British musical life irrevocably – as well as setting an otherwise improbable number of musical masterworks in the English language. As Shaw wrote in 1913, 'Handel is not a mere composer in England: he is an institution. What is more, he is a sacred institution.'[2]

The other iconic visitor was Felix Mendelssohn, who made the first of several visits to England in 1829 at the age of twenty and gradually endeared himself not only to the public but to the Queen as well. He too is credited with an influence far beyond his own musical activities, as his exemplary behaviour, his family's cultural and financial status and especially the Queen's favour played a significant role in helping to make composers more respectable in society. For better or worse, these two remained closest to Victorian hearts; London taste, in particular, was conservatively attached to Mendelssohnian style for decades, and massed choirs throughout Britain are still singing *Messiah* to this day.

So no doubt Crowest was right about Great Britain's vast expenditure on music; in fact, he was echoing composer William Sterndale Bennett's rhetorical question to a London Institute audience in 1858: 'What country pays more for music than England?'[3] A new seriousness in cultural production in general, around the time of Victoria's accession, may have helped generate the increasingly urgent thirst for music. But it was frequently observed (and still is) that this development may owe as much to the moral preoccupations of mid-Victorians, about which I shall have more to say below, as to an actual fondness for the sound of music.

By the last decades of the century things had changed somewhat: widely respected professional composers of British birth had begun to appear, whose works have remained, to some extent, in the canon, including Arthur Sullivan (b. 1842), Hubert Parry (b. 1848), Charles Villiers Stanford (b. 1852) and Edward Elgar (b. 1857). Some controversy has arisen about the genesis and authenticity of this so-called 'English musical renaissance', given its emergence just as issues of nationalism and imperialism came especially vividly to the fore.

There is no question that this generation of composers was widely seen as the long-looked-for answer to England's problem: to find a genuine, native musical voice, to counter once and for all the exclusive influence of the 'parade of foreigners' that marked the nation's foremost arena of cultural insufficiency. But was it, as some have suggested, a deliberately staged and politically motivated pageant of nationalism, even jingoism, or was it simply a normal development of musical culture – which does, after all, have a history of its own? In any event it is these composers, and Elgar in particular, who became associated with Britain's growing world empire during their careers and have sometimes found themselves playing slightly Kiplingesque roles subsequently.

Public and domestic music

Just as elsewhere in Europe, concert music in Great Britain in the nineteenth century underwent a profound and sometimes awkward transition from aristocratic patronage to the robust development of a middle-class audience, with commensurate changes in musical style and in the sheer size of both compositions and performing forces. A pertinent comparison might be between the eighteenth-century Concerts of Antient Music, which came to an end in 1848, having operated by aristocratic subscription and marked by nostalgic taste and a fairly amateur performance standard, and the Philharmonic Society, founded in 1813 by professional musicians, which played recent and current music to high professional standards, addressing its programmes to and relying on the developing middle-class audience.

During the middle of the century, music was undergoing the same process as other callings, becoming increasingly professionalized, with training and certification eventually provided by specialized educational institutions founded for the purpose. Although the demarcation between public and private became increasingly rigid as the century went on, musical activity burgeoned in both to an almost astonishing degree.

The significant increase in public concert activity in Britain, especially in London, really started in the 1830s as Victoria's reign began, and saw an especially vigorous growth after 1870. Seen through a typical Victorian eye, this expansion of musical life was widely taken as a sign of the emergence of a splendidly unified, like-minded society without serious rifts of class or political interest; an anonymous writer in *Macmillan's Magazine* in 1875 called music the 'panegyric', which could 'bring the largest gathering of people into conscious and intelligent sympathy'[4] – the quintessential Victorian public event.

One after another, performance venues and organizations appeared, notably John Ella's Musical Union, founded in 1845 for the performance of chamber music, and the 'Monday Pops' (popular concerts) at St James's Hall, started in 1859 and lasting for forty years. Of special significance, however, was the Crystal Palace. After the Great Exhibition of 1851, the building was dismantled and rebuilt in Sydenham, where it opened in 1854 as a permanent site for public events of many sorts, and quickly became the most important place in Britain for public music-making. Its performance spaces were continually renovated and enlarged, including at one point the installation of the largest organ in the country, until it had halls suitable for musical events of various sizes. Most highly regarded were the large-scale orchestral programmes of the Saturday Concerts, started in 1855 and continuing until the end of the century. Perhaps the huge and persistent success of the Crystal Palace partially explained why there was no really satisfactory concert hall in London until quite late in the century, although several fine ones had been built in other cities; orchestral concerts, even wildly popular ones like Louis Jullien's 'promenade concerts', took place in theatres.

The splendid musical career of the Palace was largely the work of one of the last of the gentleman-amateur generation, George Grove, a passionate and unusually knowledgeable music lover (trained, however, as an engineer), who served as the secretary of the Crystal Palace Company. Later in his unusual career, Grove became the editor of *Macmillan's Magazine*, the initiator of what is still the predominant music reference book in English, *Grove's Dictionary of Music*, and ultimately the first director of the Royal College of Music.

But it was not as a venue for orchestra concerts that the Crystal Palace became most famous. Rather, it could hold the thousands of performers and listeners who participated in the 'monster' oratorio presentations that were, perhaps, the iconic Victorian musical events. Choral festivals and competitions had taken place all over Britain at least since the previous century; best known were the 'three choirs' festivals held in the cathedral cities of Gloucester, Worcester and Hereford, and other festivals took place in Leeds, Birmingham and Norwich. But oratorio on a truly massive scale took off during the Victorian period, spurred by the early craze for public singing classes, part of (in some minds a substitute for) the push for public musical education. In the so-called 'Tonic Sol-Fa' movement, John Hullah and his methodological rival John Curwen and their disciples taught thousands of middle- and working-class Britons around the country (and in many parts of the empire as well) to sing, and to enjoy singing together. Triennial Handel Festivals at the Palace lasted for several days and presented oratorios with 'monster' choruses and orchestras of several thousand. At the centenary celebration of Handel's death in 1859, a chorus of 2,700 and an audience of over 81,000 were recorded.

It was characteristic of Victorian ideas about music that the oratorios served both musical and religious purposes; indeed, there was much debate about the propriety of their double nature. Just as, in an earlier period, oratorio had provided a satisfactory dramatic substitute for theatrical performances banned during Lent, during the nineteenth century mass audiences could feel that a day's jaunt to Sydenham had, in some sense, provided them with a religious experience – and one which, furthermore, could be shared by establishment and Nonconformist churchgoers together. In his days as a music critic, G. B. Shaw attended many such events and skewered them as religious 'humbug'. A typically sardonic comment appeared in a June 1890 column in *The World*: 'It was prime, no doubt, at the Crystal Palace on Saturday, to hear the three thousand young ladies and gentlemen of the choir, in their Sunday best, all shouting "Stone him to death; stone him to death."'[5]

Not to be forgotten in any assessment of the development of Victorian public music are the considerable economic consequences of this enormous increase in demand: not only was there more work for musicians and for music teachers – hence, eventually, the need for conservatories and training schools – but vigorous growth in the markets for printed music and for the manufacture of musical instruments also followed. The removal in 1860 of protective tariffs on the importation of musical instruments had a significant influence on both public and domestic music-making. Periodicals multiplied, first those addressed to professional musicians and then those for the general music-loving public.

Music-making in the home also underwent explosive development during the period and was largely responsible for the enormous demand for music teachers, printed music and keyboard instruments. It is not at all clear (indeed, to the contrary) that these practices were driven by any widespread passion for the music itself. Professional musicians tended to see domestic musical activities as unserious and conducive to bad taste, but social reformers thought otherwise, confident that playing and listening – unless to hopelessly vulgar music in hopelessly dangerous venues – were good for the soul.

Bourgeois daughters at the keyboard dominated the field, just as so many Victorian novels have portrayed or caricatured them; I will have more to say about this phenomenon below, but here I want only to point to its astonishing ubiquity and almost frightening social stranglehold. The musical repertory itself was moulded by the phenomenon, since amateur pianists at home demanded pieces that were 'brilliant but not difficult', to use a catchphrase of the day; we are reminded of the 'brilliant' and 'triumphant voluntary'[6] with which Becky Sharp marked her social ascent. For the most part, instead of the sonatas we would think of as staples, girls played fantasias or variations on currently popular tunes, most likely tunes taken from favourite operas, and learned to accompany dances and popular ballads for singing.

The situation of domestic chamber music is slightly anomalous; while new research is demonstrating that it was not as entirely absent as has been thought, nonetheless the British prejudice against music as a pursuit for gentlemen was powerful and militated against the development of chamber playing as a family pastime or as a masculine social activity, as was common on the continent. Rumour had it that a taste for music was considered a tragic development, or even a disgrace, in a male child.

General music education remained meagre during most of the nineteenth century but was a frequent topic of concern and debate, understandably so given the qualities that Victorians thought music could impart. When school music began to grow after the 1830s it did so because of the success of arguments that it would wean children's minds from 'vicious and sensual indulgences',[7] as the Committee of Council on Education said in 1841, and that it could be of central importance in forming an industrious and loyal working class. As the century went on, musical skill began to emerge as a means of social emulation, especially for girls, and it gradually found its place in public school curricula as well. By the 1870s, anonymous writers in the shilling monthlies were beginning to congratulate themselves that even Oxford and Cambridge undergraduates knew something about music.

Professional musical education was transformed during the Victorian era as well, swept up in the larger national drive for British superiority and the self-consciousness about the nation's poor musical reputation. The Royal Academy of Music, founded in 1822, was in that period largely ineffective, for many reasons including its reliance on aristocratic subscription and the lack of professional standards; similarly, an abortive National Training School for Music (1873) did not thrive because of its dependence on fee-paying students whose aspirations were limited to drawing-room culture. But the Royal College of Music, opened in 1883 in South Kensington, finally provided a serious conservatory for the preparation of professional musicians; an alternative venue for the training of military musicians was founded at Kneller Hall. Both of these institutions are still in operation.

Industry and progress

In the 'century of progress', we could hardly be surprised to discover that musical life was assessed, continuously and self-consciously, in the same terms as industry or military success. In an 1897 issue of the *Fortnightly Review* dedicated to assessing the development of the nation during the Queen's reign, critic Francis Heuffer asserted that no other art, indeed no other field excepting the natural sciences, had made so much progress in that period as music.

Musical 'progress' could mean various things: that the demand for professional music was increasing; that the middle-class audience was becoming more sophisticated in its taste; that performance standards were improving; that some native-born compositional talent was beginning to appear; or finally that the knowledge of art music, together with bourgeois taste, was seeping down into the lower classes. It seldom, and then only among professional musicians, referred to progress in musical style itself, at least until the end of the century when Wagner and 'the music of the future' became topics of general controversy. Music played a role as well in more general assessments, as the 'handmaid' of social progress and the achievement of social goals such as improvements in education and class relations.

The impact of industrialization is visible everywhere in the history of Victorian music, central as it was to the growth of musical audiences and mass participation in any number of ways. The urbanization that accompanied industrialization had implications for both concert life and popular musical activity that cannot be exaggerated. Standardization of production brought musical instruments within the budgets of vast numbers of consumers. Pianos, with their large array of identical moving parts, became the iconic musical product of industry; while it has been calculated that a pre-industrial piano maker, say a master employing a handful of craftsmen and apprentices, could produce around fifty pianos each year at the most, even at the turn of the nineteenth century the Broadwood factory could produce several hundred. What was more, the British products were widely acknowledged to be of higher quality, and British manufacturing methods were gradually copied elsewhere.[8] Factories made other instruments as well, mechanical instruments like music boxes, player pianos, and far more elaborate devices, and of course instruments for the brass band in great numbers.

Rationalized industrial work shifts, bringing increased leisure time on standardized schedules, made large middle- and working-class publics available for promenade concerts, excursions to the Crystal Palace and large-scale band or choral rehearsals. And, of course, there began to be discretionary income to spend on musical activities: leisure time and spending money together created a public for music. A good deal of the mass activity that became possible was also aided and abetted by the 'rational recreation' movement, a meliorist social philosophy that saw a stark choice for workers between a concert in the park and an evening in the pub, and often provided financial incentives to nudge them towards the right choice. Outside London, especially in the north, manufacturers themselves were the patrons of working-class musical activities, intended among other things to keep workers out of trouble and to gain their loyalty and gratitude.

And then there were the railroads. Since the Crystal Palace was outside London, concert life and transportation had perforce to develop together. The railroad companies built special spurs, scheduled special trains and even eventually constructed a second station to bring the enormous crowds to Sydenham, and for some years the concert programmes listed the times of departing trains. The *Musical Times* reported on one day in 1859 when 'for some hours during the morning the passengers delivered exceeded 12,000 per hour, or 1,000 every five minutes'.[9] Good railroad service was also necessary for the flourishing of provincial choral festivals and the nation-wide travel of band members to competitions.

Common and distinct musical cultures

British Victorians shared a lively and surprisingly common musical culture, which is not to say either that it was experienced by everyone in the same way or that distinct musical subcultures were lacking. The emergence of a classical music canon or 'standard repertory' began around the middle of the nineteenth century, and its notional segregation from 'popular music' was not firm until the turn of the twentieth. Until then, familiarity with the concert and opera repertory – even if sometimes in makeshift form – was very general in the population, and musical mixtures and crossovers were numerous and fruitful. The commonalities resulted from the ways in which music circulated in Victorian life: in many guises it resounded outdoors and in large public spaces, travelling throughout the country and through much of the empire.

To begin we might mention the choral singing movement and choral festivals; choral societies were enormously popular in all parts of the country and strikingly pervasive through the class structure. Gradually, too, they even played a role in the 'renaissance' of English composition, since they provided a ready-made and massive performance opportunity for composers including Arthur Sullivan and his contemporaries. Choral events, especially festivals, became iconic as instances of British national, even patriotic, expression.

Ballet and opera functioned as popular and money-making activities. Although performances were not of course financially available to the lowest classes, plenty of parody versions, especially of Italian operas, were found in music halls and variety theatres, where they came to be known by a very diverse public, and in fact helped in turn to generate enthusiastic audiences for the originals.

Although the ballroom dance world was strictly, and often explicitly, segregated by class and dance venue, its musical repertory was much less so; most people would know the same waltzes and familiar traditional dances like 'Sir Roger de Coverley'. Similarly, from the 1830s on promenade concerts, taking place in city parks and seaside resorts, drew enormous crowds. Conductor Louis Jullien became famous (in some circles infamous) for his showmanship and favourite gimmicks like the jewelled baton he reserved for Beethoven; nonetheless his programmes included complete symphonies along with the usual pastiches of lighter music, and he familiarized large publics with mainstays of the concert repertory.

Patrons of the most familiar forms of popular music, theatre and music hall were less stereotypically lower class than is sometimes assumed nowadays; rather, the halls were frequented by a mix of classes that became increasingly broad and gradually included women. As the music halls became established, they began to feature a familiar array of opera tunes, even whole scenes from operas, until curbed by regulation. There were reports of newsboys in the streets whistling tunes from *Faust*. Late in the century, increasingly frantic attempts were made to establish regulatory barriers between music hall and legitimate theatre, limiting the kinds of presentations the music halls could offer. An 1892 Select Committee recommended 'an absolute distinction between the theatre and the music-hall, that the theatre is the representative of cultured dramatic feeling, and that the music-hall is a place where you primarily go to drink and smoke, and where there happens to be a performance as well'.[10]

Eventually such legislation did change the atmosphere and the music heard in the halls.

Forms of popular music were also part of the general culture. So-called 'royalty songs' became common musical heritage just like their American equivalents from Tin Pan Alley, and during the 1870s and 1880s the Gilbert and Sullivan operettas were relied upon as family entertainment in wide swathes of the public. It is bemusing today to encounter the disdain with which the critical press reacted to these pieces and their runaway popularity; they were very widely held to be financial rather than artistic gambits, and – most ironically – they were dismissed as 'ephemeral'. While it would be foolish to suggest that members of all classes could see the shows at the Savoy Theatre, it was nevertheless the case that sooner or later everyone knew the good tunes.

Even street music, excoriated as it was by Babbage, Dickens and others trying to do serious work inside their London homes, made its contribution to the spread of a common musical culture. While it has been suggested by some scholars that many of these musicians were only extorting payments for silence from neighbourhood residents, others were in fact immigrant musicians from Europe whose repertory was firmly based in the classical tradition, which they played so frequently and so ubiquitously that the music became literally inescapable.

Despite the strength and vivacity of this common musical culture, it is nonetheless the case, as I suggested above, that not everyone in Victorian society experienced it in the same way. It is well understood, vividly from literary sources, that girls and women had their own peculiar relationship to musical culture. At the root of the peculiarity were Romantic and Victorian values that associated music with female nature at a very deep level, an aura that did not entirely dissipate until twentieth-century rock performers vaporized it. English men in particular worried about music's feminizing effects; perhaps they still took to heart Lord Chesterfield's advice to his son, in a letter of 1749, that 'it puts a gentleman in a very frivolous, contemptible light'.[11]

Bourgeois daughters were expected to provide their families with entertainment, while always bearing in mind that musical entertainments were to be edifying and uplifting. Conduct books, of which Sarah Stickney Ellis's *Daughters of England* (1842) is only one typical example, reiterated endlessly the gravity of this responsibility and the benefits families could expect: fathers soothed on return from the office after a hard day's work, brothers kept out of gin palaces and reconciled to family life, mothers relieved of their cares about making ends meet, invalids charmed out of their pain; it is easy to forget, nowadays, how seriously all this was taken in a certain segment of society.

Daughters' sacrificial hours upon the piano bench also represented the family's aspirations to gentility and upward class mobility. The entire complex of practices constructed girls as dutiful and marriageable rather than as musical – not to be taken seriously in the musical arena – and no doubt for many of them turned music into a hated obligation and source of perpetual embarrassment.

On the other hand, profoundly associated with music though they were, middle-class women at the start of Victoria's reign were very limited as to where and when they could hear it: they could attend an orchestra concert, opera or oratorio, if accompanied, but seldom encountered other musical phenomena besides their own parlour playing. As the century went on, though, women's options increased; they could walk more freely in the streets or hear popular songs first-hand in music halls. While according to social stereotypes women were not expected to claim professional status as musicians, and most especially not as composers, as a matter of fact they outnumbered men in the profession by the end of the century, working mostly as music teachers in schools or as private piano teachers making house calls.

Many writers of the period did not see, or pretended not to see, music cultures of any value emerging from the working class; their focus tended to be entirely on the 'progress' workers were making in developing bourgeois taste – what they referred to as becoming musical. But in hindsight it is easy to see creative verve and musical innovation amid a burgeoning working-class musical sensibility.

It is crucial to note, though, that mapping musical repertories on to economic classes is a dicey business, seldom very reliable and even less so in a context like Victorian Great Britain, where the crossovers were so very rich. To complicate the categories even further, folklorists characterize this as a moment of transition in which the presumably authentic folk music of an earlier and more rural time becomes enmeshed in developing capitalist modes of marketing music to a mass audience, blurring the line between folk and popular song. There are urban folk music practices as well. We may take as exemplary the survival (or perhaps revival) of the broadside ballad from Elizabethan times, in which news and events of the day, including the grievances of protest movements, were carried into working-class slums. Broadsides relied on a substantial repertory of tunes that were familiar to everyone, since they carried only printed words and the name of the tune to which the words fit. The practice survived at least until the time of the Crimean War, gradually disappearing then in favour of large-circulation newspapers and a music hall repertory that served similar purposes of topical humour and social commentary.

The crown jewel of working-class music was certainly the brass band, and sociologist Dave Russell even says categorically that 'the brass band represents one of the most remarkable working-class cultural achievements in European history'.[12] Although the bands originated in factories in the industrial north as 'improving' activities sponsored by the company owners, the players took hold of the opportunity and ran with it; they jealously guarded their organizational autonomy from their bosses, choosing their repertory, organizing rehearsal times and arranging to participate in the competitions that multiplied from their origins in the 1810s through their heyday in the 1860s and beyond. At that point, a band competition might see as many as sixty-five bands with over a thousand players, performing first as a single massed group and then in competition that reputedly became somewhat energetic. A few of the bands, like the familiar Black Dyke Band, founded around 1816, are still in existence today.

Music in the Victorian churches represents another set of distinct cultures which, however, grew closer to commonality towards the end of the century. Church music was the one arena in which Britain had always been exempt from its poor musical reputation; it remained renowned for both its composers and organists, although even here some of the lustre was left over from earlier centuries. World-famous church composers including Samuel Wesley and his son Samuel Sebastian were closely associated with the service music of the Anglican Church, especially the cathedrals. Today, music historians who wax enthusiastic about Victorian religious music are usually describing the most rarefied of high church practices, those of cathedral or university chapel, but the experiences of others could be very different, for the dissenting churches brought along with them dissenting musical practices, and just as religious differences were a constant topic of debate and argument, especially in the first half of the century, musical differences were their persistent accompaniment.

There were several bones of contention, of which arguably the most vexed was the appropriate extent of congregational participation – this was a doctrinal point with Nonconformists, but to the establishment it often translated as contempt for aesthetic values. It followed that hymns themselves, ideal for congregational singing, became a derivative issue, as opposed to composed services or to the efforts of various groups to promote the adaptation of plainchant in modern setting, both characteristic of Anglican worship. High churchmen often tended towards the medieval in ritual and garb as well as in liturgy, but when George Eliot's Dinah Morris, as she preaches, also encourages her listeners to join her in singing a hymn, she is faithful to Methodist practice. By the end of the century, to be sure, a more common interest in hymns had developed, and the publication in 1860 of Sir Henry Baker's *Hymns Ancient and Modern* helped to begin the reclamation of congregational singing for the established church.

This musical dispute could be framed in other terms as well. The 'battle of ancient and modern music' probably also carried a whiff of nostalgia for the sublime sound of the seventeenth- and eighteenth-century church composers – Gibbons, Purcell, Boyce – who represented Britain's musical golden age. Thereby another question arose, whether music in church ought have its distinct and reverent sound and style, or whether the appropriation of current popular musical styles would be more effective in luring people to worship. Folk wisdom had it that 'the devil has all the good tunes', and dissenters and evangelicals – notably the Salvation Army – found it a useful tactic to deprive him of them.

Inevitably, cultural (and literary) stereotypes developed, particularly because in Victorian Britain religious difference always entailed class difference; dissenters as well as Anglican evangelicals were perceived as noisy, 'enthusiastic', somewhat lumpen and uncultured. Charlotte Brontë's *Shirley* (1849) offers one such vignette in its sketch of a Whitsuntide procession in which the members of several Anglican parishes are confronted by a crowd of dissenters singing a 'dolorous' hymn. Although in this case the Anglicans reply arrogantly with 'Rule, Britannia' – itself a revealing response – in truth the Nonconformists' comfort with congregational hymn-singing might well have seemed primitive and unruly to establishment parishioners accustomed to having a sedate and well-trained choir do the singing for them.

Music, meaning and morals

During the nineteenth century, British philosophers shared with their continental counterparts in the general disputation about the meaning of music: its capability for extra-musical representation, the significance of its skill at emotional arousal and, in the intense debates occasioned by Darwin's *The Origin of Species* (1859), its genesis and evolutionary purpose. Over the length of the century there was a general shift from viewing music simply as decor or entertainment to awarding it significant weight as a channel of ineffable truth. A culmination of sorts was reached in Walter Pater's 1873 dictum that 'all art constantly aspires towards the condition of music',[13] a catchphrase that stresses the high significance and the indefinable aesthetic power that the Victorians attributed to the art, before yet another shift occurred at the turn of the century, towards the aesthetic philosophy that considered 'art for art's sake'.

The Victorian public, for its part, remained entirely convinced that music's significance was moral, construing it as a kind of sub-department of religion or of social work, as we have already seen. Frederick Crowest's 1881 history expressed the conviction that music was 'the mightiest among the Arts and one to which we must look for the largest refining and enlightening influence' and anticipated further progress in 'its civilising and health-giving mission'[14] if deployed diligently in society.

The *locus classicus* for this argument in its fullest form was the Reverend Hugh Reginald Haweis's *Music and Morals* (1871), one of the most influential books of the late century, which went through at least fifteen editions in his lifetime and was still being issued for years afterwards. Haweis was not an acerbic or censorious individual, like many contemporaries who warned of the dire results of musical misbehaviour, but a progressive and genial fellow whose primary interest was to encourage music for its spiritual benefits, in which he had enormous confidence and to which he had a dramatically strong personal attachment: he found himself entranced by, indeed often carried away by, music's power.

This very prevalent attitude towards the societal effects of music had both general implications and very specifically class-bound ones. In general, it sustained efforts on behalf of musical education and towards the support of musical institutions, especially the monster oratorio presentations; the widespread middle-class enthusiasm about the singing-class movement was also substantially bolstered by belief in music's moral influence, and both Curwen and Hullah promoted their classes with references to the ethical purposes of singing.

Turning the lens on the same idea, musicality could serve as an index of character or moral purpose. For this reason, music-making in a Victorian novel can never be taken lightly, since its iconic role can replace the proverbial thousand words as moral monitor or diagnostic tool. Reading

Daniel Deronda, we can learn all we need to know about the differences between Gwendolen Harleth and Mirah Lapidoth by the kinds of music they sing and their attitudes towards singing it: the one delighted to become the centre of drawing-room attention with music that Klesmer says 'makes men small',[15] the other only diffidently offering Handel and Beethoven to carefully chosen groups of sympathetic listeners.

A different light is thrown on these Victorian attitudes by their use of music as a means of social reform, a major front in what has been called 'the battle for the working class soul'. It was very widely believed that the promotion of musical activity – in particular, opportunities to hear the 'higher sorts' of music – would guard against an 1848-style revolution or perhaps Chartist-inspired class warfare. The Temperance movement also relied heavily on the promotion of choirs, bands and concerts in the park as activities workers could substitute for drinking.

It has proven nearly impossible for later historians to tease apart the motivations behind such meliorist ventures as the 'Music for the People' campaign of the century's last three decades, the foundation of the Kyrle Society by Octavia Hill's sister Miranda to bring beauty into the lives of the poor in the form of art, music and green spaces, or the presentation of free Sunday-afternoon concerts at Toynbee Hall, founded in 1884 in Whitechapel. It is certainly tempting to take the cynical view; on the other hand, considering the strength in Britain of religious prohibitions of musical performances or other forms of recreation on Sundays, the fact that so many such events occurred at all testifies to the gravity and earnestness of the public approbation of music.

A piquant demonstration of this gravity arose soon after mid-century when the case of Richard Wagner and the 'music of the future' burst upon British consciousness. A problematic figure everywhere, Wagner became a musical lightning rod in England. Part of the reason may have been that his provocative writings – egocentric, arguably racist and threatening to rewrite the entire history of music in favour of his own self-serving notions of musical progress – became known long before any of his music-dramas were performed in their entirety in London. But when they were, with their extended delirious love scenes and their passionate depiction of Walsung incest, the fraught situation did not improve.

Even in the professional music press, which remained largely conservative and resistant to Wagner's musical innovations for a long time, there was an echo of the uproar: was he a genius and musical reformer, or was he just morally disreputable and musically unintelligible? Sterndale

Bennett's account was typical, commenting that 'his aesthetic opinions, as well as the merits of his operas, have become the subjects of a violent and widespread controversy'.[16] The *Musical Times* for June 1898 quipped about J. W. Davison, *The Times*'s music critic, that 'when the name of Wagner was mentioned [he] would cry *"Police! Police!"*'.[17]

Wagner became a kind of flash-point in the music-moral arena, partially because of his musical ideas and the disturbing nature of his music itself, but first and foremost because of the moral atmosphere publicly associated with him in his personal life and perceived within his music. Such moral fixations relaxed later in the century, of course, but even as late as 1888, when Mrs Humphry Ward tells us in *Robert Elsmere* that one of her sister heroines is a violinist who plays 'the music of the future',[18] she is also letting us know that Rose is not only modern in outlook but passionate and slightly racy as well.

In short, just as it is difficult to overestimate Victorian earnestness about moral life and the rapidly changing social fabric, so also the belief that music played an extensive and unique role in both is central to understanding Victorian thought. Charles Kingsley let us understand the degree to which it mattered in a Christmas Day sermon entitled 'Music'. Music, he preached, is 'a pattern of the everlasting life of heaven'.[19]

Notes

1 Friedrich Nietzsche, *Beyond Good and Evil*, trans. Marion Faber (Oxford: Oxford University Press, 1998), 144; Ralph Waldo Emerson, *English Traits* (Boston and New York: Houghton Mifflin, 1903), n. 1 to 251; Frederick Crowest, *Phases of Musical England* (London: Remington, 1881), vii; Oscar A. H. Schmitz, *The Land without Music*, trans. H. Herzl (London: Jarrolds, 1925; orig. pub. 1914).

2 George Bernard Shaw, *Shaw's Music*, ed. Dan H. Laurence, 3 vols. (New York: Dodd, Mead, 1981), II, 638.

3 'On the State of Music in English Private Society and the General Prospects of Music in the Future', lecture of 8 Apr. 1858; William Sterndale Bennett, *Lectures on Musical Life*, ed. Nicholas Temperley (Woodbridge: Boydell, 2006), 32.

4 'Notes on Mr. Tennyson's "Queen Mary"', *Macmillan's Magazine,* 32 (1875), 434.

5 *Shaw's Music*, ed. Laurence, vol. II, 97.

6 William Thackeray, *Vanity Fair*, Project Gutenberg, www.gutenberg.org.

7 E. D. Mackerness, *A Social History of English Music* (London: Routledge and Kegan Paul, 1966), 154.

8 Arthur Loesser, *Men, Women and Pianos: A Social History* (New York: Simon and Schuster, 1954), 234.

9 Michael Musgrave , *The Musical Life of the Crystal Palace* (Cambridge: Cambridge University Press, 1995), 45.

10 Cyril Ehrlich, *The Music Profession in Britain since the Eighteenth Century* (Oxford: Clarendon, 1985), 57.

11 Philip, Earl of Chesterfield, *Letters to his Son on the Fine Art of Becoming a Man of the World and a Gentleman*, letter LXVIII, Apr. 1749. Project Gutenberg, www.gutenberg.org.

12 Dave Russell, *Popular Music in England, 1840–1914: A Social History* (2nd edn, Manchester: Manchester University Press, 1997), 205.

13 Project Gutenberg, www.gutenberg.org.

14 Crowest, *Phases of Musical England,* 145.

15 Project Gutenberg, www.gutenberg.org.

16 Bennett, *Lectures on Musical Life*, 77.

17 Percy A. Scholes, *The Mirror of Music, 1844 1944: A Century of Musical Life in Britain as Reflected in the Pages of the* Musical Times, 2 vols. (Oxford: Oxford University Press, 1947), vol. I, 255.

18 Project Gutenberg, www.gutenberg.org.

19 Charles Kingsley, *The Good News of God: Sermons* (London: Parker, 1859), 167.

7
———————

Theatre

What we think of as the Victorian theatre emerged from the late Romantic period, and the aesthetic and political anxieties of the early decades of the nineteenth century were woven into the legislative, industrial and aesthetic characteristics of that theatre throughout the rest of the century. Many of the enduring debates about the theatre – about its audiences, texts and performance practices – were first broached in the late Romantic period, when the break between popular and high culture was institutionalized and embedded in ideologically loaded hierarchies of aesthetic value. These hierarchies are still with us today: whenever impassioned public debate erupts over the place of Shakespeare's plays in English-speaking national schools curricula, or the advisability of the (British) National Theatre staging *Oklahoma* in a state-subsidised theatre, or the paucity of new plays which are not musicals on Broadway, we are re-enacting Victorian debates about the competing roles and values of theatre as entertainment, or art or education. Abiding anti-theatrical concerns that theatre professionals value art over entertainment, evident in the assumptions and actions of state funding bodies (where these exist), and the suspicion that performance for the sake of pleasure (entertainment) is somehow both ethically and aesthetically 'wrong', are views inherited from the nineteenth century. And canonical literary histories of the Victorian period – the privileging of some narratives over others – have reinforced these ideological and aesthetic anxieties.

To discuss the Victorian theatre, we really need to think about Victorian *theatres*. From the early years of the century, the British theatre industry (my account here will largely focus on London) was stratified into the 'legitimate' and the 'illegitimate' theatres through a complex web of legislative and customary practices which regulated them. By the

1830s, the legal meaning of the term 'legitimate' had been combined with aesthetic and even moral judgements of plays, theatres and audiences, to signify class differences in popular entertainment. Working-class entertainment was rarely given serious attention in public critical discourse. The fashion for melodramas about the lives of the city's poor was cause for castigation of the whole mentality of the minor theatres in the 1840s:

> When no less than seven minor theatres adopt a French melo-drama of crime and wretchedness, such as 'The Bohemians, or the Rogues of Paris', which was first introduced at the Adelphi a few weeks ago – a medley of horrors and vulgarities, with something of 'Jack Sheppard' and 'Tom and Jerry' in its composition – there is little chance for the Shakespearian drama in those quarters.[1]

This comment reveals the distance between the denizens of 'those quarters' of the minor theatres, and the opinion-forming classes, in a discursive process which Jim Davis and Victor Emeljanow argue constitutes an orientalizing of the working-class audience as a different type of people, strange and remote.[2]

However, the practices and effects of the divisions within the theatre industry were not always those articulated or valued at the time, and there were times when similarity was more evident than division. The quality and variety of play scripts, for example, thought to be one of the ways in which the legitimate theatre was superior to that of the illegitimate (or 'minor') theatre, is not borne out by an analysis of theatre repertoires or individual plays. Indeed, if the early twenty-first-century criterion of innovation in new writing is applied, then the minor theatres offer significant innovation throughout the period, in their inventive manipulations of genre, adaptation and spectacle, particularly through hybrid forms such as melodrama and burlesque. Notwithstanding dismissive comments about 'minor' theatres, even elite critical opinion grudgingly accepted that Shakespeare was a playwright of the people: an *Athenæum* critic fantasized that if Shakespeare were alive in the nineteenth century he would write 'immortal libretti for operas, or pathetic melodramas or farces'.[3] And in London particularly, with its burgeoning theatre industry, there were regular instances of novelties – adaptations of popular novels, spectacles, pantomimes, new melodramas – which originated in the minor theatres, and were copied across the range of theatres from West End to East End and the South Bank, as the production history of Douglas Jerrold's melodrama *Black-Ey'd Susan* or the domination of East

End and West End by *Lady Audley's Secret* and *East Lynne* in the 1860s, demonstrates. The theatres of London may have been divided according to class and reputation, but there are significant moments across the century when they all seemed to be playing the same show.

The legal regulation of theatre in Britain has a complex history, with state control of public entertainment having a specific impact on the Victorian theatre. This regulation started in the late sixteenth century, when the Office of the Revels took titular control of the public theatres, and each actors' company was required to perform under the patronage of a member of the Royal Household.[4] The development of the Lord Chamberlain's role in regulating public performance (originating in the Office of the Revels) indicates the seriousness with which policy makers regarded the entertainment business, and suggests the importance of theatre as a national cultural institution in Great Britain, and particularly its connection with the monarchy. The story of increasing power invested in the Lord Chamberlain's office throughout the nineteenth and into the twentieth century is usually told in relation to the overt powers of political censorship awarded to the Lord Chamberlain in the 1737 Theatres Bill. However, for the Victorian theatre, the re-establishment of the public theatres in London in 1660, through the Letters Patent from Charles II, is just as significant, as the monopoly powers thus awarded, and reiterated in the 1790s, became a central issue in both the aesthetic valuation and legislative regulation of the theatre in the nineteenth century.

The Letters Patent, given to Thomas Killigrew and William Davenant by Charles II, awarded them a monopoly on the management of public theatre in London, and the Royal imprimatur for its performance.[5] This was substantial economic and cultural capital. The Patent, and the monopoly it legislated for, became a property – inheritable and with an exchange value – and part of the complex legislative and customary practice which regulated the London theatre industry. Drury Lane and Covent Garden (and the Haymarket in the summer season by the Victorian period) were established as the 'Theatres Royal', with monopoly rights to produce the extant repertoire of English spoken drama, and new plays as they were written. As well as the title 'Theatre Royal', the Drury Lane and Covent Garden theatres were variously known as the Patent theatres, the monopoly theatres, the National theatres, the majors or the legitimate theatres. This plethora of naming indicates the extent to which the original Royal licence had become entwined in a complex system of legislation, customary practice and economic reality, which resulted in the merging of aesthetic value and legal status in the concept of the 'legitimate theatre'.

By default, then, other theatres in London were 'illegitimate' or 'minor' theatres, with all the force of inferiority and disempowerment that those descriptions suggest. However, as London audiences grew in the early nineteenth century, entrepreneurs saw opportunities in catering for this new popular audience in the minor theatres, established outside of the monopoly and its aesthetic constraints. These new theatres challenged the dominance of the Patent theatres. But the conflict signified more than economic competition, as Jane Moody argues: 'Theatrical warfare between minor and patent playhouses . . . dramatised . . . an ideological struggle about relationships between social classes and cultural interests.'[6] The language used in public debates around the regulation of the theatre indicates this ideological battle, and the slippage between 'illegitimate' as a description of the Minor theatres' legal position, and as a description of their aesthetic and social status, is one of the cultural frames of the Victorian theatre industry. Furthermore, the regulation of the *theatre* as an industry has had an impact on the reception of the *drama* as literary and performance text: valuations of the written drama in the nineteenth century have long been caught up in debates over legitimacy, to the detriment of our understanding of the scope and impact of the theatre in Victorian culture.

The 1832 House of Commons Select Committee Inquiry into the Laws Affecting Dramatic Literature (hereafter the Select Committee) offers an important starting point for exploring the effects of the complexities of the legal and customary organization of the theatres in the late Romantic and early Victorian periods.[7] The industrial and aesthetic ideologies and practices it encapsulates drove the Victorian theatre in its aesthetic and economic aspirations. The Select Committee was set up in the aftermath and the spirit of the 1832 Reform Act, by Edward Lytton Bulwer, one of the Radical MPs elected in the wake of the First Reform Act, and part of that 'radical fraction' of new middle-class intellectuals claiming a place in British culture as arbiters of aesthetic values.[8] The Minutes of Evidence of the 1832 Select Committee records direct testimony of those involved in the debates over the aesthetic, legal and customary practices of the English theatre. Managers, playwrights, actors, theatre proprietors and owners were asked (often leading) questions about the regulation of the theatres under the 1737 Theatres Act, and the advisability of lifting the monopoly of the Patent theatres on presenting the spoken or legitimate drama. The recommendations of the Select Committee emphasize the principles of free competition, public choice and elevation of the intellectual and literary qualities of the drama. Arguing that 'the exclusive privileges claimed by the two Metropolitan Theatres of Drury Lane and Covent Garden . . . have neither preserved the dignity of the Drama, nor . . . been of much advantage to the Proprietors of the Theatres' (5), the Committee recommended that 'that the interests of the Drama will be considerably advanced by the natural consequences of a fair competition in its Representation' (2). As contemporary polemic phrased it, the Drama should be 'thrown open' to all. And by these means, the Committee hoped, the status of the 'National Drama' and the playwright would be raised:

> In regard to Dramatic Literature, it appears manifest that an Author
> at present is subjected to indefensible hardship and injustice; and the
> disparity of protection afforded to the labours of the Dramatic
> Writer . . . seems alone sufficient to divert the ambition of eminent
> and successful Writers from that department of intellectual exertion.
>
> (5)

The underlying agenda is one of modernization, attuned to contemporary radical Benthamite or utilitarian approaches to reform of the British public sphere. The terms in which the Committee represented the work of the playwright became central to the ongoing debate about the theatre, its status in Victorian culture and the aesthetic and educational values the theatre offered its audiences. This part of the argument was accepted. Although the monopoly rights of the Patent theatres were not removed until the Theatres Act of 1843, the rights of playwrights were swiftly protected under the 1833 Dramatic Authors' Act, which regularized royalty payments to them.

For all its reformist zeal, the 1832 Select Committee made recommendations that were based on a set of class assumptions about the state of the theatre in 1832. The Committee assumed that the theatre was in decline, and dramatic writing in need of improvement. These assumptions emerged from a largely middle-class point of view, which valued literariness, the conventional forms of the five act verse tragedy and the three act 'high' comedy, seriousness, and sought an improving and educational purpose for the theatre. In other words, Bulwer Lytton and his colleagues were seeking to establish the model of the literary, legitimate drama as the hegemonic form for Victorian theatre. However, the minor theatres of London were certainly not in decline in any material way – they were expanding, entrepreneurial and innovative. Theatres including the Adelphi, the City of London, Astley's Amphitheatre, the Surrey, the Coburg (now the Old Vic) and later the Britannia were thriving. Their repertoires were characterized by mixed generic modes, sometimes slapdash production practices, interspersed with flashes of genius of managerial and performative invention – the very opposite of middle-class homogeneity and hegemony. As Simon Shepherd and Peter Womack argue, in the Victorian period 'there were probably more performances in more theatres seen by more people than at any other period, including the present. But next to none of it seems to be either natural or proper – as if English theatre was under occupation by an alien culture.'[9] Throughout the Victorian period, theatre critics wrote about the working-class audiences as if they were living in another country, orientalizing their social and entertainment desires and practices. The division between the legitimate and the illegitimate, enacted aesthetically, socially and economically, together with the condemnation of the illegitimate in public critical discourse, is the principal faultline of the Victorian theatre, influencing Victorian attitudes towards playwrights and the theatre, both then and now.

The standard narrative of the Victorian theatre is one which has been accepted relatively uncritically. It echoes Victorian anxieties about the growing influence of the 'illegitimate' theatre and drama, and the apparently profligate spectatorial tastes and desires of the new mass audience in London in the period. This narrative charts a decline in English dramatic writing from the heights of English comedy in the eighteenth century, and from the tragedies of the Renaissance and Jacobean periods. The 'decline of the drama' was accompanied by a decline in performance standards, production practices and audience behaviour. The sense of decline was all the more marked because of a consciousness of the heights which English drama had reached: Sheridan, Wycherly, Congreve in comedy, and Webster, Marlow, Jonson in tragedy; these were names to conjure with, but dominating them all was William Shakespeare. It is a truism to acknowledge the powerful impact of Shakespeare's legacy on English dramatic literature, particularly in the Romantic inheritance of his work as a model of 'the National Drama,' and the reification of Shakespeare himself as the 'National Poet' after the Jubilee celebrations in 1763.[10] But Shakespeare's significance to the practice and discourse of the Victorian theatre cannot be underestimated. The ghost of Shakespeare haunted public debates about legitimacy and the state of the drama and shaped critics' views of a desirable theatre throughout the nineteenth century. Shakespeare's plays were invoked as the model of tragedy which served as the highest form of drama to which an English writer could aspire, as did poets such as Robert Browning, who wrote several verse tragedies for William Macready, and aspirants to legitimate theatre such as Mary Russell Mitford, who wrote for Charles Kemble at Covent Garden.[11]

Notwithstanding the claims of the legitimate theatre on Shakespeare – and technically, until 1843 only the Theatres Royal could legally perform his plays – Shakespeare's legacy was, however, claimed by theatre professionals working in both the legitimate and the minor theatres. In the minor theatres, Shakespeare became a key part of the mix of political and aesthetic debate over the rights of their managers and audiences to participate in the National Drama, and also a talisman for the progress of knowledge and understanding among the working-class audiences of the East End and south of the Thames. As a playbill for the Surrey Theatre proudly proclaimed:

> In nothing has the 'March of Intellect' been more palpably exemplified than in the steady and progressive improvement, which has, of late years, raised the character of the MINOR THEATRES of the Metropolis, to their present unexpected elevation. Bursting from the trammels of mere 'Sound and Show', they have dared to emulate the reputation of the Major Houses: instead of the jingling doggerels, that so offended all ears of taste, the flowing lines of SHAKSPEARE and of MASSINGER, of OTWAY and of ROWE, have been placed in substitution, and Decorum has now firmly established her empire, where before, were Riot and Confusion.[12]

The right to see Shakespeare's plays, even in cut down or burlesque form, was an important element of English identity for the new working-class audiences of the minor theatres. Such theatre-going, and the campaign for it to be legitimized, was part of broader working-class political agitation for representation and participation in the public life of the nation.

For the rest of this chapter I want to offer an alternative account of the Victorian theatre to that of the standard narrative of decline and abjection which has tended to dominate the way we think about the theatre in Victorian culture. Rather than seeing the popular Victorian theatre as the 'fat, puffy, unwholesome, dropsical brother' of dramatic art,[13] I argue that the Victorian theatre was uniquely sensitive to the material conditions and anxieties of its society. As an art form, theatre is about active presence; it is also a communal art form which relies on the exchange between audience and performer, in which audience members participate in making meaning. One of theatre's powerful characteristics is its ability to make visible and present our cultural blind spots: theatre reflects us back to ourselves, in a reconstruction of a world which is simultaneously fantastical and recognizable. The Victorian theatre offered its audiences texts and performances which responded nimbly to the vast social and cultural changes of the nineteenth century, in staged explorations of the physical world of the city, the representation of changing social relationships between classes and genders and the playing out and resolution of social anxieties and problems. The Victorian theatre was innovative, adaptive and, most of all, contemporary.

Melodrama was the great dramatic and theatrical innovation of the nineteenth century, and a performance genre which has proven enduring and popular to the present day, particularly in its rapid adoption by screen media. English melodrama emerged from the illegitimate combination of *mélodrame* from revolutionary Paris with the peculiarities of the English licensing and monopoly laws described above. The French term literally means 'music with drama', and refers to the practice of accompanying long sections of action and dialogue with music, and interspersing dialogue and action with set-piece song and dance numbers. In this way, managers of the minor theatres circumvented the Patent monopoly, because, technically, dialogue spoken with music underneath was not the 'spoken drama', but regarded by the Lord Chamberlain's office as 'burletta'. The mixed modes of melodrama also offered a structure for spectacular entertainment, in a fast and topical format which allowed actors to show off their versatility in both 'light' and 'heavy' scenes, to dance and sing, as well as declaim highly coloured prose of great feeling.

However, melodrama would not have survived for so long, and against the odds of critical disdain and legal pressure, if it were simply a way for managers and playwrights to avoid restrictive licensing laws. The generic characteristics of melodrama have long been recognized as central to Victorian art and thought, as the choice between opposing absolutes becoming the 'archetypal pattern of nineteenth-century response'.[14] Wylie Sypher argues that much of Victorian thought offers a melodramatic choice between extremes, citing the theories of Marx and Darwin as examples of theories of human life and society expressed dialectically, while Elaine Hadley links the ethical worlds of melodrama with Victorian political tactics and a performative culture, seeing in the melodramatic mode 'a polemical response to the social, economic, and epistemological changes that characterized the consolidation of market society'.[15] Peter Brooks provides a psychological corollary to political readings of melodrama, linking the genesis of melodrama in the French Revolution with the revolutionary dispersal of traditional institutions and the literary genres which relied on those institutions for their authority. Melodrama, according to Brooks, offered post-revolutionary society a set of ethical responses with which to negotiate the new world.[16] Melodramatic ethics and justice have also been characterized as '*the Naturalism of the dream world*',[17] offering its audiences the world they 'want but cannot get'.[18] In all of these broad descriptions, melodrama is defined as a dramatic form which offers a truncated dialectic of moral choice between good and evil, dramatized simply, directly and effectively. Characters are good or bad – a virtuous black-eyed Susan or an evil Lady Audley (in the stage version). Action is uncompromising, final and devastating, its resolution inevitable. Desire is made palpable, and politicized as the desire of the feeling man for justice, of the working woman for freedom, of the poor family for security.

This superstructure of melodrama and the world of the 'moral occult' (to use Brooks's phrase) it dramatized worked so powerfully because playwrights, actors and theatre managers were able to connect melodramatic moral absolutes with the quotidian details of contemporary life. In the hands of British playwrights throughout the century, melodrama became 'domestic drama', focused on the family, English village or town life and the daily life of working people. In terms of academical hierarchies of art, aligned, for example, with Joshua Reynolds's *Discourses*, this focus on the everyday life of ordinary people presented a significant challenge to the cultural capital invested in tragedy. The challenge to aesthetic and social hierarchies posed by melodrama should not be underestimated: in placing the working man or woman in the role of hero, melodramatists were not only contradicting established Aristotelian dramaturgy, but also traditional class-based assumptions of moral worth attaching to economic power.

In this overview of Victorian theatre, a brief discussion of the work of one playwright will need to stand for the literally thousands of melodramas written and produced in the period. Douglas Jerrold, playwright, comic novelist and journalist, founder of *Punch* and doughty champion of authors' rights, claimed that he invented the domestic drama.[19] He certainly wrote one of the most popular melodramas of the century, *Black-Ey'd Susan*, which had regular revivals across London and regional theatres until at least 1896.[20] It is a melodrama typical of its time: neatly combining the popular character type of the stage sailor, the sentimentality of the beleaguered hard-working couple and an ending which combines natural justice with the rule of law, yet action which incorporates a challenge to authority by a working man. It is a play which has also come to represent all that is seen as clichéd and stereotypical of Victorian melodrama. However, a century's dismissal of its sentimentality has perhaps overshadowed a much more politically engaged and complex set of thematic concerns. The happy ending neatly ties up the loose ends of the plot concerning the central couple – William and Susan – who had been separated by the press ganging of William into the navy, and the threatened eviction of his wife Susan by her landlord and uncle, Doggrass, and by harassment from William's commanding officer. The play aligns poverty and moral worth, and contrasts those values with the alliance of wealth with corruption. This moral order validates the politicized protest William makes against the power of wealth and rank, in a way which is now seen as predictably melodramatic, but should be recognized as part of the process of democratization across the Victorian period.

What is particularly significant about *Black-Ey'd Susan*, and the many melodramas for which it stands here, is the refinement of the general melodramatic formula to enable playwrights and theatre managements to deal with issues of contemporary concern, and initiate the representation of contemporary life on the popular stage. Dickens satirized this in *Nicholas Nickleby*, with Mr Crummles's commission of Nicholas to write a play which included the 'practicable pump' Crummles had acquired. But in the practices and politics of the Victorian theatre, such topicality was a significant factor in the centrality of melodrama in popular entertainment. The theatre could act as a newsreel of sorts for the performance of topical debates: the Poor Laws and the Factory Acts as dramatized in plays such as *The Climbing Boy* (a partial source for *Oliver Twist*)[21] and *The Factory Strike*; the Crimean and the Indian wars in spectacles which used every bit of stage technology and real army kit available.[22] In even the most spectacular dramas, stories of everyday life engage ideologically with Victorian culture and society. These melodramas stage, again and again, a crisis in the domestic life of an innocent, hard-working family, in which their security – economic and moral – is threatened. The crisis is resolved by the extraordinary fortitude of the hero and heroine, in plots which unambiguously connect heroism with working people. While it is tempting to dismiss melodrama as ultimately conservative, shoring up unchallenged a moral order which preserves a pre-revolutionary moral *status quo,* such a judgement overlooks the political and moral complexities enabled by melodramatic dramaturgy. In looking at domestic melodrama we can see how the positioning of the feeling individual of humble circumstances at the centre of the plot offers a politically charged challenge to Aristotelian dramaturgy, which maintained that only high-born heroes could elicit sympathy. To assert that the humbly born could equally be objects of audience sympathy was to challenge the abjection and orientalizing of the poor and the working classes so prevalent in public discourse in the nineteenth century.

The Victorian investment in a grand narrative of progress is ever present in the theatre: in its practices and its history. In 1899, Clement Scott wrote in *The Drama of Yesterday and Today*, that: 'We have arrived, step by step, steadily and by slow degrees, at the year 1865, which is a landmark in the history of the English stage during the Victorian Era.'[23] The 'landmark' was Marie Wilton's 'discovery' of playwright T. W. Robertson. Later, critic William Archer was to identify Robertson at the centre of the first of three stages of the 'rehabilitation of the British drama'.[24] Robertson's plays *Caste*, *Society* and *Ours* were associated with Marie Wilton's management of the Queen's, a minor theatre just off the Tottenham Court Road, and her transformation of it into the Prince of Wales, a comfortable theatre attracting new middle-class audiences. Robertson's plays were a hybrid of social comedy and melodrama, dramatizing the domestic lives of middle-class families in realistic settings, and with a subdued performance style. If Scott and Archer saw Robertson as a saviour of the drama, they did so with dramaturgical tools familiar to his audience from melodrama.

Robertson's and Wilton's emphasis on staging an immediately recognizable and contemporary reality was also familiar to audiences from the welter of farces and comedies which flooded the London stage throughout the 1840s and 1850s. Until the long run of a single play became standard in the 1860s, a typical bill would include three, and sometimes four, pieces, including the central play, framed by a variety of mixed generic pieces which might include *divertissement* of song and dance, an opening or closing farce, a 'petite comedy' or a burletta. The short one-act comic piece, either farce or burletta, became a mainstay of writers' incomes and managers' playbills. These short farces and comedies were always given a domestic setting,[25] and their attention to the detail of language, while not literary, required audiences to be literate, even while groaning at the word play and punning dialogue. Victorian farce and comedy writers, including John Maddison Morton, in *Box and Cox* (1847) and the comic opera adapted from it by Francis Burnand and Arthur Sullivan (1866), or Joseph Sterling Coyne's *Did You Ever Send Your Wife to Camberwell?* (1846) celebrated the confusions of modern life, even if that detail included desperate devices for hiding apparent wrong doing, through clumsy plot devices of mistaken identity, misheard words and letters falling into the wrong hands. The frenzied activities to which the landlady in *Box and Cox* resorts to disguise her corrupt practices in letting the same bed to two tenants, or the extravagant response of a husband to observing a woman whom he mistakes for his wife entertaining another man in Catherine Gore's farce, *A Good Night's Rest*, are examples of the ways in which Victorian farce and comedy took the material of melodrama, and turned it on its head. The ridiculous brinksmanship of farce played – often quite daringly – on Victorian anxieties about respectability, sexual conduct, marital relationships, landladies and cooks. The humour of these farces works off their characters' neurotic insistence on the proprieties of bourgeois domesticity even when the lower-middle-class communal life of boarding houses, genteel poverty and the presence of over-close neighbours work against maintaining such respectability. These are the plays which might entertain a Mr Pooter, even as they parody his attempts at gentility.

Farce and comedy sliced into Victorian anxieties about conduct in lower-middle-class private life in the new suburbs, laying open the perils of modern life with a daring that was all the more audacious in its insouciance. The sensation drama and the problem play of the late nineteenth century offered further compelling combinations of serious moral debate with visceral and heightened emotional experience. The English problem play of the last two decades of the nineteenth century was hailed as the native version of naturalist and realist drama from continental Europe. Critics including Henry Arthur Jones, Clement Scott and William Archer (one of the champions of Henrik Ibsen in Great Britain) welcomed plays by Arthur Wing Pinero and George Bernard Shaw, and Jones himself, as further stages in the progress of the drama. Yet even as he praised the intellectual improvement offered by Shaw's work, Archer returned to the same dichotomies between popular entertainment and art, between performance and the literary drama which so exercised early Victorian critics.

Unlike the work of Robertson and Pinero, which 'came from within the theatre itself', the 'Shaw drama'

> proceeded from without. It was an intellectual movement and a movement of intellectuals. Its leaders, with one exception, were men of letters before they became men of the theatre. Economically, it was at first, and has continued to be in some measure, an endowed movement . . . if the Shaw drama had been forced to pay its way, as were the Robertson drama and the Pinero drama, it would long ago have died of starvation.[26]

Yet the English problem play – represented by plays including Pinero's *The Magistrate* (1885) or *The Second Mrs Tanqueray* (1893), or Shaw's *Widower's Houses* (1893) or *Arms and the Man* (1894) – owes as much of a debt to sensation melodrama as it does to Ibsen.[27] Sensation drama broke new ground for English writing, by introducing complex female protagonists caught in morally ambiguous situations, which were shown explicitly, rather than by allusion. Not only were such fictions bracing antidotes to the infantilization and desexualization of the Victorian woman otherwise so prevalent in popular culture, they prepared the way for what Katherine Kelly suggests was the contemporary definition of modern drama in the late nineteenth century: the 'male authorship of woman-centred plays'.[28] At the same time, their reliance on the visceral sensation and suspense of murder, adultery and bigamy remind us of the importance of sensory experience and popular appeal in the English theatrical tradition, in spite of critics' encouragement of the literary drama.

Adaptations of three sensation novels, *Lady Audley's Secret*, and *Aurora Floyd*, both by Mary Elizabeth Braddon, and Ellen Wood's *East Lynne*, dominated the London stage in 1863 and 1864. Adaptations of *East Lynne* in particular travelled the English-speaking world, emphasizing the extent of globalization in Victorian popular culture. *Lady Audley's Secret* was first published in book form in October 1862, and by March 1863, adaptations appeared on five stages in London, filling both West End and East End theatres, in a cross-class theatrical phenomenon. Such was the play's ubiquity that a burlesque version (always an indication of a play's impact), *Eighteen Hundred and Sixty Three; or, The Sensations of the Past Season, with a Shameful Revelation of 'Lady Someone's Secret'*, opened on Boxing Day, 1863.[29] The first verifiable performances of adaptations of *East Lynne* were given in New York at the Brooklyn Academy of Music in January 1863. Like *Lady Audley's Secret*, a burlesque version of this production appeared in 1866,

East Lynne; or, The Great Western. The subtitle referred to star actress Lucille Western who played the role many times until her early death, using *East Lynne* as a convenient and lucrative filler in her seasons.

Underlying both sensation drama and the problem play was a deep anxiety about the nature of femininity. In the last three decades of the nineteenth century, gender replaces class as the arena for ideological debate in the theatre. The structures of Victorian dramaturgy, founded in the dialectical oppositions of melodrama, work in fascinating paradoxes to perform these debates. The moral transgressions of the central female characters are staged, bodily and overtly: we see Lady Audley push George Talboys into the well, we see and hear Levinson's seduction of Isabel Vane. In Pinero's iconic problem play, *The Second Mrs Tanqueray*, Mrs Patrick Campbell playing Paula Tanqueray, confronts her husband with her past: 'I'm tainted through and through; anybody can see it, anybody can find it out.'[30] Lyn Pykett has described melodrama in fiction as the 'irruption into the narration of that feeling . . . which is repressed in the narrative'.[31] In the heightened and transgressive plots of sensation drama and the problem play, this feeling is quite literally staged, made manifest in a set of gestures, vocal usages and physical poses, which show the female body and mind under stress. Through their impassioned speeches delivered in the heightened acting style of the period, female characters indicated realms of experience and emotion beyond the quotidian and limited notion of the domestic sphere. In this gesture towards broad experience, they provided a partial model for liberation for female experience.

Sensation and problem plays place the female performing body at the centre of the theatrical event, emphasizing the physical and visceral nature of performance. Yet such excitements are partial, and closed down by the punishment of the female protagonist for her ideological subversion. Paula Tanqueray commits suicide after the realization that there is no future for a 'woman with a past'. Famously, Isabel Vane dies in *East Lynne*, lamenting that her son is 'dead, dead, dead! and he never knew me, never called me mother!'. In stage versions of the story, Lady Audley dies mad, her secret monopathy publicly revealed at the fall of the final curtain. In this context, we can appreciate the revolutionary dramaturgy of George Bernard Shaw and Oscar Wilde, who – each in his different way – resist the closure of the melodramatic mode in their comedies and dramas. Shaw puts a brothel keeper centre-stage in *Mrs Warren's Profession*, and persuades us that her intellectual daughter, Vivie Warren, just down from Cambridge, is not just a prude, but as complicit in the deeper immoralities of capitalism as is her mother's work as a prostitute and madam. In *Lady Windermere's Fan*, Mrs Erlynne, a 'woman with a past', sacrifices her reputation for her daughter's, in an intriguing echo of the *East Lynne* plot, which offers the fallen woman as a morally complex construction.

The plays of Shaw and Wilde are often paired with those of Sheridan and Congreve as the bookends of readable drama on a century of dross. As numerous critics and historians have argued, the theatre in the Victorian age was often the lens through which Victorians viewed their world. Yet, the power of canonical literary judgements of the majority of Victorian dramatic writing as simply 'bad writing' has inhibited a full exploration of just what the importance of the theatre might have meant for Victorians. As I have argued, this view of the Victorian theatre is no longer sustainable: it does not accord with the information we have about Victorian audiences, their pleasure in spectacle and variety and their desire for performances which reflected back to Victorians the exciting, modern world in which they lived.

Notes

1 *Athenæum*, 2 Dec. 1843, 1073.
2 Jim Davis and Victor Emeljanow, *Reflecting the Audience, London Theatregoing, 1840–1880* (Iowa City: University of Iowa Press, 2001), 46–8.
3 17 June 1843, 573–4.
4 J. Leeds Barroll et al., *The Revels History of Drama in English*, vol. III: *1576–1613* (London: Methuen, 1975), 14 and ff.
5 'Bill for Restraining the Number of Houses for Paying of Interludes, and for the Better Regulating Common Players of Interludes', in Vincent J. Liesenfeld (ed.), *The Stage and the Licensing Act, 1729–1739* (New York: Garland 1981), n.p.
6 Jane Moody, '"Fine Word, Legitimate!": Toward a Theatrical History of Romanticism', *Texas Studies in Literature and Language*, 38, 3/4 (1996), 232.
7 British House of Commons, Sessional Papers, *Report from the Select Committee on Dramatic Literature: With the Minutes of Evidence*, vol. VII, 1831–2.
8 Dewey Ganzel, 'Patent Wrongs and Patent Theatres: Drama and Law in the Early Nineteenth Century', *Publications of the Modern Language Association*, 76, 4 (1961), 384–96; and J. S. Bratton, 'Miss Scott and Miss Macaulay: "Genius Cometh in All Disguises"', *Theatre Survey*, 37, 1 (1996), 59.
9 Simon Shepherd and Peter Womack, *English Drama: A Cultural History* (Oxford: Blackwell, 1996), 219.
10 For recent discussions of the importance of Shakespeare in the nineteenth century, see Jane Moody, 'Romantic Shakespeare', and Richard S. Schoch, 'Pictorial Shakespeare', in Stanley Wells and Sarah Stanton (eds.), *Cambridge Companion to Shakespeare on Stage* (Cambridge: Cambridge University Press, 2002).

11 Katherine Newey, *Women's Theatre Writing in Victorian Britain* (Basingstoke: Palgrave, 2005), 44–50.

12 Surrey Theatre, 15 Sept. 1832, *Playbills and Programmes from London Theatres 1801–1900 in the Theatre Museum, London* (Cambridge: Chadwyck-Healey, 1983).

13 Henry Arthur Jones, *The Renascence of the English Drama* (London: Macmillan, 1895), 11.

14 Wylie Sypher, 'Aesthetic of Revolution: The Marxist Melodrama', *Kenyon Review*, 10 (1948), 431.

15 Elaine Hadley, *Melodramatic Tactics: Theatricalized Dissent in the English Marketplace, 1800–1885* (Stanford: Stanford University Press, 1995), 3. For recent studies of the performative culture of the Victorian period, see Tracy C. Davis and Peter Holland (eds.), *The Performing Century: Nineteenth-Century Theatre's History* (Basingstoke: Palgrave, 2007).

16 Peter Brooks, *The Melodramatic Imagination: Balzac, James, and the Mode of Excess* (New Haven: Yale University Press, 1976), 20.

17 Eric Bentley, *The Life of the Drama* (London: Methuen, 1965), 205 (his emphasis).

18 Michael R. Booth, *English Melodrama* (London: Jenkins, 1965), 14.

19 Jerrold is reported to have said 'A poor thing, but mine own', in one sentence claiming a major genre of the nineteenth century and strategically linking himself with Shakespeare. Cited in Walter Jerrold, *Douglas Jerrold, Dramatist and Wit*, 2 vols. (London: Hodder and Stoughton, n.d.), vol. i, p. 211, and W. Blanchard Jerrold, *The Life of Douglas Jerrold* (London: Bradbury, Evans, 1869), 82.

20 Donald Mullin, *Victorian Plays. A Record of Significant Productions on the London Stage, 1837–1901* (Westport: Greenwood, 1987), 29–30.

21 Katherine Newey, 'Climbing Boys and Factory Girls: Popular Melodramas of Working Life', *Journal of Victorian Culture*, 5, 1 (2000), p. 32.

22 J. S. Bratton, 'Theatre of War: The Crimea on the London Stage, 1854–5', in David Bradby et al. (eds.), *Performance and Politics in Popular Drama* (Cambridge: Cambridge University Press, 1980), 119–137, and Michael R. Booth, *Victorian Spectacular Theatre, 1850–1910* (London: Routledge and Kegan Paul, 1981), 69–70.

23 Clement Scott, *The Drama of Yesterday and Today*, 2 vols. (London: Macmillan, 1899), vol. i, 471.

24 William Archer, *The Old Drama and the New* (London: William Heinemann, 1923), 338.

25 On the importance of the domestic in Victorian farce, see Michael R. Booth, 'Comedy and Farce', in Kerry Powell (ed.), *The Cambridge Companion to Victorian and Edwardian Theatre* (Cambridge: Cambridge University Press, 2004), 131 and 139.

26 Archer, *The Old Drama and the New*, 338.

27 Nina Auerbach explores this connection in more detail in 'Before the Curtain', in Powell (ed.), *Cambridge Companion to Victorian and Edwardian Theatre*, 10–13.

28 Katherine E. Kelly (ed.), *Modern Drama by Women, 1880s–1930s* (London: Routledge, 1996), 1.

29 Reprinted in Richard W. Schoch (ed.), *Victorian Theatrical Burlesques* (Aldershot: Ashgate, 2003), 53–94.

30 Arthur Wing Pinero, *The Second Mrs Tanqueray*, in Michael R. Booth (ed.), *English Plays of the Nineteenth Century*, vol. ii: *Dramas, 1850–1900* (Oxford: Oxford University Press, 1969), 328.

31 Lyn Pykett, *The 'Improper' Feminine. The Women's Sensation Novel and the New Woman Writing* (London: Routledge, 1992), 97.

8

Popular culture[1]

In 1894, the publisher John Lane issued a prospectus regarding his forthcoming periodical *The Yellow Book*. In it, he encourages the notion that the volumes' physical surfaces and reputation will mark their owners as discriminating connoisseurs. According to the prospectus, the quarterly would 'depart as far as may be possible from the bad old traditions of periodical literature', and 'provide an Illustrated Magazine which will be as beautiful as a piece of book-making, modern and distinguished in its letter-press and its pictures'.[2] The pages of the first volume, Lane ensures readers, are 'now being especially woven' and the book will be 'bound in limp yellow cloth'. In reality, the periodical was produced with paper that was not unique; for example, it is not rag (that is, it is not made entirely of cotton or linen) and it has no watermark or other indication of special manufacture.[3] The image of exclusivity fabricated through the prospectus reflected neither the material resources nor the cost of production. Lane's language makes apparent not so much the preciousness of the objects as his desire for potential purchasers to expect them to be precious. The rhetoric also captures the popularization of the image of exclusivity that was a driving force behind the rise of commodity culture.

At the same time that Lane issued the prospectus, he also paid to have information about the forthcoming journal appear in other periodicals. This tactic, as Margaret Stetz and Mark Samuels Lasner point out, reflects the populist aspirations on the part of Lane who 'took every opportunity to insist upon the significance of this venture and to instruct readers in the proper way of receiving it'.[4] In light of Matthew Arnold's well-known descriptions in *Culture and Anarchy* (1869) of upper-class refinements as exclusionary and useless, and of the 'raw and unkindled masses of humanity' as incompetent at discerning cultural value,[5] Lane's effort to fuse high-culture tastes with mass appeal can appear to be an enterprise destined to failure. But while *The Yellow Book* did last for only thirteen volumes, the cause of its demise was not its effort to combine refinement with broad consumption. This mix had arisen within Victorians' notions of popular culture decades earlier. In fact, Lane's marketing methods for the periodical echoed those he himself had already deployed in other ventures with his previous co-publisher Elkin Matthews.

Lane neatly captures his fusion of specialist tastes and populist intentions when he declares in the prospectus that *The Yellow Book* is not to be simply popular, but 'popular in the better sense of the word'.[6] The 'popular' is constituted here not as an undifferentiated hodgepodge of events, occasions and objects, but as having its own internal demarcations of quality. Lane shifts emphasis from the objects and experiences in question to the expectations, demands and interests of the people consuming them. On this occasion, his own sensitivity to varying qualities of the popular is explained, in part, by the fact that he was venturing into the realm of the periodical. This is the very medium to which people frequently turned when pointing out the moral dangers of mass entertainment. One need only read mainstream commentators' discussions of popular culture, and the role and influence of its periodicals in particular, to realize that Victorians in general already conceptualized popular culture as more than a category of a society's production. As these writings demonstrate, people of the era recognized it to be a site of ideological contestation for control of the hegemonic understanding of class, age, gender, commerce, morality and education. Indeed, it is within these confrontations that one locates the edifying middle-class intentions that first gave shape to the modern notion of popular culture itself. And within them, as well, one finds the impetus that eventually led to the conflation of these intentions with the new consumerist ethos signalled by marketing strategies such as Lane's.

Edification and the creation of a culture for the masses

The term 'popular culture' is widely understood today to refer to those beliefs, practices and forms of entertainment and leisure activity that are common to the general population, and not specific to any single class field. Within the Victorian context, scholars see these as including mainstream, everyday activities and objects of pleasure and leisure such as street ballads, broadsides, melodrama and music halls. Popular culture is also understood to include other perhaps less obvious phenomena, from domestic practices including cooking and knitting to folk traditions including pagan beliefs and Morris dancing. Victorians, however, had their own conceptions of both 'popular' and 'culture' so that, as they came to use the new term 'popular culture', they imbued it with values and concerns that are not as apparent in our own general understanding of it.

Within nineteenth-century analyses of popular culture, a topic that arose particularly often was that of positive influence, which was closely aligned with public education, or 'popular education' as it was often called. In 1977, Harold Silver called for a scholarly approach to Victorian education history that gave less attention to policy formation and administrative developments and, instead, emphasized the exploration of the education system's reciprocal relationship with other cultural and social developments.[7] John Morley's 'On Popular Culture: An Address', which appeared in the *Fortnightly Review* in 1876, suggests just how entwined education and popular culture were during the period. Morley originally presented his argument as a talk in his role as president of the Birmingham and Midland Institute, founded in 1854 for 'the Diffusion and Advancement of Science, Literature and Art amongst all Classes of Persons resident in Birmingham and the Midland Counties'.[8] Other than in the title of his piece, Morley never mentions the term 'popular culture', demonstrating the ubiquity with which it was used to refer to education for the masses – Morley's focus. The main point of his talk is that education must be recognized as more than a tool for developing culture among the general population, becoming ideally an everyday, uplifting aspect of all people's lives.

In accord with Morley's message, it was common during the Victorian era to use the term 'popular culture' to refer not to the practices, values and entertainments favoured by a considerable portion of the general population but to those that the middle classes advocated as tools for giving those people whom they saw as beneath them civilizing and moral inspiration. 'Plenty of people', Arnold cautions in *Culture and Anarchy*, 'will try to give the masses, as they call them, an intellectual food prepared and adapted in the way they think proper for the actual condition of the masses. The ordinary popular literature is an example of this way of working on the masses.' He then rewords his warning more forcefully, declaring that 'Plenty of people will try to indoctrinate the masses with the set of ideas and judgments constituting the creed of their own profession or party.'[9] In this sense, popular culture is primarily the result of not working-class but middle-class ideology, forming what Michael Warner theorizes as a 'mass subject' – an amorphous entity whose influence (and, for the middle classes, potential threat) is enhanced by its dislocation from reality.[10]

This infusion of ideological instruction into mass entertainment was a manoeuvre Victorians did not reserve for literature, as demonstrated by Clement Scott's 'The Modern Music-Hall' (1889). In his analysis of the social function of the music hall, Scott does not condemn such broadly appealing entertainment outright. Rather, he argues that all humans have instincts for positive development and self-enrichment, but that these internal moral monitors have been stifled in contemporary society by amusement laws which are too strict:

> You may turn every beer-barrel and wine-cellar into the Thames and you will not check some form of drunkenness. You may shut up every theatre and music-hall in the kingdom and you will not prevent depravity. The thing to do is to give people good drink and to teach them to use it in moderation: to give people good amusement and to encourage them to value it: to counteract the tediousness of toil with the soul-inspiring medicine of wholesome entertainment.[11]

Despite Scott's critique of puritanical proselytizers, he is not in direct conflict with their position, agreeing that the unrefined music halls and theatres are blights on English society. Rather than removing them, however, he recommends taking advantage of their mass appeal by converting them into a civilizing influence. Scott's readers are told to 'teach' and 'encourage' fans of the music halls to turn to morally superior forms of entertainment. Taking language usually used in support of popular education, he adapts it to articulating strategies for forming a respectable culture that the masses would *choose* to adopt, what he would call a 'popular culture'.

Demonstrating the commonness of this form of mass persuasion, T. C. Horsfall – whose writings drew on the work of John Ruskin – makes a comparable argument for painting which notably, unlike music halls, was recognized as an aspect of high culture. In 'Painting and Popular Culture' (1880), Horsfall states that contemporary painting fails in the task of giving 'noble pleasure to a large proportion of the intelligent people of their race'[12] because, unlike literature, it does not relate to 'some body of vital knowledge', which he describes as recorded wisdom that is sustained for a large portion of society through 'habitual thought and feeling' (850). In order to make visual art as morally influential as contemporary literature, Horsfall proposes that the Royal Academy reserve some rooms in its annual show for visual art specifically addressing a well-known written work such as a book of the Old Testament or something by Shakespeare, Wordsworth or Eliot (853). He speculates that each year this project would familiarize almost as many people with 'fine thought and feeling finely expressed' as 'one of our little wars, or a famine, or some other great calamity, now makes familiar with the geography of a distant country or the manners of a barbarous race' (855). Moreover, such inter-artistic referencing would be more effective at 'bringing the classes together' than anything else except 'perhaps an invasion' (855–6).

Horsfall's shift into metaphors of war, invasion and foreign barbarians imbues the edifying role of popular culture with a nationalist potency. The article was published in 1880, with Britain in the thick of a series of conflicts in southern Africa. Sir Theophilus Shepstone, the British Secretary for Native Affairs in Natal, had annexed the South African Republic (or Transvaal Republic) in 1877. Britain then invaded Zululand in 1879. The successful defeat of the Zulus was quickly followed by the Transvaal War (or First Boer War) of 1880–1. Echoing Britain's efforts to enforce a united British colony in southern Africa, Horsfall attempts in his article to transpose an ideal of a nation unified in spirit and aim on to painting by making the latter a form of uplifting culture for the entire populace. The benefits would be immense both for the artist – whose work would become widely appreciated and a form of vital knowledge – and for the nation, because the art 'would give noble pleasure to a large proportion of the intelligent people of their race' (856). With this closing image, Horsfall leaves his readers with a notion of popular culture as a mode of mass edification that elevates the collective morality of the nation and reinforces its political cohesion on the international stage. Not only vital knowledge, popular culture has become – in Horsfall's model – a vital duty.

A culture *of*, rather than for, the masses

As suggested by the political connotations of much of the edifying discourse that dominated initial discussions of popular culture, middle-class Victorians did recognize the presence of values, tastes and interests arising from the masses themselves but they usually chose to ignore or diminish their relevance. It appears promising, then, when Thomas Wright opens his essay 'On a Possible Popular Culture' (1881) by explicitly stating that the term 'culture' refers not only to a higher, aesthetic sense unfamiliar to the working classes, but also to a 'more robust' sense that would apply to them.[13] He notes that there has been a growth in public museums and art galleries in his time (37), an increased view that the age is 'emphatically an age of progress' and extensive recent attention to 'the question of popular education' (25) – all things, he argues, that would lead one to assume that most working-class people are cultured in the 'more robust' sense. It is clear to him, however, that this is not the case. Although Wright begins his argument by suggesting the potential presence of a culture created by the lower classes, he ultimately argues that it does not in fact exist.

In Wright's conception of popular culture, things such as folklore, folk tradition and entertainments originating with the masses are not given a place, because, for him, the working classes have no intrinsic means of becoming cultured. External encouragement, especially of their reading ability, is required. Concluding that the education system has done no more than make the masses able to consume 'the lower types of weekly newspapers, and willing to read little else' (26), Wright turns away from an attempt to define and analyse culture to the familiar subject of the role of reading in popular education. Again, we hear that the working classes need our 'judicious guidance, and not too obtrusive supervision', a key concern being the wave of 'trashy – and often worse than trashy – "boy" dreadfuls and serials' (31). Due to an educational style that is draining and unappealing, the young never learn to read well. Eventually, the inexpensive magazines known as penny dreadfuls – characterized by exciting adventure stories and crude visuals – usurp 'the place of the only reading by which, practically speaking, the foundations of a cultured taste could be laid, and the means to the end of a new happiness created' (36).

Although Wright implies throughout the article that it is the working-class individuals who lack culture, towards the end of the piece he also considers its absence among the higher classes: 'Their working-time, it is said, is devoted exclusively to money-making, and their leisure hours to amusements and competition in social displays' (39). Wright accepts this argument that the middle class is engrossed by a consumerism motivated by competitive self-display, but he counters that the deficiency of culture in the higher classes does not justify its absence in the working classes. Bourgeois entertainments are generally expensive, he observes, but an education will give the working classes access to culture that does not cost money. Indeed, pleasures that cost money – so many of which prove to be no more than passing fashions – are not culture at all. The 'higher, healthier, simpler' culture that Wright proposes for the masses would be substantial and long term. It 'would require no hyper-æsthetical jargon to expound it. Nor would it have any tendency to seek outlets in crazes for crockery, or exhibitions of oddity in art, or house furnishing' (43). The Aesthetic Movement, avant-garde art and the 'house beautiful', he implies, are all to be avoided for their faddishness. Underlying Wright's criticism is also an assault on the rise of consumer culture and commodity fetishism.

The curious result of this attack on consumerist trends is that culture for the masses has, in Wright's paradigm, now taken the position of being superior due to its long-term, historical associations. Should the edifying plans he proposes be followed and prove successful, England would become a nation where the lower classes would be more cultured than those fad-devoted people with money. With this formulation of a wealth-based distinction within the uncultured collective, Wright suggests an important new perspective on the ownership of respectable popular culture. It would ultimately be the working classes that would be most invested in its content, signalling a shift in managerial authority away from the middle classes who instigated the modern formulation of the concept as a tool of ideological management.

Throughout his article, Wright never drops his association of culture with moral development. Nevertheless, his consideration of such things as artistic innovation, house furnishing and passing trends reflects the fact that Victorians were developing a growing awareness of a spectrum of items as cultural beyond those marked as traditional entertainment or High Art. The importance of this awareness is apparent in Elizabeth Robins Pennell's 1886 article 'The Modern Comic Newspaper'. Pennell situates the public analysis of popular culture firmly within the contemporary materials with which Wright was most concerned. Collaborator with her husband, the artist and writer Joseph Pennell, biographer of James McNeil Whistler and close friend of numerous people involved in Aestheticism, Pennell was a distinguished contributor to the Aesthetic Movement. She also published considerably on less refined subjects including music halls, cooking and comics. The innovative perspective on culture that allowed her to take interest in such a range of items is apparent in her description of her book, *The Feasts of Autolycus* – a collection of essays on food and cooking – as a guide to 'the Beauty, the Poetry, that exists in the perfect dish'.[14] The combination of popular and refined tastes echoes those of John Lane, the book's publisher.

In 'The Modern Comic Newspaper', Pennell has no interest in disparaging mass entertainments of her own time, but instead challenges the tendency of contemporary commentators to turn to historical works as sources for defining culture. Pennell summarizes her initial thesis by paraphrasing the character Mr Rose in W. H. Mallock's well-known satire *The New Republic* (1878), having the aesthete bewail the fact that 'the cultured of to-day linger so long in the boundless gardens of the past, that they forget to enter the house of the present'.[15] As most of her readers would have known, however, Mr Rose was a parody of Walter Pater, the strongest voice of Aestheticism at the time and, as works by him such as the essay collection *Studies in the History of the Renaissance* (1873) and the novel *Marius, the Epicurean* (1885) attest, a person who was actually heavily invested in history. In fact, in the passage from *The New Republic* that Pennell misleadingly paraphrases, Rose does not offer a detraction of history but actually meanders off into a comic celebration of it.[16] While one character concludes that Mr Rose is 'a little off his head', another declares that they 'now see something of the way in which history gives us culture' and that 'in history, and many other things as well, books are only the telescopes through which we see distant facts'. Pennell inverts Pater's investment in a view of history as something living and all-important in order to challenge what she sees as 'a contemptuous indifference to the modern world'.[17] It is this recognition of the importance of current, vital creations of pleasure that is her article's key contribution to the Victorian understanding of popular culture.

In Pennell's view, the contemporary creation that is the most genuine reflection of the English masses is the cartoon character Ally Sloper. Bumbling, lazy and in debt, he was far from the ideal artefact for those advocating a civilizing and morally uplifting model of popular culture. His drunkenness was as blatant a marker of his nonconformist ways as anything, alcohol consumption – as Scott suggests in the article discussed above – itself being seen as both an important aspect of Victorian working-class men's leisure and a sign of the mass's inability to manage itself.[18] First appearing in the magazine *Judy* in 1867, Ally was invented by Charles H. Ross and drawn with the aid of his wife Emilie de Tessier, who eventually took over the series entirely. Pennell suggests that Ally's success, like that of old masques, arises from the fact that he typifies 'infirmities and absurdities based, not upon fashion, but upon human nature and [is] in sympathy with the unlettered majority as well as the cultured elect'.[19] In this rare positive valuation of a contemporary piece of mass entertainment by someone familiar with the scholarly debates in the area, Pennell celebrates Ally for embodying qualities that the majority of Victorians would have recognized as 'popular' in the sense of 'well known', but not as 'culture', the latter term still carrying connotations of edification. Pennell, however, is critical of popular education itself, arguing that it 'will destroy whatever is peculiar to the thoughts and beliefs of the masses of to-day, just as the railroad is rapidly reducing costume and customs to uniformity'. She directly contrasts respected works such as Swinburne's poetry and Pre-Raphaelite painting with 'the expression of [the masses'] mental or moral attitude', arguing that these last are 'of more value relatively than the representative work of the educated' because of its intrinsic merit. In accord with this position, Pennell is not interested, in her article, in proposing methods for improving the moral foundation of the nation or the masses. Instead, she turns her energies towards analysing a form of culture that appeals to the masses in order to gain a greater understanding of past and present societies. Although she never uses the term 'popular culture' in the article, Pennell nevertheless offers an entirely modern approach to what would become the field of popular culture studies.

Capitalism's investment in popular culture

Pennell's and Lane's social circles overlapped considerably, but the two had distinctly differing views on popular culture. As The Yellow Book's marketing history suggests, Lane's populist interests were strongly influenced by financial concerns. Linda K. Hughes has recently noted that Lane and the quarterly's letter-press editor Henry Harland displayed an 'eclectic editorial strategy, which was designed to market the journal and Bodley Head books to a broad array of readers'.[20] Even elements that would be recognized as decadent, Laurel Brake points out, were actually used 'to create large readerships seeking titillation through writing which is commodified as "news" through its notoriety'.[21] In light of Lane and Harland's desire to have the quarterly develop a broad appeal, it is curious that they would have, as the opening piece of writing in the ninth volume, an attack by Harland on what was recognized, even in its own time, as one of the best examples of late Victorian popular culture.

An irony-laced 'Birthday Letter' written by Harland under the pseudonym of 'The Yellow Dwarf', the work is in large part an attempt to disparage George Du Maurier's novel *Trilby* for setting new records in Britain and the United States as a best seller. Even Du Maurier lamented the bizarre popularity of his novel. 'I never took myself *au sérieux* as a novelist', he declared; 'Indeed, this boom rather distresses me when I reflect that Thackeray never had a boom. And I hold that a boom means nothing as a sign of literary excellence, nothing but money.'[22] Harland explains *Trilby*'s popularity in part by the fact that Du Maurier was already well known for his many cartoons in *Punch* and in part by its being 'an amiable, sugar-and-watery sort of book.'[23] But the main cause of its success was somewhat more menacing. For Harland,

> the silliness of *Trilby* is a more insidious kind of silliness, its vulgarity a more insidious kind of vulgarity, its slipshod writing a more insidious kind of slipshod writing, than the feeble-minded multitude have been baited with before, in a novel. The writing, for instance, if you will study it, resembles no other form of human writing quite so much as that jauntily familiar, confidential, colloquial form of writing which all lovers of advertisements know and appreciate in the circulars of *Mother Seigel's Syrup*.   (15)

Today, we would see Mother Seigel's Syrup as a bit of popular culture in its own right. It was a well-known pseudo-medicine claiming to cure a variety of ailments including dyspepsia, gout, indigestion and piles. The breadth of ills the syrup allegedly remedied contributed to its success and, in Harland's letter to the editor, it functions as a metaphor for popular entertainment that operates as a cure-all whose superficial sweetness dangerously conceals the long-term effects of commercial exploitation.

The source of *Trilby*'s triumph was, more specifically, the author's adaptation of advertising techniques that manipulated the feeble minds of the masses. There is no record of whether Harland tweaked to the irony that the prospectus of *The Yellow Book* that he co-edited had adopted a similarly coercive strategy. Recognizing that Du Maurier probably had not consciously chosen to construct his novel as its own promotional medium, Harland argues that the novelist adopted an attitude of 'Me-and-Youness' or 'Wegotism' that 'flatters the self-conceit' of 'your average plebeian American or Briton, your photographer, your dentist.'[24] 'Sometimes, for brief intervals', he laments, 'one forgets how elementally imbecile our Anglo-Saxon Public is.'[25] For Harland, this weakness

lies primarily in the unrefined tastes of the growing population of consumers who, due to sheer numbers, have the power to dictate what will
become successful.

An 1887 *Punch* cartoon by Harry Furniss entitled 'How We Advertise
Now' (Figure 4) suggests just how thorough an influence such low fare
was seen to be having.[26] The image depicts a wall over 20 feet high covered
in posters advertising a variety of popular products, including theatrical
productions, performing animal shows, soap and even advertising itself.
The dominant threat of this collection hovering over the heads of passers-
by is cheap entertainment. We see an advertisement for the Theatre of
Horrors; one for something called 'The Hangman'; another revealing only
a series of shapely legs with the words 'Theatre Royal Tights'; and another
for the Newgate Theatre (a reference to the *Newgate Calendar* and Newgate
novels that dominated the pulp-fiction market early in the Victorian era).
In front of this looming wall of promotional materials is a spectrum of
city life – a woman and child attempting to pass a hawker wearing an
advertising placard for 'bogus water', a police officer standing nearby,
a horse and carriage being disturbed by an advertiser in an elephant
costume, and so on.

The individuals at the base of the image are roughly the same size as
many of those portrayed in the giant posters, resulting in a visual blurring
of the people and the popular culture they consume. This conflation of
popular culture and personal subjectivity is even more fully embodied by
those individuals in the image who are actually wearing advertising and
whose livelihood is promotion. Other people in the cartoon, meanwhile,
come across as cringing victims of commercial abuse. Not only is the
visibility of musical theatre, pulp fiction and other trashy entertainment
interpreted as an intrusion on their space, but the very chaos of urban
life is being caused by it. As Lynda Nead observes, 'the commercial street
culture of the 1850s and 1860s was an assault on the senses. Ugly images,
poorly made, bombarded unsuspecting pedestrians from all directions'.[27]
Furniss's comic mockery is not directed at these forms of popular culture,
however, so much as at the visual excess of the marketing devices used to
promote them. As with Harland's reference to the advertising for Mother
Seigel's Syrup, the dominant concern in this image is with the influence
of commercial culture on the minds of the general population.

Furniss's cartoon comes to the defence of the lives and identities of
everyday Londoners. Similarly, *Judy* struck a popular chord with Ally
Sloper's utter disregard for the middle class's preferred image of the

HOW WE ADVERTISE NOW.

Figure 4. 1887 *Punch* cartoon by Harry Furniss: 'How We Advertise Now'.

worker as a productive contributor to consumerist industry. For Pennell, Ally was a success because he was a common citizen; his full name is Alexander Sloper, FOM (Friend of Man). Of equal influence on his popularity, however, was the fact that he existed within a periodical. Unlike any of the edifying articles, Ally resurfaced in people's lives on a regular basis, turning the charming experience of the first encounter into a pleasurable habit. And yet in contrast to Ally's attitude, *Judy*'s own success was based on the heavy promotion of consumerism, with even the front cover of the publication often being overwhelmed by advertisements. The paradoxical reliance on consumerism's funds and marketing to sell a momentary release from the burden of capitalist industry had, by this time, become common practice, and nowhere more so than in the periodical industry. It is appropriate, then, that Pennell's prime example of the cultural embodiment of her society came from a periodical. After all, it was trash publications such as penny dreadfuls that proved the greatest impetus for the debates that eventually gave shape to modern notions of popular culture. At the same time, it was primarily within periodicals that the debates themselves took place.

Periodicals and the dangerous boom of cheap entertainment

During the Victorian era, working-class wages gradually rose such that, 'by the last decade of the century, transports of delight appeared accessible to all, regardless of class or gender.'[28] Just as the working classes increased their proportion of readers more than the middle and upper classes, the young increased theirs more than the adult community. Literacy among working-class children had grown substantially during the first half of the Victorian era, but it received a major boost from the passage of Forster's Education Act in 1870. The act made publicly funded education available to all children in England and Wales between the ages of five and thirteen.

   Not surprisingly, as Marysa Demoor observes, 'Concurrent with the rise of a mass readership was a growing unease and a sense of doom on the part of the previously privileged, highly educated classes. The masses were considered a danger and threat by many intellectuals.'[29] Moreover, the increasing impact of written works on the working classes marked, as Morag Shiach has noted, 'the beginning of an argument about the relationships between technological development and cultural decline'.[30]

Despite the rise in literacy, short works with bold, emotional narratives and vivid visuals – first made popular through the *Newgate Calendar* – remained favourites among the poor, the working classes and the young, and new technological developments were simply making more of these readily available. As with street ballads early in the period, this continued attraction was, in part, because the brevity of much of the material allowed semi-literate people to read it and made it easier for poor and illiterate people to consume the material aurally. The practice of story-sharing is suggested by the cartoon accompanying an 1845 *Punch* piece entitled '"Parties" for the Gallows' (Figure 5). The cartoon depicts a boy buying a penny newspaper while his friends hover at the shop doorway.[31] The purchaser's semi-literacy is suggested by his heavy accent and weak grammar, bringing to mind Wilkie Collins's claim in his essay 'The Unknown Public' (1858) that the general population is 'in a literary sense, hardly beginning, as yet, to learn to read'.[32] Collins meant that the masses lacked the ability to distinguish quality, being 'still ignorant of almost everything which is generally known and understood among readers whom circumstances have placed, socially and intellectually, in the rank above them'. His claim also has validity, however, in the more direct sense that the audience for cheap periodicals included people who were barely or not at all literate.

In her well-known essay 'Byways of Literature: Reading for the Millions', Margaret Oliphant refers to the reading tastes of the masses as a product of the 'popular mind', but she also describes the works they consume as 'publications popular in this enlightened nineteenth century which reject the aid of mind'.[33] In the face of the hardships and poverty these people face on a daily basis, she suggests, it is understandable that the growing lower-class reading population rejects the notion of mental stimulation such as that proffered by philosophy, choosing instead stories that are sheer entertainment. Despite her sympathy, Oliphant's piece accords with Collins's warning that the 'largest audience for periodical literature, in this age of periodicals' is the readers of the dangerous penny journals (even if the penny newspapers are excluded from the calculation).[34]

These publications were frightfully well distributed, appearing, Collins declares, in stationer's shops, in tobacconist's shops, 'in fruit-shops, in oyster-shops, in lollypop-shops'.[35] Penny journals seemed to beckon incessantly from all directions – a nightmarish goblin market of bad writing: 'Buy me, borrow me, stare at me, steal me – do anything,

"PARTIES" FOR THE GALLOWS.

Newsvender.—" Now, MY MAN, WHAT IS IT ?"
Boy.—" I VONTS A NILLUSTRATED NEWSPAPER WITH A NORRID MURDER AND A LIKENESS IN IT."

Figure 5. Cartoon for '"Parties" for the Gallows', from *Punch* (June 1845).

O inattentive stranger, except contemptuously pass me by!' The source of Collins's anxiety is not this 'locust-flight of small publications', but the three million people who, he calculates, must be buying the products. While these readers were usually envisioned as primarily poor, young, inadequately educated males,[36] detractors also saw the appeal of penny journals as threatening to overpower the bourgeoisie as well. The dangerous amorphousness of this mass subject is apparent from Collins's and others' alarm over their difficulty in distinguishing the demographics of the penny-journal readership, as well as the dangerous overlap in content among not only the dreadfuls, other penny journals and penny newspapers, but also more expensive journals and newspapers.

Writing in 1895, Henry Chisholm offers an example of the ethical slippage across a spectrum of potential consumers resulting from these sorts of ambiguities. Chisholm observes that, 'when we have taught small boys and girls to read, their natural inclination will often be to read what is not good for them.'[37] It is primarily a class problem, he says, like premature smoking and continual spitting, all of which leads to children of the poor 'degenerating'. Chisholm then offers a cultural context for this youthful practice of reading trash that fills in the spaces between the lines. 'Coming so soon after the exposure of the abominable immoralities of an accomplished producer of non-moral literature for the upper circles of the reading world', he argues, 'it is not surprising that there should be an outcry against such publications as these.'[38] Only a few months before Chisholm's column appeared, London's attention had been focused on Oscar Wilde's conviction for gross indecency, newspapers taking advantage of the public's attraction to sensationalism by reporting on some ambiguous acts he and young, lower-class men had conducted in private rooms. What exactly went on in these rooms was left, for the most part, to readers' imaginations. Chisholm sees no problem in transposing the public attitude towards Wilde's private life on to the man's writings. And he is equally comfortable in conflating Wilde's 'literature for the upper circles' with dreadfuls because they are both, in his view, immoral. Chisholm proposes that the youthful consumption of popular literature will lead to crimes akin to Wildean gross indecency. In fact, Chisholm implies that Wilde and young readers belong to the same category of criminal.

Commercial considerations further complicated Victorian views of the popular literary market, as W. T. Stead demonstrates. In an article in his infamous 'Maiden Tribute to Modern Babylon' series, Stead notes that a procurer of girls for prostitution claimed she kept up on legal developments in her field through the numerous articles on the subject that she found in her Sunday reading of newspapers.[39] The complexity of the marketplace manoeuvring becomes apparent when one realizes that, just the day before this particular article appeared, Stead – a major influence on journalism reform – had published another in which he took advantage of the sensationalist tradition that he clearly condemns in the later article. In the earlier 'We Bid You Be of Hope', he promises that his upcoming report 'will be read to-day with a shuddering horror that will thrill throughout the world'.[40] 'After this awful picture of the crimes at present committed as it were under the very aegis of the law has been fully unfolded before the eyes of the public', he says tantalizingly, 'we need not doubt that the House of Commons will find time to raise the age during which English girls are protected from inexpiable wrong.' Through strategies similar to those Lane applied in his prospectus to *The Yellow Book*, Stead both lures readers with the upcoming sensual thrills of his text, and instructs them on how to consume it. He sanctions their reading of the material as the responsible act of a self-improving citizenry. Of course, self-education is the very reason the procurer gave for her own reading of crime reports. When Stead was found guilty of abduction and indecent assault, after he had arranged to have the young Eliza Armstrong kidnapped so that he could describe the process in his 'Maiden Tribute' serial, the judge chastised him for his 'articles so filthy and disgusting that one cannot help feeling that they may have suggested to innocent women and children the existence of vice and wickedness which had never occurred to their minds before'.[41] In this example, one sees the infection of salacious imagination moving from the sexual abusers to the edifying journalist and then, through his seductive rhetoric, to the general public. Stead demonstrates the invested interest that seemingly morally conscientious members of society had in abetting popular writing's propagation not only among a broad audience but also within assumedly reputable publications and genres including journalistic reporting.

As both Chisholm and Stead suggest, the segregation of immoral popular culture that Collins attempted did not become easier over time. James Payn explicitly revisited the questions in Collins's 'Unknown Public' twenty three years later in his 1881 'Penny Fiction', and Thomas Wright did so again two years after that, with both men ultimately offering an equally amorphous sense of the readership of popular culture as regards gender, class and age.[42] Wright emphasizes the notable number of women reading penny periodicals, a view echoed by George R. Humphery, who declares that dreadfuls are dangerous to both men and women,[43] and May Hely Hutchinson, who criticizes female servants specifically for reading dreadfuls.[44] In 'What the Working Classes Read' (1886), Edward Salmon concludes that most consumers of periodicals are men, while 'penny novelettes' are the domain primarily of 'shop-girls, seamstresses, and domestic servants'.[45] A few months later, however, in 'What Girls Read' (1886), he declares that many girls read books intended for boys. He even suggests that authors writing for young females could learn from their

male-oriented counterparts: 'Girls' literature would be much more successful than it is if it were less goody-goody.'[46] Literature of adventure
and daring, Salmon argues, not only appeals to young readers of either
sex, but also has the potential of encouraging moral development.

Salmon was not alone in recognizing that, rather than attempting
to stymie the tastes of the masses, their entertainments might be used
as media for the dominant ideologies of their society. Indeed, writing
at roughly the same time as Salmon, the anonymous author of 'Boyish
Freaks' (1888) suggests they already are. The author first notes various
recorded historical cases in which boys pursued adventure, usually with
a stolen pistol in one pocket and a penny dreadful in the other. While
predominantly condemnatory of such exploits, the author concludes by
noting the overlap between the actions and character traits often celebrated in dreadfuls and those admired by mainstream society: '[M]ay not
the enthusiasm which undertakes them prove the germ of the same old
spirit which animated the death-defying adventurers who have made this
country renowned, and to whose names on the roll of fame we can point
with pride and triumph?'[47]

The same valorizing interpretation of the impact of dreadfuls is offered
by Edward Viles, in this case an author and advocate of such works. In a
defence of readers of these stories, Viles extrapolates on the social function
of characters such as his daring highwayman:

> Were scenes of violence alone depicted, the only feeling that would be
> called into existence would be disgust at his atrocities. Such, then,
> being the case, it must be self-evident that it is not his obnoxiousness
> to the laws of the land nor the crimes of which he may have been
> guilty, that rivets the attention of the reader, but his courage, address,
> single-mindedness, and opposition to all kinds of oppression.[48]

These noble characteristics are most common in the anti-heroes of late
Victorian works, figures who are part of the lawless underworld they
patrol and whose virtues are not clearly those emulated by critics of
popular entertainment. It is these characters' skills in operating within
middle-class society while seemingly able to calculate justice from outside
the logic of the dominant legal order that endows them with the ability to
oppose 'all kinds of oppression', including those arising from the middle
class itself.

In works including Salmon's, Viles's and Pennell's, as in Ross's character of Ally Sloper, mass entertainment is imbued with the potential

for liberating the moral authority of the masses from that prescribed by the dominant order. Meanwhile, the anxiety that the preferences of the poorly educated and semi-literate were influencing the tastes and interests of the middle classes is, in itself, a confirmation that it was so. Various members of the middle class therefore tried to articulate a conceptual containment of the tastes and entertainments of the masses, with the hope of thereby also stalling the mass subject's growing cultural force. As such political manoeuvring suggests, popular culture was seen as far more than just a set of objects and practices. The notion of 'popular culture' arose as a realm of strategic contest through which the masses themselves were to be shaped in accord with middle-class interests and values. By the end of the century, however, Victorians saw this edifying conception eroded not only by the acknowledged influence of the lower classes on English culture but also by the boom of consumerism.

Notes

1 The research for this article was made possible by a grant from the Social Sciences and Humanities Research Council of Canada and a Visiting Scholar position at the University of Exeter, where I conducted research in the Chris Brooks Collection of Victorian Culture and the Bill Douglas Centre for the History of Cinema and Popular Culture.

2 John Lane, Prospectus to *The Yellow Book* (London: Elkin Mathews and John Lane, 1894), 29.

3 I thank Mark Samuels Lasner for information on the materials with which the volumes were made.

4 Margaret D. Stetz and Mark Samuels Lasner, *The Yellow Book: A Centenary Exhibition* (Cambridge: the Houghton Library, 1994), 7–8.

5 Matthew Arnold, *Culture and Anarchy: An Essay in Political and Social Criticism* (London: Smith, Elder, 1869), 47.

6 Lane, Prospectus, 1.

7 Harold Silver, 'Aspects of Neglect: The Strange Case of Victorian Popular Education', *Oxford Review of Education*, 3, 1 (1977), 57–69.

8 'About the B.M.I', The Birmingham and Midland Institute, www.bmi.org.uk, Accessed 12 Mar. 2008.

9 Arnold, *Culture and Anarchy*, 48.

10 Michael Warner, 'The Mass Public and the Mass Subject', in Craig Calhoun (ed.), *Habermas and the Public Sphere* (Cambridge, MA: MIT Press, 1992), 377–401.

11 Clement Scott, 'The Modern Music-Hall', *Contemporary Review*, 56 (1889), 683–90, at 688.

12 T. C. Horsfall, 'Painting and Popular Culture', *Fraser's Magazine*, 101 (June 1880), 849–56, at 856.

13 Thomas Wright, 'On a Possible Popular Culture', *Contemporary Review*, 40 (1881), 25–44, at 25.

14 Elizabeth Robins Pennell, *The Delights of Delicate Eating*, 1896 (Urbana: University of Illinois Press, 2000), 8. *The Feasts of Autolycus* was reprinted in the United States in 1901 under the title *The Delights of Delicate Eating*.

15 Elizabeth Robins Pennell, 'The Modern Comic Newspaper', *Contemporary Review*, 50 (1886), 509–23, at 509.

16 W. H. Mallock, *The New Republic: Or Culture, Faith, and Philosophy in an English Country House*, 1877 (Gainesville: University of Florida Press, 1950), 121.

17 Pennell, 'The Modern Comic Newspaper', 510.

18 J. M. Golby and A. W. Purdue, *The Civilization of the Crowd: Popular Culture in England: 1750–1900* (London: Batsford Academic, 1984), 116–25.

19 Pennell, 'The Modern Comic Newspaper', 515.

20 Linda K. Hughes, 'Women Poets and Contested Spaces in *The Yellow Book*', *Studies in English Literature*, 44, 4 (2004), 849–72, at 849–50.

21 Laurel Brake, 'Endgames: The Politics of *The Yellow Book* or, Decadence, Gender and the New Journalism', *Essays and Studies* (1995), 38–64, at 59.

22 Quoted in Robert Sherard, 'The Author of "Trilby": An Autobiographic Interview with Mr. George M. Du Maurier', *McClure's Magazine*, 4 (Apr. 1895), 391–400, at 399–400.

23 Henry Harland, 'A Birthday Letter', *The Yellow Book*, 9 (Apr. 1896), 11–22, at 13.

24 Ibid., 17.

25 Ibid., 18–19.

26 Harry Furniss, 'How We Advertise Now', *Punch* (3 Dec. 1887), 262.

27 Linda Nead, *Victorian Babylon: People, Streets and Images in Nineteenth-Century London* (New Haven: Yale University Press, 2000), 152.

28 David Vincent, *Literacy and Popular Culture: England 1750–1914* (Cambridge: Cambridge University Press, 1989), 212.

29 Marysa Demoor, 'Introduction', in Marysa Demoor (ed.), *Marketing the Author: Author Personae, Narrative Selves and Self-Fashioning: 1880–1930* (Basingstoke: Palgrave Macmillan, 2004), 2.

30 Morag Shiach, *Discourses on Popular Culture: Class, Gender and History in Cultural Analysis, 1730 to the Present* (Oxford: Polity, 1989), 72.

31 Cartoon for '"Parties" for the Gallows', *Punch* (June 1845), 147.

32 Wilkie Collins, 'The Unknown Public', *Household Words*, 18 (Aug. 1858), 217–22, at 222.

33 Margaret Oliphant, 'The Byways of Literature: Reading for the Million', *Blackwood's Edinburgh Magazine*, 84 (Aug. 1858), 200–16, at 204, 202.

34 Collins, 'The Unknown Public', 222.

35 Ibid., 217.

36 Scot McCracken, *Pulp: Reading Popular Fiction* (Manchester: Manchester University Press, 1998), 3.

37 Hugh Chisholm, 'How to Counteract the "Penny Dreadful"', *Fortnightly Review*, 64 (Nov. 1895), 765–75, at 771.

38 Ibid., 765.

39 W. T. Stead, 'The Maiden Tribute of Modern Babylon – II', *Pall Mall Gazette* (7 July 1885), 1–6.

40 W. T. Stead, 'We Bid You Be of Hope', *Pall Mall Gazette* (6 July 1885), 1.

41 Quoted in Alison Plowden, *The Case of Eliza Armstrong: A Child of 13 Bought for £5* (London: BBC, 1974), 123.

42 James Payn, 'Penny Fiction', *Nineteenth Century*, 9 (Jan. 1881), 145–54; Thomas Wright, 'Concerning the Unknown Public', *Nineteenth Century*, 13 (Feb. 1883), 279–96.

43 George R. Humphery, 'The Reading of the Working Classes', *Nineteenth Century*, 33 (Apr. 1893), 690–701.

44 May Hely Hutchinson, 'Female Emigration to South Africa', *Nineteenth Century and After*, 51 (Jan. 1902), 71–87, at 73.

45 Edward Salmon, 'What the Working Classes Read', *Nineteenth Century*, 20 (July 1886), 108–17, at 112.

46 Edward Salmon, 'What Girls Read', *Nineteenth Century*, 20 (Nov. 1886), 515–29, at 515.

47 'Boyish Freaks', *Chambers's Journal of Popular Literature, Science and Arts*, 5 (Apr. 1888), 252–55, at 255.

48 Quoted in Kevin Carpenter, *Penny Dreadfuls and Comics: English Periodicals for Children from Victorian Times to the Present Day* (London: Victoria and Albert Museum, 1983), 27.

9

Satirical print culture

One of the most notable innovations in nineteenth-century literary culture was mechanical rather than imaginative: the printing machine introduced by the London-based German inventor Friedrich Koenig in 1811. It replaced the old-fashioned rectangular hand-press with a more efficient, steam-powered, cylinder, thereby hugely increasing publishing capacity. Over the succeeding decades technology developed to the point that by the mid-1850s the wonderful machine had increased production ten-fold and beyond, from around 500 printed sheets per hour to more than 8,000. To give but one instance, the most successful London daily newspaper, *The Times*, saw its print capacity multiplied at a stroke as a result of these innovations. Pre-Koenig, in the first decade of the nineteenth century, the paper had daily runs of between 2,500 and 3,000 copies, but by 1855 it sold around 60,000 *per diem*. This rapid growth in sales of the 'Thunderer', as it was nicknamed, is indicative of the expansion of print culture in the Victorian era. From the 1830s onwards there was both an insatiable appetite for print and, for the first time, the means to satisfy that craving, making this period the first era of mass-market publishing in Great Britain.

Facilitated by the contemporary industrialization – as it might be called – of print culture, some entrepreneurial publishers turned their attention to the needs of what E. P. Thomson has taught us to think of as the newly made working class. If the era from the 1720s to the 1740s – according to orthodox literary history – was the period in which the emergence of the English novel catered to the cultural tastes of a newly literate middle class, then, a century later, the decades from the 1820s to the 1840s are often seen as the age in which, in analogous fashion, 'penny literature' served the literary appetites of a nascent working-class reading public. Some of this was directed in worthy and earnest directions, servicing the intellectual life of the British working classes, and feeding the taste for self-improvement evident among a population with rising levels of literacy. Popular editions of Shakespeare and of the British poets, particularly the works of Burns and the Romantics, sold in large numbers, as did improving and indubitably informative periodicals such as *Chambers' Edinburgh Journal* and the *Penny Magazine* established by socially aware publishers. Similarly, the English novel began to sell in numbers unprecedented, whether in reprints of the eighteenth-century classics, Fielding, Goldsmith and Smollett, or in the work of the contemporary notables of Victorian fiction. From the wild success of Boz's *Pickwick Papers* (1836–7) onwards, best-selling novelists, some, like Dickens, copying the part-work serial publication first utilized to popular acclaim by Pierce Egan's *Life in London* (1821), managed significantly higher print runs than in the days of the 'Great Unknown' only two or three decades earlier. There Sir Walter Scott's triple-decker novels, published in editions of 2,000 or 3,000 expensive copies, could still be considered a publishing triumph.

The proliferation of print culture in the first half of the Victorian age is apparent in the healthy sales and critical esteem of renowned novelists such as W. M. Thackeray, Wilkie Collins and that master of prose narrative Charles Dickens. However, it was also manifest in what might be seen as some of the less dignified print subcultures of the age. 'The world impolite', writes the aforesaid Thackeray in his survey of cheap literature, 'A Half-Crown's Worth of Cheap Knowledge', published in *Fraser's Magazine* in 1838, 'has a literature of its own'.[1] To illustrate contemporary popular-cultural tastes, Thackeray lists the purchases, some fifteen in number, which his two-and-sixpence had bought from the street bookseller's cart. Here were two sporting journals, the *Sporting Gazette* and the *Sporting World*; a literary miscellany, the *Weekly Magazine*, a cheap version of the likes of the society publisher Henry Colburn's *Literary Gazette*; several satirical journals such as the *Penny Satirist* and the *London Satirist*; *Oliver Twiss*, a chapbook imitation of Dickens ('a kind of silly copy of Boz's admirable tale' (285)); two miscellanies of society gossip, crime and scandal, the *Fly* and the *Town*; the *Poor Man's Friend,* the successor to the *Poor Man's Journal*, the notorious unstamped newspaper published by fearless Radical and political gaolbird Henry Hetherington; the *Moral Reformer*, a journal conducted by pro-Temperance zealot Joseph Livesey; and, finally, straightforward sheets of narrative both fictional and factual: the *Penny*

Storyteller, which speaks for itself, the *Wars of Europe,* tales of derring-do among the soldiery during the Napoleonic Wars and the *Penny Gazette of Varieties*, part compendium of stories, both serious and whimsical, and part satirical journal. This last was, in the words of its subtitle, 'illustrated with cuts comic and satirical' and was edited by the Radical iconoclast John Cleave who also published *Cleave's Weekly Police Gazette*, a journal set up as a rival to the official police organ the *Hue and Cry*, and which managed 40,000 copies a week in its heyday. The *Police Gazette* combined the moral force of Chartist views with lurid and detailed crime reports, though without glamourizing the constabulary (Thackeray says Cleave portrayed the average policeman as 'a "bloody bludgeon-man" – a kind of ogre, invented by Sir Robert Peel to swallow or imprison poor Englishmen' (281)).

Surveying the good things which his thirty pennies had bought him, Thackeray scoffs at the optimistic 'progress-of-mind' narratives which some contemporary middle-class liberals had seen as being evident among the lower orders' newish taste for print, declaring that he found little evidence of 'the "March of Intellect" which we have heard so much about' (279). Indeed, the essayist sees nothing to suggest that populist tastes in the new Victorian age were currently changing for the better or were likely to alter any time soon, as if the late Georgian literary appetite for satirical character assassination, cruel sports and society tittle-tattle had all of a sudden been replaced by a self-improving thirst for the plays of the Bard of Avon, treatises on political economy and the works of Jeremy Bentham (1748–1832) on utilitarianism: 'Is it unfair to conclude', Thackeray asks, 'that the people, for whose special benefit penny literature has been invented, do not care much for politics or instruction, but seek chiefly for amusement in exchange for their humble penny?' (283).

In his catalogue of cheap literature, Thackeray is right to emphasize the importance of certain key strands within the print subculture of the early Victorian age: of graphic and literary satire, of comic writing devoid of moral design, of a widespread appetite for writing about sport and of a taste for lurid reporting of felony, whether sexual or sociopathic, and whether in high or low circles. Such were the preoccupations of popular culture at the start of the Victorian age, and so they continued, both in penny literary form and, indeed, in periodicals aimed at middle-class audiences. We should not automatically assume that there was so great a divide in literary tastes between readers of different brows.

Renton Nicholson's notorious scandal-sheet the *Town*, which Thackeray dismisses in *Fraser's* as full of matter which would not 'bear repetition in this Magazine' (290), attracted bourgeois as well as artisan readers, and the popular newspapers established in the 1840s and beyond such as the *News of the World* and *Lloyd's Weekly* (both first published in 1843) were aimed at all classes: in its prospectus, the former declared that it wished to achieve 'a very extensive circulation' by targeting 'the general utility of all classes'.[2] Furthermore, recent criticism in Victorian studies has taught us not so readily to assume an unbridgeable gap between cultures ostensibly high and ostensibly low. Dickens, the most notable novelist of the age, was also someone who participated in the wider print subculture in his capacity as popular journalist, satirist and crime writer. And his first masterpiece grew out of the comic writing about sport which had been so popular in the late Georgian period. In all of its publishing diversity and variety, the Victorian era was very much that of the polymath Dickens, and in more ways than we might customarily think.

Her Imperial Majesty excepted, Charles Dickens was perhaps the most emblematic figure within Victorian culture. Its first literary genius, an author whose debut novel, the *Pickwick Papers*, completed its serial publication in the very year of the Queen's coronation, Boz was the boy wonder turned literary celebrity of the age. At just twenty-five, he bestrode a literary world that he would dominate until his relatively early death some thirty years later. If we consider the opening decades of the nineteenth century as the heyday of the Romantic poets, we also think of Dickens introducing the great period of the nineteenth-century novel that was manifested in the work of the sisters Brontë, George Eliot, Elizabeth Gaskell and Thomas Hardy. This notion of prose summarily displacing poetry as the most significant cultural formation of the age has frequently been viewed as the central epochal shift of Victorian literature. It seemed so to many at the time, and it did so very quickly. Only six years after the appearance of *Pickwick*, the change of key was seen as near-proverbial: Abraham Hayward noted in the *Edinburgh Review* in 1843 that 'The present, however, is an unpoetic age [which] decidedly prefers prose to poetry; [Wordsworth's] *Excursion* . . . has no chance at all against the *Pickwick Papers* or *Oliver Twist*.'[3]

Historically, critical opinion has tended to endorse the notion of a clear rupture between a Romantic sensibility and the literary mentality of the Victorian era. However, this is an opposition which decidedly fails to account for the literary antecedents of Charles Dickens, whom

Andrew Sanders, following the logic of the conventional view, has called 'the man from nowhere'.[4] If we assume that the first decades of the nineteenth century were purely defined by high Romantic argument, by the poetry of sensibility, nature and the creative imagination and so on, then this is undeniably so. However, if we see the 1810s onwards as a Koenigian rather than a Wordsworthian age, with a proliferation of popular-cultural literary forms, then we can understand how the context of late Georgian print provided formative influences that both shaped the development of Charles Dickens's work and also fashioned modes of popular publishing which continued well into the Victorian period. Recent criticism has problematized the notion of a clear and untroubled division between 'Romantic' and 'Victorian', arguing instead for a sense of continuum rather than fracture. This position might be further refined into an argument that popular Victorian print culture, whether high or low in tone, whether by Dickens or by anonymous pressmen lost to history's chronicle, was a development and extension of the burgeoning print industry of the later part of the Romantic period, some of it Radical in character, some of it purely commercial. Charles Dickens emerged from a culture of print ephemera attuned to a different key from what the author once labelled 'the muse's lyre',[5] from Wordsworth's and Coleridge's emphasis on poetic selfhood and the sublime, for instance, or Shelley's neo-Platonism or Keats's preoccupation with the nature of art. While Sanders is right to say that Dickens 'blazed on to the early Victorian literary firmament like a meteor',[6] this trajectory owes something of its movement to the publishing conditions of post-Napoleonic England, notably in print satire but also in other aspects of Thackeray's impolite canon: in Radicalism, the representation of crime and the literature of sport. What is generally seen as the high point of Victorian literature publishing, the novel, was just the meringue peak of a wealth of styles and forms of print.

Charles Dickens, like the Radical penny publishers, borrowed from a much older literature of the street in adapting the concerns of sensationalist broadsides, Newgate chapbooks and murder ballads. In doing so, as Sally Ledger has written, the author was 'able . . . to transcend the boundaries between high and low culture'. Ledger argues, rightly, that Dickens 'was able to promote popular radical cultural traditions at the same time as commercially exploiting them and becoming a rich man'.[7] For some, though, commercial success required relinquishing precisely those traditions. The *News of the World*, as Virginia Berridge has argued, adopted a superficial radicalism as a matter of expedience before, in the end, dispensing with it in favour of sensationalism, news and sport.[8] The success of such publications eventually did for the Radical press, ultimately entailing a decline in political partisanship and a march towards an apolitical and sometimes conservative popular press.

Berridge's argument, in effect describing the Pyrrhic victory of the Radical press, is decidedly less optimistic than Ledger's narrative of its triumphant transmogrification in the work of Charles Dickens. That said, it does not take away from Boz's sincerity in his own indebtedness to the late Georgian print tradition of Radical satire, a tradition with which he, at times, clearly identified himself. This crucial business of satire is an example of the way in which one of the key aspects of Romantic era print culture continued and mutated into the Victorian age in Dickens and elsewhere. We too easily think that nineteenth-century satire expired with the late Georgians. Undeniably the period which we now label 'Romantic' was possessed of a raucous satirical vigour: the powerful graphic satire of Gillray, Rowlandson and Cruikshank; the Tory satirists William Gifford and T. J. Mathias who were so influential in the 1790s 'Revolution Controversy'; the post-Napoleonic Whig and Radical wits Lord Byron, Thomas Moore, Leigh Hunt and William Hone; and the satirical magazines that spanned the age from the *Anti-Jacobin* (1797–8) to the Regency journals the *Satirist* and the *Scourge* and through to the early years of *Blackwood's Edinburgh Magazine*. However, this rich satirical tradition did not die out with the dimming of the Romantic day but survived in mutated form in Dickens's novels, as well as resounding through particular aspects of Victorian periodical culture.

Romantic era satire shaped Dickens, and Dickens, in turn, shaped Victorian satire. We know of his early prose satire on the law, prison conditions and female poetasters in the *Pickwick Papers* and of his indictment of the abuses of Yorkshire boarding schools in *Nicholas Nickleby* (1838–9), but less well acknowledged is his self-alignment with the tradition of Radical verse satire. Certain aspects of Leigh Hunt's personality may have provided the raw material for Dickens's unflattering portrait of Harold Skimpole in *Bleak House* (1852–3), but it should also be acknowledged that the poet represented rather more than that to our author. Hunt's potent occasional satires provided a model for Dickens in his own efforts as a verse satirist. Even in his pomp, Dickens, whose earliest days as a pressman were spent working for the ultra-Radical newspaper the *New Sun*, was not above composing verse for oppositionalist periodicals. In

August 1841, for example, he contributed an anonymous squib, 'The Fine Old English Gentleman', to the *Examiner*, Hunt's vehicle of subversion during the Regency. The lampoon berates the recall of the Tories – after the fall of Lord Melbourne's administration in the previous month – as a return to the bad old days of reactionary Toryism:

> The good old laws were garnished well with gibbets, whips, and
>   chains,
> With fine old English penalties, and fine old English pains,
> With rebel heads and seas of blood once hot in rebel veins:
> For all these things were requisite to guard the rich old gains
>   Of the fine old English Tory times;
>   Soon may they come again![9]

Dickens's poem is a comic imitation of 'The Fine Old English Gentleman', a burletta aria which had become one of the most widely published broadside ballads of the first half of the nineteenth century. In the formal model, the old gentleman – like Scrooge reborn on Christmas morn – though rich, is a friend to the people: 'When winter cold brought Christmas old,/He opened house to all . . . Nor was the houseless wanderer/Then driven from the hall.' 'While he feasted all the great', says the ballad, 'He ne'er forgot the small.' However, in Dickens's version the story is upended. To the satirist, who to some establishment figures was not quite above the salt, the notion of a 'Tory gentleman' was a contradiction in terms. Re-establishing Toryism was the worst form of atavistic blundering, taking the nation back into an age of merciless political oppression. Dickens laments that the return of the Tories, in power over forty years after the rise of William Pitt, will cause social fracture, political violence and hunger in Great Britain and Ireland:

> The bright old day now dawns again; the cry runs through the land,
> In England there shall be dear bread – in Ireland, sword and brand;
> And poverty, and ignorance, shall swell the rich and grand,
> So, rally round the rulers with the gentle iron hand,
>   Of the fine old English Tory days;
>   Hail to the coming time!   (276)

It might be noted that the 'fine old English Tory times' spoken of so ironically here were actually within the living memory of some readers of the *Examiner*. Dickens refers not to the days of some pitiless medieval tyrant, but to the 1790s and 1800s, in which Billy Pitt, as all good Radicals knew, used cruel and savage means to repress the starving populace:

> The good old times for cutting throats that cried out in their need,
> The good old times for hunting men who held their fathers' creed,
> The good old times when William Pitt, as all good men agreed,
> Came down direct from Paradise at more than railroad speed.
>   Oh the fine old English Tory times;
>   When will they come again!   (275)

Dickens's choice of publication for his satire is significant. The *Examiner* was the site of some of the most significant freedom-of-the-press heroics of the Romantic era. The high point of the newspaper's history had been during the Regency, when Leigh and John Hunt had landed up in prison as a consequence of their entertainingly libellous attack on the Prince Regent, 'The Prince on St Patrick's Day', in which the former mocked flatterers of the corpulent royal womanizer (reminding them that this '"*Adonis in Loveliness*" was a corpulent gentleman of fifty') and dismissed Prince George as 'a violator of his word, a libertine, over head and ears in debt and disgrace [and] a despiser of domestic ties'.[10] The *Examiner* was still a force to be reckoned with in the early Victorian age and it is telling that Dickens sought out the foremost newspaper of the late Georgian middle-class Radical tradition and positioned himself within that tradition. Indeed, Dickens makes his identification with Leigh Hunt explicit, going so far as to refer directly to the plight of the Hunt brothers in his reference to Tories 'shutting men of letters up, through iron bars to grin,/Because they didn't think the Prince was altogether thin.'[11] That Dickens was assuming Hunt's mantle is also demonstrated by the fact that the elder satirist had several times imitated broadside balladry in his own *Examiner* satires, in such stuff as 'A-Hanging we will go' (1821). Here Dickens makes the same imitative gesture.

'By Jove, how radical I am getting!',[12] Charles Dickens wrote to John Forster the week after his squib was published in the *Examiner*. The author was consciously identifying himself with a tradition of nineteenth-century oppositionalist satire that was then beginning to adapt into its particularly Victorian shape, whether echoing through Chartist periodicals including Feargus O'Connor's *Northern Star* and the 1840s satire of Ebenezer Elliott, the anti-Corn Law rhymester, or, indeed, in the middle-class periodical culture best exemplified in a journal founded in 1841 – the year of 'The Fine Old English Gentleman' – to which Dickens had close connections. The most famous Victorian comic magazine, *Punch, or The London Charivari*, was established in the month before the novelist waxed subversive in the public prints. This, too, initially adopted a Radical, or at least liberal, political perspective, and was, from the start, politically engaged: '*Punch*, like Melbourne', a banner to one of the early numbers declared, 'is JUST OUT.' The joint editors of the journal were three press-men dramatists: Dickens's friend Mark Lemon, the social reformer Henry Mayhew and Joseph Stirling Coyne, who had contributed articles to *Bentley's Miscellany* during Dickens's editorship. Its earliest staffers included the indefatigable journalist, playwright and Radical Douglas Jerrold, later to take *Lloyd's* to a weekly readership of over 500,000 copies a week, and Gilbert à Beckett, who had made his name as a principal co-adjutor in Boz's collaborator's money-making jest-book *Cruikshank's Comic Almanack* (1835–53). Luminaries including Thomas Hood and W. M. Thackeray soon joined the comical ranks (though the latter had reservations about being 'in the same boat as such a savage little Robespierre'[13] as Jerrold), with all working alongside those gifted and now well-known artists John, later Sir John, Tenniel and John Leech, then strongly attached to the liberal cause, who provided memorable illustrations, farcical, satirical, grotesque.

Punch commenced with a *de facto* manifesto, 'The Moral of Punch', written by co-editor Lemon, a document that brings to mind the prospec-tuses to both the *Anti-Jacobin* and the *Examiner* before it, and which declared *Punch* would consist of satire as well as purely comic whimsy: 'trifles that have no other object than the moment's approbation' would be set alongside 'graver puppetry'. Lemon's very title is significant; satire is, after all, comedy with a moral purpose and *Punch* revelled in satirical assaults on what it saw as the widespread corruption and injustice around it: the failings of the House of Lords and the judiciary, the sufferings of the people during the 'Hungry Forties', the iniquities of the Corn Laws (less cherished by posterity are its campaigns for 'No Popery' and delight in goading the Irish). However, one should not overestimate the extrem-ity of *Punch*'s radicalism. In general it railed against 'seditionists' and the Chartist leaders, especially physical-force champions including the Irish leader Feargus O'Connor, who was dismissed as a bombastic and violent demagogue (Chartist workers themselves were, in general, more sym-pathetically treated, portrayed as honest men too often led by knaves). This notwithstanding, an early historian of *Punch* is correct to remark that during the 'forties *Punch* doubled the rôles of jester and political pamphleteer, and in the latter capacity indulged in a great deal of vehement partisan rhetoric'.[14]

Punch's 'partisan' polemicism was not uncontentious. In 1847, one contemporary commentator wrote disapprovingly that 'the present . . . is constantly viewed as food for satire'[15] in its pages; 'Satire', it railed, 'must always fail as the preacher of truth'.[16] The Roman satirist Juvenal (c. AD 60–c. 136) would have been unconvinced. And certainly *Punch* swatted aside such criticism, continuing to turn the handle of its satirical barrel organ. It strongly condemned – in the manner of Dickens's contemporaneous satire – the mistreatment of children, the horrors of the workhouse and the plight of the poor, both rural and metropolitan. In 1848, for instance, in its famous 'Model' series, it offered an ironic depiction of the life of a labouring man:

> He supports a large family upon the smallest wages. He works from twelve to fourteen hours a day . . . He prefers his fireside to the alehouse, and has only one pipe when he gets home, and then to bed. He attends church regularly, with a clean smockfrock and face on Sundays, and waits outside, when service is over, to pull his hair to his landlord, or, in his absence, pays the same reverence to the steward. Beer and he are perfect strangers, rarely meeting, except at Christmas or Harvest time; and as for spirits, he only knows them, like meat, by name. He does not care for skittles. He never loses a day's work by attending political meetings . . . This is the MODEL LABOURER, whose end of life is honourably fulfilled if he is able, after a whole life's sowing for another, to reap a coffin for himself to be buried in![17]

The humble, forelock-tugging, politically docile peasant drudge, the Tory model of a labourer, is rewarded, like George Orwell's Boxer in *Animal Farm* (1945), only by the knacker's yard. Figure 6 shows John Leech's dark cartoon 'The Poor Man's Friend' (1845) which, ploughing the same ideological furrow, deals with (grim) reaping: death is seen as a blessed release for the pauper, for the famished and oppressed and for the poor people of England.

Punch had much in the way of satirical and philanthropic preoccupations in common with Charles Dickens. Their ethical coincidence was reinforced in the mid-1840s, when the journal invoked and, indeed, strengthened, the novelist's radical squib of 1841 in its own satirical imitation of 'The Fine Old English Gentleman':

THE POOR MAN'S FRIEND.

Figure 6. John Leech, 'The Poor Man's Friend', from *Punch* (1845).

I'll sing you a fine old song, improved by a modern pate,
Of a fine Old English Gentleman, who owns a large estate,
But pays the labourers on it a very shabby rate.
Some seven shillings each a week for early work and late,
Gives this fine Old English Gentleman, one of the present time.

...

In winter's cold, when poor and old, for some assistance call,
And come to beg a trifle at the portals of his hall,
He refers them to the workhouse, that stands open wide for all;
For this is how the parish great relieve the parish small,
Like this fine Old English Gentleman, one of the present time.[18]

Here *Punch* echoes the *Examiner*'s great contributor. Whether or not this is a conscious or unconscious allusion to Dickens's poem, it undeniably resounds with the concerns of the novelist's early fiction. The horrors of the workhouse, the relationship of *noblesse oblige* between high and low, the 'shabby' treatment of the rural poor, sweated labour: Dickens, the consciously post-Georgian satirist, had constructed a path for his contemporaries to follow.

As far as the poor of the metropolis were concerned, it was Thomas Hood who contributed the most well-known politically charged poem of *Punch*'s early days. Those famous verses 'The Song of the Shirt' were published in the Christmas number for 1843, and movingly articulate the suffering of a worn-out seamstress paid a pittance for her piecemeal work:

With fingers weary and worn,
With eyelids heavy and red,
A Woman sat, in unwomanly rags,
Plying her needle and thread –
Stitch! stitch! stitch!
In poverty, hunger, and dirt,
And still with the voice of dolorous pitch
She sang the 'Song of the Shirt!'
. . .
– With fingers weary and worn,
With eyelids heavy and red,
A Woman sat, in unwomanly rags,
Plying her needle and thread –
Stitch! stitch! stitch!
In poverty, hunger, and dirt,
And still with a voice of dolorous pitch, –
Would that its tone could reach the Rich! –
She sang this 'Song of the Shirt!'[19]

The sheer familiarity of Hood's work should not blind us to the Juvenalian power and effectiveness of the piece, which was brilliantly illustrated by Leech. (Testimony to the poem's impact is its representational currency; it was later treated in oils by Richard Redgrave (1844), G. F. Watts (1850) and Anna Elizabeth Blunden (1854).) The poem indulges in soapbox verse oratory, and is, perhaps, none the worse for that: 'It is not linen you're wearing out/But human creatures' lives.'

The success of *Punch* begat many imitators over the succeeding decades. 'At this period', wrote the Victorian journalist James Hannay, 'the British public was rabid for comic literature. To do the B.P. justice, it is always willing to be amused, and liberal to its buffoons. But in those days it bought funny journals and little books with voracity, and funny journals and little books were showered upon it accordingly.'[20] Some of these titles were short-lived, including the *Great Gun* (1844–5), the *Comic News* (1864–5) and *Mash; A Humorous and Fantastic Review of the Month* (1868). Others were more long-lasting, notably *Fun*, established in 1861 by Tom Hood, the son of the author of 'The Song of the Shirt', which expired as late as 1900; *Funny Folks* (1874–94), edited by William Sawyer, 'a Weekly Budget of Funny Pictures, Funny Notes, Funny Jokes [and] Funny Stories', and *Judy, or the London Serio-Comic Journal* (1867–1907). Let us take this last journal, founded in the late 1860s, as representative of the comic papers of the second half of the Victorian period (it also seems appropriate to follow discussion of *Punch* by considering the periodical named after the hook-nosed truncheon wielder's long-suffering wife). The London correspondent of the *New York Times* jested in 1891 that the average Englishman was 'a grim melancholy person, who only smiles when beating his wife', and, certainly, the trope of domestic violence raised a smile in some of the periodical culture of the Victorians. The prospectus to *Judy* declared the eponymous one's antipathy to 'our caitiff husband, PUNCH', whom it described as 'wasting his substance in riotous living to the great discomfort of ourself, his lawful wife'. (Judy, like Punch, was a central figure in her own periodical, generally represented on the cover and frequently referred to in the copy – in the meta-comical manner of the day – as if she were its actual editor. Figure 7 shows the cover of the 'half-jubilee' number of *Judy*, dating from 1892.)

Judy was initially edited by Charles Henry Ross, who was a gifted caricaturist, and it was he who was responsible for first sketching the best-known corner of the magazine, the misadventures of its famous anti-hero Ally Sloper, a figure who first appeared in the number for 17 August 1867. Alexander Sloper, a boozy, bald, work-shy schemer and social climber, dressed in heavy boots and a battered hat, with a bottle of something generally tucked in his pocket, was comically known as 'Ally Sloper', a reference to his tendency to dodge the bailiffs by running

Figure 7. Artist unknown. Cover from *Judy* (1892).

down the nearest back lane. Sloper, clearly a raffish and less good-natured imitation of Dickens's Mr Micawber, drank, skived and boasted in the pages of *Judy* to the entertainment of a large audience. It was Sloper's comical doings, featuring one boldly drawn cartoon per page and generally spanning between six and a dozen pages (though occasionally more), which individuated *Judy* – which otherwise had a similar mixture of comic poems, prose and cartoons – from the comic horde.

In 1884, Gilbert Dalziel purchased the paper and the character from C. H. Ross, and in so doing then owned both of *Punch*'s principal rivals (he had bought *Fun* from Tom Hood in 1870). This entrepreneur of comedy promptly launched an even more successful spin-off, *Ally Sloper's Half-Holiday* (1884–1923), the pioneering comic in British print culture, and a journal which lasted for nearly forty years. In its pages, Ally, alongside a large cast of family (Mrs Sloper, racy daughter Tootsie, naughty Master Alexander), his pet dog and his disreputable friends (Snatcher, Isaac 'Iky' Moses and Mr McGoosele), made merry, supped, avoided his creditors and was frequently beaten up.

In the early numbers of *Judy*, beginning with 'Some of the Mysteries of Loan and Discount', in which Moses – a Jewish conman and the second most important character in the strip in its early days – and Sloper, both down-on-their-luck scoundrels, set up a 'Loan Office'. It claimed to have 'Capital, One Million' when in fact their safe only contained a pipe, a loaf of bread and a stinking fish (one is reminded here of *Martin Chuzzlewit*'s Anglo-Bengalee Disinterested Loan and Life Assurance Company). Sloper has a series of further misadventures: he is physically assaulted for cheating at cards but manages, on the other hand, to earn pots of cash tossing up with his 'famous double-headed penny'; he poses as a gentleman of property when Iky establishes a Matrimonial Agency to assist 'ladies of property who would very much like to get married' (only for the 'long-lost MRS SLOPER' to turn up and assault him up with her umbrella), and is flattened by an irate customer when he and Iky, after pretending to be trained hairdressers, scalp an extravagantly hirsute customer. Ally tours Europe from Le Havre to Constantinople ('JUDY', of course, 'found the bulk of the travelling expenses'), and joins the crowd at the Epsom Derby ('SLOPER was always a patron of sport') where he sets himself up a tipster ('Werry simple'), with the usual concussive results. He is further sponsored by *Judy* to meet Dr Livingstone in 'darkest' Africa where he engages in a bigamous marriage ('"Hallo! I say –"'. But then, after all, one must conform to the customs of the country'), sells cosmetics and 'toilet requisites [to] the fair black sex', and plays find the penny with stereotypical bulging-eyed, sloping-foreheaded and big-lipped 'Negroes'. The catalogue of roguery goes on; Sloper masquerades as a sightless beggar ('BLIND but honest'), contrives to get drunk at the Teetotallers' Fête at the Crystal Palace and tries to steal the boots from a sleeping member of the soldiery after which he is, as a predictable consequence, duly bashed up.[21]

What does this rascal Sloper represent? For some, not very much. When it troubled to consider the matter, late Victorian opinion frequently saw the character and, indeed, the strip as little more than foolish triviality and, worse, as indicative of a decline in contemporary literary standards: 'To devour *Ally Sloper* and *Tit Bits*', declared one earnest magazinist: 'is not to read. Nothing can be more enervating to the mind than this class of literature, if literature it may be called. Such sheets as these destroy the appetite for real reading, and the healthful hunger for books.'[22] Though the 'this country's going to the dogs' tone of this bromide is somewhat risible, the question of Ally Sloper's inanity bears inspection. Is he the knockabout incarnation of the triumph of non-satirical comedy in the second half of the Victorian period? Berridge, as we have seen, argues that popular Radicalism was ultimately displaced by a less politically engaged, mass-market newspaper tradition and, perhaps, a similar process might seem to be at work in the age's comic literature, with an analogous decline in partisanship manifesting itself as the Victorian age developed. There is much evidence to support this. Charles L. Graves, for instance, noted the gradual move away from satirical engagement in the most signifi-cant example of that literature, in his argument that there was a 'gradual cooling of *Punch*'s democratic ardour'[23] in the late 1850s and beyond. Satirical rage, similarly, does not run through the veins of *Fun* magazine, despite its editor's Liberal politics. Likewise, whereas *Punch*'s 1841 ardu-ously democratic prospectus proclaims its willingness to wield the sword of satire in the cause of justice, *Judy*'s 1867 effort expends itself in self-referential jests about the comic press and in a consciously commercial attempt to attract its profitable rival's readership. Perhaps appropriately, given his journal's positioning against *Punch*, Judy's founding editor was Conservative in politics. But *Judy* had a commercial rather than a political agenda. Consider the tumultuous advertising which threatens to overrun the cover reproduced above, which might be seen as indicative of its pur-pose to address a consumer rather than an ideological culture. '*No moral, as usual*', says the last line of an early 1868 Sloper strip in *Judy*, and this might be seen as symptomatic of the depoliticization of comic writing in the second half of the century.

The *Judy* front covers, those cornucopias of advertising copy, bark for, among other products, Nestlé's baby food. And it might be argued that Ally Sloper represented the infantilization of Victorian comic writ-ing, both in a move away from the tradition of political satire and in the conscious appeal to a youthful audience that was evident in the

Half-Holiday and in *Fun* and *Funny Folks*. The puerile journal – in a non-offensive sense – the *Boys' Brigade Gazette* certainly saw the Sloper franchise as a childish business, speculating in 1893 that a boy, possessed of rather less pocket money than W. M. Thackeray fifty years before, would spend his little mite on comics, including here the *Half-Holiday*: 'Give him 3d. to expend on current literature and he will probably select *Scraps*, *Ally Sloper*, *Comic Cuts*, the *Joker*.'[24] The late Georgian satirist William Hone had adapted nursery rhymes, children's bestiaries and infants' chapbooks in the Radical pamphlets that he devised with George Cruikshank in the post-Napoleonic period including *The Political House that Jack Built* (1819) and *The Political Showman at Home!* (1821). Perhaps in *Judy* and, in particular, *Ally Sloper's*, we see the most notable comic literature of the late Victorian age, in a similarly populist, but apolitical, gesture, in addressing children rather than borrowing their literature to serve a satirical thesis.

But this is not wholly so. The British have, it seems, long had a fondness for boozy chancers from Sir John Falstaff to Derek 'Del Boy' Trotter, someone who 'could smell a fiver in a force nine gale'.[25] The 'industrious' Victorians were no exception, and one might make a case for a satirically engaged reading of Ally Sloper. David Kunzle has labelled the strip 'a satire on the Victorian work ethic',[26] seeing Sloper as, in effect, Samuel Smiles's parodic alter-ego. That said, one might also interpret the failure of Sloper's 'get-rich-quick' schemes as a conservative rebuke, reminding the reader that hard work alone was the key to wealth and prosperity[27] (the possibilities multiply: to a Bakhtinian, Sloper's antics could signify a carnivalesque nose-thumbing of conventional authority, while a Foucauldian might equally interpret his frequent bashings as the re-establishment of that authority after a certain licensed naughtiness). Indeed, there were some contemporaries of Ross and Dalziel for whom Sloper, far from representing a decline in the Georgian tradition, actually marked its continuance. Hume Nesbit, the Victorian historian of graphic satire, writing in 1892, specifically identified the *Half-Holiday* as the modern equivalent of the eighteenth- and nineteenth-century satirical canon:

> *Ally Sloper* is the only paper of the present day to which the peculiar genius of the old caricaturists has descended; the Hogarthian satire and Rabelaisian humour is, in this much-illustrated weekly paper, reproduced in modernised costume and surroundings . . . blend[ed] with the broad buffoonery with which Cruikshank delighted his audience of the past generation.[28]

George Cruikshank was the interdependence of late Georgian and early Victorian satire incarnate, from his brilliant collaborations with Hone in the 1810s and 1820s to those with Boz in the 1830s and early 1840s. However, his work is also sometimes seen as emblematic of the supposed decline of satire as the nineteenth century wore on, as he became increasingly preoccupied with Temperance (Dickens and others felt he had transformed into an anti-boozing 'fanatic'). Still, a change of target does not necessarily entail a weakening of satirical potency: his great picture 'The Worship of Bacchus' (1860–2) is no less powerfully Juvenalian for wearing temperate clothes. While historically satire possesses greatest political force in times of war and social fracture, it could still prosper, as the work of Cruikshank demonstrates, in a time of relative political settlement.

Charles Dickens, who worked with Cruikshank on *Oliver Twist* and elsewhere, was, as I have said, to some extent a product of literature impolite. Sally Ledger is right to emphasize his indebtedness to the Radical print culture. However, Dickens also owed much to some distinctly less noble print traditions – pot-boilery and hackwork – in writing advertisements, and in the literature of crime and sport. It may be that Dickens's first literary role was that of copywriter (according to his uncle, he wrote advertising jingles for Warren's Blacking Factory, some years after his father's financial collapse forced him to work there as a child). Either way, Dickens's early work is much concerned with the print subculture of contemporary advertising. Similarly, his writing is informed by the contemporary fascination with crime in popular culture. In *Oliver Twist*, Fagin 'with a horrible grin' is depicted as 'deeply absorbed in the interesting pages of the Hue-and-Cry' and it might be argued that the novelist wrote an elevated form of crime literature in *Oliver Twist* and *Edwin Drood* and detective fiction, of a sort, in *Bleak House*.[29]

Dickens also owed something to the standby of street literature, sport, and here again we see the importance of satirical culture in his work. His first book, as G. K. Chesterton once said, was the production of a 'hand-to-mouth journalist',[30] initially conceived by Chapman and Hall as a contribution to the existing 'Cockney sporting' genre. In the figure of Mr Winkle, the *Pickwick Papers* joined a tradition of texts that laughed at metropolitan blunderers ill at ease in the countryside, who shoot beaters, grandmothers and their hunting dogs, mistake crows for pheasants and get hauled before magistrates for their misdemeanours. This was evident in the graphic satire of Henry Bunbury and James Gillray in the late eighteenth century, in that of Henry Alken and Robert Seymour (Dickens's initial collaborator in the *Pickwick Papers*) in the 1810s and 1820s and in the Jorrocks novels of Dickens's immediate predecessor, R. S. Surtees. Dickens's first novel emerged, in part, from this broad satire. Out of the hackneyed conventions of the amusing Cockney sportsman came the seed of Boz's great work. The *Pickwick Papers* took a collection of generic conventions from eighteenth-century picaresque and Romantic era sporting satire, and fashioned them anew. The novel saw the transmogrification of the Cockney sportsman genre: in transcending the conventions of late Georgian sporting satire, Charles Dickens ushered in the first literary and satirical Victorian masterpiece.

And yet, perhaps, there is more to say. The *Pickwick Papers* pointed both backwards and forwards. The novel is in many ways proleptic and ground-breaking, but there is also something culminatory about Dickens's early work. Victorian commentators, who did not, as we have seen, speak unanimously about the satire of their period, were divided on this issue. While Hume Nesbit, in 1892, saw the tradition of Cruikshank et al. surviving into the late Victorian period in the figure of Ally Sloper, Andrew Lang, on the other hand, writing in 1886, viewed Dickens as the last gasp of that tradition. Addressing the shade of Dickens, Lang saw the young novelist at one with the late Georgian age's dark comedy, sharing Gillray's sense of caricature, delighting in Cockney jokes with Bunbury and Surtees and drawing on Cruikshank's preoccupation with low-life. Baudelaire, in his remarks on satire, wrote that 'When it comes to caricature, the English are "extremists"',[31] but by the end of the nineteenth century, in Lang's account, they had renounced the satirical poniard, along with the rest of the Georgian enormities. The 'broad blown comic sense' has gone the way of public executions and bull-baiting:

> How very singular has been the history of the decline of humour. Is there any profound psychological truth to be gathered from consideration of the fact that humour has gone out with cruelty? . . . Fifty years ago we were a cruel but also a humorous people. We had bull-baitings, and badger-drawings . . . and prize-fights, and cock-fights; we went to see men hanged . . . With all this we had a broad blown comic sense. We had Hogarth, and Bunbury, and George Cruikshank, and Gillray; we had Leech and Surtees . . . and, above all, we had you. From . . . broad caricature, [and] Cockney jokes . . . from these you derived the splendid high spirits

and unhesitating mirth of your earlier works. Mr Squeers, and Sam Weller, and Mrs Gamp, and all the Pickwickians . . . these and their immortal companions were reared, so to speak, on the beef and beer of that naughty, fox-hunting, badger-baiting old England, which we have improved out of existence.[32]

Beginning or end? This question has no definitive answer. To some, Dickens ignited the Victorian torch of satire which blazed on until the 1890s; to others, he was – however heroic – the carrier of a light that fell. In this, as in so much, Charles Dickens was the emblematic figure of Victorian satire.

Notes

1 *Fraser's Magazine*, 17 (Mar. 1838), 280.
2 Quoted in George Boyce, James Curran and Pauline Wingate, *Newspaper History from the Seventeenth Century to the Present Day* (London: Sage Publications, 1970), 70.
3 *Edinburgh Review*, 77 (Feb. 1843), 3–4.
4 Andrew Sanders, *Dickens and the Spirit of the Age* (Oxford: Oxford University Press, 1999), 17.
5 Charles Dickens, *Selected Journalism, 1850–1870,* ed. David Pascoe (Penguin: Harmondsworth, 1997), 355.
6 Sanders, *Dickens and the Spirit of the Age*, 17.
7 Sally Ledger, *Dickens and the Popular Radical Imagination* (Cambridge: Cambridge University Press, 2007), 3.
8 Virginia S. Berridge, 'Popular Journalism and Working Class Attitudes, 1854–1886: A Study of Reynolds' Newspaper, Lloyds' Weekly Newspaper and the Weekly Times', 2 vols., Ph.D. Dissertation, University of London, 1976.
9 John Strachan (gen. ed.), *British Satire 1785–1840*, 5 vols. (London: Pickering & Chatto, 2003), vol. i, 275.
10 *Selected Writings of Leigh Hunt,* gen. eds. Robert Morrison and Michael Eberle-Sinatra, 6 vols. (London: Pickering & Chatto, 2003), vol. i, p. 221.
11 Strachan (gen. ed.), *British Satire 1785–1840*, vol. i, 275.
12 *The Letters of Charles Dickens*, 12 vols. (Oxford: Clarendon, 1965–2002), vol. ii, ed. Madeleine House and Graham Storey (1969), 357.
13 Marion Harry Spielmann, *The History of Punch* (London: Cassell, 1895), 323.
14 Charles L. Graves, *Mr Punch's History of Modern England*, 4 vols. (London: Cassell, 1921), vol. i, v–vi.
15 *North British Review*, 7 (May 1847), 122.
16 Ibid.
17 *Punch*, 14 (1848), 259.
18 Quoted in Graves, *Mr Punch's History of Modern England*, vol. i, 19–20.
19 Thomas Hood, *Complete Poetical Works*, ed. Walter Jerrold (Oxford: Oxford University Press, 1920), 625.
20 George J. Worth, *James Hannay* (Lawrence, University of Kansas Press, 1964), 27.

21 All of these happenings are to be found in strips published in the first five years of *Judy*'s existence.

22 *Central Literary Magazine*, 13 (1897), 243.

23 Graves, *Mr Punch's History of Modern England*, vol. I, 18.

24 *Boys' Brigade Gazette*, 8 (1893), 7.

25 The memorable words used to describe the market trader by his brother Rodney in the British sitcom *Only Fools and Horses* (1981–2003).

26 David Kunzle, 'The First Ally Sloper: the Earliest Popular Cartoon Character as a Satire on the Victorian Work Ethic', *Oxford Art Journal*, 8 (1985), 40–8.

27 The first of the Ally Sloper books, published in 1873, and featuring strips reproduced from *Judy* is, not insignificantly, entitled *Ally Sloper: A Moral Lesson*.

28 *Gentleman's Magazine*, 272 (Mar. 1892), 267.

29 For a discussion of this subject, see Philip Collins's *Dickens and Crime* (1962) (3rd edn, New York: St Martin's Press, 1994).

30 G. K. Chesterton, *Charles Dickens* (London: Methuen, 1936), 52.

31 Charles Baudelaire, *Selected Writings on Art and Artists*, trans. Patrick Edward Charvet (Cambridge: Cambridge University Press, 1981), 143.

32 Andrew Lang, *Letters to Dead Authors* (London: Longman, 1886), 13.

10

Journalism

The Victorians witnessed a boom in the volume of affordable books, magazines and newspapers produced to satisfy the demands of the first mass reading public. Wilkie Collins described this new audience as the 'Unknown Public', the millions of readers of cheap print who were more likely to acquire their literature from the tobacconist's shop than the circulating library.[1] Collins's surprise at discovering this audience suggests how quickly affordable print had spread to sectors of the population formerly overlooked by publishers. Nearly everyone was exposed to print of some kind during an era offering over 25,000 different journals to the growing reading public.[2] Periodicals, not books, were the most widely read genre of the nineteenth century. The innumerable kinds of prose writing by Victorian authors extended well beyond the novel, which was just one among many forms of print favoured by Victorian readers as a way of spending their leisure time. The ephemeral publications of this period capture in their pages nearly every aspect of Victorian culture. Journalism at this time encompassed a wide range of formats, from the quarterly review to the monthly magazine to the daily newspaper. While the term 'journalism' first entered the English lexicon in the 1830s, by the end of the century it had become one of the most distinctive features of the Victorian era. As one contributor to the *Cornhill Magazine* predicted in 1862: 'Journalism will, no doubt, occupy the first or one of the first places in any future literary history of the present times, for it is the most characteristic of all their productions.'[3] If journalism's place in literary history is assured, the specific ways in which journalism was characteristic of the times as well as the reasons why its influence has often been underestimated by modern readers are topics that have only recently come to the attention of literary historians.

Victorian print culture has emerged as a lively field of research in recent decades despite the difficulties in working with ephemeral texts. The earliest research using nineteenth-century periodicals was hampered by access to poorly preserved materials. A former editor of the *Manchester Guardian* once compared newspapers to butterflies and mushrooms for the manner in which some rise to glory while others leave behind little more than mouldy remains.[4] Fortunately a number of resources now make access to periodicals easier than ever before. The study of print culture owes much to Richard Altick's *The English Common Reader* (1957), an encyclopaedic study of the printed texts consumed by ordinary readers in nineteenth-century Britain. Altick's pioneering work inspired subsequent scholars to revisit the archives and form the Research Society for Victorian Periodicals, an interdisciplinary organization dedicated to all aspects of the nineteenth-century press. Some of the most useful resources for print historians include *The Waterloo Directory of English Newspapers and Periodicals, 1800–1900*, a bibliographical record of thousands of English serial publications, and *The Wellesley Index to Victorian Periodicals, 1824–1900*, which identifies the authors of anonymous and pseudonymous contributions to numerous periodicals. Information about aspects of the press overlooked by traditional bibliographical resources is now available online via the *Dictionary of Nineteenth-Century Journalism*. A number of individual resources formerly available in print can also be searched electronically through ProQuest's *C19: The Nineteenth Century Index*. Many researchers no longer need to visit archives at all thanks to the massive amount of print digitized by the British Library as part of the projects *19th Century British Library Newspapers* and *19th Century UK Periodicals*. These virtual databases are in addition to the ever-growing body of resources devoted to individual titles, topics and journalists. Researchers who once faced the problem of too little access to periodicals now face the opposite problem of information overload.

There was little separation between journalism and literature at a time when the most celebrated Victorian prose authors wrote for the periodical press. One has only to take the example of Charles Dickens, who worked in journalism in some capacity throughout his entire career. The young Dickens read Addison's *Spectator* alongside 'penny dreadfuls' like the *Terrific Register*, whose macabre tales made him 'unspeakably miserable' as a schoolboy.[5] His career began as a freelance journalist writing anonymous reports for the morning paper *The British Press*. After learning shorthand, Dickens worked as a parliamentary reporter for *The True Sun* and the *Mirror of Parliament* amid fervent debates over electoral reform. The descriptions of urban life he wrote as a reporter for the *Morning Chronicle* were afterwards republished under the title *Sketches by Boz*. Journalism continued to play a prominent role in Dickens's life as he pursued a career as a novelist. His first story appeared anonymously in *The Monthly Magazine* in 1833. Four years later, *Bentley's Miscellany* under Dickens's editorship serialized *Oliver Twist*, a novel born out of the Mudfog papers originally published under a journalistic pseudonym. He edited a newspaper for a short period of time in the 1840s and two family magazines in the following decades. The miscellaneous contents of *Household Words* (1851–9) and its successor *All the Year Round* (1859–95) encompassed fiction, verse, science, politics and documentary reportage of the sort that had long featured in Dickens's fictional narratives. Nowhere else could readers get first sight of the serialized novels *A Tale of Two Cites* (1859) and *Great Expectations* (1860–1). Lord Northcliffe later eulogized Dickens as the greatest magazine editor the world had ever seen.[6] This involvement with journalism was the rule rather than the exception for Victorian novelists, virtually all of whom wrote for the press at some point during their literary careers. The sheer volume of journalism produced at this time makes even the Victorian novel look slim by comparison.

Some of the most memorable prose literature from the Victorian period first appeared in the pages of magazines. Readers encountered Elizabeth Gaskell's *North and South* (1854–5), Anthony Trollope's *Framley Parsonage* (1860–1), George Eliot's *Romola* (1862–3), Joseph Conrad's *Lord Jim* (1899–1900) and Arthur Conan Doyle's *The Hound of the Baskervilles* (1901–2) in periodical instalments prior to their republication in the volume format to which we are accustomed today. The serial narrative differed substantially in some instances from the revised volume, as in the case of Thomas Hardy's *Tess of the d'Urbervilles* (1891), which first appeared in a censored version in the illustrated journal *The Graphic*. Publication in parts made fiction affordable at a time when few families could afford to purchase a three-volume novel outright. Serial publication extended the market for fiction well beyond the metropolitan papers through commercial fiction syndicates. In 1873, William Tillotson's Fiction Bureau purchased the serial rights to some of the era's most popular authors for a syndicate of provincial papers among towns such as Dundee and Sheffield. Best-selling sensation novelist Mary Elizabeth Braddon first published at least twenty-five of her novels among the provincial press in this way. Long poems including Arthur Hugh Clough's *Amours de Voyage*

(1858) likewise appeared over a span of several months in the pages of an American magazine, and much of the most influential prose of the nineteenth century first appeared in periodicals: Matthew Arnold's *Culture and Anarchy* (1867–8), John Ruskin's *Unto this Last* (1860) and Walter Pater's *The Renaissance* (1873), to name a few. Although the serial form was used prior to the Victorian era, this was the first period in which the methods of serial publication became so widespread. Annual, quarterly, monthly, weekly, daily: serials appeared at intervals of increasing frequency throughout the century as the audience for cheap reading material continued to grow.

Serial publication influenced the reception of literature in a number of ways not always evident to modern readers accustomed to inexpensive trade editions. This method of publication shaped the form of these narratives to a great extent since the periodical was not the product of a single author but a collaboration among proprietors, editors, writers, illustrators and even advertisers. A fictional tale such as Dickens's *Hard Times* might even be interpreted differently when read in the context of articles on the Preston strike appearing alongside it in several issues of *Household Words*. More important, a novel could take years instead of weeks to finish when appearing in instalments. Hence the passage of time in the narrative corresponded to some extent with the passage of time in the reader's own life. The serial's intermittent publication schedule generated suspense in order to maintain interest during intervals by way of the cliff-hanger, an unresolved dramatic incident whose outcome would not be known until the following issue. It was no accident that one instalment of Thomas Hardy's *A Pair of Blue Eyes* (1873) ended with the novel's protagonist literally hanging from a cliff. This format persists among many of today's television serials. The serial format has even been used by BBC television adaptations such as Andrew Davies's *Bleak House* (2005), which recuperated the rhythm of parts publication through biweekly half-hour episodes paired with the long-running soap opera *EastEnders*. Victorian readers looked forward between instalments to 'magazine day', the first day of the month when new issues appeared in bookstalls across the country. Serial publication fostered a community of readers whose simultaneous reception of the narrative allowed them to experience events at the same time as fellow readers and share reactions during the interval between instalments. The London weeklies nourished these conversations by regularly reviewing individual instalments long before the narrative's completion. For instance, the *Era* described the latest instalment of one Dickens novel as 'a fresh subject for dinner parties' until the publication of its sequel the following month.⁷ Serial publication made authors susceptible to outside influence such as declining sales and poor reviews since individual chapters came out before the completion of the story. Sometimes pirated adaptations with invented endings appeared on stage before the novel's final instalment. Personal appeals to spare the life of a favourite character from impending disaster were not uncommon either, though authors could react to unsolicited advice in unexpected ways. Trollope claimed to have 'killed' the memorable character Mrs Proudie after overhearing the complaints of a pair of clergymen reading the latest instalment from the Barchester series.⁸ She was dead by the next issue.

Periodicals were an equally important venue for non-fiction. The quarterly reviews offered serious discussion of a wide range of subjects in journals closely aligned with political parties from the turn of the century. The Whiggish *Edinburgh Review* was founded in 1802 as a forum for literary and political discussion, including among its contributors Sir Walter Scott, Thomas Babington Macaulay and Thomas Carlyle. The *Quarterly Review* (1809–1967) began as a Tory alternative to the Whig politics of the *Edinburgh*, as did *Blackwood's Edinburgh Magazine* (1817–1905). Jeremy Bentham and James Mill's *Westminster Review* (1824–1914) offered a radical alternative to the other quarterlies through reform-minded contributions from George Eliot, Harriet Martineau and Herbert Spencer. The most characteristic form of nineteenth-century journalism may have been what Walter Bagehot called 'the review-like essay and the essay-like review' ushered in by the quarterlies.⁹ The title under review was little more than a pretext for the reviewer to digress on topics bearing little relation to the matter at hand in many of these pieces. Such essays among the quarterlies had the benefit of making specialist knowledge accessible to non-specialist audiences. Cardinal Newman noted the influence of these periodicals in instructing audiences 'what to think and what to say'.¹⁰ The legacy of the quarterlies was a tradition of 'Higher Journalism', prose written for discriminating audiences at a time when newspapers were still suspect in many circles. The quarterlies lost much of their influence from the 1840s onwards, however, when the daily press began to play a greater role in the political sphere. Monthly and weekly publications eventually supplanted the role of the quarterlies albeit for a broader, less high-minded readership. The intellectual weeklies providing informed opinion on politics and literature included the *Athenaeum* (1828–1921), *Saturday Review* (1855–1938) and *Spectator* (1828–1925). The new class of shilling monthlies devoted to leisure pursuits not accommodated by the daily press included Thackeray's *Cornhill Magazine* (1860–1975), Braddon's *Belgravia* (1866–99) and Mrs Henry Wood's *The Argosy* (1865–1901). The less sectarian approach among these journals courted the growing number of female readers in particular through a literary emphasis. The first number of the *Cornhill* sold nearly 120,000 copies in part through contributions from Ruskin, Thackeray, Trollope and Elizabeth Barrett Browning.

Anonymity was the rule for most periodicals until *Macmillan's Magazine* (1859–1907) and the *Fortnightly Review* (1865–1934), founded by G. H. Lewes and Anthony Trollope, became the first major journals to promote signed contributions as their editorial policy. The quarterlies had by long tradition published articles anonymously instead of alongside the signatures of individual contributors. There were compelling arguments on both sides of the debate over anonymous publication. Supporters of unsigned contributions argued that the policy invested articles with the corporate authority of the journal as a whole rather than a fallible individual. According to this perspective, the collective editorial 'We' operated as an impersonal, disinterested instructor to the public and allowed the article to be judged on the basis of its contents rather than its author. In Trollope's words, 'The newspaper is not a lamp lighted by a single hand, but a sun placed in the heaven by an invisible creator.'[11] Public figures were likewise able to speak their minds under the cloak of anonymity without risk to their reputations. By contrast, advocates of signed articles argued that signature would hold contributors accountable for statements that might otherwise be said with impunity. To take one example, Robert Buchanan's notorious attack on the Pre-Raphaelite poets as the 'Fleshly School' initially appeared under a pseudonym in 1871.[12] An author's qualifications were thought by many to be relevant in assessing the merits of an argument. Signature advocates insisted that the best way to ensure quality was to give authors the incentive of public recognition. Public interest in individual correspondents ultimately may have been the most significant factor in tipping the scales towards signature since sales drove most editorial decisions. Newspapers alone among periodicals refrained from using by-lines until the appearance of 'From Our Own Correspondent' tags toward the end of the century. A decade after the monthlies began using signed contributions on a regular basis, the *Contemporary Review* (1866–1988) and *Nineteenth Century* (1877–1950) were already recruiting celebrity contributors to boost circulation: William Gladstone, Petr Alekseyevich Kropotkin, Cardinal Manning and

Alfred Lord Tennyson were just a few of the names displayed to entice readers.

The man of letters was not the only one who sought to influence public opinion through the columns of the newspaper. An unintended bene-fit of anonymity for women was access to the press and, consequently, to a voice in public discourse from which they ordinarily would have been excluded on the basis of gender. Journalism was noteworthy for its employment of women even if their contributions have often been over-looked by traditional histories of the profession. Harriet Martineau was one such woman to begin her career by writing anonymous contributions before proceeding to author over 1,600 leading articles on topics ranging from slavery to political economy for the *Daily News*. Writing for the press frequently meant adopting a male persona for the purpose of fitting in among the paper's other male voices. Consequently, the actual authors behind anonymous contributions complicate any straightforward dis-tinctions among journalistic writing in terms of gendered identity even when the editorial 'we' was presumed to be male. Geraldine Jewsbury, George Eliot, Eliza Lynn Linton, Frances Power Cobbe and Margaret Oliphant all published prolifically in journals anonymously or under pseudonyms. Editors did not always conform to gendered expectations either: Christian Isobel Johnstone edited *Tait's Edinburgh Magazine* (1832–61); Oscar Wilde served as editor to *Woman's World* (1887–90).

As the latter title suggests, the expanding female readership could choose from among an assortment of women's magazines, ranging from Samuel and Isabella Beeton's *Englishwoman's Domestic Magazine* (1852–90), with its advice on household management, to the *Woman's Suffrage Journal* (1870–90), with its campaigns on behalf of women's rights. While the contents of magazines aimed at a female readership were typically moral, sentimental and, above all, apolitical, even the Beetons organized essay competitions on such controversial topics as women's rights. The peri-odical press provided a forum for women to participate in debates over the changing role of women in public life. One of the most controver-sial columns on this subject was Eliza Lynn Linton's 'Girl of the Period', which makes an unflattering comparison between modern women and the modest English ideal of former times. The column's hostility towards feminism provoked responses from all sides of the political spectrum in numerous periodicals after its initial appearance in the *Saturday Review* in 1868.[13] Despite conservative attitudes towards the workplace, women were sufficiently numerous among the press to establish the Society of

Women Journalists in 1895. Women's roles were not always restricted to stereotypically feminine subjects, either, once the press expanded towards the end of the century, providing opportunities for women to work as interviewers like Hulda Friedrichs or even foreign correspondents like Flora Shaw.

While the earliest periodicals appealed almost exclusively to an upper-middle-class male readership, the audience for print expanded throughout the century following technological improvements in the publishing industry. One of the most striking aspects of the periodical press was the variety of material produced for readers formerly ignored by publishers: women, children, tradesmen, servants and other marginal groups. The initial success of family magazines during the 1830s demonstrated the demand among the working classes for entertaining literature at an affordable price. In 1832, *Chambers's Edinburgh Journal* (1832–1956) claimed to reach an audience spanning the drawing rooms of high society to the lowly shepherd on the mountainside with its instructive programme. That same year, the Society for the Diffusion of Useful Knowledge's *Penny Magazine* (1832–45) appealed to a public unaccustomed to reading through plentiful woodcut illustrations chosen with an eye towards self-improvement. High costs along with a utilitarian refusal to print fiction resulted in the magazine's succession by the illustrated weeklies *The London Journal* (1845–1906), *Reynolds's Miscellany* (1846–69) and *Cassell's Illustrated Family Paper* (1853–67). Even the crossing-sweepers interviewed by Henry Mayhew for his survey of the metropolitan poor admitted to finding time after work to read *Reynolds's Miscellany*.[14] In contrast to family magazines oriented towards enrichment, the weekly illustrated magazine *Punch, or the London Charivari* (1841–1992) provided humorous treatment of current events at odds with the stereotypical sobriety of the middle classes. Drawing its name from the slapstick puppet, *Punch* differed from its comic predecessors by avoiding the scurrilous humour responsible for barring their entry to polite drawing rooms. The magazine's satire was offensive only to the sanctimonious prig, a favourite target of its caricatures.

At the same time, many publishers turned away from general interest periodicals by tailoring publications to the tastes of niche readerships as the market for print continued to grow in size. Few groups lacked a magazine of their own according to the catalogue of titles generated by the Victorian publishing world. Discouraged from reading any but the most pious literature, the large evangelical audience indulged in narratives illustrating a moral lesson in the Religious Tract Society's *Leisure Hour* (1852–1905) and *Good Words* (1860–1906), endorsed by the Society for Purity in Literature. Even children had journals of their own by the end of the century. The *Boy's Own Paper* (1879–1967) and *Girl's Own Paper* (1880–1908) amused juvenile audiences with tales of imperial adventure for boys and domestic utility for girls, though anecdotal evidence suggests that the actual readership for these journals may have been more mixed than their titles suggest. The Brontë children even created their own 'Young Men's Magazine', which contained pseudonymous reviews, serialized fiction and made-up advertisements in imitation of their father's copies of *Blackwood's*. Other magazines sought audiences on the basis of potential interest to advertisers. Special interest publications catering to specific consumer groups emerged with increasing frequency towards the end of the century by way of titles such as *Amateur Gardening* (1884–1969), *Horse and Hound* (1884–1912) and *Autocar* (1895–1988).

Unlike the penny magazines, newspapers were simply too expensive for most people to purchase until the second half of the nineteenth century. What opponents called the 'taxes on knowledge' restricted the circulation of newspapers by requiring the payment of prohibitive stamp duties on any publications containing news. The taxes were not removed until the 1850s after long debate. According to advocates of the stamp duty, taxation ensured the press would circulate only among the respectable classes. Politically radical publications known as the unstamped press, in attempting to reach the poorer classes who were unable to afford the expensive stamped press, risked prosecution. According to opponents of the duty, market competition would increase the number of politically stable newspapers by eliminating the repressive conditions responsible for the radical press. Campaigns on behalf of press freedom eventually succeeded in removing the last duty in 1861, ensuring the press was free from fiscal restrictions for the first time since the reign of Queen Anne.[15] The reduction in price resulting from the tax repeal enabled the newspaper to evolve from a luxury item read by an elite into an essential component of daily life taken by readers of all classes by the century's end.

Advertisement revenue allowed the press to become increasingly independent of political control and market-oriented throughout the century. The newspapers representing rival political parties satirized by Dickens as the *Eatanswill Gazette* and *Eatanswill Independent* in the *Pickwick Papers* (1836–7) became less influential once editors realized that political involvement was to some extent a liability in pursuit of a large readership. As James Fitzjames Stephen emphasized in 1862, 'a newspaper is beyond everything else a commercial undertaking'.[16] Financial security enabled the press to refashion itself as a means of communicating information to the public rather than as a mouthpiece for political sedition. The reputation of journalists as 'the lowest hacks of literature', in John Stuart Mill's words, gradually improved once journalism gained recognition as a legitimate profession independent of party influence.[17] This was partly brought about by improved methods of reporting. The term 'reporter' at this time referred primarily to a member of the press who transcribed official proceedings for the newspapers. The courts of law and parliament were the chief arenas reported by the press for most of the century. Reporters were permitted to publish transcripts of most legal trials without interference after the 1790s. The Sunday papers in particular attracted large readerships through amusing reports of the police courts. Forbidden entry throughout the eighteenth century by Standing Order, the press has been admitted to the House of Commons for parliamentary debates since 1802. Court and parliamentary reporting involved taking notes of speeches to be written up verbatim for publication in *Hansard* or other journals. Shorthand systems devised by Thomas Gurney and Isaac Pitman improved the accuracy and speed of writing through the use of an abbreviated, symbolic notation method humorously portrayed by Dickens's *David Copperfield* (1849–50), written shortly after the author's own stint as a parliamentary reporter. Not until the last decades of the nineteenth century would the role of reporting extend to investigative reports and eyewitness accounts. The establishment of the National Association of Journalists in 1884 (renamed the Institute of Journalists in 1890) enhanced the professional identity of newspaper employees. While the press initially struggled to fashion itself as a credible Fourth Estate, a watchdog of abuse acting on behalf of the public, its power by the end of the century was beyond question, if not reproach. Oscar Wilde quipped that the Fourth Estate was now the only estate: 'It has eaten up the other three.'[18]

The incremental removal of taxes between 1833 and 1861 on each occasion led to increased circulations through reductions in price. With the exception of *The Times* (1785–), the London dailies reached audiences of only several thousand before the tax repeal, though some observers estimated that a single newspaper might be read by up to thirty people through reading rooms and public houses.[19] Nicknamed 'The Thunderer' for its influential leading articles, *The Times* sold nearly twice as many copies as its rivals until the first penny dailies emerged after the removal of the taxes on the press. The competitive field ushered in by the tax repeal ensured no single paper would ever again secure the influence wielded until that point by *The Times*. *The Daily Telegraph* (1856–) was the first penny paper to reach circulations of over 100,000 readers through greater sensational coverage of events than had been the custom in the more expensive papers preceding it. The paper sought to reflect the attitudes of its audience through topical discussions of social issues such as the 'Marriage or Celibacy?' debate taking place in the correspondence columns of the *Telegraph* in 1868. A subsequent debate on the question 'Is Marriage a Failure?' initiated by the feminist Mona Caird two decades later attracted over 27,000 letters.[20] Here at last was a paper designed for clerks and shop keepers, according to one journalist.[21] The penny press appealed in particular to readers who had seldom or never before read newspapers. These papers were written for 'the million', a term for the growing number of readers who would actually reach this mythic number by the end of the century.[22]

The penny papers appealed to the crowds through an emphasis on human interest stories and public campaigning adopted from the Sunday papers, which were the first to reach genuinely mass readerships by renovating the staid format of the respectable dailies for an economically diverse readership. The enormous popularity of these publications from early in the century confirmed the existence of a large market for print if delivered at an affordable price. Cost was always more of an obstacle than literacy when it came to selling newspapers. The Sunday papers appealed to the populist sentiments of a mass readership by taking up the polemical tradition of the unstamped press for profit rather than politics. While some legislators originally envisioned the press as a paternalistic source of moral instruction, the Sunday press pandered to audiences with unwholesome entertainment according to the timeless formula of sex, sport and scandal. The weekly format appealed in particular to working-class readers who could afford a newspaper no more than once a week. The *News of the World* (1843–1960), *Lloyd's Illustrated London Newspaper* (1842–1931) and *Reynolds' Weekly Newspaper* (1850–1967) all anticipated the mass circulation daily papers of the twentieth century in their mixture of news and entertainment. These were the first papers to reach circulations of one million readers at the turn of the century alongside the halfpenny *Daily Mail*.

One of the most widely read features of the penny press was its coverage of the newly established Divorce Court. Every major newspaper covered the notorious Yelverton trial in 1861, for example, for its revelations of bigamy committed by an unrepentant aristocrat. The Matrimonial Causes Bill of 1857 made divorce available as long as petitioners were willing to subject the most intimate details of their personal lives to public scrutiny. Many daily papers turned judicial proceedings into spectacles by placing the divorce reports on the front page. The reports were particularly scandalous since the only grounds for divorce was adultery. Sexual behaviour likely to be censored from a novel was on display in newsprint for all to see as private diaries were read aloud and embarrassing personal questions submitted to those called to testify before the court (including Prince Albert in one trial). The frank discussion of taboo sexual practices including bigamy unsettled conceptions of matrimony, giving rise to opportunistic *roman à clef* novels with titles such as *Can Wrong be Right?* (1862) and *A Wife and not a Wife* (1867). Stories of unhappy marriages told on a daily basis by the press made the discrepancy between the marriage ideal and its reality all too clear. Queen Victoria herself asked the Lord Chancellor to prevent the newspaper reports of divorce proceedings from being brought into the home in order to safeguard national character.[23] This was a particular problem since divorce trials, unlike those in the Criminal Courts, often involved prominent citizens rather than members of the lower classes. One contemporary source suggested that future historians would learn more about Victorian society from the divorce cases involving Sir Charles Dilke and Lord Colin Campbell than from any other document of the period.[24] Divorce trials are just one example of the intensified interest shown by the cheap press in sensational trials of all kinds that would bring the newspaper ever closer in its content to fiction, to the point that sensation novelist Charles Reade kept entire notebooks full of news cuttings on which to base his 'improbable' plots. Tabloid journalism confirmed on a daily basis that truth was indeed stranger than fiction.

Telegraph and undersea cable communication dramatically increased the coverage of news from around the empire during these same decades. One Newcastle editor described his role as 'running the British Empire from Northumberland Street'.[25] Letters from foreign correspondents could take months to reach home by ship before the advent of telegraph networks accelerated the pace of news distribution from the late 1840s onwards. Whereas news of the Battle of Waterloo took five days to reach the newspapers in 1815, a telegram from abroad took only minutes to reach the printer by the century's end. The provinces in particular benefited from immediate access to current events without needing to rely on metropolitan papers distributed by the rail network. The widespread supply of newspapers across the country was vital to the formation of a genuinely national daily press from the mid-century. The press played a crucial role in forging national identities by allowing readers to conceive of themselves as part of a community made up of people whom they had never met but considered to be members of the same group on the basis of shared 'Britishness'. A submarine telegraph cable linked Dover and Calais in 1851, followed by the first telegraph link between India and Europe in 1856. Still, reports were often impeded by expense and infrastructure. After the outbreak of the Indian Mutiny in 1857, for example, reports of the relief of the siege of Lucknow did not reach Britain for over a month due to difficulties in delivering information to telegraph networks. From the 1860s, the expansion of the cable infrastructure and the organization of syndicated news agencies such as Reuters led to increased coverage of imperial events back in Britain.[26] Use of the telegraph influenced the style of news reporting as well. It was not long before long descriptive letters were replaced by brief impersonal telegrams in a prose referred to by critics as 'telegraphese'.

War correspondents provided British readers with reports from colonial conflict zones such as Zululand and the Sudan for the first time during the second half of the nineteenth century. One of the first noteworthy war correspondents was William Howard Russell, sent by The Times to cover the Crimean War in 1854. Whereas previous newspapers had relied on the foreign press or letters from soldiers, this was the first conflict in which the press designated a journalist to report the war to the civilian population at home. Russell's dispatches shocked many readers back in Great Britain with graphic descriptions of the battlefields. His account of a disastrous but heroic British cavalry charge directly into Russian artillery during the Battle of Balaclava inspired Tennyson's poem 'The Charge of the Light Brigade'.[27] News reports of the appalling conditions endured by troops inspired Florence Nightingale and Mary Seacole, among others, to follow the army abroad in an attempt to reform the medical services for wounded combatants. The government's mishandling of affairs throughout the conflict led to the resignation of the cabinet after exposure by the press. It would be over half a century before journalists were granted such liberty again following a general order prohibiting correspondents from publishing strategic details at risk of removal from the front in response to press reports by Russell and other correspondents. While the decision had little effect on the Crimean War, the precedent established a form of military censorship that continued through to the First World War.

A transatlantic cable installed between America and Britain in 1866 permitted rapid communication across the Anglophone world. One of the first stories to be reported simultaneously on both sides of the Atlantic was Henry Stanley's so-called rescue of David Livingstone in Africa with the famous greeting: 'Dr Livingstone I presume?' After entering Africa as a Protestant missionary, Livingstone undertook several journeys across the continent documented in *Missionary Travels* (1857), the enormously popular account of his sixteen years abroad. The Scotsman had been presumed dead for several years until being located in Ujiji (now Tanzania in East Africa) by the American correspondent in November 1871. The *New York Herald* was the first paper to report the meeting under the cross-head 'LIVINGSTONE' before sharing Stanley's account with London papers the following day. The encounter preoccupied the press in America and Britain throughout the summer of 1872. The famous engraving of the two explorers meeting for the first time with a gentlemanly doff of the cap in the *Illustrated London News* was reproduced across the world in publications such as *L'Illustration*, *Illustrazione Popolare*, *Illustrierte Zeitung*, *Harper's Weekly* and the *Canadian Illustrated News*. This story raised public awareness about the slave trade in Africa to a greater extent than any number of editorial campaigns.

The use of illustrations to accompany news stories was hardly new. The increasingly pictorial character of the press throughout the century allowed it to reach a broader market by appealing to audiences lacking basic literacy or formal education. Wood engraving permitted a tradition of illustrated periodicals long before the development of satisfactory techniques for the reproduction of photographs at the end of the century. The first graphic newspapers emulated the successful formula of the illustrated family magazines during the 1830s. In 1842, the *Illustrated London News* (1842–1988) appeared weekly with thirty-two woodcut illustrations on its sixteen pages for the price of 6*d*. Its engravings were measurably superior to the coarse woodcuts of gruesome crimes and other marvels available in the form of street ballads. Up to this point, occasional woodcuts used to depict singular events including the Greenacre murder, a violent crime involving a widow's dismemberment, and Queen

Victoria's coronation were exceptions among the press. The *Illustrated London News* was selling more than ten times the daily sale of *The Times* by the next decade. As one of the first graphic newspapers, it introduced a model for combining journalism and illustration adopted by a host of imitators. Photography was not used by the press until the 1890s, when the halftone permitted images of higher quality and lower cost than the woodcut. The newspaper page traditionally had consisted of a page of uninterrupted letterpress prior to satisfactory techniques for reproducing photographs. The *Daily Graphic* (1890–1926) and the *Sketch* (1893–1959) were the first newspapers to use halftone blocks for the swift reproduction of photographs. A few years later this technology made it possible to use photographs effectively in daily journalism, paving the way for the increasingly visual formats of the twentieth-century press.

Marketing tactics adopted from the North American press gave rise to the controversial 'New Journalism' of the 1880s and 1890s. 'New' was hardly a complimentary term for Matthew Arnold, who coined the phrase in a much-quoted piece describing modern journalism as '*feather-brained*' in its pursuit of profit and populism.[28] While many of its supposedly modern methods had been used by mid-Victorian papers and their American counterparts for some time, this phase of journalism achieved unprecedented commercial success by making papers more appealing to a readership whose numbers would nearly quadruple by the start of the First World War. Many features associated with the twenty-first-century press were used for the first time during this period: banner headlines, brief paragraphs, correspondence columns, personal interviews, profuse illustrations. The daily paper's front page increasingly featured news instead of advertisements, a layout to that point used only by disreputable weekly papers. The unbroken columns of small type inherited from the era of high taxation likewise gave way to visual formats appropriate for commuters who took their news on the train or omnibus. The change in style corresponded to a change in substance. In 1888, the first issue of one evening newspaper announced: 'We believe that the reader of the daily journal longs for other than mere politics.'[29] Political speeches once reported verbatim were replaced by abridged versions or even the parliamentary sketch, in which the speaker's personality was more likely to feature than the speaker's address to the House. An emphasis on human interest stories confirmed that it was not necessary for the newspaper to instruct as well as amuse. Notoriety given to the 'Jack the Ripper' murders in 1888 by even the most respectable papers at this time shows how integral scandal had become to the press. The respectable press had finally decided to adopt the methods used for decades by the popular press.

Star editor T. P. O'Connor distinguished between the old and new journalism in terms of 'the more personal tone' of the modern press.[30] This brand of personal journalism was evident in the use of signed articles, personal interviews and a colloquial style cultivating an intimate relationship with readers even as newspapers became more commercial in scope. These trends are exemplified by George Newnes's *Tit-Bits* (1881–1956), a digest of previously published items, and Alfred Harmsworth's *Answers to Correspondents* (1888–1955), a forum in which advice was sought by readers (many of whose letters were actually written by the magazine's editors). True to its motto 'a picture on every page', the *Strand Magazine* (1891–1950) owed much of its early success to an intimate series of 'Illustrated Interviews' portraying celebrities amid the splendour of their homes. A similarly personal rhetoric lay behind a form of campaign journalism allegedly expressing the will of the people, whose interests were inadequately represented by parliament. One of the most notorious campaigns was W. T. Stead's 'Maiden Tribute of Modern Babylon' exposé of juvenile prostitution in the *Pall Mall Gazette* in 1885. The account of Stead's procurement of a child prostitute from a London brothel under the subheading 'A Child of Thirteen Bought for £5' ensured the story's scandalous reception, which resulted in parliamentary legislation for the protection of minors as well as the editor's brief imprisonment in Holloway Prison.[31] Stead used this enforced sabbatical to write a pair of articles advocating the replacement of parliament by the press, which, in his opinion, had become more effective than the House of Commons in representing public interests. His controversial opinions were hardly representative themselves.[32]

The growing influence of the periodical press throughout the century elicited both optimism and anxiety on the part of onlookers. In fact, it would be difficult to understand debates over the influence of the media in the twentieth and twenty-first centuries without first understanding how this debate emerged in the nineteenth century. While some celebrated the democratization of the press for allowing a more inclusive political nation, others, including Arnold, expressed alarm about the deteriorating standards of mass culture. George Gissing's portrait of a literary sphere driven by commercial interests in *New Grub Street* (1891) memorably depicted the widening divide between journalism and serious literature at this time. The rise of the mass press during the last two decades of the century in particular corresponds to a declining faith in the capacity of the press to invite new readers into deliberations on matters of national interest. Above all, observers blamed the apparent decline of serious purpose in reading on the daily newspaper. In this sense, the launch of the *Daily Mail* on 4 May 1896 marked a movement towards the mass media of the twentieth century by becoming the first daily paper to reach a million readers a few years later during the Second Boer War. It did so largely through the tabloid formula of the paper's editor Alfred Harmsworth (later Lord Northcliffe), whose success owed much to economy in the use of words – the fewer the better. Joseph Pulitzer's *New York World* afterwards invited Northcliffe to introduce his version of tabloid journalism to the American public, momentarily reversing the flow of transatlantic media influence in 1901.[33] The hostile reaction by the writers of later centuries towards the mass media emerging at this time is in part responsible for the retrospective demotion of nineteenth-century periodical writing in favour of privileged artistic forms such as the novel. This is unfortunate since the vast range of prose enjoyed by Victorian readers bore some relationship to the periodical press in terms of subject, style or source. Those who overlook the prominent role played by periodicals during the nineteenth century risk missing out on the favourite literature of the Victorians.

Notes

1   Wilkie Collins, 'The Unknown Public', *Household Words,* 18 (1858), 217.
2   This estimate is taken from Walter Houghton, 'Periodical Literature and the Articulate Classes', in Joanne Shattock and Michael Wolff (eds.), *The Victorian Periodical Press: Samplings and Soundings* (Leicester: Leicester University Press; Toronto: University of Toronto Press, 1982), 3.
3   James Fitzjames Stephen, 'Journalism', *Cornhill Magazine*, 6 (1862), 52. Many of the most significant pieces on Victorian journalism have been reprinted in Andrew King and John Plunkett (eds.), *Popular Print Media, 1820–1900*, 3 vols. (London: Routledge, 2004).
4   A. P. Wadsworth, 'Newspaper Circulations, 1800–1954', *Transactions of the Manchester Statistical Society* (1954–5), 1.
5   John Forster, *The Life of Charles Dickens*, vol. i (Philadelphia: Lippincot, 1874), v.
6   Edgar Johnson, *Charles Dickens: His Tragedy and Triumph*, vol. ii (London: Gollancz, 1953), 717.
7   'Literature', *The Era*, 14 Mar. 1852, 10a.
8   Anthony Trollope, *An Autobiography*, ed. Michael Sadleir and Frederick Page (Oxford: Oxford University Press, 1999), 275.
9   Walter Bagehot, 'The First Edinburgh Reviewers', *National Review,* 1 (1855), 256. Reprinted in Norman St. John-Stevas (ed.), *The Collected Works of Walter Bagehot*, 15 vols. (London: Economist, 1965), vol. i, 308–41.
10   Quoted in Houghton, 'Periodical Literature', 8.
11   Anthony Trollope, 'On Anonymous Literature', *Fortnightly Review*, 1 (1865), 493.

12 Thomas Maitland [Robert Buchanan], 'The Fleshly School of Poetry: Mr. D. G. Rossetti', *Contemporary Review*, 18 (1871), 334–50. For an account of the controversy, see J. B. Bullen, *The Pre-Raphaelite Body: Fear and Desire in Painting, Poetry, and Criticism* (Oxford: Clarendon, 1998), 149–216.

13 See Eliza Lynn Linton's 'The Girl of the Period', *Saturday Review*, 25, 14 Mar. 1868, 339–40. The ensuing controversy is discussed in Elizabeth K. Helsinger, Robin Lauterbach Sheets and William Veeder (eds.), *The Woman Question: Society and Literature in Britain and America 1837–1883*, vol. I (Chicago: University of Chicago Press, 1989), 103–25.

14 Henry Mayhew, *London Labour and the London Poor*, vol. II (New York: Dover, 1968), 474.

15 Richard Altick, *The English Common Reader: A Social History of the Mass Reading Public, 1800–1900* (2nd edn, Columbus: Ohio State University Press), 354.

16 Stephen, 'Journalism', 53.

17 Quoted in Lenore O'Boyle, 'The Image of the Journalist in France, Germany, and England, 1815–1848', *Comparative Studies in Society and History*, 10, 3 (1968), 316.

18 Oscar Wilde, 'The Soul of Man under Socialism', in *De Profundis and Other Writings* (London: Penguin, 1973), 40.

19 See Gibbons Merle, 'Weekly Newspapers', *Westminster Review*, 10 (Apr. 1829), 477.

20 See the correspondence collected in Harry Quilter (ed.), *Is Marriage a Failure?* (London: Sonnenschein, 1888).

21 H. W. Massingham, *The London Daily Press* (London: Religious Tract Society, 1892), 91.

22 [Margaret Oliphant], 'The Byways of Literature: Reading for the Million', *Blackwood's Magazine*, 84 (1858), 202.

23 See Barbara Leckie, *Culture and Adultery: The Novel, the Newspaper, and the Law, 1857–1914* (Philadelphia: University of Pennsylvania Press, 1999), 93. Anne Humpherys documents the court's establishment in 'Coming Apart: The British Newspaper Press and the Divorce Court', in L. Brake, B. Bell and D. Finkelstein (eds.) *Nineteenth-Century Media and the Construction of Identities* (Basingstoke: Macmillan, 1944), 220–31.

24 'Should Scandals in High Life be Hushed Up?', *Pall Mall Gazette*, 4 Feb. 1887, 1a.

25 Raymond L. Schults, *Crusader in Babylon: W. T. Stead and the Pall Mall Gazette* (Lincoln: University of Nebraska Press, 1972), 79.

26 See Simon J. Potter, *News and the British World: The Emergence of an Imperial Press System 1876–1922* (Oxford: Clarendon, 2003).

27 The full account is reprinted in Russell's *Despatches from the Crimea 1854–1856*, ed. Nicolas Bentley (London: Deutsch, 1966).

28 Matthew Arnold, 'Up to Easter', *Nineteenth Century*, 21 (May 1887), 639.

29 'Our Confession of Faith', *The Star*, 1, 17 Jan. 1888, 6f.

30 T. P. O'Connor, 'The New Journalism', *The New Review*, 1 (Oct. 1889), 423.

31 The full text of this report is reprinted in W. T. Stead, *The Maiden Tribute of Modern Babylon: Report of the Secret Commission*, ed. Antony E. Simpson (Lambertville, NJ: True Bill, 2007). Judith Walkowitz discusses the cultural context of the campaign in *City of Dreadful Delight: Narratives of Sexual Danger in Late-Victorian London* (London: Virago, 1992), 101.

32 For more details on Stead and journalism, see above, pp. 150–3.

33 Reginald Pound and Geoffrey Harmsworth, *Northcliffe* (London: Cassell, 1959), 266.

11

Art

Since the Renaissance, the British had the reputation of being a literary, but assuredly not a visual, nation. Thus the sudden flourishing of visual art in Victorian Britain could seem an astonishing development. Certainly the French thought so, when they encountered the fine arts of Great Britain at the Exposition Universelle held in Paris in 1855. This was the first of the great international exhibitions to make a feature of fine art (the Great Exhibition of 1851, for which the Crystal Palace was built in Hyde Park, excluded painting). 'An English painting is as modern as a novel by Balzac', wrote Théophile Gautier, who began his two-volume collection of reprinted press notices with ten chapters on artists of the British school, among them Mulready, Landseer, Grant, Millais, Hunt, Egg, Frost, Hook, Webster, Leslie – 'the truly original talents, the incontestable glories of England'[1] – names strange to the French in 1855. And when Baudelaire reviewed the Paris Salon four years later, he began by lamenting the absence of the British, again listing the strange names: Leslie, the two Hunts, Maclise, Millais, Chalon, Grant, Hook, Paton, Cattermole. Some rumour had led Baudelaire to hope for a sight of 'these devotees of the imagination and of exotic colour, . . . these favourites of the fantastic muse; but alas', the British did not appear, and Baudelaire addresses them in disappointment: 'Were you so badly received then the first time . . . and do you consider us unworthy of understanding you?'[2]

The responses of Gautier, Baudelaire and the other French critics of 1855 now produce a defamiliarizing effect. Not only do many of the names in the long lists remain strange, a century and a half later, but the characterization of the British school contradicts all of our received ideas about Victorian art. Modern, original, independent, distinctive in imagination – it comes as a shock to see these terms, which today's art historians associate with the most progressive French art of the period since 1850, applied instead to British art, and by the very same French critics who championed incipient (French) modernism. Indeed, we share not only the French critics' surprise, but to a large extent their perspective: since the Bloomsbury generation at the beginning of the twentieth century (of which more below), French art has unequivocally taken the lead in discussions of modernity and modernism, not only among scholars and historians, but also in art criticism and museum practice. Like the French critics of 1855, we come to Victorian art with Francophile eyes and expectations.

The sheer volume and diversity of British art that nonplussed critics in 1855 remains intractable to scholarship, which has only begun to scratch the surface of the art production of the Victorian period. Partly this is a simple matter of the rapid expansion of the art world: the number of fine artists in census returns jumped from about 4,000 in 1841 to nearly 14,000 in 1901, with particularly striking growth in numbers of women artists, from fewer than 300 to 3,700 in the same period.[3] But the British art world also differed in character from that of France, despite the superficial similarity between the art institutions of the two countries. Indeed, the Royal Academy had been founded in imitation of continental academies such as that of France, and the *Discourses* delivered between 1769 and 1790 by its first president, Joshua Reynolds, recommend a hierarchy of pictorial types and a set of academic precepts more lucid and eloquent than those of any single French treatise. But the Royal Academy was established late – in 1768, well over a century after Louis XIV set up his Académie Royale – and on inhospitable territory, at least as far as the grand traditions of continental painting were concerned. Thus, the higher genres recommended in the *Discourses*, based on subjects from history and Scripture, failed to supplant the longstanding British predilection for portraiture, as Reynolds's own highly successful practice demonstrated. Paradoxically, the relative weakness of Britain's latecoming academic tradition meant quicker modernization than in France. In the absence of state and church patronage, the Royal Academy adapted quickly to the new, early Victorian generation of private patrons from the industrial and commercial middle classes, and the Academy's continuing hegemony over British art in the first half of Victoria's reign was a matter as much of market dominance as of either cultural privilege or intellectual authority. The character Oswald Millbank, in Disraeli's novel *Coningsby* of 1844, is a portrait of the new kind of patron:

The walls of the dining-room were covered with pictures of great merit, all of the modern English school. Mr. Millbank understood no other, he was wont to say! and he found that many of his friends who did, bought a great many pleasing pictures that were copies, and many originals that were very displeasing. He loved a fine free landscape by Lee, that gave him the broad plains, the green lanes and running streams of his own land; a group of animals by Landseer, as full of speech and sentiment as if they were designed by Aesop; above all, he delighted in the household humour and homely pathos of Wilkie.[4]

As Gautier put it in 1855, British pictures were adapted to modern life in cities.[5] They were moderate in scale, anecdotal in subject-matter, meticulous and detailed in execution to suit both close viewing and patrons' demands for value-for-money.

These factors help to explain the long, and somewhat miscellaneous, lists of artists in the French reviews: French critics simply failed to find the clear hierarchies, either of artists or of pictorial types, to which they were accustomed. The French section of the Exposition was organized to celebrate the nation's canonical masters, with large retrospective displays for Jean-Auguste-Dominique Ingres, Eugène Delacroix and Horace Vernet – grandees of French art, and practitioners of the highest genres. It was far harder to name the great masters of the British school; Gautier devoted a chapter to the English love of animals partly to account for the prominence of Sir Edwin Landseer, whose dogs and horses, exquisitely painted though they were acknowledged to be, failed to meet any of the traditional criteria for artistic importance.[6] Critics acknowledged the excellence of the Irish painter William Mulready, who was made Chevalier of the Légion d'Honneur, but his work was too diverse to be easily classified. As well as a genre picture showing a bully threatening a small boy, piquantly entitled *The Wolf and the Lamb*, Mulready showed a female nude, *Bathers Surprised* (Figure 8). Here at last was a rare example of a pictorial type to which academic art theory could give high place, and there was widespread admiration for Mulready's skill, for example in the drawing of the difficult poses of the background nudes, scrambling up the bank to find their clothes as a male intruder is glimpsed in the far distance. But this intruder is an Actaeon only by way of analogy: startlingly, Mulready's nudes inhabit a modern scene, surrounded by a variegated landscape and scudding clouds much in the manner of watercolour (a medium revealed at the Exposition to be a particular British strength). Mulready's painting also appeared untraditional in technical terms: the

Figure 8. William Mulready, *Bathers Surprised*, 1852–3, oil on panel, 59.1 × 43.8 cm, National Gallery of Ireland, Dublin.

bright key and clear colours made Gautier think of pastel rather than the shadowy tones typical of oil paintings in the Old Master tradition. Indeed, this supremely experienced critic was at a loss to account for the paradoxical combination of delicacy of handling with solidity of drawing, and attributed it to some ineffable Englishness: 'a skin of cold cream [Gautier uses the English expression, untranslated] and virginal milk rendered with the most English exactitude'.⁷ Of all the British pictures, Mulready's had perhaps the clearest claims to represent the kind of subject sanctioned by the European High Art tradition – even so, it appeared startlingly modern. Perhaps there was a tinge of xenophobia in the readiness with which critics linked the paintings' modernity and originality to the stereotype of English eccentricity. However it came about, though, British art and modernity were powerfully associated in this, the first international competition for the fine arts.

In standard histories of artistic modernism, the Exposition Universelle features for a different reason: the oppositional action of the painter Gustave Courbet, who held a simultaneous exhibition of his own, entitled 'Pavilion of Realism,' an event enshrined in art history as a founding moment for avant-gardism. Yet Courbet was a lone rebel, and the first of the group exhibitions held by the artists we now call impressionists was still nineteen years in the future. In 1855, the English already had an avant-garde group, although the term was not yet in use. Gautier instead referred (in the parlance of his own, Romantic generation) to a '*petite chapelle*' comprising William Holman Hunt and John Everett Millais (Dante Gabriel Rossetti had ceased to exhibit in public after the first, controversial seasons of the Pre-Raphaelite Brotherhood, and did not show in Paris).⁸ Gautier and other French critics gave prominent notice to these young rebels, who attracted further coverage in subsequent years.⁹ The obvious hypothesis must be that the English Pre-Raphaelite Brotherhood served as an influential precedent for the later, French avant-garde groupings that have dominated art-historical textbooks so thoroughly.

William Michael Rossetti (himself one of the original seven members of the Pre-Raphaelite Brotherhood, brother of Dante Gabriel Rossetti, and now an art critic) readily recognized the parallel between Courbet and the Pre-Raphaelites, in his review of the Exposition Universelle for the *Spectator*. Courbet, he wrote, holds 'in France, as the apostle of "Realism", a position somewhat analogous to that of the Praeraphaelites in England'. 'Realism', then, was the rallying cry for the avant-garde on both sides of the channel, although as Rossetti stresses, the term meant very different things in the two cases: Courbet's realism is 'the roughest of the rough' in execution, capturing just what he sees before him, while that of the Pre-Raphaelites, 'the most exquisite of the elaborated', pushes to the limits of human vision and penetrates beyond superficial appearances.¹⁰ Rossetti's contrast owes much to the discussions of 'truth' in the first volumes of John Ruskin's *Modern Painters* (1843 and 1846; two more volumes were to appear in 1856 and the last in 1860) – perhaps the most compelling, and certainly the most comprehensive, work of criticism to argue for a modern art based on realism, on either side of the channel.

Ruskin's title chimes intriguingly with that of Baudelaire's essay, 'The Painter of Modern Life', not published until 1863 but begun in 1859 when, as we have already seen, British painters were on his mind. Indeed, Baudelaire's stirring call for a modern art links the two capitals: he writes of a Parisian graphic artist, Constantin Guys, who worked for the London paper, the *Illustrated London News*. The fast pace of life in the modern city, the rapidity of the graphic medium and the representation of modern fashions and habits are bound together in Baudelaire's essay, which has come to seem the crucial founding text for French modernism through its influence on artists of the impressionist generation. Yet Ruskin's five volumes make an equally powerful case for a modern art. Like Baudelaire, Ruskin builds his argument around the work of a particular artist, his revered J. M. W. Turner (not included in the Exposition Universelle since he died in 1851), and one who worked in a genre – landscape – that did not have high status in traditional hierarchies and could accordingly be presented (like Guys's magazine illustration) as quintessentially modern. From 1851 Ruskin extended this championship to the Pre-Raphaelites, whose work is frequently mentioned in the later volumes of *Modern Painters* and Ruskin's other writings. Baudelaire's essay is, like the rapid drawing he recommends, vivid and summary in its celebration of aspects of the modern city. Ruskin's magisterial volumes, on the other hand, are as detailed and comprehensive as a Pre-Raphaelite landscape that omits no blade of grass. While Baudelaire emphasizes modern-life subject-matter (which remained much more controversial in France, where the traditional hierarchy of genres was more entrenched, than in Great Britain), Ruskin instead grounds artistic modernity on truth-to-nature:

> The conclusion, then, to which we are led by our present examination of the truth of clouds is, that the old masters attempted the representation of only one among the thousands of their systems of scenery, and were altogether false in the little they attempted; while we can find records in modern art of every form or phenomenon of the heavens from the highest film that glorifies the aether to the wildest vapour that darkens the dust, and in all these records, we find the most clear language and close thought, firm words and true message, unstinted fulness and unfailing faith.[11]

The enormous prestige of Baudelaire's essay, in art-historical scholar-ship, has helped to confirm the dominance of Paris, and particularly of the painting of subjects from modern life, in standard accounts of artistic modernism. But Ruskin's volumes are more revolutionary in that they not only present a sophisticated theoretical rationale for mod-ern art, but also reconfigure the entire tradition of Western painting in consequence.

Clearly, the standard assumption of twentieth-century art-historical orthodoxy – that Paris was the cradle of modernism in the visual arts, with Victorian England lagging somewhere behind – must be challenged. The responses of the French critics to British art in 1855 are sufficient to prove the limitations of that view; indeed, part of the shock, particularly for those French critics who had been advocating realism and modernity against academic tradition, must have been to see those concerns already so much to the fore in a contemporary art world of which they had been virtually ignorant. Nonetheless, it would be equally mistaken to ignore the genuine differences that the French critics stress, sometimes explicitly and sometimes through their real puzzlement. If it is illogical to deny Pre-Raphaelitism its chronological priority, it would make no better sense to assimilate it, in any simple fashion, to standard accounts of artistic modernism, based largely on French examples. In many respects not only Pre-Raphaelitism, but other contemporary and succeeding developments in Victorian art, conflict dramatically with modernism as it has been configured in art-historical orthodoxy. Thus the difference of Victorian art from what has come to seem the modernist mainstream has important implications not only for our understanding of Victorian culture, but also for wider debates about modernism and modernity.

Victorian literary painting

British critics often complained that the *grandes machines* of French paint-ing – vast canvases of historical or scriptural subjects – were bombastic, superstitious in their Catholicism, histrionic or gory. French critics, on the other hand, complained that it was impossible to understand British pictures without a detailed knowledge of British novels, plays and poems. The novelist William Makepeace Thackeray, who had trained as a painter in Paris in the 1830s, played wittily on both stereotypes in the series of exhibition reviews he contributed to *Fraser's Magazine* between 1838 and

Figure 9. John Everett Millais, *Mariana*, 1850–1, oil on mahogany panel, 59.7 × 49.5 cm, Tate collection (London).

1845. Under the pseudonym Michael Angelo Titmarsh, he satirized both French pretension and British anecdotalism, developing a running joke about the preponderance of subjects from Goldsmith's novel, *The Vicar of Wakefield*, at British exhibitions.[12]

Yet literary subject-matter was a prolific source of innovation in Victorian painting, something that Gautier was perhaps acknowledging when he wrote that a British picture was 'as modern as a novel by Balzac'. A particularly complex example is Millais's *Mariana* of 1851 (Figure 9). The primary reference is to Tennyson's poem 'Mariana', about a woman, deserted by her lover, and living apart from society in a dilapidated farm-house. The pose Millais invents for his Mariana, standing up from her tapestry-work to stretch, is unconventional and not particularly graceful, but it captures the mood of Tennyson's refrain:

> She said, 'I am aweary, aweary,
> I would that I were dead!'

And Millais even includes a piquant detail from the poem:

> the mouse
> Behind the mouldering wainscot shrieked,
> Or from the crevice peered about.[13]

But Tennyson's poem, and through it Millais's painting, also refers to Shakespeare's *Measure for Measure*, in which Mariana has been abandoned by the mercenary Angelo because her dowry has been lost at sea. And Millais incorporates aspects of another poem by Tennyson, 'Mariana in the South', in which, with Roman Catholic overtones, Mariana prays to the Virgin; the little domestic altar in the background, which the then-evangelical Ruskin famously called an 'idolatrous toilet table',[14] alludes to Mariana's devotions, and the stained glass window shows the angel Gabriel in the left light and the Virgin on the right. There may be further literary references: the heraldic stained glass, to the right of the Annunciation scene, features a snowdrop, the flower of St Agnes, which suggests either the poem by Keats, 'The Eve of St Agnes', or Tennyson's 'St Agnes' Eve', both of which revolve around the tradition that, on the eve of St Agnes's feast day, maidens will dream of their future lovers. Perhaps wisely, Millais sent the more familiar Shakespearean subject, *Ophelia* (1852, Tate), to the Exposition Universelle; the complex of literary references in *Mariana* would surely have baffled the French and other foreign critics of 1855.

But bafflement may be no bad thing, if it encourages the viewer to pay closer attention in the attempt to make sense of what is seen. Nor is that inconsistent with Victorian 'literary' painting; such close looking might be described as the lesson of Ruskin's writings, in a nutshell. 'Examine it well inch by inch', he writes of another Pre-Raphaelite painting in 1856; 'Give it much time.'[15] *Mariana* requires its viewer to follow Ruskin's advice. It is not particularly large, and certainly not by the standards of French High Art – about 60 by 50 centimetres. Thus the scale of the details is exceedingly small, like the fine-grained painting of Jan van

Figure 10. Jan van Eyck, *The Arnolfini Portrait*, 1434, oil on oak panel, 82.2 × 60 cm, National Gallery, London.

Eyck. Indeed the basic organization of the picture is very like that of the painting by van Eyck now known as the *Arnolfini Portrait* (Figure 10), which entered London's National Gallery in 1842, and which Ruskin singled out for 'technical perfection' in an influential review of 1848, just at the time when the Pre-Raphaelite Brotherhood was formed.[16] In both paintings there is a window, that is a strong light source, on the left; a bed with hangings on the right; and in the centre background an array of intricately crafted objects including glinting metalwork and a hanging light. In both, too, there is an animal in the foreground and an expanse of floorboards, with minutely painted woodgrain, which serves to establish the perspective of the interior domestic space. In other words, Millais is working within the visual world of the van Eyck, and that is no inert art-historical comparison. Realism of van Eyck's special kind is important to the painting not merely as a display of skill, but more significantly as an invitation to linger in the viewing, and to ponder the implications of what is seen.

All accounts of *Mariana* quote Ruskin's phrase 'idolatrous toilet table' – this is witty, to be sure, but also much more. In just three words Ruskin captures the undecidability of the collection of objects on the background table; are they accessories of religious devotion, or of personal adornment? The darkness in this area is so deep that the white tablecloth appears to levitate in mid-air, and we must peer into the gloom for some time to make out the objects.[17] Intellectually, one would expect to see a shrine laid out symmetrically, but the visual evidence confounds expectations. The hanging candle ought to be central, but the orange patch represent-ing its cast light is just to our side of the vertical crease in the table-cloth, and the gleaming silver castor; either the castor and the crease, or the lamp, is off-centre. Again, the orange glow on the left wall appears centred above the triptych, turned into such sharp perspective that its imagery is indecipherable, but then the little stained glass window must be out of alignment with the table. These spatial oddities might be dis-missed as typical Pre-Raphaelite quirks, distracting details that result from an overly slavish attention to observed fact. But a more searching interpretation would see them in relation to one of Ruskin's most impor-tant didactic projects. They demonstrate that, when looking, we cannot rely on our preconceptions, but must rid our minds of what we thought we should find; then we might see something else, something different. That also helps to explain the fascination with van Eyck, at this historical moment. The uncanny precision of detail, far from being merely 'realis-tic' in some mundane sense, constantly surprises the viewer with what things *look like*, as opposed to what we *thought they were like*.

For Ruskin what we see is not merely truer to nature than what we thought we should see; it is also more productive of meaning, and *Mari-ana* encourages the viewer to tease out the intellectual complexities of the scene in the very process of deciphering its visual imagery. Throughout the painting, religious imagery appears in close contiguity with visual cues to ideas about marriage and sexuality, which not only respond to, but also extend upon, the ideas suggested in the texts of Tennyson, Shakespeare and Keats. In this light, all of the Marianas become intriguing for their differences. Shakespeare's Mariana receives the full development of a drama, with a beginning, a middle and an end. Tennyson translates this into lyric; he elaborates the middle moment of Mariana's solitude to dwell on her longing for a death that would end her weariness, but which never comes; the seven poignant stanzas manage magically to make poetry of nothing happening. Millais, finally, makes his Mariana visible, and invents a visual world, based on a vibrant contrast of complementary blues and red-oranges, in which to realize the tensions and nuances of her story.

Thus, Millais is not simply 'illustrating' a prior literary text. On the contrary, he constructs his painting so as to yield its 'literary' meanings only to the most dedicated visual scrutiny. Such procedures came under heavy attack in the modernist art theories that have been dominant since the early twentieth century; according to these, any intrusion of literary content sullied the simplicity and purity of painting as a visual art form. Yet an art of complexity might be equally appropriate to the modern world, and consistent with the alternative modernism of Ruskin's *Modern Painters*:

> But I say that the art is greatest which conveys to the mind of the spectator, by any means whatsoever, the greatest number of the greatest ideas; and I call an idea great in proportion as it is received by a higher faculty of the mind, and as it more fully occupies, and in occupying, exercises and exalts, the faculty by which it is received.[18]

Ruskin draws on the language of High Art theory. But he transforms its import to emphasize the proliferation and fecundity of ideas, rather than hierarchical ordering. This is distinct, on the one hand, from the generalization and idealization recommended by Reynolds, and on the other from the simplification required by modernist art theory. Literary painting came low in the traditional hierarchy of genres, and it fared no better in relation to modernist demands for the purity of the visual. But it could meet Ruskin's criteria for great art, by creating a vast expansion not merely in the range of subjects available to visual art, but also in the kinds of associated ideas that could be conveyed to the spectator.

Aestheticism and the art of the past

Another reason for the equivocal reputation of Victorian art within standard histories of modernism has been its seeming dependence on the art of the past. We have already seen examples of this. For all the modernity that startled the French critics, Mulready's *Bathers Surprised* borrows the pose of its principal figure from a famous painting by Titian, the *Venus Anadyomene*, then in the collection of the Earl of Ellesmere (now in the National Gallery of Scotland). Ruskin's *Modern Painters* built its case for a modern art through sustained juxtaposition with the art of the Old Masters and van Eyck's *Arnolfini Portrait* which was crucial to the development of Pre-Raphaelite style. While the Pre-Raphaelite Brotherhood chose their name in defiance of the academic tradition descending from Raphael, their project can seem merely to substitute an alternative artistic precedent – the art of the period before Raphael – rather than to make the radical break with the Western artistic tradition that has been taken to characterize the French avant-garde movements.

The problem is compounded when we come to the art of the succeeding generation, in which the detailed realism of mid-century gives way to an array of artistic projects that take their cue from the art of the past rather than from the natural world. The sensual women of Titian and Giorgione are reincarnated, from 1859 onwards, in Rossetti's series of paintings of single female figures surrounded by gorgeous flowers. The Elgin Marbles, sculptures from the Parthenon on display at the British Museum since 1817, find echoes in the classical revival of the 1860s, led by Frederic Leighton and George Frederic Watts. Renaissance drawings seem to inspire the beautiful, androgynous figures of Simeon Solomon and Edward Burne-Jones. Botticelli, Mantegna and Piero della Francesca, artists of the late fifteenth century who had been underappreciated in earlier generations, are rediscovered in the work of Burne-Jones and his many followers of the later Victorian period. Velázquez becomes a crucial inspiration for artists such as Millais and James McNeill Whistler. And Reynolds, Gainsborough and Lawrence inspire a dramatic revival of Grand Manner portraiture, led by John Singer Sargent in the 1880s and 1890s. Reminiscences of the art of the past would seem to have overwhelmed the modernity so notable to the critics of 1855.

Yet eclecticism, from a different perspective, can be seen as a prolific source of stylistic innovation, parallel to the expansion of subject-matter through literary reference. Throughout the Victorian period, contemporary art production was in constant negotiation with the simultaneous construction of the history not just of Western art, but also of world art, as the arts of India, the Near and Far East became familiar in exhibitions and museums throughout the United Kingdom. The British Museum, founded in 1753, was joined in 1824 by the National Gallery, in 1852 by the South Kensington (now Victoria and Albert) Museum, and then by dozens of municipal art galleries in the burgeoning cities of Britain and its empire. These new institutions not only patronized Victorian artists, but employed them as advisers and officials; at the same time, they increased the need for scholarship and interpretation. The magisterial histories of Italian art, published between 1864 and 1871 by Joseph Archer Crowe and his Italian collaborator Giovanni Cavalcaselle, established newly rigorous standards for 'scientific' attribution and connoisseurship. The literature of the history of art flourished, from Anna Jameson's popular books on sacred art in the 1840s and 1850s through to the four meticulous volumes on the arts of eighteenth-century France, published by Lady Dilke from 1899 to 1902. These museological, scholarly and commercial activities were supported by new techniques of mechanical reproduction, in the widest variety of printmaking and photographic media, again in tandem with contemporary art practice. The innovative fine art photographer Frederick Hollyer, for example, pioneered techniques for reproducing the delicate drawings of Simeon Solomon which became indispensable for documenting the art of past ages and remote cultures.

The developing network of museums, dealers, critics and scholars was increasingly international, like the contemporary art world after the middle of the century. Yet the dialogue between contemporary art and the art of the past was a distinctive feature of ambitious painting in Victorian Great Britain. This has made Victorian art appear too backward-looking to constitute a fully fledged modern art. Yet a different story can be told, in which the art of Victorian Great Britain can be configured as radical in another sense: modern art might mean a wholesale reconfiguration of the relationship between the new work of art and the entirety of its past tradition, which changes on both sides with the creation of every new work. Such a story would help to make sense of Aestheticism, the diffuse collection of art forms and trends in fashion that does duty for the principal vanguard movement in British art between Pre-Raphaelitism and early modernism. When Oscar Wilde introduced the new movement to American audiences, on his lecture tour of 1882, he called it 'The English

Renaissance of Art'. The title succinctly suggests a relationship between the new vanguard and the historical art of the period christened 'the Renaissance' in nineteenth-century scholarship; at the same time, it calls attention to the innovative aspect of the movement, a second 'rebirth' of Western art in the new context of Victorian Britain. As Wilde noted, the English Renaissance 'has been described as a mere revival' of the art forms of the past: 'Rather I would say that to these forms of the human spirit it has added whatever of artistic value the intricacy and complexity and experience of modern life can give'.[19] Wilde's title also pays homage to the volume of essays by Walter Pater, *The Renaissance*, on which he drew heavily for the aesthetic theory that underpins his account of recent developments in art practice. It is telling that Pater's volume, a set of studies of the art and literature of the fifteenth and sixteenth centuries, came to serve as a kind of manifesto for the progressive art circles of the later nineteenth century. To the aesthetic critic, as Pater wrote in his Preface, 'all periods, types, schools of taste, are in themselves equal'.[20] Pater's explorations of the art of the Renaissance form a link between the broader development of art-historical and museological scholarship, on the one hand, and Aestheticism as a vanguard movement on the other.

It is possible to trace this link in detail, for example in the striking rise to prominence of the late fifteenth-century Florentine painter Botticelli. Stirrings of interest in Botticelli's art are first apparent in the art and writing of the Rossetti circle in the 1860s. Pater's essay of 1870, 'A Fragment on Sandro Botticelli' (subsequently included in *The Renaissance*) transformed the critical reputation of the artist: what had seemed merely quaint or 'Gothic' in the previous generation becomes, in Pater's account, the expression of a new and complex sense of inexplicable melancholy – this reinterpreted Botticelli is still familiar in today's criticism. Also in 1870, the Arundel Society published a chromolithograph of the great Botticelli of the Uffizi Gallery in Florence, *The Birth of Venus*, making it available for the first time in colour reproduction. Immediately, the National Gallery began to acquire important works by Botticelli: *Venus and Mars* in 1874, and the *Mystic Nativity* in 1878. In the next few years, artistic responses to the National Gallery pictures began to appear in the London exhibitions. These are just a few of the events in a complex history, in which art-historical scholarship, art dealing, reproductive technology and museology were in constant interplay with art practice and creative critical interpretation.[21] The result was not merely to elevate Botticelli to

Figure 11. Evelyn Pickering (later De Morgan), *Ariadne in Naxos*, c. 1877, oil on canvas, 60.3 × 99.7 cm, the De Morgan Foundation, London.

the position he still holds in the art-historical canon, but also to revitalize both art and taste in the later nineteenth century and beyond.

At the first exhibition of the new Grosvenor Gallery, founded in 1877 and greeted in criticism as a progressive alternative to the Royal Academy, the twenty-two-year-old Evelyn Pickering (later De Morgan), showed *Ariadne in Naxos* (Figure 11). The High Art subject from classical mythology is a sign of the growing ambition of women artists; ten of the sixty-four artists invited to participate in this elite new exhibiting venture were women. Yet Pickering's project is more complex than a mere reversion to High Art tradition, for she combines her classical story with a conspicuous visual reference to Botticelli's *Venus and Mars*. The painting is not just backward-looking in a single sense, but doubly so. In another way, though, Pickering's painting is thoroughly up-to-date. Not only was the Botticelli a recent arrival on the London art scene, but Pickering's painting participates in, and contributes to, the aesthetic debates that surrounded the rise of interest in Botticelli. Pickering re-imagines the Renaissance rediscovery of classical antiquity that inspires Botticelli's work in Pater's essay: 'a record of the first impression made by [the Hellenic spirit] on minds turned back towards it, in almost painful aspiration, from a world in which it had been ignored so long'.[22]

As president of the Royal Academy from 1878 until his death in 1896, Frederic Leighton lectured to the Academy students, in the tradition of the *Discourses* of his illustrious predecessor, Reynolds. Yet rather than

Figure 12.   Frederic Leighton, *Flaming June*, c. 1895, oil on canvas, 119 × 119 cm, Museo de Arte de Ponce, Fundación Luis A. Ferré, Ponce, Puerto Rico.

offering an art theory illustrated by examples for emulation or rejection, Leighton's *Addresses* amount to a comprehensive and scholarly history of art, astonishingly catholic in its scope, as if to leave the students free to choose whatever they wished from the array of artistic precedents. Leighton's *Flaming June* (Figure 12), exhibited the year before his death, summarizes the results of a lifetime's study. The massive bodily forms, revealed through endlessly rippling drapery, derive from the pediment figures of the Elgin Marbles. The pose takes its cue from the series of male nudes that twist and turn on Michelangelo's ceiling for the Sistine Chapel. And perhaps the burning reflection of the sun on water, painted in startlingly thick impasto, recalls the work of Turner. These allusions are to the most sublime monuments of the Western tradition – ancient, Renaissance, and modern – the works revered above all for their grandeur or power. Intellectually, it would seem surprising to deploy them in a painting that represents nothing more than a girl, asleep in the hot June sunshine. Visually, though, the effect is anything but eclectic. The tight interlocking of the limbs within the square format, the infinite modulations of orange and gold hues, the light that seems to emanate from somewhere within the glossy paint surface cohere in an image suggestive at once of deep repose and overwhelming radiance. Michelangelo never saw the Parthenon sculptures, and Turner was notorious for his summary drawing of the human figure; yet Leighton's painting reinterprets these precedents to establish a new relationship between modern art and its tradition. In its reconciliation of seemingly divergent artistic qualities, Leighton's work brings to mind the web of interconnections, prospective and retrospective, that Pater traced in his essay on Michelangelo:

> That strange interfusion of sweetness and strength is not to be found in those who claimed to be his followers; but it is found in many of those who worked before him, and in many others down to our own time, in William Blake, for instance, and Victor Hugo, who, though not of his school, and unaware, are his true sons, and help us to understand him, as he in turn interprets and justifies them. Perhaps this is the chief use in studying old masters.[23]

A willingness like Leighton's or Pickering's to absorb styles and motifs from the past may perhaps be described as the counterpart, in art practice, of the special receptiveness to aesthetic experience that Pater seemed to be advocating as a philosophy of life, in the controversial 'Conclusion' to *The Renaissance*: 'While all melts under our feet, we may well grasp at any exquisite passion, or any contribution to knowledge that seems by a lifted horizon to set the spirit free for a moment, or any stirring of the senses, strange dyes, strange colours, and curious odours, or work of the artist's hands, or the face of one's friend.'[24] From the perspective of twentieth-century modernism, there was something passive, or feminized, about both the eclecticism of the visual arts, in the Aesthetic Movement, and the aesthete's devotion to beauty and art rather than manly action and engagement in the world's affairs. The sensational trials of Oscar Wilde in 1895 reinforced a sense, implicit in the criticism of Aestheticism since its beginnings in the 1860s, that there was some underlying link between aesthetic sensitivity and effeminacy (following two well-publicized trials, Wilde was convicted of gross indecency and sentenced to two years' hard labour). Indeed, there is some truth to the stereotypical association of Aestheticism with unmanliness. The prominence of women artists in Aestheticism has already been noted, and its male leaders tended to have public images at odds with conventional British masculinity: not only the brilliant young Jewish artist Simeon Solomon, arrested in 1873 for homosexual activities, but Whistler, the dandified American, the reclusive poet-painter Rossetti, the cosmopolitan Leighton and Pater, the refined Oxford don. Thus the reluctance to enrol Victorian Aestheticism among the modernist avant-garde movements carries tinges of both misogyny and homophobia. Paradoxically, though, the apparent withdrawal of Aestheticism into a feminized realm of art and beauty, routinely stigmatized in twentieth-century criticism as 'escapist', may constitute precisely its claim to represent a genuinely oppositional avant-garde.

Victorian, modern, postmodern

William Orpen's painting of 1900, *The Mirror* (Figure 13), demonstrates the complexity of the British art world at the end of the Victorian period. First displayed at the New English Art Club, a progressive exhibiting society founded in 1886 by artists sympathetic to the latest developments in French art, the painting displays a simplicity of design, bright tonality and expressive brushwork that can readily be associated with modernism. Yet the work also looks back to an eclectic range of artistic precedents: the circular mirror, with its reflection of the artist at his easel, is borrowed from van Eyck's *Arnolfini Portrait*, and the placement of the seated figure in profile against a flat back wall instantly recalls Whistler's famous portrait of his mother, by this date a modernist icon in the French national collection; there are glances, too, at Rubens's *Chapeau de Paille*, acquired by the National Gallery in 1871, and at Reynolds's reinterpretations of the motif of the hat shading the face. The painting explores the relationship between artist and model, a preoccupation in British art at least since Rossetti, yet the model's deadpan expression and the tiny scene in the mirror do not readily yield a legible anecdote. Roger Fry noted the revival, in Orpen's work, of the British tradition of genre painting stemming from Hogarth, but stressed at the same time his refusal to indulge in anecdotalism.[25]

Fry's own career, as painter, critic, scientific connoisseur and museum professional, ties together many of the developments in the art world of

Figure 13. William Orpen, *The Mirror*, 1900, oil on canvas, 50.8 × 40.6 cm, Tate collection (London).

the preceding few decades. In 1900, he succeeded F. G. Stephens, one of the original seven members of the Pre-Raphaelite Brotherhood and one of the first British writers to make a career of art criticism, as regular art critic for the *Athenaeum*, and in the next six years wrote nearly 500 articles on contemporary art, Old Master exhibitions, museum acquisitions and every other aspect of the art world. In the pages of his reviews are lists of artists even less familiar than those of half-a-century earlier. Orpen is just one example, taken almost at random – a painter of distinction whose name is now known only to specialists. No more than a handful of the 14,000 artists recorded in the census of 1901, or the hundreds discussed in Fry's criticism, has ever been the subject of a scholarly article; until such research gets underway, any pretence to offer a summary of the artistic scene at the end of the Victorian period would be irresponsible.

Fry was, then, the last of the great Victorian art critics. But he is more famous as the first of the great modernist art critics, and the moving force behind the exhibition, *Manet and the Post-Impressionists*, which brought French avant-garde art before the London public in 1910. Fry's reputation and that of his Bloomsbury circle for plunging Victorian art into ignominy is oversimplified. Clive Bell's influential volume, *Art* (1914), retains traces of respect for Pre-Raphaelitism and Aestheticism. Nonetheless, in its zeal for the new French art it over-states its case with polemical brilliance: 'Except stray artists and odd amateurs, and you may say that in the middle of the nineteenth century art had ceased to exist. That is the importance of the official and aca-demic art of that age: it shows us that we have touched bottom.'[26] By 1940, when the American critic who would become the most powerful proponent of modernism, Clement Greenberg, echoed Bell's categorical denunciation, all distinctions have been lost: 'academicians sank paint-ing to a level that was in some respects an all-time low. The name of this low is Vernet, Gérome, Leighton, Watts, Moreau, Böcklin, the Pre-Raphaelites, etc., etc.'[27] All of Victorian art – even the Pre-Raphaelites – had become synonymous with retrogressive academicism.

There is nothing surprising about the repudiation of Victorian art in criticism designed to effect a drastic change in taste. What is stranger is the tenacity of the tastes of Fry, Bell and Greenberg, even after mod-ernism and its art theories came under comprehensive attack. Since the 1970s, the rise of the social history of art to dominance among the methods of Anglo-American art history ought, in all logic, to have put paid to the devaluation of Victorian art once and for all. It would be absurd to deny the utility of Victorian works of art as documents of the period's social, cultural and political ideologies. Yet today's textbooks of nineteenth-century and modern art continue to give overwhelming priority to the French paintings seen to take the cue of Baudelaire's 'The Painter of Modern Life'. Manet and Cézanne remain the heroes of the social history of art, just as they were in the formalist history of modernism.

Will postmodernism finally come to the rescue? Modernism and the social history of art both emphasized a restricted canon of artists, along with a strong conception of national identity, whether that was understood in terms of national schools of artists or in those of nationalist cultural politics. The appearance of Bell's *Art* in 1914 coincided with the abrupt curtailment of the internationalism that had characterized the art worlds of the later nineteenth century. Now, at the beginning of the twenty-first century, it may at last be possible to return to the spirit of the great international exhibitions; the watchwords are globalism, diversity, eclecticism. This is a world in which Leighton's catholic history of art, or Pater's welcoming of 'all schools of taste', may have something important to offer. *Flaming June*, which disappeared from public view sometime in the early twentieth century, resurfaced towards the 1960s, when the reputation of Victorian art had struck bottom; more than one connoisseur has claimed to have seen it on sale for £50, on a market-trader's stall or in a frame-maker's shop, where it was priced for its gilded neoclassical frame, the painting itself being considered worthless. Perhaps these stories are exaggerated, but there is no doubt about the painting's spectacular rise to fortune once it entered the Museo de Arte de Ponce, Puerto Rico, founded by the enterprising collector Luis Ferré. Now the painting is an art-historical icon, reproduced on countless posters, greetings cards and websites.

Does that mark the return of *Flaming June* to High Art esteem? Or does its new-found popularity merely confirm its status as kitsch, a demerit under modernism that is playfully reversed in postmodernism? Only time will tell. But the fortunes of *Flaming June*, together with innumerable other Victorian paintings now featured on popular websites, demonstrate one crucial similarity between the Victorian and the postmodern art worlds: the willingness to question hierarchical canons. Modernism vaunted itself on its opposition to the hierarchies of the academic tradition; thus it produced a new canon, but arguably it remained in thrall to the kinds of hierarchical and exclusionary thinking that characterized the very tradition it pretended to overthrow. Perhaps, then, it is no bad thing to share the confusion of the French critics, when they encountered British art at the Exposition Universelle in 1855. We do not know yet whether posterity will accord Victorian art a place alongside the Parthenon sculptures, Michelangelo and Turner at the summit of artistic achievement; but it has at least the value of testing our received ideas about artistic merit and about what a modern art might look like.

The current state of research on Victorian art is almost laughably backward, in comparison to the vast and sophisticated literature on French modernism. Not just to correct the record, then, but also to expand and refine our ideas about both art and modernity, there is every incentive to promote new scholarship in the field; indeed, in its absence, the current revival of interest in Victorian art will never amount to more than post-modern playfulness. Ruskin's teaching will still serve. If we discard what Francocentric modernism has taught us we ought to think, we can learn to see Victorian art differently.

Notes

1 Théophile Gautier, *Les beaux-arts en Europe 1855*, 2 vols. (Paris: Lévy, 1855–6), vol. I, 7, 18.

2 Charles Baudelaire, *Art in Paris 1845–1862: Salons and Other Exhibitions*, trans. and ed. Jonathan Mayne (Oxford: Phaidon, 1965), 145–6.

3 Numbers are for England and Wales and because of recording variations are approximate. See Statistical Abstracts printed for Her Majesty's Stationery Office: *Abstract of the Answers and Returns: Occupation Abstract, 1841*, 31; *Census of England and Wales 1901: Preliminary Report and Tables*, 257 (Table 34).

4 Benjamin Disraeli, *Coningsby: Or The New Generation* (London: Davies, 1927), Bk IV, ch. IV, 182.

5 Gautier, *Beaux-Arts*, vol. I, 9.

6 For more on Landseer, see below, p. 257.

7 Gautier, *Beaux-Arts*, vol. I, 23–4.

8 Ibid., 8.

9 See Jacques Lethève, 'La connaissance des peintres préraphaélites anglais en France (1855–1900)', *Gazette des beaux-arts*, 53 (May–June 1959), 315–28.

10 William Michael Rossetti, *Fine Art, Chiefly Contemporary: Notices Re-Printed, with Revisions* (London: Macmillan, 1867), 112.

11 John Ruskin, *The Works of John Ruskin (Library Edition)*, ed. E. T. Cook and Alexander Wedderburn, 39 vols. (London: Allen, 1903–12), vol. III, 415.

12 See Judith L. Fisher, 'The Aesthetic of the Mediocre: Thackeray and the Visual Arts', *Victorian Studies*, 26 (1982), 65–82.

13 Christopher Ricks (ed.), *The Poems of Tennyson* (London: Longmans, 1969), pp. 188–90.

14 Ruskin, *Works*, vol. XII, 320.

15 Ibid., vol. XIV, 60. Ruskin is commenting on Henry Wallis's *Chatterton* (Tate).

16 Ibid., vol. XII, 256–8 (quotation on 257; from 'Eastlake's History of Oil-Painting', *Quarterly Review*, Mar. 1848).

17 I am indebted to the fine discussion of *Mariana* in Paul Barlow, *Time Present and Time Past: The Art of John Everett Millais* (Aldershot and Burlington, VT: Ashgate, 2005), 22–9.

18 Ruskin, *Works*, vol. 3, III, 92.

19 Oscar Wilde, 'The English Renaissance of Art' (1882), in John Wyse Jackson (ed.), *Aristotle at Afternoon Tea: The Rare Oscar Wilde* (London: Fourth Estate, 1991), 3.

20 Walter Pater, *The Renaissance: Studies in Art and Poetry: The 1893 Text*, ed. by Donald L. Hill (Berkeley: University of California Press, 1980), XXI.

21 See Michael Levey, 'Botticelli and Nineteenth-Century England', *Journal of the Courtauld and Warburg Institutes*, 23 (1960), 291–306.

22 Pater, *Renaissance*, 46.

23 Ibid., 76.

24 Ibid., 189.

25 [Roger Fry, published anonymously], 'The New English Art Club', *Athenaeum*, 3834, 20 Apr. 1901, 505.

26 Clive Bell, *Art* (London: Chatto and Windus, 1927), p. 192.

27 Clement Greenberg, 'Towards a Newer Laocoon' (1940), repr. in Clement Greenberg, *The Collected Essays and Criticism*, ed. John O'Brian, 4 vols. (Chicago: University of Chicago Press, 1986–93), vol. I, 27.

12

Domestic arts

The idea of the Victorian home

In her 1928 fantasy novel *Orlando*, Virginia Woolf offered a parodic version of the cultural shift from the eighteenth to the nineteenth century:

> The hardy country gentleman, who had sat down gladly to a meal of ale and beef in a room designed, perhaps, by the brothers Adam, with classic dignity, now felt chilly. Rugs appeared; beards were grown; trousers were fastened tight under the instep. The chill which he felt in his legs the country gentleman soon transferred to his house; furniture was muffled; walls and tables were covered; nothing was left bare. Then a change of diet became essential. The muffin was invented and the crumpet. Coffee supplanted the after-dinner port, and, as coffee led to a drawing-room in which to drink it, and a drawing-room to glass cases, and glass cases to artificial flowers, and artificial flowers to mantelpieces, and mantelpieces to pianofortes, and pianofortes to drawing-room ballads, and drawing-room ballads (skipping a stage or two) to innumerable little dogs, mats, and china ornaments, the home – which had become extremely important – was completely altered.[1]

Woolf foregrounds those elements of Victorian domestic culture that her own generation found so repugnant: the clutter and kitsch, the obsession with objects and cosiness. There is also an implied objection to the femininity of this new domestic space – to the muffins and coffee that replace the ale and beef of the eighteenth century.

The negative image of the Victorians that prevailed so long into the twentieth century is, of course, largely the creation of the disgruntled late Victorian children of Woolf's generation, who rebelled so gladly and grandly against what they saw as the stuffiness and hypocrisy of their parents and grandparents. Yet Woolf is absolutely right about one thing: the home had indeed become important. A new emphasis on the importance of home is a key element in Victorian culture. Historians concur that this change is the result of a number of factors: the rise of the evangelical movement, with its emphasis on quiet, domestic virtues; the improving child mortality rates, which produced an increasingly child-centred culture; the huge changes brought about by industrialization, which separated home from workplace and the related expansion of the suburbs that meant that many middle-class men worked at some distance from their homes. The middle-class Victorian woman lived increasingly apart from the arena of work, her role as domestic doyenne bolstered by any number of texts selling her the image of herself as 'the angel of the hearth': household manuals, cookery books, women's magazines, sermons and literature extolled the wife and mother as the repository of the moral values of the family and nation, salver of worldly hurts, source of sustenance both material and spiritual. One of the most influential writers was Sarah Ellis, whose many popular books on the morals and behaviour of women (*The Women of England: Their Social Duties and Domestic Habits* (1845); *The Daughters of England: Their Position in Society, Character and Responsibilities* (1842); *The Mothers of England: Their Influence and Responsibility* (1844)) sought to establish a correct code of conduct for the dutiful, Christian middle-class woman:

> [W]here . . . the individuals who compose the household are thrown upon the consideration of the mothers, wives, and daughters for their daily comfort, innumerable channels are opened for the overflow of those floods of human kindness which it is one of the happiest and most ennobling duties of women to administer to the weary frame, and to pour into the wounded mind.[2]

The key figure for the next generation was Isabella Beeton, whose *Household Management* (1861) offered detailed advice on every aspect of running a home, from the hiring and management of servants to the etiquette of dining, from caring for infants to paying social calls. For a long time, historians and literary critics took such discourses at face value, constructing a model of 'separate spheres' in which the public sphere belonged to the male and the domestic to the female, seeing the Victorian woman as a virtual prisoner in the home, like Tennyson's Mariana in the moated grange moaning 'I am aweary, aweary,/I would that I were dead!'[3] But in recent decades there has been a number of challenges to this model, voices pointing out that just because advice manuals prescribed a certain form of behaviour, which is no guarantee that people actually observed these prescriptions: that such books are always interventions, attempts to alter the *status quo*, rather than clear windows on to the past.[4] Furthermore, close study of the prescriptive texts themselves reveals that what are often taken for monoliths of narrow social control are often much more subtle, polyvalent and self-contradictory.[5]

At the heart of the ideal Victorian home constructed in domestic texts is the figure of the woman. The home gathers its meaning from her presence, and she is responsible for 'making' that home, pouring moral, spiritual, emotional and physical energy into it, in a process of continual refashioning. The most extreme statement of this view, in Ruskin's formulation, sees 'home' as an idea absolutely contained in the feminine, not even needing bricks and mortar: 'Whenever a true wife comes, this home is always around her. The stars only may be over her head; the glow-worm in the night-cold grass may be the only fire at her foot, but home is yet wherever she is.'[6] The notion that the woman *makes* the home is a crucial one for understanding both the power of the pro-domestic discourses and their provisionality. The home imagined in these discourses is not a fixed, static entity – it is continually changing, always in a process of being re-made, even while certain elements of the fantasy – the hearth, the woman – remain constant. This chapter will consider some of the key activities involved in that re-making, examining handicrafts, cookery, entertaining, household management and home decoration to elucidate the paradoxes and complexities tied up in these domestic arts.

Managing the home

> Such weighing and mixing and chopping and grating, such dusting and washing and polishing, such snipping and weeding and trowelling and other small gardening, such making and mending and folding and airing, such diverse arrangements, and above all such severe study. (Charles Dickens, *Our Mutual Friend* (1864–5))

The newly married Bella Rokesmith enters on the task of keeping house with much pleasure but also great puzzlement: she 'was under the constant necessity of referring for advice and support to a sage volume entitled The Complete British Family Housewife, which she would sit consulting, with her elbows on the table and her temples on her hands, like some perplexed enchantress pouring over the Black Art.'[7] The nineteenth century saw a dramatic increase in such instructive texts: the very notion of household management is peculiarly Victorian in its sense that running a home is a specific and uniquely complex activity, rather than simply part of a woman's life.[8] The ordering of the domestic sphere suddenly becomes a subject for study and instruction rather than familial received wisdom because the women of the Victorian middle class were living rather different lives from those of earlier generations. Located mostly within or on the outskirts of large cities, surrounded by strangers, dealing with a mass of shop keepers and trades people rather than the trusted few that would have been found in a small provincial town, the mistress of a Victorian house could be forgiven for feeling in need of some expert guidance. The handling of servants was a particular problem because many were the first in their family to keep more than a single servant, and because the relationship between mistress and maid differed from even a generation earlier. Most particularly, the management of the home became a science because one's home was a key marker of status in a world where middle-class identity was both constantly shifting and enormously important. The middle class expanded hugely over the course of Victoria's reign: in the twenty years between 1851 and 1871 it tripled in size.[9] It was a time of extremely rapid class mobility, with many opportunities both to make and lose fortunes, and there was a nagging awareness that a fall in status was as possible as a rise. It is a truism of historical study that the middle class has been rising for the past 500 years, but the Victorian middle-class expansion was unique because it was taking place at the same time as a massive process of industrialization and urbanization. New jobs in industry and trade created a distinctly different middle class whose interests and identity were often at odds with those of the old professional class with whom they were notionally merging – a tension that is repeatedly worked through in the fiction of the period. Advice books of all types were read most particularly by this new sector of the middle class, although they invariably professed to be speaking to people considerably higher up the social scale.

Household management seems to have been an exclusively middle-class subject. Writers for working-class readers concentrate on the basics, while those for the upper classes assume these details are already known – and that the management will, in any case, be carried out by someone other than the mistress of the house. The chef Alexis Soyer, author of a series of cookery books devoted sequentially to each section of the market, only addresses the issue of the running of the house in his book for the middle classes, *The Modern Housewife* (1850), in which domestic and culinary advice is transmitted to the reader through a series of letters exchanged between two fictional friends, Mrs B. ('Hortense') and Mrs L. ('Eloise').[10] Mrs B., who is acclaimed by all who observe her elegant economy as 'the Model Housekeeper', takes it on herself to instruct her friend in her secrets. Chief among them is the efficient deployment of the household income for maximum effect: close attention is paid to the pennies and the details in order that a better show may be made to her husband's friends and business associates. Far from functioning as a 'separate sphere', the management of the home is explicitly linked to the family's worldly success. The text captures the middle-class woman at the very moment of transition between two modes of being. Mrs B. had worked – 'been in business' – alongside her husband early in their marriage; now his business is separate from their home she enjoys the appearance of leisure, but Soyer wants to make it very clear that her gentility is in no way compromised by her active involvement in all the affairs of the household. Writing only a decade later, Isabella Beeton, while no less meticulous in her outlining of the many domestic duties of the mistress of the house, has to be much more respectful of her readers' notions of their own gentility. *Household Management* is masterly in its treatment of class, offering much tactful elevation of its readers' status. The book begins with two separate chapters – one addressed to the Mistress of the house, and concerned with matters such as social calls, conversation and dress, and the other addressed to the Housekeeper, and covering issues such as accounts, ordering of servants and the keeping of the larder. In fact, virtually no middle-class household would have employed a housekeeper, unless the wife was deceased. The existence of the two chapters is more than flattery of the reader: it is part of the means by which Beeton manages to maintain the polite fiction that middle-class women need not soil their hands with physical work, while actually providing them with copious instructions for how to do such work well.

If Beeton's book pays lip service to the notion of separate spheres, it is also clearly the product of a woman who took women's work very seriously (and who worked herself in her husband's publishing enterprise throughout her short married life).[11] From its first sentence there is a determined talking-up of the status, challenge and importance of domestic management: 'As with the commander of an army, or the leader of any enterprise, so it is with the mistress of a house.' In seeing the home as a prison for middle-class women, earlier critical readings of Victorian domestic ideology tended to miss the extent to which it was also a kingdom. The sheer pleasure to be taken in being mistress of one's own domestic domain is one that is explored by a number of novelists: think of the sense of empowerment with which Esther Summerson shakes the bunch of keys that symbolize her stewardship of Bleak House, and of the exuberance with which Jane Eyre plans the preparations to welcome her cousins back home:

> My first aim will be to clean down (do you comprehend the full force of the expression?) – to clean down Moor House from chamber to cellar; my next to rub it up with beeswax, oil, and an indefinite number of cloths, till it glitters again; my third to arrange every chair, table, bed, carpet with mathematical precision, afterwards I shall go near to ruin you in coals and peat to keep up good fires in every room.[12]

It is not by chance that this description of tending to a house makes it sound like a piece of machinery – 'clean down', 'rub up', 'glittering', 'mathematical precision' – far from dividing the home off from the world of industry, the discourse of household management began to borrow its metaphors, its ideas and even its techniques. In breaking down the servants' day into fifteen minute chunks of manageable time, Mrs Beeton imitates the division of labour and rule by the clock of the Victorian factory. She also offers an enthusiastic fanfare for its products.

Cooking and entertaining

The kitchen was the place in the Victorian home where the products of the industrial revolution were most clearly in evidence. Beeton, writing at the moment when these products were beginning to be available in significant quantities, is largely in favour: she discusses the merits of commercially bottled sauces and relishes and is excited about the development of aerated bread production techniques. New cookers are described in lascivious detail, with pictures, prices and names of suppliers provided. Mrs A. B. Marshall, writing two decades later, goes much further: as well as writing best-selling cookery books, she also markets her own commercial food products and kitchen equipment – Marshall's Baking Powder,

Marshall's Crème de Riz, Marshall's Patent Freezer – as well as running a cooking school and a domestic agency.[13] These products were seized with such alacrity because they promised to save time – and, despite what advice books might profess, the time to be saved was actually the mistress's own.

If middle-class women invariably took on the role of the housekeeper, they also very often performed the function of the cook. According to Isabella Beeton's own table of servants' wages, a household would not employ a cook until they had a – substantial - annual income of about £500 a year. This would exclude all of the extremely numerous lower middle class, whose incomes were in the region of £100–£300 per annum. It is notable that Beeton herself, for almost all of her married life, employed one or two maids and no cook.[14] In practice, the mistress of the average home would do much of the cooking herself, with her maids carrying out the 'rough' work of preparation and the less delicate tasks. For an earlier generation than Beeton's, this fact was not a particularly uncomfortable one. The writer of the most important early Victorian cookery book, Eliza Acton, treated the preparation of food in a way that made it clear that creative pleasure was to be gained from the activity. Her *Modern Cookery for Private Families* (1845) provides a striking contrast with Beeton's, despite the fact that Beeton unashamedly 'borrowed' a hefty proportion of her recipes from the earlier book. Acton's prose is opinionated, colourful and meticulous, joyfully revelling in the physical experience of cooking. Beeton's is determinedly colour*less*, ruthlessly excising all adjectives, opinions and personality from the recipes and directions. This is no accident – Beeton, who obtained almost all her recipes from other sources, put an enormous amount of energy into reducing recipes to something close to scientific formulae. There was no room for personality, for variations of taste, for pleasure: the purpose was not enjoyment but efficiency.

Where there is excitement in Beeton's text is in the notion of entertaining. Food in itself is not particularly pleasurable. But there is a great deal of libidinal energy invested in the social function it can perform. Where Acton's recipes, designed for a less socially fluid, more self-confident early Victorian upper middle class, tend to be consistent in terms of expense and extravagance, Beeton's are wildly disparate. Her long chapter on Dinners and Dining juxtaposes table plans for hugely extravagant banquets – 'Bill of Fare for a Ball Supper for 60 Persons (Winter)' – with grimly practical weekly plans for 'Plain Family Dinners' which make scrupulous use of leftovers. These different models of eating are not intended for different audiences: one of the key features of the life of the mid-Victorian middle classes was that they entertained. Formal dinners would be held on at least a monthly basis, a fixed item in the household budget because they had an overt purpose: to consolidate and advance the family's social position. We can probably dismiss the plans for grand entertainments as part of Beeton's campaign of reader flattery (of a piece with the recipe for Turtle Soup – so complex and expensive that it was usually reserved for the annual Lord Mayor's Banquet, or that for Truffles in Champagne), but the fact that she devotes so much time and attention to the meal plans for dinners for eight, ten, twelve and eighteen persons suggests that she considered such events a significant part of her readers' lives. Victorian fiction is full of scenes of entertaining – from grand formal occasions in Trollope and Thackeray to those wonderful moments in Dickens when everything goes wrong: Dora and David Copperfield giving their first dinner party in their first married house and serving unopened oysters; David throwing a party in his lodgings and the landlady failing to cook the meat (though all ends well with one of the most mouth-watering scenes of *cooking* in Victorian fiction, as the whole party joins in grilling slices of meat on a gridiron over the fire). The utter familiarity of such scenes leads us to assume that the middle-class dinner party was an established convention, but in fact, as with so much else that the Victorian novel focuses on, it was a facet of culture in the process of construction, with rules and modes in a process of continual evolution. The disproportionate amount of energy given to the activity of entertaining suggests that the Victorian home, far from being the place of inward familial comfort and retreat celebrated in the 'official' domestic ideology, was in fact a place of show, a sort of theatre for the enactment of performances of successful family life.[15] The same tendency can be seen in the ways in which the home was prepared for public view.

Decorating the home

The Victorian home, as Woolf's caricature suggests, was full of stuff. Recent cultural historians have increasingly devoted attention to these 'Victorian things' (in Asa Briggs's highly influential formulation), looking at the catalogues of the 1851 Great Exhibition, at the contents of Victorian museums and amateur collections, at furniture, textiles and the hordes of display cabinets, ornaments, knick-knacks, craft-objects and souvenirs that survive from the nineteenth century, and asking how we should read both the objects themselves and the economy of their deployment in the home.[16] It is notoriously hard to make sense of the Victorian room – particularly those public rooms designed to display the family to its contemporaries. The temptation is simply to list all the heterogeneous objects – the clocks and fans and firescreens, the antimacassars and rugs and mats – that would have been found in the typical home. But just to re-amass the clutter of the Victorian interior does not get us very far in understanding its cultural significance. We need to consider where the objects came from, and the role that they play in the way the Victorian middle classes imagine themselves.

One of the most satisfying historical explanations for the rise of the apparently idle, economically unproductive middle-class woman at exactly the moment that industrialization went full throttle is that she now had a new economic function: her role was to buy things. We see in the Victorian age the birth of the modern consumer economy, with the continual proliferation and innovation of products and the development of advertising. Many goods were exported overseas, but the main British purchasers of the nation's industrial products were women. Shopping became an increasingly complex activity, and one which legitimated the presence of the respectable middle-class woman on the streets of the city. Advice books offered tips on negotiating the shopping experience: ascertaining the appropriate price for goods, dealing with shop keepers, budgeting, avoiding extravagance and exercising good taste. The last was one of the thorniest of issues, as what was tasteful was contingent on income and social mobility: it was important to avoid the drab but also the flashy. The home was an emblem of social status, but also the means of subtly advancing it. Furnishings, decoration and style needed to be up to – and perhaps a touch beyond – the mark (Mrs Ellis thought it 'scarcely necessary . . . to point out . . . the loss of character and good influence occasioned by living below our station'),[17] but not noticeably out of keeping with the householder's rank and income. Literary texts are full of examples of those who go too far. The social-climbing Veneerings in Dickens's *Our Mutual Friend* are 'bran-new people in a bran-new house in a bran-new quarter of London': 'in the Veneering establishment . . . all things were in a state of high varnish and polish. And what was observable in the furniture, was observable in the Veneerings – the surface smelt a little too much of the workshop and was a trifle sticky.'[18] Like the reproduction furniture their name references, the Veneerings look like the 'real' thing – the aristocrats and gentry whose modes and manners they imitate – but overdo it. Household furnishings are also the downfall of another couple trying to establish their place in society: Rosamond and Tertius Lydgate in George Eliot's *Middlemarch* (1871–2) bankrupt themselves buying 'essentials' for their new married home; the threat of the loss of the furniture which is so important to his wife leads Lydgate to accept a loan from the unscrupulous Bulstrode – a decision that brings him to the brink of personal and professional ruin. A number of writers express concern over the susceptibility of customers – particularly female ones – to the persuasions of shop keepers. Charles Eastlake's influential *Hints on Household Taste* (1868) is explicitly devoted to reforming the taste of women, which he sees as having been misdirected by shop keepers and upholsterers. He is particularly scathing about the influence of fashion on interior design – the idea that the newest thing is always the best. In this he is fighting a rear-guard action against the nascent operations of consumerism – and it is notable that in offering a revised aesthetic model (which favoured oak and a solid Jacobean style over curvilinear 'foreign' styles and imported woods), he himself contributes largely to the next shift in decorative fashions.

Interior design was by no means a static entity in the Victorian period – it was one of the most hotly contested of all areas of culture. The 'battle of the styles' that informed public debates about architecture had its interior dimension. There is no space here to enter into a detailed discussion of the many succeeding and overlapping decorative styles adopted, often as a heterogeneous mixture, by middle-class Victorian householders. We can simplify matters by boiling down the prevailing tastes into two broad tendencies: the first was the rococo revival of the earlier part of the century, with its taste for 'realistic' natural images: 'gigantic flowers, pansies as big as peonies; cabbage roses that deserve the name, suggesting pickle rather than perfume; gracefully falling fuchsias as big as handbells'.[19] The taste for carpets patterned with flowers was particularly reviled by the representatives of the second tendency: the group of design reformers who emerged in the 1850s in association with the Great Exhibition and the establishment of the new museum at Kensington. Notable among them was Henry Cole, whose prescriptions on taste are amply caricatured in Dickens's *Hard Times* (1845), when the 'third gentleman' visiting Gradgrind's school interrogates and instructs the hapless Sissy Jupe on the subject of carpets:

You are not to have, in any object of use or ornament, what would be a contradiction in fact. You don't walk upon flowers in fact; you cannot be allowed to walk upon flowers in carpets. You don't find that foreign birds and butterflies come and perch upon your crockery; you cannot be permitted to paint foreign birds and butterflies upon your crockery . . . This is the new discovery. This is fact. This is taste.[20]

The attitudes of design reformers coalesced in the years after the Great Exhibition into what became known as the Aesthetic Movement, with its rediscovery of the medieval and artisanal, its belief in functionality and material 'honesty' and its avoidance of direct natural imitation. Most of the commentators on aesthetics who emerged from the late 1850s onwards belonged to this tendency – John Ruskin, William Morris, Charles Eastlake and William Pater to name the most significant. As well as being heavily influenced by their idealized version of the medieval, the ideas of the design reformers were significantly formed by the stylized natural images of first India and later Japan. Indian designs featured heavily in the objects shown at the Great Exhibition (a whole treatise could be written on the cultural place of the Indian shawl in mid-Victorian Britain); Japanese designs began to appear as trade with Japan opened up in the late 1850s, with fans and distinctive blue and white china proving particularly popular (Arthur Liberty was highly impressed by the stand of Japanese objects at the London exhibition of 1862, and his department store became one of the foremost importers of such goods).[21] Large numbers of the objects thronging the Victorian interior were of foreign origin: Indian screens, Japanese fans, oriental china, souvenirs from all over Europe and the empire. Critics are divided on how to read this accumulation of foreign objects, with some, including David Brett, seeing it as 'the face of imperial rapacity', and others arguing that the foreign object has a more ambiguous presence in the Victorian home –'tamed' of its exoticism but simultaneously an emblem of 'otherness', of a life beyond the domestic sphere. As such, it might be said to function as an icon of imaginative escape for women (just as the young Jane Eyre, unhappily enclosed in Gateshead Hall, reads Bewick's *History of British Birds* for its exhilarating depiction of the arctic wastes).[22]

One reason for the massive proliferation of objects in the Victorian home is the rapidity with which the women of the house produced them. The following is a brief selection of the domestic objects for which patterns are given in one needlework guide of the period: wall pockets, handkerchief cases, postcard cases, stools, wastepaper baskets, cushions, lamp mats, chair backs, pen-wipers, ornamental meat safes, mantel borders, chair covers, napkin rings, letter bags, manuscript bags, portfolios, magazine racks, antimacassars, firescreens, woodbaskets, bootbags, window blinds, tables (with the embroidery nailed down with decorative studs), card baskets, photograph stands, serviettes, napkins, doilies, bed linen and glass cloths.[23] Such objects far outweigh any other category of needlework in the book: there are a few instructions for personal items such as handbags, slippers and clothes, but the home, rather than the people in it, was by far the greatest beneficiary of the craft of its female occupants. Most striking of all is the huge number of needleworked objects designed to aid in the occupation of needlework: pincushions, work bags, work baskets, needlebooks, scissor cases and thimble holders testify to something disturbingly circular in this most fundamental of Victorian feminine occupations.

Fancy work

Anyone researching Victorian domestic crafts will be quickly overwhelmed by their plenitude. Every women's magazine offered patterns and instructions for crafts and books on the subject abounded. It is not possible to give an exhaustive list of the crafts practised at even a representative moment in the nineteenth century; the forms of needlework alone could easily fill a six-volume work such as the 1882 *Dictionary of Needlework*, which, among thousands of others, has entries on Aloe Thread Embroidery, Antwerp Lace, Appliqué upon Satin, Bead Mosaic Work, Berlin Work, Braid Work, Brighton Towelling Embroidery, Carnival Lace, Carrickmacross Guipre Lace, China Ribbon Embroidery, Crochet, Knitting, Macramé, Drawn Work and Tatting. Other popular crafts included shellwork (making flowers, and decorating boxes with shells), pokerwork (burning patterns on wooden objects with a red-hot poker), marquetry (the construction of pictures out of thin veneers of differently coloured woods) and the making of wax flowers and fruits.

Fancy work, like home decoration, was a much-debated facet of Victorian culture. Sarah Ellis, at the beginning of the period, worried that middle-class women would adopt the indolence and self-gratificatory habits of the aristocracy along with their occupations. Her solution was that women should craft only in the proper spirit – for other people.

It is almost certainly due to the influence of Ellis and other evangelical writers that so little space proportionately is given in books and journals to fancy work to adorn the self. Middle-class needlework was to be devoted towards the comfort of the family; it was to be a crucial element in that process of continually re-making the home: '[Needlework] brings daily blessings to every home, unnoticed, perhaps, because of its hourly silent application; for in a household every stitch is one for comfort to some person or other and without its ever watchful care home would be a scene of discomfort indeed.'[24] Ellis's writings made overt something that was implicit in all the conflicting discourses about women's domestic activity: that needlework was *work*. 'Work', indeed, is the term most often used in literary texts to describe the craft activities of women. Yet the phrase 'fancy work' is richly self-contradictory, with the adjective challenging the noun with its implications of something trivial, purely decorative, and also in its sense of imaginative excess. Work is serious, real; the fancy is excessive, unnecessary. The duality of the term contains within it some of the many ideological complications posed by women's activities at home. For Ellis, it was important that needlework be defined as a form of work rather than pleasure – but work that carried no financial reward; that was, in fact, a solid sign of familial affection, a mark of a woman's love. But as a sign of upward mobility, needlework had another, contradictory function to perform: it had to stand as a emblem of leisure, an indication that the family was sufficiently advanced in rank that the woman of the house did not have to labour. Poised between these apparently contradictory imperatives to duty and to pleasurable excess, needlework had a great deal of ideological work to manage.

Many commentators worried about the effect of needlework on its practitioners. Women writers employ a repeated trope in which the needle is compared to the pen – the one an instrument of enforced passivity and wasted talent, the other a source of emancipation. For Elizabeth Barrett Browning's eponymous writer-heroine Aurora Leigh, needlework is institutionalized time-wasting, a symbolizing of the futility and irrelevance of women's lives:

> The works of women are symbolical.
> We sew, sew, prick our fingers, dull our sight,
> Producing what? A pair of slippers, sir,
> To put on when you're weary – or a stool
> To stumble over and vex you . . . 'curse that stool!'

Or else at best, a cushion, where you lean
And sleep, and dream of something we are not
But would be for your sake. Alas, alas!
This hurts most, this – that, after all, we are paid
The worth of our work, perhaps.[25]

This comes as the culmination of a passage on the emptiness of female education, sharply counterbalancing the writerly education that Aurora surreptitiously supplies for herself. In a verse-novel deeply concerned with the social, emotional and economic price at which women's freedom might be bought, Aurora's futile stitching contrasts with the stitching of another woman – the working-class Marian Earle, whose life threatens to follow the conventional Victorian narrative of the sempstress – seduced, ruined and ending in prostitution and death. For nineteenth-century feminists, the trope of the middle-class woman's symbolic enslavement to her needle is always haunted by the resolutely unsymbolic slavery of another class of stitchers.[26] In many women's novels needlework functions as an index of character – rebellious women rail against its petty, painstaking demands, while the more conventionally feminine are happy, or at least willing, to devote themselves to its intricacies: so in Charlotte Brontë's *Shirley* (1849), Caroline Helstone endures many hours of wearisome stitching under the watchful eye of her aunt, while the rebellious Shirley refuses to stitch at all, until she falls in love with the socially inferior Louis Moore and accords him the mastery she had previously assumed herself. It is at this point that she is to be seen sewing: 'Mr Moore leaned back in his chair, and folded his arms across his chest; Miss Keeldar resumed her square of silk canvas, and continued the creation of a wreath of Parmese violets.'[27] The embroidery functions as a prop by means of which Shirley can conduct a masquerade of feminine meekness, allowing a symbolic transfer of power. Novelists and artists are fascinated by the postural implications of stitching: the dutifully bent head that reveals the erotically charged nape of the neck; the still body contrasted with the busy hands; the woman physically present yet also inwardly absorbed.

If embroidery represented a conventionally feminine passivity, in the second half of the period it began also to represent a direct form of empowerment, as it started to be possible for a respectable woman to earn money through her labour without automatically losing caste. The Art Needlework movement, founded by the Royal School of Needlework, established a discourse of needlework as an ancient and sophisticated art which to some extent disguised the School's primarily commercial function.[28] Impoverished gentlewomen could see themselves akin to the talented medieval ladies whose crewelwork the School revived. From about the 1860s onwards, we increasingly find textual representations of middle-class women earning through their needle. The virtuous Meyrick sisters in *Daniel Deronda* (1876) are first depicted in an iconic portrayal of home, the ideality of which is not undermined by the fact that their crafts are designed for the market:

> Mrs Meyrick's house was not noisy: the front parlour looked on the river, and the back on gardens, so that though she was reading aloud to her daughters, the window could be left open to freshen the air of the small double room where a lamp and two candles were burning. The candles were on a table apart for Kate, who was drawing illustrations for a publisher; the lamp was not only for the reader but for Amy and Mab, who were embroidering satin cushions for 'the great world'.[29]

For the 'New Woman' novelist Sarah Grand, writing at the end of the century in *The Beth Book* (1897), art needlework and writing are equally valorized as means for her heroine to buy her way out of her abusive marriage.

What sense are we to make of the overflowing excess of women's handicrafts as both activity and objects? Feminist historians of the 1960s and 1970s were inclined to read middle-class women's crafts as a shameful index of their oppression, a useless repetitive activity designed to keep them busy and out of trouble.[30] But explanations that see craft work straightforwardly as an instrument of patriarchy ignore the extent to which it was frowned on by social commentators, its products mocked and reviled.[31] They also leave out of account the creative pleasure that many Victorian women seem to have taken in these activities. A materialist explanation for the over determined nature of fancy work might look to its relation to the industrial revolution. It is surely no accident that at exactly the moment that mass-produced goods became cheaply and widely available, the middle classes developed a taste for the home-made and hand-made article. Yet domestic handicrafts were not simply positioned in an antithetical relationship to the mass-produced object: they made use, to a striking extent, of industrial products. The fabric and thread they used was produced using the bright new aniline dyes, while other popular crafts involved gluing printed images to screens and boxes, embroidering over printed fabric, making lace from machine-made ribbon and so on. Domestic handicrafts re-made and re-humanized the industrial product. Conversely, many other crafts took objects from nature – shells, feathers, flowers, beetles' wings, fish scales – and made from them objects that resembled the mass produced. In this sense, the Victorian fancy-worker stands at the intersection of the industrial and natural worlds, re-making and harmonizing their products with her (unacknowledged) labour.

Constantly in a process of being re-made and re-imagined, both the Victorian home and the woman who makes it are required to perform acts of ideological transformation: the woman enacting a masquerade of leisure even as she ceaselessly labours; the house performing as a stage set on which dramas of social stability and unchanging domestic bliss could be enacted. Together they are a machine that re-forms the brash new products of the industrial age into something altogether more soothing to the nation's self image.

Notes

1 Virginia Woolf, *Orlando* (Oxford: Oxford University Press, 1992), 218.

2 Sarah Ellis, *The Women of England: Their Social Duties and Domestic Habits* (London: Fisher, 1845), 30.

3 Christopher Ricks (ed.), *The Poems of Tennyson* (London: Longmans, 1969), 188–90.

4 See Monica F. Cohen, *Professional Domesticity in the Victorian Novel: Women, Work and Home* (Cambridge: Cambridge University Press, 1998); Elizabeth Langland, 'Nobody's Angels: Domestic Ideology and Middle-Class Women in the Victorian Novel, *PMLA*, 107 (1992), 290–304; Amanda Vickery, 'Historiographical Review: Golden Age to Separate Spheres? A Review of the Categories and Chronology of English Women's History', *Historical Journal*, 36 (1993), 383–414.

5 See the work on Sarah Ellis in Karen Chase and Michael Levenson, *The Spectacle of Intimacy: A Public Life for the Victorian Family* (Princeton: Princeton University Press, 2000), and my own work on Isabella Beeton in *Culinary Pleasures: Cookbooks and the Transformation of British Food* (London: Faber, 2005), and in my edition of *Household Management* (Oxford: Oxford University Press, 2000).

6 John Ruskin, 'Of Queens' Gardens', in *Sesame and Lilies: Two Lectures* (London: Smith, Elder, 1865), 149.

7 Charles Dickens *Our Mutual Friend* (London: Chapman and Hall, 1903–7), 796.

8 Dena Attar's *Bibliography of Household Books Published in Britain 1800–1914* (London: Prospect Books, 1987), lists more than 500 books.

9 The 1851 census recorded 272,000 professional workers; that in 1871 showed three times as many.

10 His other works included *The Gastronomic Regenerator* (1846), addressed to the chefs of the upper classes, and *Shilling Cookery for the People* (1854) which attempted to reform the diet of the poor.

11 Isabella was married at twenty, wrote *Household Management* in her early twenties, gave birth to four children and was dead before her twenty-ninth birthday.

12 Charlotte Brontë, *Jane Eyre* (Harmondsworth: Penguin, 1985), 416.

13 Agnes Marshall, *Mrs A. B. Marshall's Cookery Book* (London: Simpkin, Marshall, Hamilton, Kent, 1888).

14 Isabella Beeton, *Mrs Beeton's Book of Household Management*, ed. Nicola Humble (Oxford: Oxford World's Classics, 2000), 15–16. See also my notes on the economic issues raised by this table, 576.

15 Chase and Levenson pursue a similar line of thought in *The Spectacle of Intimacy*.

16 See Asa Briggs, *Victorian Things* (London: Batsford, 1988); Steve Dillon, 'Victorian Interior', *Modern Language Quarterly*, 62 (2001), 83–115; Inga Bryden and Janet Flood (eds.), *Domestic Space: Reading the Nineteenth-Century Interior* (Manchester: Manchester University Press, 1999); Andrew H. Miller, *Novels behind Glass: Commodity Culture and Victorian Narrative* (Cambridge: Cambridge University Press, 1995).

17 Sarah Ellis, *The Wives of England: Their Relative Duties, Domestic Influence, & Social Obligations* (London: Fisher, 1843), 219.

18 Dickens, *Our Mutual Friend*, 20.

19 Reverend T. James, 'Church Work for Ladies: A Paper Read to the Architectural Society of the Archdeaconry of Northampton', *The Ecclesiologist*, 16 (1855), 379, cited in B. Morris, *Victorian Embroidery* (London: Jenkins, 1962), 26.

20 Charles Dickens, *Hard Times* (Harmondsworth: Penguin, 1985), 52. Cole apparently took the caricature with good humour – see his letter to Dickens, 17 June 1854.

21 Briggs, *Victorian Things*, 85.

22 David Brett, *On Decoration* (Cambridge: Lutterworth, 1992), 42; Susan Stewart, *On Longing: Narratives of the Miniature, the Gigantic, the Souvenir and the Collection* (Durham, NC: Duke University Press, 1993), 148; Thad Logan, *The Victorian Parlour* (Cambridge: Cambridge University Press, 2001), 196–7.

23 S. F. A. Caulfield and Blanche C. Saward, *The Dictionary of Needlework: An Encyclopaedia of Artistic, Plain, and Fancy Needlework*, 6 vols. (2nd edn, London: Cowan, 1884–7).

24 Mrs Warren and Mrs Pullen, *Treasures in Needlework* (London: Ward Lock, 1855), cited in Rozsika Parker, *The Subversive Stitch: Embroidery and the Making of the Feminine* (London: The Women's Press, 1984), 154.

25 Elizabeth Barrett Browning, *Aurora Leigh* (1856), Book I, ll. 456–65.

26 On the subject of those for whom needlework was work rather than domestic art see Beth Harris (ed.), *Famine and Fashion: Needlewomen in the Nineteenth Century* (Aldershot: Ashgate, 2005); and Lynn M. Alexander, *Women, Work, and Representation: Needlewomen in Victorian Art and Literature* (Columbus: Ohio University Press, 2003).

27 Charlotte Brontë, *Shirley* (Harmondsworth: Penguin, 1974), 477.

28 Lady Alford, one of the founders of the school, bolstered its position with her weighty study of *Needlework as Art* (London: Sapson Low, Marston, Searle and Rivington, 1886).

29 George Eliot, *Daniel Deronda* (Harmondsworth: Penguin, 1995), 196.

30 See, for example, Jenni Calder, *The Victorian Home* (London: Batsford, 1977), 105.

31 Including, energetically, by Ruskin in, for instance, 'Of Queens' Gardens'.

13

Victorian literary theory

It is the fashion to try to trace things to remote origins, and show more or less plausibly how complex products have evolved from beginnings held for simple, – we say held for simple, because the egg is in reality as complex as the chick; and as Dogberry said, 'it will go near to be thought so' before long.[1]

Readers of Victorian culture may feel that they have a pretty good idea of what Victorian literary theory looks like. Compared to our own 'complex' theories, derived from post-structural thinkers including Derrida, Foucault, Jameson, Bhabha and Butler, the Victorians' theory seems 'simple' by comparison: evaluative and prescriptive, concerned aesthetically and morally with what literature 'should' do. Skirmishes including Robert Buchanan's assault on 'The Fleshly School of Poetry' and Dante Rossetti's response, 'The Stealthy School of Criticism', for example, are entertaining to read; they present thinly veiled personal attacks on the poet coupled with sarcastic commentary on the poetry itself. Buchanan attacks Rossetti for his sonnet 'Nuptial Sleep':

> Here is a full-grown man, presumably intelligent and cultivated, putting on record for other full-grown men to read, the most secret mysteries of sexual connection, and that with so sickening a desire to reproduce the sensual mood . . . that we merely shudder at the shameless nakedness. We are no purists in such matters . . . but it is neither poetic, nor manly, nor even human, to obtrude such things as themes of whole poems. It is simply nasty.[2]

Unsurprisingly, Rossetti felt impelled to respond in kind; in his essay he outs Buchanan, who wrote 'The Fleshly School' under a pseudonym, accusing him (not untruthfully) of quoting out of context and, worse, of using his pen names to write favourable reviews of his own work.[3]

These exchanges look very little like our critical 'conversations' today, which develop or challenge theoretical positions of previous critics and rarely if ever make evaluative judgements about the quality of the writing, either of the literary or the theoretical texts they discuss. Our own debates may or may not have personal animus underlying them, but if they do, it is unlikely to be evident in the texts themselves. How is it, one might ask, that we have so far 'evolved' from 'naïve' criticism like Buchanan's to our current theoretical sophistication? The answer, to borrow from W. B. Rands's 1880 essay 'The New Fiction', is that 'the egg is in reality as complex as the chick', and we should not assume that the Victorians' literary theory *was* more naïve than ours.

We should, rather, understand that narratives of the progressive development of literary studies, however historically accurate they may be, are also, as Kathy Psomiades notes in '"The Lady of Shalott" and the Critical Fortunes of Victorian Poetry', 'rhetorically satisfying'.[4] The satisfaction of 'today's' theorist comes from his or her superior relation to past theorists. For example: in the 1920s and 1930s the New Critics (unfairly) devalued much Victorian literature as simple, naïve, sentimental and 'commercial', whereas they privileged substantial portions of modernist literature as complex, sophisticated, ironic and 'difficult'. The advent of cultural studies in the latter decades of the twentieth century allowed scholars to appreciate the Victorians anew: to see the complexities of their social discourses and to value their literature as part of those discourses – on empire, the Woman Question, industrialization, religion, evolution and so forth. Within this progressive narrative it is difficult to 'rediscover' the sophistication of the Victorians' theory without also accusing the New Critics, and even more recent twentieth- and twenty-first-century scholars, of overlooking their complexity; this difficulty leads to some interesting equivocation. As Edwin Eigner and George Worth write in the introduction to their anthology *Victorian Criticism of the Novel*: 'It has become usual to begin such discussions as this by contesting the traditional view that there was no valuable criticism of British fiction before Henry James. Both commonplaces, the usual *and* the traditional are valid.'[5]

One of the problems with taking the 'traditional' view of Henry James as the origin of 'valuable' literary theory is that in doing so one takes him at his own word. As he writes in 'The Art of Fiction': 'Only a very short time ago it might have been supposed that the English novel . . . had no air of having a theory, a conviction, a consciousness of itself behind it.'[6] Undoubtedly in defining psychological realism James articulates something nascent in fiction in the latter decades of the nineteenth century, and certainly this shift to psychological reality, in opposition to 'incident', became one of the defining features of modernist writers including Virginia Woolf. But, it is important to understand that James is taking a rhetorical position, just as critics before and after him, likewise, have articulated their own projects as improvements on those of their predecessors and 'retrograde' contemporaries. In fact, his 'new' theory was the outgrowth of lively, far-reaching debates throughout the nineteenth century about the role of literature in culture.

Recent scholarship including Amanda Anderson's *The Powers of Distance* (2001), David Wayne Thomas's *Cultivating Victorians* (2004) and Suzy Anger's *Victorian Interpretation* (2005) examines the Victorians' critical concerns and draws connections between nineteenth-century and current literary theory. As Anger argues: 'In contemporary debate, self-reflexivity about the processes of understanding is pervasive: knowledge is historically and culturally situated . . . subjectivity is involved in all representation; in short interpretation is always at work. What is not so often noticed is that Victorians were equally concerned with the general character of human knowledge and understanding.'[7] Likewise in this chapter I present a view of Victorian literary theory in which the 'remote origins' of our own theories are not as distant as they might seem. Victorian literary theory, like the post-structural and cultural studies theories that inform literary studies today, was deeply concerned with literature's ability to produce culture and with literature's relationship to subjectivity, knowledge and representation.

A couple of things will be useful in understanding Victorian literary theory: context and genre. In the first place, readers of Victorian literary theory would do well to pay attention to the ways in which pieces of literary theory reached the public. For example, John Ruskin's influential *Sesame and Lilies* (1865) was originally delivered as lectures, as were Thomas Carlyle's *Heroes and Hero-Worship* (1841), William Morris's 'Art, Wealth, and Riches' (1883) and 'Of the Origins of Ornamental Art' (1886), and Anthony Trollope's 'On the Higher Education of Women' (1869) and 'On English Prose Fiction as a Rational Amusement' (1870). In other words, issues of literacy, literature, art and culture were pervasive in the public consciousness throughout the Victorian period, and literary authors and critics appeared as public authorities, their works constituting current events as well as interventions in literary discourse.

Likewise, the growth of literacy in the nineteenth century, which occurred concomitantly with the proliferation of the periodical press,[8] meant not just that questions of reading practices and populations were important to Victorian thinkers but that literary theories were being articulated, often self-reflexively, in a wider and wider array of media, addressing a wider and wider range of audiences. Literary criticism was a regular feature of journals from the conservative *Blackwood's Edinburgh Magazine* to the radical *Westminster Review*, and the 'family-oriented' *Cornhill Magazine*. Some of the most famous pieces of theory were originally published, in part or in whole, in periodicals, including Matthew Arnold's 'The Function of Criticism at the Present Time' (1864) and *Culture and Anarchy* (1869), Walter Pater's *The Renaissance* (1873), Henry James's 'The Art of Fiction' (1884) and Oscar Wilde's 'The Critic as Artist' (1891). Moreover, many literary critics were also authors of political and economic treatises (John Stuart Mill, Walter Bagehot), of social theory and art criticism (John Ruskin, William Morris), of psychological and philosophical essays (E. S. Dallas, G. H. Lewes). Many theorists were themselves literary authors (Matthew Arnold, George Eliot, Margaret Oliphant, George Meredith, William Morris and Oscar Wilde). And their works often spoke across disciplines and genres to one another even as they addressed different specialized and general audiences.

Yet, readers today are far more likely to have experienced these texts either as stand-alone books, or in the collected works of their authors, or, more problematically, as excerpts in anthologies. As Mark Turner notes: 'Periodicals scholars have long argued against the smash-and-grab approach to using the material, pointing out the intellectual limitations of going to a title, pulling out a specific contribution from it, and using it in isolation from any discussion about its periodical source.'[9] In other words, one gains a more nuanced understanding of individual pieces of literary criticism by examining them within the context of the entire periodical, including advertisements, illustrations, literary instalments, legal and political discussion, scientific debates and so forth. In this way, we can see more clearly the interconnections among myriad social and literary discourses. And, asking questions of the publishing practices of journals allows scholars to form a more comprehensive idea of how an essay might fit into these discourses. What audiences are addressed by the publication? What political sympathies or editorial 'vision' did the journal have? Did it publish its essays anonymously, or were its authors' identities known to the public?

With the growing availability of digitized texts, online in archives and through initiatives including Google Books and the Internet Archive, students and scholars will find it increasingly easy to explore these questions.[10] A search in Google Books, for example, for William Morris's socialist essay 'Art, Wealth, and Riches' yields an 1883 issue of the *Manchester Quarterly*, where the essay first appeared in print, after having been delivered as a lecture at the 'joint conversazione' of the Manchester Literary Club, the Manchester Academy of Fine Arts and the Manchester Art Museum Committee. The essay was published alongside the following (among other things): an essay 'Concerning Style', by Alfred Owen Legge, author of *The Growth of the Temporal Power of the Papacy* (1870) and, pseudonymously, the novel *Manslaughter: A Chronicle* (1876); an analysis, 'On Some Marginalia Made by Dante G. Rossetti in a Copy of Keats' Poems', by George Milner, president of the Manchester Literary Club and apologist for the Lancashire dialect poets; a description of 'The Marquis Morante: His Library and Catalogue', by Richard Copley Christie, bibliophile, philanthropist and reviewer for the *Spectator*. What might be gleaned from the convergence of these authors, subjects and the social, political and aesthetic interests they represent? How was the readership of the *Manchester Quarterly* influenced by these essays together? How did these authors envision their own criticism as cultural work? These are questions readers of Victorian literary theory, particularly outside England, would have found it much more difficult even to have asked before the issue was digitized. But, as I will argue, these kinds of questions were fundamental to the Victorians' own literary and theoretical projects. In the following three sections, I will examine (1) productive theories of literature, or theories about how literature makes subjects; (2) embedded theories, or self-referential theories that were articulated within the literature itself; (3) theories about theory, or Victorians' meditations on literary criticism itself as a genre and as an intellectual and cultural practice.

Productive theories

I want you to feel, with me, that whatever advantages we possess in the present day in the diffusion of education and of literature, can only be rightly used by any of us when we have apprehended clearly what education is to lead to, and literature to teach.[11]

Many Victorian literary theories are concerned with the power literature has to shape subjects and, by extension, society. This idea is central to John Ruskin's *Sesame and Lilies,* which originally comprised the two lectures on reading 'Of Kings' Treasuries' and 'Of Queens' Gardens', and to Matthew Arnold's *Culture and Anarchy*, which became one of the foundational apologies for the importance of liberal arts education as it still operates – or endeavours to – in some university curricula today.

In *Culture and Anarchy* Arnold defines culture as 'the pursuit of light and perfection, which . . . consist, not in resting and being, but in growing and becoming, in a perpetual advance in beauty and wisdom'.[12] He argues that the '*study of perfection*' produces 'the moral and social passion for doing good'.[13] In other words, an appreciation for culture, or 'the *best* knowledge and thought of the time', leads to the refinement of civilization and, thus, away from anarchy.[14] For Arnold the pursuit of culture is the cultivation of 'disinterestedness' – that is, a mode of active intellectual inquiry unhampered by the personal prejudices, partisan loyalties and unexamined beliefs that foster complacency.

In *Sesame and Lilies* Ruskin criticizes the worship of wealth and, like Arnold, extols the 'cultural capital' offered by books as the means not just of self-improvement, but of social progress. In 'Of Kings' Treasuries', he remarks: 'the more I see of our national faults and miseries, the more they resolve themselves into conditions of childish illiterateness and want of education in the most ordinary habits of thought'.[15] Ruskin's two lectures offer gender-specific guidelines for reading that are founded in 'natural' differences between the sexes, but, according to him, both kinds of 'correct' reading will teach individuals sympathy, which he defines as 'the "tact" or "touch-faculty", of body and soul . . . fineness and fulness of sensation, beyond reason; – the guide and sanctifier of reason itself', and, thereby, allow England to address social ills.[16]

Today *Culture and Anarchy* and *Sesame and Lilies* may strike readers as old-fashioned or elitist. Arnold's work has served as a bulwark of the 'Great Books Curriculum', which largely excludes works by women and minorities. And *Sesame and Lilies* – especially 'Of Queens' Gardens' – has often been held up as an example of the 'conservative' doctrine of the separate spheres, though this view has now been comprehensively challenged.[17] Yet, both sat (however uneasily) at the intersection of multiple Victorian discourses on gender, class, education and culture. Both seem to express anxiety about individuals' 'unconscious' susceptibility to cultural influences, even as they suggest that the right kind of culture has

the power to train individuals to be critically observant of, while ethically invested in, the world around them. Both understand literature
as bound up in contemporary social issues and they grapple with questions of individual agency in relation to productive power/knowledge in
ways similar to those we see today in Foucauldian and post-Foucauldian
scholarship.[18]

Arnold's and Ruskin's texts are, perhaps, the most famous articula-
tions of a Victorian theory of cultural production, but numerous other
theorists proposed a link between the cultivation of literary taste and
the progress of civilization. In 'What is Poetry?' John Stuart Mill argues
that an appreciation for poetry, as opposed to fiction, represents not just
psychological maturity in individuals but a more advanced level of civilization: 'In what stage of the progress of society . . . is storytelling most
valued, and the story teller in greatest request and honour? In a rude state;
like that of the Tartars and Arabs at this day, and of almost all nations
in the earliest ages.'[19] Similarly, if more humorously, Eliza Cook argues
in 'People Who Do Not Like Poetry' that these flawed people 'know not
that poetry is co-existent with a flourishing state and a great people' and
concludes: 'They may be useful and necessary – so may the cholera; but
in honest simplicity, we desire to keep clear of both afflictions.'[20] Mill
and Cook echoed earlier Romantic period views of the poet as someone,
in Arthur Henry Hallam's words, 'whose senses told them a richer and
ampler tale than most men could understand' and of poetry as the con-
duit whereby ordinary people could 'understand [the poet's] expressions
and sympathize with his state'.[21]

Apologists for the novel, likewise, staked out cultural terrain. George
Eliot, in 'Silly Novels by Lady Novelists' (1856), argues that realist fiction, as opposed to didactic novels of the '*mind-and-millinery* species', is
conducive to cultural refinement.[22] According to Eliot, the hubris of the
under-educated lady novelists – who believe their partial grasp of philosophical, political and social issues authorizes them to instruct others –
not only produces bad fiction, but amounts to a breakdown of culture. 'A
really cultured woman', Eliot writes,

> does not make [her knowledge] a pedestal from which she flatters
> herself she commands a complete view of men and things, but makes
> it a point of observation from which to form a right estimate of
> herself . . . She does not give you information, which is the raw
> material of culture, – she gives you sympathy, which is its subtlest
> essence.[23]

Moreover, Eliot argues, for readers to accept 'silly' novels from lady novelists is to accept that women are not capable of better and to contribute to women's continued social denigration. George Meredith in his 1877 *An Essay on Comedy* makes a similar feminist claim for comedy (which he defines as salutary social critique). Meredith argues that women cannot be free in societies that prefer sentimental or melodramatic fiction to comedy: 'There has been fun in Bagdad. But there never will be civilization where comedy is not possible; and that comes of some degree of social equality of the sexes.' He urges 'cultivated women to recognize that the comic Muse is one of their best friends'.[24] Meredith's progressive view of literary consumption engages with evolutionary theories of culture articulated by men of science including Charles Darwin, Herbert Spencer and Francis Galton.[25]

The flip side of these progressive-productive theories of literature can be seen in rhetoric about the ability of 'bad' literature to 'poison' its readers, the best-known instance of which is the furore surrounding sensation novels in the 1860s. Margaret Oliphant argues in 'Sensation Novels' (1862) that novels including Wilkie Collins's *The Woman in White* (1860) and Ellen Wood's *East Lynne* (1861) are dangerous because they make bad behaviour exciting and attractive. This danger, she argues, is exacerbated by 'the violent stimulant of serial publication – of *weekly* publication, with its necessity for frequent and rapid recurrence of piquant situation and startling incident'.[26] Oliphant claims, likewise, in 'Novels' (1867) that 'light' popular literature written by women is dangerous precisely because we might be inclined to doubt its ability to influence:

> It may be possible to laugh at the notion that books so entirely worthless, so far as literary merit are concerned, should affect any reader injuriously . . . but the fact that this new and disgusting picture of what professes to be the female heart, comes from the hands of women, and is tacitly accepted by them as real, is not in any way to be laughed at.[27]

What Oliphant decries is sensational literature's ability to be more exciting than 'the monotony of ordinary life',[28] and, through repeated exposure, to distort (female) readers' sensibilities, and to lead, thereby, to social degeneration.

Similarly, in *Fiction, Fair and Foul*, which appeared in *The Nineteenth Century* in instalments between June 1880 and October 1881, Ruskin connects the taste for 'literature "of the prison house"' to the degeneration of modern urban society. With much more pessimism than he shows in *Sesame and Lilies*, Ruskin argues that

> the thwarted habits of body and mind, which are the punishment of reckless crowding in cities, become, in the issue of that punishment, frightful subjects of exclusive interest to themselves; and the art of fiction in which they finally delight is only the more studied arrangement and illustration . . . of the daily bulletins of their own wretchedness.[29]

Using Dickens's *Bleak House* as an example, he claims that modern fiction's preoccupation with death and suffering is the result of the 'hot fermentation and unwholesome secrecy of the population crowded into large cities'.[30] Ruskin's distaste for urbanization is linked to his nostalgia for the 'wholesome' literature of authors including Sir Walter Scott – or at least Scott's early work before his agrarian sensibility was 'destroyed, by the modern conditions of commercial excitement'.[31] And, as his metaphor of compost heap decay shows, Ruskin saw literature as organically, if tragically, connected to social ills.

It is true that a literary theorist today would be unlikely to suggest that one genre can produce the right kind of culture, or that another genre can destroy it, but in these examples we can see that the Victorians' concern with the complex interconnections among publishing and reading practices, access to 'culture' and individual agency are not unlike those that inform much Victorian scholarship, and more general reflections on the role of literature in culture, today. In short, the essays discussed here are all about how literature *makes* subjects and, in turn, has the power to aid (or impede) civilization.

'Embedded' theories

> The successful application of any art is a delightful spectacle, but the theory, too, is interesting.[32]

In 'The Art of Fiction' Henry James remarks that

> it would take more courage than I possess to intimate that the form of the novel, as Dickens and Thackeray . . . saw it, had any taint of incompleteness. It was, however, *naïf* . . . and, evidently, if it is destined to suffer in any way for having lost its *naïveté*, it has now an idea of making sure of the corresponding advantages.[33]

Dickens and Thackeray, he claims, wrote when 'there was a comfortable, good-humoured feeling abroad that a novel is a novel, as a pudding is a pudding, and that this was an end of it'.[34] Yet, a novel like *Vanity Fair* (1848) seems very much to have 'an air of having a theory' about novels and novel readers. Indeed, some of the most interesting examples of literary theory from the period appear in the literature itself. Far from offering the intellectual equivalent of dessert to an unreflective readership, much Victorian literature, rather, demands that readers engage in rigorous analysis – of text and self alike.

In Chapter VI of *Vanity Fair* the narrator begins with the disclaimer: 'I know the tune I am piping is a very mild one (although there are some terrific chapters coming presently), and must beg the good-natured reader to remember, that we are only discoursing at present about a stockbroker's family in Russell Square'. He remarks,

> We should easily have constructed a tale of thrilling interest, through the fiery chapters of which the reader should hurry, panting. But my readers must hope for no such romance, only a homely story, and must be content with a chapter about Vauxhall, which is so short it scarcely deserves to be called a chapter at all. And yet it is a chapter, and a very important one too. Are not there little chapters in everybody's life, that seem to be nothing, and yet affect all the rest of the history?[35]

This passage plays with multiple meanings: chapters of books and chapters of life are collapsed so that book chapters that do not, formally speaking, fit the definition of a chapter are authorized because they mimic life chapters which, because real, fail to conform to novelistic conventions. The story *Vanity Fair* presents is not a romance, but only a humble story; however, by the end of the passage, it is more than a story; it is a history.

Thackeray's digression from the plot is the very thing that Henry James calls 'a betrayal of a sacred office' in 'The Art of Fiction'.[36] However, the detour does more than destroy the illusion that real events are being narrated. Here, as throughout the novel – even from the subtitle, 'A Novel Without a Hero' – Thackeray asks his readers to think about form as well as content: with whom does one identify in a novel without a hero? What should a chapter look like if not like the Vauxhall chapter? What might be the trade-offs for reading a sensational romance, as opposed to a 'mild' story about a 'stockbroker's family in Russell Square'? By calling attention to his refusal to provide the familiar conventions that his readers may expect or desire Thackeray demands that readers examine the power of literature to fabricate those expectations and desires.

If Thackeray proposes realism as a superior means of shaping subjects, Robert Browning in his long poem *The Ring and the Book* (1868–9) suggests that the subjective nature of experience renders truth in representation impossible. In his 1912 lecture 'The Novel in "The Ring and the Book"', Henry James praises Browning's poem *as* a novel, thus recasting Oscar Wilde's snide comment in 'The Critic as Artist' (1891) that '[George] Meredith is a prose Browning, and so is Browning.'[37] As Herbert Tucker notes, James admired '[t]he staging that Browning gave to his poem's inescapably documentary and hermeneutic origins'.[38] Ironically, James admires in Browning the same kind of self-reflexivity that he derides in novelists like Thackeray and Trollope.

The Ring and the Book is the story of the seventeenth-century trial of Count Guido Franceschini for the murder of his wife Pompilia. Franceschini's defence rested on accusing his wife of adultery with a priest, Giuseppi Caponsacchi, while the prosecution argued that Caponsacchi had helped Pompilia escape from the Count's abuse. The source for the story was an old volume of trial documents that Browning found in a used bookstall in Florence. What is most interesting, theoretically speaking, is Browning's treatment of the source documents and the process by which he transforms them into his creative work. Book I of the twelve-book poem describes the finding of the 'Old Yellow Book' in the bookstall. The poet-speaker, likening the writing of the poem to forging a gold ring, tells his auditors:

> From the book, yes; thence bit by bit I dug
> The lingot truth, that memorable day,
> Assayed and knew my piecemeal gain was gold, –
> Yes; but from something else surpassing that,
> Something of mine, which, mixed up with the mass,
> Made it bear hammer and be firm to file.
> Fancy with fact is just one fact the more;
> To-wit, that fancy has informed, transpierced,
> Thridded and so thrown fast the facts else free.[39]

Browning, accordingly, gives his reader a layered effect: we are reading him reading and interpreting the original documents just as we are reading and interpreting the poem.

Framed by the poet-speaker's discussion of the work in Books I and XII, the poem is a series of dramatic monologues from the conflicting viewpoints of the key figures in the trial (including Pompilia herself, who lived long enough to serve as witness to her own murder), as well as of 'Half-Rome' and 'The Other Half-Rome', the voices of public opinion on the *cause célèbre*. As such it repeatedly appeals to imaginary auditors, thereby prompting the reader to scrutinize the contingent nature of the narrative. For example, the speaker in Book II, 'Half-Rome' (the half sympathetic to the husband) reports gossip heard from 'Curate Carlo':

> We looked he'd give the history's self some help,
> Treat us to how the wife's confession went
> (This morning she confessed her crime, we know)
> And, may-be throw in something of the Priest –
> . . .
> The gallant, Caponsacchi, Lucifer
> I' the garden where Pompilia, Eve-like, lured
> Her Adam Guido to his fault and fall.
> Think you we got a sprig of speech akin
> To this from Carlo, with the Cardinal there?
> Too wary, he was, too widely awake, I trow.
> He did the murder in a dozen words.[40]

The speaker's bias in this passage is clear, and, just as clearly, it shapes the expectations for the narrative; that Carlo delivers 'the murder in a dozen words' instead of fulfilling his audience's desires leaves the reader of the poem in the position of the imaginary auditor, no wiser about what really happened in the events leading up to the trial than before. We only 'know' what one faction of the public may have imagined was the course of events, and we can imagine what prejudices shaped this version of the narrative. Browning's poem provides a complex meditation on the insufficiency of representation, on the contingent nature of all knowledge, all history. Yet, as the poet-speaker of Book XII urges, artistic interpretation is a kind of truth itself: 'Art may tell a truth/Obliquely, do the thing shall breed the thought,/Nor wrong the thought, missing mediate word/ . . . So write a book shall mean, beyond the facts.'[41]

Browning's self-reflexive narrative is reminiscent of Thomas Carlyle's strange novel *Sartor Resartus* (1833–4), which is framed as an Editor's commentary on a fictitious volume, *The Philosophy of Clothes*, by the equally fictitious German philosopher, Diogenes Teufelsdröckh. The novel was published in instalments in *Fraser's Magazine*, which publishing decision the Editor explains in Chapter Two, 'Editorial Difficulties', when he ponders how best to convey Teufelsdröckh's wisdom to the English public. 'The first thought naturally', he says, 'was to publish Article after Article on this remarkable volume, in such widely-circulating Critical Journals as the Editor might stand connected with, or by money or love procure access to'. But the philosophy is so revolutionary, and English journals so partisan that if

> the whole Journals of the Nation could have been jumbled into one Journal, and the Philosophy of Clothes poured forth in incessant torrents therefrom, the attempt had seemed possible. But, alas, what vehicle of that sort have we, except *Fraser's Magazine?* A vehicle all strewed (figuratively speaking) with the maddest Waterloo-Crackers, exploding distractively and destructively, wheresoever the mystified passenger stands or sits![42]

The Editor's discussion of *Fraser's* as a vehicle of the bizarre – in addition to being, perhaps, Carlyle's dig at the journal, which had rejected an earlier version of *Sartor Resartus*[43] – makes it a character *in* the novel, in turn subjecting it to the reader's interpretation. Carlyle, accordingly, not only encourages an analysis of publishing practices, but offers a treatise on how interpretation happens. It is this consideration of 'how interpretation happens' that is the focus for the authors I will discuss in the final section.

Theories on theory

> Still greater is the advantage of 'our limits'. A real reviewer always spends his first and best pages on the parts of a subject on which he wishes to write . . . The formidable difficulties which he acknowledges, you foresee by a strange fatality that he will only reach two pages before the end.[44]

Given the sheer volume of literary criticism being produced in the periodical press in the nineteenth century, in literature and elsewhere, it would be surprising if the Victorians did *not* also take the time to consider the practice of criticism itself. Three of the best-known examples of what we might call Victorian meta-theory are Matthew Arnold's 'The Function of Criticism at the Present Time', Walter Pater's *The Renaissance* and Oscar

Wilde's 'The Critic as Artist', all of which offer epistemological explorations into the scope of human perception and understanding, and all of which attempt to define the critic as the ideal observer.

In 'The Function of Criticism', Arnold argues that the critic must 'see the object as in itself it really is'.[45] As in *Culture and Anarchy*, here the critical ideal is 'disinterestedness', which seeks not to do things in the world but to observe and analyse impartially: 'Criticism must maintain its independence of the practical spirit and its aims. Even with well-meant efforts of the practical spirit it must express dissatisfaction, if in the sphere of the ideal they seem impoverishing and limiting.'[46] It is not that criticism is divorced from the real world, but that the disinterested critic, through contemplating 'the best that is thought and known in the world', is saved from 'a self-satisfaction which is retarding and vulgarizing'.[47] Arnold offers a poignant example of the dangers of this kind of self-satisfaction by juxtaposing several articles from contemporary papers; in them the 'exuberant self-satisfaction' of politicians who applaud the English as '"the best breed in the whole world"' is set against a three-line report of a child murdered by its mother, which ends bleakly with the statement '"Wragg is in custody."'[48] For Arnold, 'Wragg is in custody' represents all the injustices and cruelties of a world that falls far short of 'ideal perfection', and it is the duty of the disinterested critic to perceive the gap between the two.

In 'The Critic as Artist' Wilde takes issue with Arnold's notion of disinterestedness. 'The Critic as Artist' is presented as a dialogue between 'Ernest', the mouthpiece of traditional views on criticism, and 'Gilbert', Wilde's iconoclast.[49] Gilbert, quoting directly from 'The Function of Criticism', claims that Arnold makes 'a very serious error and takes no cognizance of Criticism's most perfect form, which in its essence is purely subjective, and seeks to reveal its own secret and not the secret of another'.[50] Wilde is drawing on Walter Pater's *The Renaissance*, a foundational text for the Aestheticism and decadence movements in England. Pater, too, grounds his theory in an objection to Arnold's formulation of the objective role of criticism. He claims that the 'impressions of the individual mind' are ephemeral, subjective: 'It is . . . with the passage and dissolution of impressions, images, sensations, that analysis leaves off – that continual vanishing away, that strange, perpetual, weaving and unweaving of ourselves.'[51] Given the supremacy of individual impressions – indeed the impossibility of knowing anything other than subjective experience – Pater argues for a critical practice that 'dwell[s] in thought on this world ... of impressions, unstable, flickering, inconsistent, which burn and are extinguished with our consciousness of them'.[52]

Developing Pater's subjective theory of criticism, Gilbert argues that criticism becomes more artistic than art, because it is one step further removed than art from the 'real life' that is the ostensible object of representation. This means that a work like Pater's *Renaissance* is not just theoretically but aesthetically notable. Wilde famously describes Pater's description of the Mona Lisa as containing 'something that Lionardo [*sic*] never dreamed of ... And so the picture becomes more wonderful to us than it really is, and reveals to us a secret of which, in truth, it knows nothing.'[53] Reading Pater's prose, one can see why Wilde claims criticism is an artistic end in itself. However, it is important to remember that Wilde's 'art for art's sake', like Arnold's notion of disinterestedness, is ethically engaged and culturally productive. As Gilbert explains to Ernest: 'It is Criticism ... that, by concentration, makes culture possible', and, further, 'If we are tempted to make war upon another nation, we shall remember that we are seeking to destroy an element of our culture.'[54] Wilde's dialogue, accordingly, ends with a meditation on criticism's role in fostering cosmopolitanism as a social and political ideal.

But, just as Henry James's 'The Art of Fiction' did not invent a theory of the novel, Arnold, Pater, and Wilde's meta-theoretical works are not exceptional in the field of Victorian literary theory. Walter Bagehot's 1855 review essay 'The First *Edinburgh* Reviewers', for example, begins with an analysis both of the generic form of the review – which, as he notes, invariably employs the 'limited space' trope, thereby enabling the reviewer endlessly to defer difficult analysis – and the material and intellectual conditions that have fostered review writing as a genre, which, he claims, 'but exemplifies the casual character of modern literature. Everything about it is temporary and fragmentary. Look at a railway stall; you will see books ... on every subject, in every style, of every opinion, with every conceivable difference ... but all small. People take their literature in morsels, as they take sandwiches on a journey.'[55] This ephemeral quality of modern literature has both created and in turn been shaped by a change in readers.

Comparing modern writing and the 'ancient volume', which was an artefact of leather binding, metal clasps and gilt pages, Bagehot argues that modern books address their readers as a contemporary 'man of the world' speaks, whereas the ancient volumes of a more 'laborious' age are like a hide-bound scholar 'who has hived wisdom during many studious years, agreeable to such as he is, anything but agreeable to such as he is not'.[56] Like the speech of the 'man of the world', modern writing imparts bits of complex ideas epigrammatically, allusively 'suggesting deep things in jest, unfolding unanswerable arguments in an absurd illustration, expounding nothing, yet really suggesting the lessons of a wider experience ... connecting topics with a more subtle link, refining on them with an acuter perception'.[57] Indeed, Bagehot argues, much as I have been arguing throughout this chapter, that the Victorians interpolated complex theories in myriad literary and critical texts.

Given the similarity of my argument to Bagehot's, the reader should not be surprised to find that, like his 'real reviewer' (and Bagehot himself in 'The First *Edinburgh* Reviewers'), I am dismayed to have reached the final pages of this chapter with so much material left to cover. Lamentably, I have not discussed George Eliot's famous digression in chapter seventeen of *Adam Bede* (1859), in which she defends realism against an imaginary reader who finds 'the world is not just what we like' and urges her: 'do touch it up with a tasteful pencil' instead of presenting it unembellished.[58] I have failed to treat 'embedded' literary theory in Mary Braddon's *The Doctor's Wife* (1864) or Oscar Wilde's *The Picture of Dorian Gray* (1891). Nor have I described E. S. Dallas's mammoth unfinished project, *The Gay Science* (1866), in which he developed a psychological theory of the pleasure of literature, arguing that: 'a science of criticism is possible, and that it must of necessity be the science of the laws of pleasure'.[59] I have covered (briefly) work by Walter Bagehot, but not by other influential 'men of letters' including George Saintsbury, Andrew Lang and Edmund Gosse. I have not described G. H. Lewes's immense influence as an editor, essayist and literary reviewer, to say nothing of his influence as George Eliot's companion and collaborator. Lastly, I have not discussed literary criticism's role in the establishment of English studies as a university discipline and that discipline's connection to the decline of the study of Classics or to the rise of adult education for women and working men in the latter half of the nineteenth century.

What I hope I have done, however, is convey a sense of the Victorians as theoretically engaged (and engaging). I began this chapter with the supposition that readers of Victorian literature and culture today may feel that our critical 'conversations' are very different from those of the Victorians. By showing that this difference is not as vast as it might seem, I hope to encourage readers to imagine that we might engage in conversation with, not just about, Victorian literary theory. If the Victorians are the objects of our study, they surely also have something to say to us about our own critical practices. For, as Wilde reminds us, 'self-consciousness and the critical spirit are one'.[60]

Notes

1 Henry Holbeach [W. B. Rands], 'The New Fiction', *Contemporary Review*, 37 (Feb. 1880), 247–62, reprinted in John Charles Olmstead (ed.), *A Victorian Art of Fiction: Essays on the Novel in British Periodicals, 1870–1900* (New York: Garland, 1979), 160.

2 Robert Buchanan, 'The Fleshly School of Poetry: Mr. D.G. Rossetti', *Contemporary Review*, 18 (October 1871), 334–50, reprinted in Thomas J. Collins and Vivienne J. Rundle (eds.), *The Broadview Anthology of Poetry and Poetic Theory* (Peterborough, Ont.: Broadview, 1999), 891.

3 Dante Gabriel Rossetti, 'The Stealthy School of Criticism', *The Athenaeum*, 2303 (1871), 792–94, reprinted in Collins and Rundle (eds.), *The Broadview Anthology of Poetry and Poetic Theory*, 1341–5.

4 Kathy Alexis Psomiades, '"The Lady of Shalott" and the Critical Fortunes of Victorian Poetry', in Joseph Bristow (ed.), *The Cambridge Companion to Victorian Poetry* (Cambridge: Cambridge University Press, 2000), 26.

5 Edwin M. Eigner and George J. Worth, 'Introduction', in Edwin M. Eigner and George J. Worth (eds.), *Victorian Criticism of the Novel* (New York: Cambridge University Press, 1985), 1.

6 Henry James, 'The Art of Fiction', *Longman's Magazine*, 4 (Sept. 1884), 502–21, reprinted in Olmstead (ed.), *A Victorian Art of Fiction*, 287.

7 Suzy Anger, *Victorian Interpretation* (Ithaca: Cornell University Press, 2005), 1. See also Amanda Anderson, *The Powers of Distance: Cosmopolitanism and the Cultivation of Detachment* (Princeton: Princeton University Press, 2001); David Wayne Thomas, *Cultivating Victorians: Liberal Culture and the Aesthetic* (Philadelphia: University of Pennsylvania Press, 2004).

8 For more on the periodical press, see above, pp. 177–94.

9 Mark W. Turner, 'Time, Periodicals, and Literary Studies', *Victorian Periodicals Review*, 39, 4 (2006), 310. See also Rosemary T. VanArsdel, 'The *Wellesley Index* Forty Years Later (1966–2006)', *Victorian Periodicals Review*, 39, 3 (2006), 257–65.

10 See Google Books: http://books.google.com/books and the Internet Archive: www.archive.org/details/texts.

11 John Ruskin, *Sesame and Lilies*, ed. Deborah Epstein Nord, Rethinking the Western Tradition Series (1865; New Haven: Yale University Press, 2002), 68.

12 Matthew Arnold, *Culture and Anarchy*, in Stefan Collini (ed.), *Culture and Anarchy and Other Writings*, Cambridge Texts in the History of Political Thought Series (1869; New York: Cambridge University Press, 1993), 95.

13 Ibid., 59.

14 Ibid., 78–9.

15 Ruskin, *Sesame and Lilies*, 59.

16 Ibid., 46.

17 See for example Dinah Birch and Francis O'Gorman (eds.), *Ruskin and Gender* (Basingstoke: Palgrave, 2002); see also Elizabeth Helsinger, 'Authority, Desire, and the Pleasures of Reading', in Ruskin, *Sesame and Lilies*, 113–41.

18 For an example of the former, see Nancy Armstrong, *Desire and Domestic Fiction: A Political History of the Novel* (Oxford: Oxford University Press, 1987); for an example of the latter, see Caroline Levine, 'Strategic Formalism: Toward a New Method in Cultural Studies', *Victorian Studies*, 48, 4 (2006), 625–57.

19 John Stuart Mill, 'Thoughts on Poetry and Its Varieties', *Monthly Repository* (Jan., Oct. 1833), reprinted in *Dissertations and Discussions: Political, Philosophical, and Historical*, 2 vols. (London: Parker, 1859), I:, 65–6.

20 Eliza Cook, 'People Who Do Not Like Poetry', *Eliza Cook's Journal*, 1 (May 1849), reprinted in Solveig C. Robinson (ed.), *A Serious Occupation: Literary Criticism by Victorian Women Writers* (Peterborough, Ont.: Broadview, 2003), 76–7.

21 Arthur Henry Hallam, 'On Some of the Characteristics of Modern Poetry', *Englishman's Magazine* (Aug. 1831), reprinted in Collins and Rundle (eds.), *The Broadview Anthology of Poetry and Poetic Theory*, 1193.

22 George Eliot, 'Silly Novels by Lady Novelists', *Westminster Review*, 66 (Oct. 1856), reprinted in Eigner and Worth (eds.), *Victorian Criticism of the Novel*, 160.

23 Ibid., 174.

24 George Meredith, 'An Essay on Comedy and on the Uses of the Comic Spirit', *New Quarterly Magazine* (Apr. 1877), reprinted in Wylie Sypher (ed.), *Comedy* (New York: Doubleday, 1956), 32.

25 Anna Maria Jones, *Problem Novels: Victorian Fiction Theorizes the Sensational Self* (Columbus: Ohio State University Press, 2007), 91–127.

26 [Margaret Oliphant], 'Sensation Novels', *Blackwood's Edinburgh Magazine*, 91 (May 1862), 568.

27 [Margaret Oliphant], 'Novels', *Blackwood's Edinburgh Magazine*, 102 (Sept. 1867), reprinted in Robinson (ed.), *A Serious Occupation*, 150.

28 [Oliphant], 'Novels', 173.

29 John Ruskin, *Fiction, Fair and Foul*, *The Nineteenth Century* (June 1880), reprinted in E. T. Cook and Alexander Wedderburn (eds.), *The Library Edition of the Works of John Ruskin*, 39 vols. (London: Allen, 1903–12), XXXIV, 276.

30 Ibid., 268.

31 Ibid., 274.

32 James, 'Art of Fiction', 288.

33 Ibid., 287.

34 Ibid.

35 William Makepeace Thackeray, *Vanity Fair* (1848; New York: Penguin, 2001), 59–60.

36 James, 'Art of Fiction', 289.

37 Oscar Wilde, 'The Critic as Artist', *Intentions* (1891; New York: Prometheus, 2004), 104.

38 Herbert F. Tucker, 'James's Browning Inside Out', *Henry James Review*, 26 (2005), 212.

39 Robert Browning, *The Ring and the Book*, ed. Thomas J. Collins and Richard D. Altick (1868–9; Peterborough Ont.: Broadview, 2001), I, 458–69.

40 Ibid., II, 162–73.

41 Ibid., XII, 855–62.

42 Thomas Carlyle, *Sartor Resartus*, ed. Kerry McSweeney (1833–4; New York: Oxford University Press, 1987), 8–9.

43 Kerry McSweeney, 'Introduction' to Carlyle, *Sartor Resartus*, xiii.

44 Walter Bagehot, 'The First *Edinburgh* Reviewers', *National Review* (July 1855), reprinted in R. H. Hutton (ed.), *Literary Studies of the Late Walter Bagehot*, 3 vols. (London: Longman's, Green, 1905), I, 148–9.

45 Matthew Arnold, 'The Function of Criticism at the Present Time', in Collini (ed.), *Culture and Anarchy and Other Writings*, 29.

46 Ibid., 47.

47 Ibid, 38.

48 Ibid., 40.

49 One of the difficulties of Wilde's dialogue is separating which statements by which character can be taken as the essay's 'argument'. Some critics take Gilbert to be Wilde's proxy in the text, but as Suzy Anger notes the dialogue is much more complicated, and careful attention to the interplay between the characters and among various viewpoints is necessary. Anger, *Victorian Interpetation*, 143ff.

50 Wilde, 'Critic as Artist', 140.

51 Walter Pater, *The Renaissance: Studies in Art and Poetry*, ed. Donald L. Hill (1893; Berkeley, CA: University of California Press, 1980), 188. Hill's annotated edition uses the 1893 fourth edition of Pater's work, which contained substantial revisions and additions from the original 1873 edition.

52 Ibid., 187.

53 Wilde, 'Critic as Artist', 141–2.

54 Ibid., 210, 212.

55 Bagehot, 'First *Edinburgh* Reviewers', 145–6.

56 Ibid., 146–8.

57 Ibid., 148.

58 George Eliot, *Adam Bede* (1859; New York: Signet, 1961), 175.

59 E. S. Dallas, *The Gay Science*, 2 vols. (London: Chapman and Hall, 1866), I, 6.

60 Wilde, 'Critic as Artist', 122.

14

The dead

'Dead', Charles Dickens's narrator says after the demise of Jo the Crossing Sweeper in *Bleak House* (1852–3) and 'dying thus all around us, every day'.[1] Dickens helped make Victorian death seem like a way of life. His celebrated death scenes – Jo, Paul in *Dombey and Son* (1846–8), Little Nell in *The Old Curiosity Shop* (1840–1) – assisted in propelling the notion of a Victorian 'sentimental' investment in death. For many decades afterwards, the Victorians have seemed to have had a peculiarly intimate relationship with, even a readiness to celebrate, mourning. The major new cemeteries – Highgate and Kensal Green, for instance, or the cemeteries of Birmingham, Leeds and Sheffield – were solemn but strangely to be enjoyed. Queen Victoria, losing Prince Albert in 1861 (perhaps to stomach cancer finished off by pneumonia or typhoid) retreated into grief. A Queen in mourning, she seemed to preside symptomatically over a culture – with its new great burial sites, notorious infant mortality rates, industrial accidents, stark gaps between rich and poor and elaborate rituals of the grave – that knew death more familiarly than any modern period. It was an age of elegy. The Queen's favourite Laureate, Alfred Tennyson, was best known for *In Memoriam* (1850), his lament on the death of his friend Arthur Henry Hallam. Even the first postage stamp was black.

Death and the Victorians are indeed peculiarly tangled. But what helps to make them so, what renders the cultural history of the Victorians and the dead distinctive and important, was not, in fact, death. It was life: eternal life. It was the period's restless probing of theological conceptions of the durability of the soul and the Christian notion of the resurrection of the dead. Around Victorian conceptions of death as an event were, accordingly, the largest questions about human purpose, the

foundations of moral living, the rewards of virtue, the intentional ordering of the Universe. Eternal life and the doctrine of the resurrection are
not the same thing. It is possible to believe in the former and doubt the
latter – and the other way round is not unheard of. But the same broad
issue of the nature of life beyond the grave matters intensely to both. For
Protestant Christians of the nineteenth century, the central authority,
the New Testament, was under new and corrosive challenge. The German Higher Critics, whom George Eliot had helped introduce to English
readers with her 1846 translation of David Friedrich Strauss's *The Life of
Jesus, Critically Examined*,[2] disputed the New Testament's veracity. The
New Geologists had earlier disputed the Old Testament's. Darwinian
evolution in mid-century added to the pressure on Christian conceptions
not least by assailing established ideas of God's creative role and his continued directing presence. It was hard for ordinary readers of *The Origin
of Species* (1859) and *The Descent of Man and Selection in Relation to Sex* (1871)
to see the old conceptions of a guiding divine mind in the biological
world at all. With the authority of the Bible under this kind of revision-
ist pressure, miraculous doctrines and histories were among the most
vulnerable. Matthew Arnold in *Literature and Dogma* (1873) and *God and
the Bible* (1875) tried to detach Christianity's claims for respect from any
miraculous basis: what mattered about religion was its moral force. The
argument for a non-miraculous but ethically compelling faith was powerful, but it was not to be long-lasting or particularly influential. Elsewhere,
Comtean Positivists, empirical scientists and the new anthropologists –
all mapping the development of human civilization as a movement away
from 'primitive' thought towards reason – agreed that supernatural or
metaphysical interpretations of phenomena signified an immature stage
of human intellectual development. John Ruskin earnestly disputed this,
among other places in *The Queen of the Air* (1869), insisting on the moral
worth of pre-Christian myth. But for others, abandoning non-rational,
non-empirical interpretations of things was evidence of human mental
progress.

It is not easy to exaggerate the significance of Christianity's changing
authority in the nineteenth century. Conceptions of the resurrection and
the durability of life were hardly the only doctrines under strain. But
the consequences of their faltering were unusually widespread.[3] Questions about life beyond the tomb that the Christian church could, for
many influential individuals, no longer confidently answer resurfaced,
in turn, in an enormous variety of Victorian cultural practices. Literary

and visual cultures, alongside moral and scientific debate in the period, were bound up with them in plural forms. And as anxieties about the tomb were felt in highly visible places, they bubbled beneath the surface of apparently remote matters too. Do the dead survive? The New Testament had promised much. Jesus on the cross, in Luke's account, had assured the malefactor with whom he was crucified: 'To day shalt thou be with me in paradise' (Luke 23:43).[4] But was eternal life a promise to be trusted? And what about coming back from the dead, not only of Jesus but the General Resurrection? Will the dead rise again? The Gospel accounts of Easter morning were interpreted by Paul as the promise of death's defeat: 'Behold, I shew you a mystery; We shall not all sleep, but we shall all be changed, In a moment, in the twinkling of an eye, at the last trump: for the trumpet shall sound, and the dead shall be raised incorruptible, and we shall be changed' (1 Corinthians 15:51–2). Hardly were there more difficult theological words for Victorians to interpret with confidence and without conflict.

Edwin Landseer's *The Old Shepherd's Chief Mourner* was first exhibited at the Royal Academy in 1837, as Victoria acceded to the throne. The painting pre-dates the resurrection and life-after-death anxieties of the Victorian age. But tranquilly, indirectly, it offers a glimpse of the matters to which Victorian artists would uneasily return. Landseer invites the viewer to think, amid his autumnal colours, and the pitiful faithfulness of the dog to the dead, about how human beings might be remembered. The painting proposes quietly the memory of a faithful dog as central to mourning a lost and unknown human life. To the lower right lie a small, thick book and a pair of spectacles, perhaps the old shepherd's, no longer needed, perhaps those of a human mourner, perhaps of a minister of the church. The volume, it may be, is the *Book of Common Prayer*.[5] But its thickness and cover suggest that it is the King James Version of the Bible. In both, anyway, the same words are to be found: John 11:25's recollection of Jesus's statement to Martha before the raising of Lazarus: 'I am the resurrection, and the life.' These are the opening words of the funeral sentences in the *Book of Common Prayer* too, and around them gathered one of the largest disputes about a miraculous religion in the Victorian period. Henry Bowler's 1855 *The Doubt: Can These Dry Bones Live?*[6] invited the viewer to contemplate resurrection and immortality directly. Jesus's words are inscribed on a tomb stone over which a woman looks thoughtfully, mournfully. Did Bowler's painting ironize 'I am the resurrection, and the life' among the bones and decay he depicted, or did the canvas simply suggest the naturalness of doubting what they meant? Frank Holl's 1872 painting, plainly titled *'I am the Resurrection and the Life'* *(The Village Funeral)*,[7] again, teased the reader to relate Jesus's statement to the scene. Does this picture depict a melancholy tableau of human loss, an image of the family bereaved, where authentic consolation is to be found in the thought of resurrection? Or is the promise of Jesus's words merely a reminder of the beginning of the funeral service? Or, worse, are those words exposed, against this sombre scene, as bitterly remote from the feelings of the bereaved?

Similar questions animated literary inquiry. Alfred Tennyson suggested the formation of a society in the late 1860s to look into the question of the immortality of the soul and ideas of miracle. The 'Metaphysical Society' that followed brought major figures with exceptionally diverse intellectual commitments – Walter Bagehot, Richard Hutton, T. H. Huxley, James Knowles, Cardinal Manning, Mark Pattison, John Ruskin – to consider the merits of materialism against non-materialism, of the testimony of reason in relation to faith. *In Memoriam* had, long before, made of Tennyson's uncertainty about his friend's soul a drama of bereavement in its dismayed contemplation of the hope that 'No life may fail beyond the grave.'[8] The elegy reached a strange climax in a visionary apprehension of Hallam's return as a living soul that flashed back to the terrestrial (see Lyric xciv). But that reassurance was doubted almost as soon as it was proposed – and *Maud* (1855), five years later, ironized and made a dark joke from the poet's 'faith' in the ways that the dead could communicate with the living. Tennyson's meditations did not stop there, though. 'In the Valley of Cauteretz' (1864), for instance, played with the notion that Hallam's voice was still audible to the living. If the mind could not reassure itself that the dead continued beyond the grave, could the ear?

> All along the valley, stream that flashest white,
> Deepening thy voice with the deepening of the night,
> All along the valley, where the waters flow,
> I walk'd with one I lov'd two and thirty years ago.
> All along the valley, while I walk'd today,
> The two and thirty years were a mist that rolls away;
> For all along the valley, down thy rocky bed,
> Thy living voice to me was as the voice of the dead,
> And all along the valley, by rock and cave and tree,
> The voice of the dead was a living voice to me.[9]

Those repeated words, 'all along the valley', at once mimicked the continuation that the poem hoped for Hallam's presence, and simultaneously
suggested that which was clogged, unable to progress, as if mirroring
an emotional state stalled by the long-ago calamity. Where, really, *was*
that heard voice and what did it signify? Was it dead or alive – the easy
exchange of 'dead' and 'living' inhibit clarity – and was it remembered
or somehow 'real'? Hallam becomes part of the environment, but is this
imagination or revelation? That final word, 'me', uncomfortably points,
perhaps, to Tennyson himself and his need to be reassured above whatever lesson the Pyrenean valley might teach about the dead.

Algernon Charles Swinburne's elegies from the 1870s onwards
exploited alternative imaginative models for the survival of the dead:
writers and artists lived through their works, he hesitantly suggested,
figuring their endurance as sound or sense or changes in the quality of
the earth's radiance. When Henry James's narrator in *The Aspern Papers*
(1888) says of the dead poet Jeffrey Aspern that 'he is a part of the light
by which we walk',[10] it was to a secular, Swinburnian metaphor of a
life's continuation that he turned. Living through books, maintaining
a sense of presence through words left behind: such an ancient idea
struck some literary Victorians with a new force as a more rationally
comprehensible notion of a form of 'immortality'. Matthew Arnold's
godfather, John Keble (1792–1866), poet, Tractarian priest and Oxford
Professor of Poetry, had dedicated his Oxford lectures to Wordsworth.
With a conventional phrase, a common label about the 'deathless' nature
of great writing, Keble had hailed the Laureate's abundant achievement
an 'immortal treasury of . . . splendid poems'.[11] This kind of vocabulary
remained across the period. Tennyson, typically, saw the limits even
to such modest, non-miraculous conceptions of 'immortality'. 'A man
of genius might be lucky', the photographer Julia Margaret Cameron
recalled him saying, 'were he remembered for 1000 years; and what, as
the psalmist asks, is a thousand years?'[12] Actually, of course, the psalms
had survived many more than a thousand years – but that was hardly Tennyson's point. Matthew Arnold in 'Haworth Churchyard' (1855) allowed
himself to think for a moment that the Brontë sisters would not die,
but, like Cathy and Heathcliff, return to the moors. Yet he promptly dismissed that idea as soon as it was mooted, ruling it out as folly in an act
of self-censorship, a prohibition even of the act of fantasizing returns.

Scenes of literal resurrection proved enticing to writers and artists
as images the culture could more easily imagine than believe. Arnold,

persistently watchful of any suggestion of miracle, preferred narratives of non-resurrection. Retelling the northern saga legend of the slain god Balder in *Balder Dead* (1855), he presented the failure of a return of the departed, despite near universal mourning. But new versions of, for instance, the Greek myth of Alcestis, rescued from the grave by the strength of Hercules, figured the alternative, a safely mythical non-Christian version of death's conquest: Browning's *Balaustion's Adventure* (1871) included a translation of Euripedes's entire version of it. Persephone, too, who returned from the kingdom of the dead for a portion of the year, re-appeared. Sir Frederick Leighton's painting *The Return of Persephone* (1891)[13] staged the emotions of return, if in a manner so faultily faultless as to leave a chill, an emotional reticence at odds with the literal scene. And if episodes of 'literal' resurrection were engaging, so too were the reinterpretations of what 'resurrection' was. The nineteenth-century realist novel, in the heart of its aesthetic, was committed to the material, the empirical, demonstrable and credible. In turn, its scenes of the 'resurrection' of life were not miraculous but moral: Silas Marner's rejuvenation by domestic affection in George Eliot's *Silas Marner* (1861); Raskolnikov's gradual transformation into ethical realization and Aleksandr Petrovich's final freedom from prison in Dostoevsky's *Crime and Punishment* (1866) and *The House of the Dead* (1862) respectively; Nekhlyudov's understanding of the consequences of ill-doing in Tolstoy's *Resurrection* (1899). For Dickens, outside that realist tradition, the return to life was the animating trope of *Little Dorrit* (1855–7) and *A Tale of Two Cities* (1859), as Mr Dorrit and Dr Manette, respectively, were brought back from the 'death' of imprisonment into a fuller sense of a life in freedom. Being 'recalled to life',[14] as *A Tale* puts it, is that novel's multiple subject, worked out in layers of the plot. With Jerry Cruncher and the body snatchers, Dr Manette's liberation and Sydney Carton's self-sacrifice to allow Charles Darnay to live, *A Tale of Two Cities* explored the affective and educative potential of re-imagined 'resurrections' that were not dependent on the New Testament's empty tomb. The legacies of such moral meanings were still potent in the early twentieth century: resurrection as a figure of freedom from constraint and of self-discovery comprised the foundation, for instance, of Ibsen's last play *Nar vi døde va °gner* (1899), published in English in 1900 as *When We Dead Awaken*.[15] August Strindberg's *Spöksonaten* (1907) – *Ghost Sonata* – interchanged the morally dead with actual death in productive confusion.

Ghosts did not necessarily suggest a theology of the afterlife. And Christian resurrection was about risen and transformed bodies, not the hauntings of the living by pale revenants. But little was more purposively instructional – descriptive of how best to live – in Dickens's *œuvre* than his conception of the role of phantoms in handling what exactly a moral revival, a moral resurrection, could really be. Ghosts allowed Dickens to deal with a robust sense of how properly to be alive (George MacDonald had a more complicated conception of this later in the century). The heartless miser, Scrooge, in *A Christmas Carol* (1843), is visited by the spirit of his former business partner Josiah Marley, who, in life, had behaved in the same cold and selfish way as Scrooge. Why am I being visited? Scrooge inquires. "'It is required of every man'", replies Marley's ghost,

> that the spirit within him should walk abroad among his fellow-men, and travel far and wide; and if that spirit goes not forth in life, it is condemned to do so after death. It is doomed to wander through the world – oh, woe is me! – and witness what it cannot share, but might have shared on earth, and turned to happiness![16]

Ghosts mark the life that was not lived; they are a posthumous function of the behaviours of the once-living. In *A Christmas Carol* and *The Haunted Man* (1848), they come to change the living too, to draw out a kindly spirit of humanity and to release the life that was not. Dickens's ghosts reinvent the notion of a moral awakening again because they are its agents, as Jarvis Lorry is in *A Tale of Two Cities*. By them are the living quickened.

The ghost story more generally, flourishing as a genre in the Victorian period, played out in an oblique form implicit questions about the afterlife in a non-Dickensian sense. Mary Elizabeth Braddon, Rhoda Broughton, Wilkie Collins, Arthur Conan Doyle, Charles Dickens, Elizabeth Gaskell, Thomas Hardy, Henry James, Sheridan Le Fanu, Rosa Mulholland, Margaret Oliphant, Mrs Henry Wood were each ghost story writers. It is a remarkable – and hardly comprehensive – list. They probed the chilling but also the domesticated tales of visitation, and the traces human misery left behind. The development of the ghost story was impelled by many forces. But it partook at the broadest level in cultural contemplations of the mystery of the grave. In those tales, however disturbing and wretched their spectral protagonists, were at least the dimmest outline of a reassurance that the dead were not wholly dead and that there was an answer of some kind to the question that Le Fanu's narrator shouts in 'An Account of Some Strange Disturbances in Aungier Street' when, in the height of anxiety and 'in a stentorian voice', he cries 'over the banisters, "Who's there?"'.[17] Henrietta Huxley, wife of Thomas Henry, wrote celebrated agnostic words that her husband took for his gravestone: 'God still giveth His beloved sleep,/And if an endless sleep He wills, – so best.'[18] But the tales of haunting formed an imaginative repository for a non-Huxleyite view. And elsewhere, outside of the generic structures of the ghost story, realist writers were, in a more subtle way, intrigued by secular, imaginative forms of the survival of the dead that was obtainable through fictional affect, through the power of imaginative prose to make things lastingly memorable. The unforgettable death scene gave, in this dimmest version of the period's fascination with survival, an aesthetic aura, an imaginative persistence, to an invented life that might remain long in the mind of the reader or viewer. Who could forget the death of Little Nell? Or, in opera, Violetta in Verdi's *La Traviata* (1853)? Or, in fiction again, Ferdinand Lopez in Anthony Trollope's *The Prime Minister* (1876)? The slow build-up to that calamity, with all its implications for the destructive power of financial speculation and technology, cannot be reproduced in critical prose. Yet the calamity itself, with Lopez at the train station, could hardly be more memorable: 'But Lopez heeded not the call, and the rush was too late. With quick, but still with gentle and apparently unhurried steps, he walked down before the flying engine – and in a moment had been knocked into bloody atoms.'[19] This is far from theology. But the attention of the realist writer to that extraordinary moment of destruction imparted a strange, unsettling persistence to the imagined dead – making a 'living' man memorable through his end – via the exceptional capacity of fiction to leave an affective impression, to allow a 'life' to remain 'after death' in the reader's imagination.

As retrospective narratives, ghost stories not infrequently narrated experiences that were recalled by speakers from long ago. In so doing, they signed memory as a retainer of the dead. But other men and women were more convinced of actual, not imaginative, survival. In the mid-nineteenth century, after the Hydesville Rappings in New York in 1848, spiritualism in Great Britain flourished. Hydesville had involved the seemingly supernatural tappings of a spirit seeking to communicate from the dead: the Fox sisters, who claimed the mediumistic powers, became the subject of international fascination. Searching matters of life and death, spiritualism thereafter conflicted for the most part with both religion and science. Natural philosophers (the term 'scientist' was not widely accepted in the period) who involved themselves in spiritualism usually faced their colleagues' suspicion: John Elliotson (1791–1868), Professor of Medicine at University College, London; William Gregory (1803–58),

Professor of Chemistry at Edinburgh and the chemist and physicist William Crookes OM (1832–1919) were among them. Yet that was not enough to prevent even so prominent a figure as the co-proponent of evolution by natural selection, Alfred Russel Wallace, from believing. Michael Faraday, investigating the claims of spiritualism in 1850, thought better education would discourage misplaced faith in things unseen – but as a Sandemanian (a Christian sect believing itself to imitate the structures and faith of the earliest Christians), he had his own Christian conception of what such things were. And well-educated men and women *did* have spiritualist faith, anyway. Elizabeth Barrett Browning, John Ruskin and William Gladstone were persuaded, at least to an extent, by spiritualism. Arthur Conan Doyle, into the early twentieth century, became one of its most energetic champions. And scientific principles *could*, some thought, be brought to bear on the life-after-death problem: that was certainly the public conviction of the founders of the Society for Psychical Research in 1882.

Extending the idea that thinking about the dead in a séance could bring them back, Conan Doyle's own supernatural stories included 'Playing with Fire' (1900). There, the act of imagining a unicorn before a séance leads, through the same principle of thought's ability to bring into actual being its subjects, to a unicorn's terrifying appearance. The tale articulated both awe at the possibilities of spiritualism, and anxiety about powers that were beyond human control. Even in narratives apparently remote from the recollections of the deceased, Conan Doyle, one of the most stimulating writers on the dead at the end of the nineteenth century, mulled over forms of return. *The Hound of the Baskervilles* (1901–2), for example, was concerned, though it might not initially seem so, with coming back from the dead. Conan Doyle had killed off his famous detective Sherlock Holmes in 'The Final Problem' in 1893. But here he was again in 1901/2. Did that mean he had come back from the dead? The date in which *The Hound* was set was omitted (the reader simply knows that the Queen is on the throne), so he or she could not be sure whether this was a 'resurrection' tale (as 'The Adventure of the Empty House' proved to be in 1903 when Holmes really did come back) or one that was intended to pre-date the detective's 'death' in the Reichenbach Falls, apparently after a fatal encounter with the master criminal Moriarty. The plot returned to issues of return as well: Stapleton is a kind of revived or reincarnated Hugo Baskerville, the wretch whose dissipation brought the Hound into being centuries before. Readers cannot know for certain, either, that

Stapleton is killed at the end – so does that mean that he might be ready to return 'from the dead' in another later tale, like a new version of the master criminal Moriarty? The reader closes the novel wondering how far it has offered a resurrected detective and a resurrectable villain.

Conan Doyle's growing commitment to, and anxiety about, spiritualism was dimly reflected in the *Hound*'s returning dead. But the idea that, in some way, Stapleton was playing out a new version of Hugo Baskerville's life was a pointer to a fictional fascination that developed more substantially among other authors, particularly in the second half of the period, as a new and startling manifestation of the cultural preoccupation with lives that outlasted the grave. Inherited histories, reincarnated men and women and strange forms of earthly immortality: these were ideas that spurred buoyant, late century imaginative versions, figurative compensations for and fantasies about, the question of life's limits. Actually, Conan Doyle, persistently thoughtful about the grave, made a brief but influential contribution to this tradition with 'The Ring of Thoth' (1890). There, an ancient Egyptian has lingered into the nineteenth century having discovered the secret of extended (but not eternal) youth. He endures through different generations, in different roles and countries. Eventually, in the Egyptian gallery of the Louvre, he is re-united with his (mummified) lover and, more importantly, the liquid that will allow him to die. The tale invites a chilly suspicion about how distant pasts could still be present in the modern world, a matter the late Victorian anthropologists considered in terms of the survival of forms of primitive culture. But other romance writers took the idea of recurrent or persistent lives and developed them into longer plots. The curious sense of a near-immortal man or woman, persisting in the modern world but ancient, was a powerful motivator for H. Rider Haggard, whose *She* novels involved reincarnational plots in which living men and women replayed, at least according to She herself, the disastrous story of the ancient Kallikrates's love. Haggard's more specifically resurrectionist novels included *When the World Shook* (1919) that narrated the recall to life of Oro and Yva after 250,000 years in a crystal tomb.

Inherited curses – a sense of one generation controlling the lives of another – were part of Wilkie Collins's *Armadale* (1866). Cathy and Heathcliff in Emily Brontë's *Wuthering Heights* (1847) had, of course, already been made to live their loves again in another generation. But the end-of-the-century romance writers took literal notions of reincarnation into more audacious territory. Contemporary culture offers many examples of plots where the past is re-enacted or partly relived: Kate Mosse's *Labyrinth* (2006) and *Sepulchre* (2008), M. J. Rose's *The Reincarnationist* (2007), Suzanne Weyn's *Reincarnation* (2008). But at the end of the nineteenth century, the plot was still surprising. George MacDonald had tested its potential in, for instance, *The Portent: A Story of the Inner Vision of the Highlanders Commonly Called the Second Sight* (1864), with its tantalizing reiteration of the word 'resurrection'. But later versions were even more startling. Most provocatively, Marie Corelli's long novel about Christian conversion, *Ardath: The Story of a Dead Self* (1889), involved a modern-day poet's discovery that he had already lived, literally, in an ancient pre-Christian city. Characteristically, the text is primarily about literary fame and its precariousness. But it is also a bold fantasy of everlasting human beings that provocatively uses a reincarnational trope to affirm the verity of Christianity and its miraculous dispensation. *Ardath* is a syncretic, prolix, exuberant and exhausting novel. But if the romance writer's end-of-century fascination with plots of human durability often suggested an imaginative compensation for the loss of the Christian promise, Corelli's text went the other way and (if opportunistically) deployed that same romance narrative to affirm the original Christian reassurance.

The promise of romance in the nineteenth century was always that the empirical world was not enough. Romance was a haven not only for adventure but for mystery, magic and enchantment. It commemorated a lost pre-Arnoldian world of miracle. And amid that mourning for lost miracles, it was to new ideas of resistance to the grave that even children's fantasy fiction sometimes turned at the close of the period. J. M. Barrie's *Peter Pan* (1911 in novel form) envisaged a hero who did not age, and in characteristically charming manner, invited its child readers to think about conundrums of survival and durability: 'every time a child says, "I don't believe in fairies"', Peter tells the children about lives one might think were immortal, '"there is a fairy somewhere that falls down dead"'.[20] Can fairies die, then? Can those who seem to have enchanted, magical, unending lives be snuffed out by thought, just as, for some, a belief in Christian resurrection had been extinguished by the critique of reason? The echoes of Victorian debates about the nature of life were faintly audible in Barrie's tale, just as the topic of fairies themselves was one that the Victorians had, earlier, made their own. In those 'strange and secret peoples', to use the title of Carole Silver's book on Victorian fairies,[21] were, among other things, fugitive hints that the new 'materialism' had not accounted for all forms of being on earth.

The technological developments of the nineteenth century helped persuade a wider public, through social and commercial advantages, of the value of an empirical, experimental and outward-facing science. Conspicuous excitement, opportunity and a glamorous sense of the modern followed in the wake of many such developments, though they were accompanied by anxiety, disorienting social change and radical shifts in the nature of work and the relationships of production too. But machines and new inventions were not merely complicated avatars of a buzzing modernity, however much the train carriage, the motor car, the telephone and the typewriting machine shifted permanently human beings' sense of space, speed and communication. It is a measure of the extent to which the nineteenth century engaged with the shifting authority of the miraculous that even machines could, at times, be incorporated into the century's discourses of fretfulness about life's end. Communication technologies, most particularly, offered new stimuli to imaginative apprehensions of how the dead might speak to the living. Swinburne's concern in the late 1870s and onwards with the migration of sound as a figure for the survival of a writer's fame after death was in curious conjunction with the development of the telephone with its capacity to carry sound across vast distances. In George Du Maurier's novel *Peter Ibbetson* (1898), new communication technology offered itself explicitly as a metaphor for strange powers of recalling the lost. Extending Dickens's notion of haunting as concerned primarily with memory, Du Maurier's novel narrates its hero's wish for a better way of contacting the past than mere conscious recollection. He discovers a faculty for 'dreaming true', allowing the past to be lived again as if really alive. In the end, he will contact his own dead lover. But, in the first stage, Du Maurier's narrator believes he has found a new way of accessing experience not consciously rememberable. 'Evidently', he remarks:

> our brain contains something akin both to a photographic plate and a phonographic cylinder, and many other things of the same kind not yet discovered; not a sight or a sound or a smell is lost; not a taste or a feeling or an emotion. Unconscious memory records them all, without our even heeding what goes on around us beyond the things that attract our immediate interest or attention.[22]

The past is preserved and the dead not wholly dead because they can be dreamed alive – and it is the modern machine that figures best that strange hope and potential.

Marcel Proust's narrator in *Le côté de Guermantes* (1920–1, *The Guermantes Way*), volume III of *À la recherche du temps perdu* (1913–27, *In Search of Lost Time*), thought speaking on the telephone recalled an ancient classical myth of loss. It was a moment the Victorians would have recognized. When he is no longer connected to his grandmother, Proust's narrator vainly repeats her name to the receiver: '"Grand'mère, grand'mère", comme Orphée, resté seul, répète le nom de la morte' ('"Grandma, Grandma", like Orpheus, left alone, repeats the name of the dead [woman]').[23] The telephone is the new ancient portal to the underworld, frantically searched by Orpheus. Words travel across space – why should they not be capable of travelling across time? Of course, literary language itself could, with a degree of plausibility, be said to 'live' across time. It was part of Proust's project in *À la recherche* to bring the past 'back' through words (as well as to mourn history's loss). But beyond Proust, the act of reading can coherently be regarded as an imaginative way of entering a domain that feels 'alive'. Reading literature permits, peculiarly, the sense of mental belonging to an alternative world, different from one's own, but vivid. And reading the words of the dead struck the Victorians as particularly like an encounter with the deceased. Reading Hallam's words, Tennyson felt him come back: 'word by word, and line by line', he wrote in *In Memoriam*, 'The dead man touch'd me from the past,/And all at once it seem'd at last/The living soul was flash'd on mine' (xcv). The poet Dora Greenwell (1821–82) wrote of looking through old letters as a revivalist moment, too:

Oh, hands that wrote these words, oh, loving eyes
That brightened over them, oh, hearts whose prize
And treasure once were these, by Time made Heir
To this your sometime wealth, with pious care
I gather in my hoards; for this is dust
Of human hearts that now I hold in trust,
And while I muse above it, spirits flown
Come back and commune with me. ('Old Letters', 1861)[24]

But for Robert Browning, writing brought back the dead in a different, more disquieting way.

Dramatic verse was, in his audacious conception, an act of rejuvenation. If literature naturally imparted a sense of a living wor(l)d, the dramatic monologue – a genre co-invented by Tennyson and Browning – suggested a peculiar sense of a living voice: charismatic, vital, asking to be heard. At the beginning of *The Ring and the Book* (1868–9), Browning's most capacious poem, a detective-novel-in-verse, the poet proposed himself as a resurrectionist with words, a writer who made the 'dead alive once more'.[25] This was an apt summary of his career to that point as a creator of vibrant speakers in volumes of dramatic work – *Dramatic Romances and Lyrics* (1845), *Men and Women* (1855), *Dramatis Personae* (1864) – that would continue until *Asolando: Fancies and Facts*, published on the day of his death in 1889. *The Ring and the Book* appropriated the vocabulary of resurrection to describe the act of writing verse. If that was a controversial proposition in the middle of the century's debates about miracle, it was one made with confidence that was almost brash. Browning's description of his own verse 'start[ing] the dead alive'[26] in *The Ring and the Book* constituted a kind of manifesto for anti-elegy, a metaphor for the exceptional imaginative life of a poet or even an oblique description of the imaginative activity Browning hoped the reader would bring to his work. Browning's daring claim for revivalist verse intrigued other writers of dramatic poetry: Kipling politicized the revivalist monologue by imagining voices not of the dead but the marginalized; John Davidson ironized its religious pretension and Christina Rossetti had, long before either, used women speaking literally from the grave to figure spiritual states and the curious power of confined female lives. Michael Field, the joint pseudonym of the two poets Katherine Bradley (1846–1914) and Edith Cooper (1862–1913), offered in their first volume *Long Ago* (1889) both a 'revived' voice of the ancient Greek poet Sappho and admitted that she was almost lost, scattered into fragments, nearly unrevivable. Browning's 'resurrectionist' poetry here was shifted into verse (read in manuscript by Browning himself, who made some minor suggestions) exceptionally conscious of the illusory nature of voices and human 'presences' obtained by words.

How aptly ironic it was that Terence Rattigan (1911–77) should use the author of *The Ring and the Book* for his play *The Browning Version* (1948) with its study of a 'dead', unhappy and unsuccessful school teacher on the verge of a precarious retirement. Browning's vibrant lives were far from Crocker-Harris's. In the nineteenth century, though, the realist tradition in fiction could deal only with multiple non-miraculous conceptions, non-Browning versions, of revival or survival. The banner of realism was persistently, definingly, the empirical and the terrestrial. There were a few 'coming back from the dead' scenes, like the Tichborne claimant,[27] to be sure – Charley Kinraid in Elizabeth Gaskell's *Sylvia's Lovers* (1863),

Allan Armadale in Collins's *Armadale* – but they were explicable, for there were to be no false promises about the end. 'Examining the world in order to find consolation', George Eliot wrote in *Impressions of Theophrastus Such* (1879), published a year after G. H. Lewes's death, 'is very much like looking carefully over the pages of a great book in order to find our own name, if not in the text, at least in a laudatory note'.[28] Browning played with the 'consolation' of revival through words. But that for a secular mind was too close to bad faith. Yet that did not mean George Eliot was indifferent to human continuations and survivals, and the ways in which men and women might, in plots at least, leave conspicuous legacies beyond their deaths. Eliot's secular sense of human persistence, enriched by a Darwinian conception of the deep consequences of the past on the present, impelled her interest in men and women who, from the grave, controlled the living. The shade of Edward Casaubon haunts the lives of Dorothea and Ladislaw in *Middlemarch* (1871–2) all but literally: he lives not through a ghost but a will, the legal dead-hand of an inhibiting financial settlement. For Thomas Hardy, the durability of the past gave it determining presence too. In the non- or anti-ghost story 'The Grave by the Handpost' (1914), the dead father shapes the life (and death) of his son not through supernatural returns but by the very force of being dead, silenced forever in the tomb. The tragedy here, in this most un-resurrectionary of stories, is deadness itself: the impossibility of rights being put wrong, apologies made, forgiveness obtained.

'The Grave by the Handpost' is a late ironization, or cauterization, of the Victorian absorption with tales of the dead, with revival and curious returns. But the ideas I have considered in my chapter were, in their full amplitude, under the early twentieth-century's surveillance. And those Victorian issues of reincarnation, ghosts, survival and the challenge of understanding what resurrection might mean in an empirical age continued to matter well beyond the formal close of the Victorian period. Ideas of the afterlife had their afterlife. James Joyce's name dimly hovers over the title of my chapter, not least because *Dubliners* (1914) and *Ulysses* (1922) were creatively engaged, at whatever cultural remove, with their nineteenth-century inheritance about loss and return. *Ulysses* extended exceptionally the realist ambitions of the nineteenth-century novel and it absorbed, too, the 'non-realist' possibilities of the dead's returns that had so compelled the age in which Joyce was born.[29] The late Victorian popular fiction enthusiasm for the ways in which the modern world might replay scenes from the ancient past – the plots of Haggard and

Corelli – faintly echoed in *Ulysses*'s shadowy replaying of Odysseus's story in the wandering of Leopold Bloom through Dublin on 16 June 1904. 'Some people believe', Bloom thinks, 'that we go on living in another body after death, that we lived before. They call it reincarnation.'[30] Haggard and Corelli knew that well, and perhaps, too, did Bloom. Victorian preoccupations with resurrection and ghosts could not be exorcised either. Maybe, at a metaphorical level, Bloom's marriage to Molly could be resurrected? And there are other, more uncanny revivals. Parnell is not dead and might come back, Bloom is told,[31] and then by strange coincidence he sees Parnell's brother, John Howard Parnell. It is like a secular, 'explicable' haunting: John Howard has, provocatively enough, a 'Haunting face'.[32] And after Paddy Dignam's funeral, Bloom muses on half-resurrectionary, half-haunting words in another probing of the posthumous: 'I will appear to you after death', he thinks, 'You will see my ghost after death. My ghost will haunt you after death.'[33]

But nowhere does *Ulysses* look back to its Victorian inheritance of anxiety about death's dominion, and the nature of resurrection or survival, more than in Bloom's private monologue about the words with which my chapter began: the statement of Jesus before the grave of Lazarus, 'I am the resurrection, and the life.' During Paddy Dignam's funeral, Bloom hears the funeral sentences. And as Jesus's words had intrigued the Victorians because they encapsulated the New Testament's boldest claims about the tomb, so the words prompt Bloom's partly comic, partly puzzled, partly troubled account of what such a miraculous event might really be: Mr Kernan said with solemnity:

> – *I am the resurrection and the life*. That touches a man's inmost heart.
> – It does, Mr Bloom said.
> Your heart perhaps but what price the fellow in the six feet by two with his toes to the daisies? No touching that. Seat of the affections. Broken heart. A pump after all, pumping thousands of gallons of blood every day. One fine day it gets bunged up: and there you are. Lots of them lying around here: lungs, hearts, livers. Old rusty pumps: damn the thing else. The resurrection and the life. Once you are dead you are dead. That last day idea. Knocking them all up out of their graves. Come forth, Lazarus! And he came fifth and lost the job. Get up! Last day! Then every fellow mousing around for his liver and his lights and the rest of his traps. Find damn all of himself that morning. Pennyweight of powder in a skull. Twelve grammes one pennyweight. Troy measure.[34]

Those Victorians with whom I have been concerned were deeply apprehensive about the nature of the miraculous and the possibility that the blunt, blank prospect 'Once you are dead you are dead' could be true. Bloom's words offer materialist, literalist – and perhaps, it may be imagined, Jewish[35] – scepticism about resurrection's probability, as devastating as they are grimly funny. And, as such, they constitute a quirky summary, in the period of high modernism, of the previous century's conflict. Leopold Bloom looks back momentarily to the age of his birth, with its demanding, dismaying encounter between the New Testament's most startling claim about the grave and the alternative arguments of materialist reason. He defuses a little of the trouble he has inherited with a fine bad joke. But the consequences for others of the great nineteenth-century problem of the dead, diversely visible across a host of Victorian cultural forms, were not so easily sealed off. In fact, it is hard to know where those consequences have even begun to end.

Notes

Some material here is considered from a different perspective in my 'Victorian Literature and Bringing the Body Back from the Dead', in Jane Macnaughton, Ulrike Maude and Corinne Saunders (eds.), *The Body and the Arts* (Basingstoke: Palgrave Macmillan, 2009), 103–15.

1 Charles Dickens, *Bleak House* (Harmondsworth: Penguin, 1971), 705.
2 Strauss's *Das Leben Jesu, kritisch bearbeitet* was published originally in 1835–6.
3 I do not, of course, mean to suggest that faith in the resurrection or in eternal life simply failed during the course of the century or that Christian theology in general shifted its emphasis towards less miraculous doctrines. For important works of theology addressing the doctrine of the resurrection, see, for instance, Brooke Foss Westcott's much-reprinted *The Gospel of Resurrection: Thoughts on its Relation to Reason and History* (1866). Arguments over cremation in the 1870s revealed a little of the depth of commitment to the resurrection of the body. See, for instance, Leopold Grindon, 'Cremation Considered in Reference to the Resurrection. By a Truth Seeker' (1874).
4 All references to the Bible are to the King James Version of 1611.
5 And if so, most likely in its most popular 1662 version (it was first published in 1549).
6 Now in the Tate Collection.
7 Now in the Leeds City Art Gallery.
8 [Alfred Tennyson], *In Memoriam AHH* (London: Moxon, 1850), LIV, 78. References subsequently are to this first edition: readers of modern editions will want to know its lyric numbers are slightly different.
9 Alfred Tennyson, *Enoch Arden, and Other Poems* (London: Moxon, 1864), 34.
10 Leon Edel (ed.), *The Complete Tales of Henry James*, 12 vols. (London: Hart-Davis, 1962–4), VI, 277.

11 John Keble, *Lectures on Poetry 1832–1841*, trans. Edward Kershaw Francis, 2 vols. (Oxford: Clarendon, 1912), I. dedication. Matthew Arnold was, one might note, the first Oxford Professor of Poetry to lecture in English.

12 Alan Bell (ed.), *Sir Leslie Stephen's 'Mausoleum Book'* (Oxford: Clarendon, 1977), 95.

13 Now in the Leeds City Art Gallery.

14 Charles Dickens, *A Tale of Two Cities* (Harmondsworth: Penguin, 2000), 12.

15 Translation by William Archer; published by London: Heinemann.

16 Charles Dickens, *Christmas Books* (Oxford: Oxford University Press, 1988), 20.

17 Sheridan Le Fanu, *Madam Crowl's Ghost and Other Stories* (Ware: Wordsworth, 1994), 74.

18 See *Poems of Henrietta A. Huxley with Three of Thomas Henry Huxley* (London: Duckworth, 1913), 52. On this topic generally, see my '"Accept Things as They Are": Reading the Agnostic Poetry of Henrietta Huxley', *Modern Believing*, 42 (2001), 39–48.

19 Anthony Trollope, *The Prime Minister* (Harmondsworth: Penguin, 1983), 194.

20 J. M. Barrie, *Peter Pan* (Harmondsworth: Penguin, 1995), 29.

21 See Carole G. Silver, *Strange and Secret Peoples: Fairies and Victorian Consciousness* (Oxford: Oxford University Press, 1999).

22 George Du Maurier, *Peter Ibbetson* (London: Harper, 1898), 208.

23 Marcel Proust, *Le côté de Guermantes* (Première partie), édition du texte, introduction, bibliographie par Elyane Dezon-Jones ([Paris]: Flammarion, 1987), 150.

24 Dora Greenwell, *Poems* (Edinburgh: Strahan, 1861), 82.

25 Robert Browning, *The Ring and the Book* (Harmondsworth: Penguin, 1971), I, 779.

26 Ibid., I, 733.

27 The Tichborne case concerned a legal claim of Arthur Orton (1834–1898) to be the missing Sir Roger Tichbourne and heir to his fortune. Orton was found to be an impostor.

28 George Eliot, *The Impressions of Theophrastus Such* (Iowa: University of Iowa Press, 1994), 10.

29 For another perspective on realism/non-realism see above, Ch. 2.

30 James Joyce, *Ulysses: The Corrected Text*, Student Edition, ed. by Hans Walter Gabler with Wolfhard Steppe and Claus Melchoir (Harmondsworth: Penguin, 1986), 4.362–3 (all subsequent references to this as *U*, chapter number, line numbers).

31 'Some say he is not in that grave at all. That the coffin was filled with stones. That one day he will come back again', says Mr Power: *U*, 6.923–4.

32 *U*, 8.502.

33 *U*, 6.1000–1.

34 *U*, 6.669–83.

35 I do not mean to overlook the matter of resurrection as a possible component of early Jewish thought.

15

Remembering the Victorians

Introduction

Writing to Virginia Woolf in 1912, Lytton Strachey tried, and failed, to imagine a time when we would love the Victorians, or at least find an acceptable way of condescending to them:

> Is it prejudice, do you think, that makes us hate the Victorians,
> or is it the truth of the case? They seem to me to be a set
> of mouthing bungling hypocrites; but perhaps really there
> is a baroque charm about them which will be discovered by our
> great-great-grandchildren, as we have discovered the charm
> of Donne, who seemed intolerable to the 18th century. Only
> I don't believe it[.][1]

The power of metaphor allows us to think of Matthew Sweet, author of *Inventing the Victorians* (2001), as Strachey's great-great-grandchild, affirming that

> Victorian culture was as rich and difficult and complex and
> pleasurable as our own; that the Victorians shaped our lives and
> sensibilities in countless unacknowledged ways; that they are still
> with us, walking our pavements, drinking in our bars, living in our
> houses, reading our newspapers, inhabiting our bodies.[2]

The three stages of Sweet's argument take us from equivalence ('as rich and difficult and complex and pleasurable as our own'), through influence ('shaped our lives and sensibilities'), to confluence ('inhabiting our bodies'). There is something creepy about the last stage, and Sweet may be thought to overplay his hand; we do not readily think of ourselves as possessed by the past in this way. The title of A. S. Byatt's neo-Victorian novel *Possession* (1990) foregrounds this anxiety both within and beyond the Victorian period. Still, the relation to the past posited by Sweet has at least the advantage of taking Victorian culture seriously, and if his were the dominant perspective the story told in this chapter would be relatively straightforward. But Strachey has had other offspring. His own lack of respect has the immediacy and force of a generational struggle, taking its cue from the first great anti-Victorian works which emerged from writers who were themselves Victorians: Samuel Butler's *The Way of All Flesh* (1903), Edmund Gosse's *Father and Son* (1907). The irreverence of these works (Butler's interpretation of Felicia Hemans's 'Casabianca', a favourite Victorian recitation piece: 'the moral of the poem was that young people cannot begin too soon to exercise discretion in the obedience they pay to their Papa and Mamma') is motivated by a specific quarrel over political, social and cultural authority, which played itself out until the First World War.[3] But what are we to make of Andrew Davies's spiced-up television adaptations of novels by Dickens, Eliot, Gaskell, Thackeray and Trollope, or of the 'Dickens World' theme park in Chatham ('jump on board the Great Expectations Boat Ride for splashing good fun'), or of a 'steampunk' computer screen framed in 'Victorian' gilt moulding?[4] These represent a tiny fraction of our multiple appropriations of Victorian themes, images, texts, characters and material remains, whose common thread is relative freedom from a strong sense of obligation. We might reflect that the Victorians invented the travesty of the past (in their appetite for historical fiction and historiography) long before we travestied *them*, and that Victorian Gothic is the steampunk of its day. But the analogy is dubious. The 'groundlessness' of postmodern appropriation is either absent from Victorian culture or present only as a faint tremor of future shock. Behind the Victorian mask there is usually a face, more or less in earnest (in earnest about masking, for one thing). Such earnestness communicated itself to their immediate heirs and detractors, but during the twentieth century it became increasingly attenuated, or rather became simply one among a number of possible, competing, but equally valid ways of imagining our Victorian 'heritage'. It is a strange journey from the purposeful hostility of the early twentieth century to the postmodern aestheticization and commodification of Victorian figures, issues, texts and style.

    This chapter attempts to chart this trajectory, examining some of the ways in which we have remembered and reconstituted Victorian culture, recycled its products and re-imagined its makers. By 'Victorian' is meant more than the neutral period descriptor for people, furniture, buildings and other aspects of culture 'belonging to, designating, or typical of the reign of Queen Victoria (1837–1901)'. The *Oxford English Dictionary* (*OED*) goes on to record the figurative usage, 'Resembling or typified by the attitudes supposedly characteristic of the Victorian era; prudish, strict; old-fashioned, out-dated'. Popular stereotypes of Victorianness – moralism, hypocrisy, sexual repression, religiosity, bourgeois respectability, the cult of 'home, sweet home', sincerity, humourlessness – have endured; a Channel 4 'Victorian Passions' season believed it still necessary to 'challenge the popular idea of Victorian Britain as a buttoned-up, unsmiling and pre-modern society' in 2008.[5] Yet the shifty indeterminacy of the signifier 'Victorian' is registered in the *OED*'s qualification 'supposedly' – an acknowledgement of historical contingency which has not always been heeded by scholars, journalists, politicians and novelists. In the course of this discussion it will be seen that the ground has shifted under the *OED*'s feet.

Even a bare list of contemporary 'Victoriana' would exceed the bounds of this chapter, and the need for a historical survey makes 'coverage' of the topic unfeasible. I have tried to indicate the main lines of historical narrative but concentrate on what seem to me the most significant features. As already suggested, one is the movement away from a polemical engagement with the period as 'other' towards an acknowledgement of likeness. Another concerns the persistent use of Victorian culture as a means of defining ourselves. This mediation is seldom straightforward, however. The period's culture is so eclectic, conflicted and heterogeneous that it can be (almost) anything we want it to be. The politically conservative can point to Samuel Smiles's *Self-Help* (1859), the liberal to Oscar Wilde's *The Picture of Dorian Gray* (1891): both are iconic 'Victorian' texts and authors, yet susceptible to oppositional counter-interpretations. Darwin has been, and continues to be, both hero and villain. Bound in stays, dragging their monstrous bustles, armoured in bombazine, Victorian ladies either embody an aberrant, exotic, bizarre sexual culture, against which we can define our own; or, on the contrary, their codes of dress and behaviour offer us a powerful symbolic repertoire for understanding ourselves. In effect, in the Victorians we find what we seek, and fabricate or 'discover' what we need.

My third keynote is the epistemological uncertainty that has marked this whole process from the beginning. 'The history of the Victorian Age will never be written: we know too much about it', is Strachey's notorious opening gambit in the preface to *Eminent Victorians* (1918); yet the statement has become so familiar that it is easy to overlook its ambiguity.[6] Does 'we know too much' mean that a definitive history is impossible because there is an overwhelming amount of material, or that for the first post-Victorian generation, the age is over-familiar, too close to home, experienced as personal rather than objective history? We can have no unmediated access to Victorian culture, and what we know about the Victorian age is not static and coherent, but dynamic and unstable, changed by every attempt to understand and engage with it, and every interpretative attempt is contingent on the status and perspective of the individual. Born in 1880, Strachey was the late Victorian product of mid-Victorian parents; the sense of history available to him, shaped by personal experience, is dramatically different from that of a twenty-first-century reader, who draws not only on primary sources, documents and objects, but on the mass of scholarly commentary and analysis produced since the birth of Victorian studies in the 1950s. We may readily assent that 'we know too much': but what we know bears little resemblance to what Strachey knew.

1901–30: modernism and anti-Victorianism

Edmund Gosse began *Father and Son* by claiming it was 'the record of a struggle between two temperaments, two consciences and almost two epochs'.[7] For the early twentieth-century generation, personal recall stands for broad analysis of ideological and cultural tendencies, and idiosyncratic single figures symbolize the age, as in Woolf's affectionate yet unsparing portrait of her parents, Leslie Stephen and Julia Duckworth, as Mr and Mrs Ramsay in *To the Lighthouse* (1927). According to Strachey, 'for the modern inquirer' the interest of Cardinal Manning's life 'depends mainly upon . . . the light which his career throws upon the spirit of his age, and the psychological problems suggested by his inner history'.[8] Needless to say such life-writing was itself a principal Victorian genre. Before *Father and Son*, Gosse himself wrote *The Life of Philip Henry Gosse FRS* (1890), an example of the 'two fat volumes, with which it is our custom to commemorate the dead' mocked by Strachey.[9] The debt to their precursors may be paid in satire and subversion, but such gestures also mask anxiety and longing.

The divided response may be traced in the narrative design of Samuel Butler's posthumously published autobiographical novel *The Way of All*

Flesh, a study of heredity across four (male) generations of the Pontifex family which Butler began working on in 1873. The ordeals suffered by Butler's alter-ego, Ernest Pontifex – bullying father (Theobald), pressure to conform to religious and social orthodoxy, sexual naiveté (mistaking a respectable woman for a prostitute leads to his imprisonment) – are the raw material on which the book works its now-famous indictments of Victorian repression and hypocrisy (the average Anglican congregation 'would have been equally horrified at hearing the Christian religion doubted, and at seeing it practised').[10] However, this armoury of wit and insight belongs not to the emotionally damaged Ernest, but to the narrator Overton, Theobald's friend and contemporary, who becomes Ernest's godfather and supporter. Overton gives a voice to Ernest's repressed inner self, reassuring the reader of the protagonist's survival, but also drawing attention to his self-division: 'as yet he knew nothing of that other Ernest that dwelt within him, and was so much stronger and more real than the Ernest of which he was conscious'.[11] Hypocrisy transmutes into self-unknowing, the object not of scorn but of pathos. Eventually Ernest's literary vocation will equip him with self-knowledge, or at least self-consciousness, but the process cannot be left to his own management.

The struggle to document an escape from parents has the ironic effect of enforcing a return to the scene of the crime – though 'enforcing' may be the wrong word here. *Father and Son*, first published anonymously, is the account of Edmund Gosse's formative years growing up in a devout Plymouth Brethren household, under the sway of his father, the zoologist Philip Henry Gosse. We are not spared the absurdity and cruelty of the father's narrow-minded fundamentalism (that the cruelty is unwitting makes it all the more exasperating) but the account is also humorous and tender; its knowingness is constrained by respect for reality. This does not mean that everything in it is factual: scholarship has uncovered inventions and improvements; the narrative mode itself privileges subjective and creative representations figuring a non-literal or poetic 'truth', art as the survivor's redemption and justification. But Gosse's representations are, so to speak, imprinted with the reality they transform, and this matters because, in the end, it is only this reality which can remember the self in writing.

The theme of the divided self, symbol of a divided age, dominates the archetypal text of modernist anti-Victorianism, Lytton Strachey's quartet of biographical essays, *Eminent Victorians* (1918). Strachey's four principal subjects (Cardinal Manning, Florence Nightingale, Dr Arnold and General Gordon) are figured as divided personalities, constantly transgressing the boundaries between their public and private selves. Their claims to selflessness form the platform for their worldly ambitions; public recognition of their sacrifice placates the demands of their egos. (The analysis and revelation of unconscious motives had been anticipated by Butler – as well as by the Tennyson of 'St Simeon Stylites' (1833).) The attributes that made the book notorious – its camp style, the technical brilliance of its pastiches, its sense of comic timing in the deployment of quotations, its disrespectful wit (for J. A. Froude, 'the loss of his faith turned out to be rather like the loss of a heavy portmanteau, which one afterwards discovers to have been full of old rags and brickbats') – all work to create the distance between author and subject in which paradox and irony flourish, not just as markers of an external judgement but as insights into the subjects themselves.[12] Take, for example, the summary verdict on Manning's conversion to Catholicism as the product of 'the two dominating forces in his nature' – his 'preoccupation with the supernatural' and 'his preoccupation with himself'; or the pointed anachronism of this description of Florence Nightingale's rhetorical technique, borrowed from a war that had not yet occurred: 'Her sarcasm searched the ranks of the officials with the deadly and unsparing precision of a machine-gun.'[13] The First World War, of course, was implicated in the intergenerational contest that Strachey and others were waging, as a monstrous plot of the fathers against the children. 'Victorian' remained a term of abuse into the 1920s, and it is striking that *The Way of All Flesh* achieved its highest critical and popular estimation in that decade. However, the indignation that fuelled the anti-Victorianism of the first two decades of the century was already shading into condescension, and condescension in turn opened the way for more complex recognitions and negotiations.

In *Orlando: A Biography* (1928), Woolf's fantastical century-hopping reinvention of the life of Vita Sackville-West, the protagonist wakes in a nineteenth century characterized by damp and cold, and choked by profuse greenery; and, Woolf remarks, 'The damp struck within.' Since Orlando, like Tiresias, is both male and female, the spectacle of sexual alienation associated with the Victorian 'separate spheres' is especially vivid to him/her: 'The sexes drew further and further apart. No open conversation was tolerated. Evasions and concealments were sedulously practised on both sides.'[14] Wedding rings fetter couples together;

relegated to the domestic sphere of emotional vacuity, Orlando finds that she cannot write: 'either she could think of nothing, and the pen made one large lachrymose blot after another, or it ambled off, more alarmingly still, into mellifluous fluencies about early death and corruption'. Ironically, Orlando chooses 'the most desperate of remedies, which was to yield completely and submissively to the spirit of the age, and take a husband'. Literature, in any case, has become professionalized and respectable, 'an elderly gentleman in a grey suit talking about duchesses'. Reading a contemporary article, she realizes that 'one must never, never say what one thought . . . one must always, always write like somebody else'.[15]

Yet Woolf does not – or cannot? – sustain this harsh note: she succumbs, several generations before Strachey thought it possible, to the 'baroque charm' of Victorian culture. Driving through St James's Park, Orlando sees

> a pyramid, hecatomb, or trophy (for it had something of a banquet-table air) – a conglomeration at any rate of the most heterogeneous and ill-assorted objects, piled higgledy-piggledy in a vast mound where the statue of Queen Victoria now stands! Draped about a vast cross of fretted and floriated gold were widow's weeds and bridal veils; hooked on to other excrescences were crystal palaces, bassinettes, military helmets, memorial wreaths, trousers, whiskers, wedding cakes, cannon, Christmas trees, telescopes, extinct monsters, globes, maps, elephants, and mathematical instruments – the whole supported like a gigantic coat of arms on the right side by a female figure clothed in flowing white; on the left by a portly gentleman wearing a frock-coat and sponge-bag trousers . . . She had never, in all her life, seen anything at once so indecent, so hideous, and so monumental.[16]

Woolf's fantasy of a monument to Victorian invention is a parody of the Queen Victoria Memorial statue outside Buckingham Palace, sculpted by Sir Thomas Brock, and unveiled in 1911 by George V. It was carved from a two-thousand pound block of solid marble, with figures representing Truth, Peace, Constancy and Motherhood, Charity, War, Architecture and Manufacture. Woolf's vision of heterogeneity, incongruity and disorder cannot resist itself: Orlando's shocked recoil (mediated by three very 'Victorian' epithets) is the flip-side of a recognition and fascinated embrace of the grotesque as part of our history and ourselves.

1930s and 1940s: nostalgia and Englishness

Woolf's association of the best and worst of the Victorian achievement with popular patriotism comes to fruition as the modernist repudiation softens in the 1930s. Two rather different allusions to Robert Browning's dreamlike quest poem, '"Childe Roland to the Dark Tower Came"' (1855), may stand for this ambivalent nostalgia. One provides the epigraph to Rudolf Besier's popular play *The Barretts of Wimpole Street: A Comedy in Five Acts* (1930), while in P. G. Wodehouse's comic novel *The Code of the Woosters* (1937), as Bertie Wooster and Jeeves approach Totleigh Towers, the 'lair' of Bertie's nemesis Sir Watkyn Bassett, Bertie reports that '"Childe Roland to the dark tower came, sir", said Jeeves, as we alighted, though what he meant I hadn't an earthly.'[17] Both contexts identify Browning's poem with a Victorian chivalric ideal that the later generation can neither take seriously nor emulate. (It is also characteristic of this period that a well-known Victorian poem is oversimplified and misunderstood.) While there are plenty of darkly humorous scenes in Besier's dramatization of the Moulton-Barretts's crippled family dynamics, the adult children kept in fearful dependence by a monstrous paterfamilias, the play is a 'comedy' because it has a happy ending in Elizabeth's elopement with Browning. Number 50 Wimpole Street is the 'Dark Tower', and Browning the heroic knight riding to Elizabeth's rescue. Jeeves, who quotes Tennyson and Browning regularly, embodies a stolid, conservative respectability that harks back to the Victorians, while comic capital is generated from Bertie's inadequacy as a romance hero. This playful use of the Victorian idealization of romance indicates that the distance between them and us aggressively asserted by the first post-Victorian generation was gradually becoming a reality.

(Auto)biographical treatments of the Victorians were superseded by a historiography committed to revising and complicating the myth of 'Victorianism'. Most influential was G. M. Young's *Portrait of an Age: Victorian England* (1936), a slender but still valuable revisionary history emulating Strachey's method of selection and ostensible 'slightness'. Introducing the second edition in 1953, Young recalled that 'I had always been convinced that Victorianism was a myth, engendered by the long life of the sovereign and of her most illustrious subjects. I was constantly being told that the Victorians did this, or the Victorians thought that, while my own difficulty was to find anything on which they agreed.'[18] Young's Victorians are diverse, eccentric and fiercely independent, and his Victorian age (at its best) is a period of spirited debate and principled opposition, resistant to univocal interpretation. While Young sought to create a more objective historical portrait, his view of the uses of history retains a Victorian moral intent. The conclusion, written in autumn 1936, is burdened with the sense of living in a world of crisis and impending disaster. Young sees the nineteenth-century's achievement as being able 'to disengage the disinterested intelligence, to release it from the entanglements of party and sect – one might almost add, of sex – and to set it operating over the whole range of human life and circumstance'. This benign project's failure in the late Victorian and Edwardian period ('the waning of a great civilization') is an inheritance that must be reckoned with: 'That time has left its scars and poisons with us, and in the daily clamour for leadership, for faith, for a new heart or a new cause, I hear the ghost of late Victorian England whimpering on the grave therof.'[19] The Victorian influence is both good and bad, 'civilization' and its failure: the current generation must fight to prevent the feared regression into barbarism.

This doubleness appears also in experimental texts in the European tradition, including Max Ernst's avant-garde collage anti-novel *Une semaine de bonté* (A week of kindness) (1934).[20] Ernst's raw materials were cheap late nineteenth-century magazines and books from second-hand bookstalls and flea-markets. He took illustrations consumed by Victorian readers and representative of their tastes and ideals – fashion plates, domestic interiors, advertising, travel, adventure – then used a scalpel to isolate, mutilate and reconfigure quotidian images to create shocking distorted reflections of the familiar. In their perverse appropriation of icons of Victorian respectability, Ernst's collages may be understood as revelations of the unconscious, making visible transgressive, aggressive and erotic drives. Yet the disturbing scenes of violence, captivity, rape and apocalypse that make up *Une semaine de bonté* read also as nightmarish projections of the increasingly unsettled and threatening European political situation.

The wider political context also inflected contemporary authors' more distanced relation to 'the Victorian', increasingly used as a generalized category signifying pastness – whether viewed as anachronistic or with nostalgia – an imaginative realm of stable and idealized moral and social values. Victorianness becomes associated with a conservative myth of English identity connoting patriotic ideals of sturdy independence and self-sacrifice, pitched against the global threat of the rise of fascism and the Second World War. But this Victorian Englishness becomes itself suspect, a delusive sign of respectability and conformity. In Graham Greene's espionage thriller *The Ministry of Fear* (1943), set in London during the Blitz, the protagonist Arthur Rowe encounters an Austrian refugee, Willi Hilfe, helping at a charity. Hilfe wears a three-piece tweed suit, and speaks an antiquated, over-precise English:

> It was as if he had come from an old-fashioned family among whom it was important to speak clearly and use the correct words; his care had an effect of charm, not of pedantry. He stood with his hand laid lightly and affectionately on his sister's shoulder as though they formed together a Victorian family group.[21]

It is not surprising that the naïve Rowe is uncertain how to evaluate Hilfe, with his 'old-fashioned' chivalric manners and resemblance to a Victorian family photograph. The mismatch between his anglophile self-representation and Austrian name and identity is unnerving. The ideal of Englishness to which he aspires is outdated, and the keywords of simile ('as if', 'as though') suggest that the likeness is a fabrication. Like Rowe, the reader is disarmed by Hilfe's melancholy imitation of Victorian gentility, and wilfully ignores the clues that hint at Hilfe's true identity as a Nazi spy. In the paranoid wartime atmosphere, adopting the persona of a Victorian gentleman both appeals to Londoners' nostalgia for a more secure, stable past, and is a coded sign of the enemy.

Traces of ambivalent nostalgia may be found in David Lean's two major film adaptations of Dickens's novels, *Great Expectations* (1946) and *Oliver Twist* (1948). Just as classic novels (especially Dickens) were favoured reading during wartime, adaptations of Victorian novels were comforting for post-war audiences, providing the romance of difference, the familiarity and escapism of costume drama. What *Great Expectations* does not, famously, provide, is the reassurance of orthodox narrative closure presided over by a just god, as formulated by Miss Prism in Wilde's *The Importance of Being Earnest*: 'The good end happily, and the bad unhappily. That is what Fiction means.'[22] Lean changed the tone of the novel's ambiguously hopeful definitive ending. In Lean's version, Pip (John Mills) dramatically rescues Estella (Valerie Hobson) from Miss Havisham's reclusive doom, forcing sunlight into the darkened rooms of Satis House, and the pair embrace and leave the house together. The heroically romantic ending is a symbolic liberation from darkness in the aftermath of war that for some readers will be shadowed by Dickens's pessimistic first version of the ending. A rather more conflicted relation between history and contemporary events is suggested by the fate of

Oliver Twist. Alec Guinness's portrayal of Fagin with an oversized prosthetic nose and thick Jewish accent copied George Cruikshank's original illustrations and Dickens's idiom; in the sensitized post-war period, it provoked controversy as anti-Semitic. Ironically, in aiming for historical accuracy, Guinness helped delay the film's US release until 1951.

1950s–1970s: Victorian studies and its consequences

The Second World War, unlike the First, could not be blamed on Victorian patriarchy. When it ended, the way was open for a more diverse response to Victorian culture. The 1951 Festival of Britain 'quoted' the Great Exhibition of 1851 without embarrassment or irony, celebrations of the modern a century apart. At the same time the period itself was receding from memory, arousing a curiosity which manifested itself at different cultural levels, from the academic to the popular. The Victorian Society was founded in 1958, with a campaigning mission to save undervalued Victorian architecture from the wrecking-ball of post-war redevelopment; exhibitions at the Victoria and Albert Museum, from 'London, 1862: The International Exhibition' (1962) to 'The Luxury of Good Taste: An Exhibition of Victorian Design, 1835–80' (1980), demonstrated a growing confidence in the period's appeal to public taste. A hitherto unthinkable revival in the market for Victorian painting (especially the Pre-Raphaelites) and sculpture began. But the real dynamic lay in the surge of Victorian artefacts – clothes, jewellery, furniture, memorabilia – released into the market by the death of their owners. Victorian ephemera flooded into flea-markets and vintage shops, appropriated by fashionable young people for whom the paraphernalia of bourgeois respectability heightened the expression of their own sexual liberation and political idealism.[23] At least one major commercial enterprise, Laura Ashley, owes its existence to the rediscovery of Victorian design: the first Laura Ashley headscarves (produced in 1953) were inspired by Victorian floral prints in the Victoria and Albert Museum in South Kensington. The long-running variety show 'The Good Old Days' (BBC, 1953–83), filmed in the Leeds City Varieties Music Hall (the only surviving music hall in the UK), created a modern pastiche of a moribund popular tradition, complete with audience in faux Victorian costume.

The distance which allowed a new generation of consumers to look with fresh eyes at Victorian material culture also affected the intellectual understanding of the period. The radical judgements of modernism had themselves become over-familiar and stereotyped, and F. R. Leavis's or

William Empson's sweeping dismissal of Victorian literature as, for the most part, fatally lacking in complexity no longer seemed self-evident.[24] Yet the academic revival, like its popular counterpart, had to come from outside the family. It is perhaps significant that the two major journals which signalled this revival originated in America – *Victorian Studies* (University of Indiana, 1956) and *Victorian Poetry* (University of West Virginia, 1962) – as did many of the books that began the critical rehabilitation of major Victorian authors and genres (Walter E. Houghton's *The Victorian Frame of Mind*, Robert Langbaum's *The Poetry of Experience*, both 1957) or broke new ground in their exploration of Victorian subcultures (Steven Marcus's *The Other Victorians: A Study of Sexuality and Pornography in Mid-Nineteenth-Century England* (1966), Richard Altick's *Victorian Studies in Scarlet: Murders and Manners in the Age of Victoria* (1970)). In the 1970s feminist scholarship recognized that the period which supposedly epitomized the sexual and social repression of women was ripe for polemical counter-readings (Elaine Showalter's *A Literature of Their Own* (1977), Sandra Gilbert and Susan Gubar's *The Madwoman in the Attic* (1979)). All these books made the Victorians more complex, less obvious, more like 'us', and therefore more interesting, but what seemed new to their readers has affiliations with earlier ways of thinking about the period. Langbaum's influential analysis of the dramatic monologue in terms of a tension between 'sympathy' and 'judgment' reprises the theme of doubleness and self-division. In their reading of *Jane Eyre* (1847), Gilbert and Gubar's recuperation of Bertha Mason as the symbolic figurehead of repressed desire attributes to Charlotte Brontë an unconscious design as profound, and as perverse, as that attributed to Florence Nightingale by Strachey.

Novelists were quick to follow scholars in recovering and reinterpreting Victorian people, texts and topics for a new generation – creating a subgenre of historiographic metafiction combining postmodern traits with a historicity redolent of Victorian fiction. Gilbert and Gubar's foregrounding of Bertha Mason also pays homage to Jean Rhys's *Wide Sargasso Sea* (1966), where Bertha appears as Antoinette Cosway, the Creole heiress who became the first Mrs Rochester. Rhys's 'prequel' to *Jane Eyre*, though technically not the first retro-Victorian fiction, was a foundational work in the scope and intensity of its re-shaping of a canonical source, as much in its divided narrative, so alien to the dominant 'voice' of Brontë's novel, as in its post-colonial perspective. *Wide Sargasso Sea* tells us that we do not know how to read, or even admire *Jane Eyre* – that we have substituted a false idol (a 'classic') for a more authentic, but more disturbing divinity.

In order to get at its imaginative truth, buried or occluded by superficial or preconceived notions, you must deconstruct the novel formally, thematically, rhetorically.[25]

This strategy was adopted and given a fresh twist in the book which came to embody the post-war, postmodern 'take' on Victorian culture, John Fowles's *The French Lieutenant's Woman* (1969). Fowles's design is radically unstable, and the author draws attention to that instability at every turn, most famously in the chapter 13 digression on narrative authority ('I live in the age of Alain Robbe-Grillet and Roland Barthes; if this is a novel, it cannot be a novel in the modern sense of the word'), and in the alternative endings.[26] A self-consciously intrusive narrative commentary prevents the reader from becoming absorbed by the plot, and the plot itself shifts between romance and a form of intellectual satire, in its depiction of Charles Smithson, a minor aristocrat and amateur palaeontologist beset by his infatuation with an apparently 'fallen' woman, Sarah Woodruff, and by his (mis)understanding of Darwin. The book has been accused of playing the Victorians for cheap laughs. But Fowles's technique faces both ways: his parodic treatment of the conventions of Victorian fiction is matched by his ironic reflection on contemporary intellectual, sexual and social conventions (the novel is set in 1867, and composed exactly a century later). There is no easy displacement of Victorian by modern ideology, and the satirical traffic moves in both directions. Using Victorian contexts and intertexts also provides ironic distance from the contemporary, giving the author a mobility that allows for both the ludic and the historically responsible.

Fowles's playground is a real place, Lyme Regis, with impeccable Victorian credentials; that is part of the book's piquancy. Brian Moore's *The Great Victorian Collection* (1975) relocates Victorian sensibility to a motel parking lot in California, an emblematic site of our dehistoricized, rootless modern cultural condition. Anthony Maloney, a Canadian historian with a research interest in Victorian culture, arrives at this motel and overnight dreams into existence a great Victorian collection, including well-known objects from museums and private collections, but also things only known through documents or by repute. The collection is fabulous, yet implacably material; it fades and loses authenticity when Maloney tries to leave or forget it, but in its historical significance and fascination for the media, the collection becomes an impossible burden of responsibility, and ultimately destroys its creator. Moore's play with questions of originality and imitation looks forward to Baudrillard, but his fantasy is grounded in a real enough phenomenon, the boom-ing transatlantic trade in Victoriana, as objects, manuscripts and books migrated from Great Britain to wealthier US institutions and private col-lectors. The collection in this sense embodies the losses and dispersals of which it is made up: its lack of authenticity is not material, but exis-tential. In the end, all that it amounts to is a spectacle, mediated to an uncomprehending public. The motel parking lot is like a laboratory in which the idea of 'the Victorian' is tested to destruction.

From the 1980s to now: Victorian values and neo-Victoriana

Myths of the Victorian are always more or less ideologically loaded, but only in the late twentieth century were they appropriated to overtly party political ends. On coming to power in 1979 Margaret Thatcher's Con-servative government proposed an agenda that the press soon tagged a return to 'Victorian values': individual responsibility, *laissez-faire* eco-nomics, law and order, sexual morality and the family. The identification of Victorian principles with an entrepreneurial free market economy was an extremely selective interpretation, not least because of the Thatcherite denial of that consummately 'Victorian' concept, society. But Victorian-ists took to heart the enlisting of their period to the right-wing cause. Conservative critics seriously proposed the Victorians as proponents of strong principles that could cure contemporary social problems.[27] David Lodge's *Nice Work* (1988), which updates Elizabeth Gaskell's industrial novel *North and South* (1855) for post-industrial Thatcherite Britain, sati-rizes Thatcherite policies (such as the erosion of higher education) but is almost as sceptical about liberal idealism as a solution to social problems. The industrial action that takes place in the key settings in Rummidge (Lodge's Birmingham) in a university and a factory is tokenistic and the protagonists' happy ending is effected, as in Gaskell, by the magic touch of an inheritance.

Nice Work anticipates the 1990s' flowering of what is now termed the neo-Victorian novel, partly stimulated by the popular success of A. S. Byatt's Booker Prize-winning *Possession: A Romance* (1990), which com-bined a page-turning detective story with high intellectual ambition characterized by allusiveness and bravura pastiches and parodies of Victo-rian texts.[28] Neo-Victorian novels wear their debt to Victorian scholarship on their sleeve, not least in their propensity for academic protagonists (from Fowles's pedantic narrator to Lodge's left-wing lecturer Robyn Penrose), but Byatt takes it further. The novel is populated by modern scholars and critics representing different (largely antagonistic) schools of thought. The plot concerns an affair between two invented Victorian poets, Randolph Henry Ash (modelled on Browning) and Christabel LaMotte (a composite of Christina Rossetti, Emily Dickinson and Elizabeth Barrett Browning), uncovered through the detective work of two young scholars, Roland Mitchell and Maud Bailey. Byatt encourages the reader's pleasure in piecing together the evidence and solving a mystery, and proposes a feminist revision of the canon: discovering LaMotte's influence on Ash has a significant impact on poetry criticism and gender studies. Yet she also denies the reader the satisfaction of definitive interpretations and easy closure. The academic characters are experts on their chosen authors, yet they cannot really know or understand them: the poets retain their mystique and authority. What first appears an exercise in postmodern playfulness – interpretative free-for-all, literary pastiche, allusiveness – cautiously reinstates a rather 'Victorian', even Arnoldian ideal of cultural value and history.

The neo-Victorian novel since *Possession* shares some features with its 1960s precursors. It exhibits metafictional formal traits, especially intertextual reference to Victorian texts. It tends to reclaim the period for a liberal agenda by privileging marginal identities and voices – servants, prostitutes, gays and lesbians, black and colonial peoples. Yet the emphasis on low-life settings, criminal gangs and other subcultures implies a rather 'Victorian' sensationalism, as well as a determination to project contemporary social concerns on to the past. Such decentring extends also to narrative voicing: the authoritative omniscient narrator is typically replaced by the individual authority of a confessional first-person narrator. However, this is not about the simple exchange of one authority for another; subjective voices are put in competition or dispute, further complicating the possibility of narrative closure.

Several types of neo-Victorian novel have emerged. A number of writers have emulated *Wide Sargasso Sea* in rewriting a specific Victorian text. Valerie Martin's *Mary Reilly: The Untold Story of Dr. Jekyll and Mr Hyde* (1990) takes a novella notorious for its paucity of female characters, and re-narrates it from a woman servant's perspective. Martin skirts the danger of being overshadowed by the precursor text by concentrating on Mary's life below stairs; her realistically brief encounters with Jekyll and Hyde, and her attempt to puzzle out the relation between them, are brought to bear on her own troubled family history. Peter Carey's *Jack Maggs* (1997) is a post-colonial rewriting of Dickens's *Great Expectations* from the perspective of the transported convict Magwitch, corrupted and betrayed by the mother country. Such revisionary rewriting of a canonical text may be distinguished from novels that appropriate real or fictional Victorian figures and invent new narratives for them, as in Lynne Truss's *Tennyson's Gift* (1996), focalized through Tennyson's circle on the Isle of Wight in 1864 (Charles L. Dodgson ('Lewis Carroll'), photographer Julia Margaret Cameron, painter G. F. Watts). An extreme example is Alan Moore and Kevin O'Neill's graphic novel *The League of Extraordinary Gentlemen* (2000), which brings together the damaged protagonists of several late Victorian fictions for a dangerous mission set in 1898: Captain Nemo, Allan Quatermain, Mina Harker, Hawley Griffin and (again) Stevenson's Dr Henry Jekyll and Mr Edward Hyde.[29] In a Victorian rewriting of comic book tradition, the heroes' superhuman qualities are inseparable from physical or psychological deformity. Most common are fictions that adopt Victorian novel conventions to construct a new Victorian fiction for our time, such as Charles Palliser's *The Quincunx* (1989), a scholarly historical pastiche and monumental *hommage* to the atmosphere, environments and social consciousness of Dickens. 'Dickensian' is the standard descriptor for these usually lengthy works packed with historical research, concrete and realistic detail, intricate plots and sub-plots – a conservatism in form that may be seen as a nostalgic or anxious assertion of a transcendent cultural standard, which also appeals to a mass readership (as in the popular success of Michel Faber's *The Crimson Petal and the White* (2002)).

The cultural value of the recent tide of neo-Victoriana has been much debated. The dense historical research on show in the neo-Victorian novel does not guard against accusations of postmodern nostalgia, in which the past is filtered through contemporary ideology, making the Victorians over in our own image, creating a pastiche that is accepted as 'true', and thereby eroding our sense of the distinction between history and fiction. We may object to the peddling of a morally irresponsible relativism, or the aestheticizing of history. But at its best the neo-Victorian novel also questions the grounds of historical knowledge in its alternative readings of the period's culture (while simultaneously reifying and preserving the past), and empowers readers to influence what constitutes 'reality'. Yet what seems most postmodern is also in essence Victorian: the nineteenth-century realist novel was just as committed to individual and personal histories (as in the privileging of Esther Summerson's subjective view above that of the omniscient narrator in Dickens's *Bleak House* (1852–3), and to positioning the reader as active and discriminating.

The pitfalls of postmodern nostalgia are largely sidestepped in *Topsy Turvy* (dir. Mike Leigh, 1999), which reconstructs the creation of W. S. Gilbert and Arthur Sullivan's comic opera *The Mikado* (1885) in the context of the late Victorian enthusiasm for oriental art and design. The film displays a care for historical accuracy and self-consciously addresses the modernity of the 1880s through the motif of reactionary responses to new technology (Gilbert's elderly father is terrified of being electrocuted by the electric doorbell at his son's house). Yet the bases of historical knowledge and personal history are addressed by Leigh's working methods, whereby actors create their roles through research and planned improvisation – a reflexive approach repeated in the film's intercutting between stage performance and behind-the-scenes action. The resulting character portraits expose secret lives: D'Oyly Carte stars George Grossmith and Jessie Bond's intravenous drug-use, the conflict between Leonora Braham's virginal stage persona as Yum-Yum and her private life as single mother. If Victorian 'issues' triangulate with our own time, it is due to our shared modernity.

The question of whether neo-Victorian novels offer a rewriting of Victorian culture so radical that they falsify history is relevant to the most critically and commercially successful example, Sarah Waters's triad of queer historical novels set in the later Victorian period, *Tipping the Velvet* (1998), *Affinity* (1999) and *Fingersmith* (2002).[30] The extent to which Waters recovers or invents occluded lesbian history is complicated by the novels' vividly realized socio-historical context and dense realistic detail. Like Byatt, Waters comes from an academic background and her fictions bear the imprint of her doctoral research on historical lesbian and gay writing, the influence of Victorian Gothic and sensation fiction (especially Dickens, Wilkie Collins and Sheridan Le Fanu) and of cultural and social history, and feminist and queer theory. *Fingersmith* is an ingenious rewriting of Collins's *The Woman in White* (1860), which also shows the influence of Marcus's *The Other Victorians* in reworking Collins's sterile connoisseur Mr Fairlie in the guise of the historical bibliographer of pornography H. E. Ashbee. Michel Foucault's *Discipline and Punish: The Birth of the Prison* (1977) is overtly referenced in the panoptical analogies between domestic and prison space in *Affinity*. The creative transformation of such scholarly sources gives Waters's writing great confidence and authority, as well as appealing to a growing university-educated readership familiar with sensation fiction and critical theory.

Although tagged 'lesbian novels', only Waters's debut has explicit lesbian sex-scenes; the other two books are more concerned with the interiority of lesbian identity and the complexities of same-sex relationships. *Tipping the Velvet*, a tour through lesbian subcultures in late Victorian London – the music hall, a secret club of aristocratic Sapphic libertines, a working-class socialist group – seeks to close the gap between historical and contemporary lesbian experience. Costume and performance license the expression of transgressive sexuality (a woman may dress as a male 'masher' on the music hall stage), and costume allows for identity shifts: lesbian protagonist Nan King dispassionately performs oral sex on a man while dressed as a guardsman, but in women's dress, shies away from prostitution. The queer polemic is at its most overt and overdetermined in this first novel, which ends (implausibly) with all the key women characters meeting at a rally in Victoria Park; the only one not to find a happy ending of sorts is the lesbian who took refuge in a conventional heterosexual marriage. The treatment of queer identity is more mature, troubling and congruent with Victorian historicity in *Affinity*, where the vulnerable prison-visitor Margaret Prior is tricked by secret lovers the spiritualist medium Selina Dawes and Prior's servant, Ruth Vigers: Selina's claimed spiritual affinity with Margaret is betrayed in the name of a more earthy passion, with tragic results. In *Fingersmith* the same-sex attraction of mistress and servant foreshadows the twisting plot's investigation of emotionally complex sororal and mother–daughter relationships. There is some justice to Waters's wry description of *Tipping the Velvet* as a 'lesbo-Victorian romp', but the other novels are serious meditations on Victorian literature and society.[31]

The centenary of Queen Victoria's death in 2001 produced a plethora of books, exhibitions and events surveying and re-evaluating the period and its afterlife, and the spirit of this revivalism was overwhelmingly celebratory. The major exhibition 'The Victorian Vision: Inventing New Britain' (Victoria and Albert Museum) explored 'vision' in the three senses of visionaries such as Ruskin, cultural perspective and visual media. The exhibition's commitment to positioning Victoria's British empire within a 'global context', where the masters' influence on the colonies was reciprocated by the Victorians becoming 'cultural and spiritual sponges, absorbing ideas from everywhere', also reflects the contemporary dominance of post-colonial discourse.[32] Asa Briggs's foreword to the exhibition catalogue acknowledged the great shift in attitudes in the previous century: 'How we describe and interpret the Victorians reveals as much about ourselves as about them. We now take them seriously: we once did not.'[33] Briggs's formula could be reversed: the modernists' satirical strategies indicate that they took the Victorians very seriously indeed, while the current phase of Victorian revivalism is more concerned with surface than substance. As Cora Kaplan warns, 'Victorian society is getting a better press than it has for a long time as a source of pride in Britain's accomplishments; this revaluation has more to do with the deep political conservatism and the profound pessimism of the present moment than a better and more balanced perspective on the injustice and inequalities of an earlier age.'[34] It is safe to say that postmodern Victoriana has much more to say about us than about them.

Notes

1 *Virginia Woolf and Lytton Strachey: Letters*, ed. Leonard Woolf and James Strachey (London: Hogarth Press, 1969), 43.

2 Matthew Sweet, *Inventing the Victorians* (London: Faber, 2001), xxiii.

3 Samuel Butler, *The Way of All Flesh*, ed. J. Cochrane and intr. Richard Hoggart (Harmondsworth: Penguin, 1986), 153.

4 www.dickensworld.co.uk, http://en.wikipedia.org/wiki/Steampunk. 'Steampunk' refers to imaginary, mock-Victorian worlds inspired by Jules Verne's and H. G. Wells's futuristic fictions, where the period's look and technology sits alongside fantastical machinery or monsters.

5 www.channel4.com/history/microsites/V/victorian-passions/promo.html.

6 Lytton Strachey, *Eminent Victorians*, ed. John Sutherland (Oxford: Oxford University Press, 2003), 5.

7 Edmund Gosse, *Father and Son: A Study of Two Temperaments*, ed. P. Abbs (Harmondsworth: Penguin, 1989), 35.

8 Strachey, *Eminent Victorians*, 9.

9 Ibid., 6.

10 Butler, *The Way of All Flesh*, 94.

11 Ibid., 158.

12 Strachey, *Eminent Victorians*, 35.

13 Ibid., 46, 112.

14 Virginia Woolf, *Orlando: A Biography* (London: Grafton, 1977), 143.

15 Ibid., 152, 175, 178–9.

16 Ibid., 145.

17 P. G. Wodehouse, *The Code of the Woosters* (Harmondsworth: Penguin, 1999), 30. Besier's epigraph is actually taken from Browning's source, Edgar's song in *King Lear*.

18 G. M. Young, *Portrait of an Age: Victorian England* (2nd edn, Oxford: Oxford University Press, 1977), vi.

19 Ibid., 163, 164.

20 Max Ernst, *Une semaine de bonté: A Surrealistic Novel in Collage* (New York: Dover, 1976).

21 Graham Greene, *The Ministry of Fear* (London: Vintage, 2001), 43.

22 Oscar Wilde, *Plays, Prose Writings and Poems*, intr. Isobel Murray (London: Everyman, 1975), 367.

23 See also the artist Tom Phillips's altered book, *A Humument: A Treated Victorian Novel* (4 editions 1970–present, online at humument.com), which 'reveals' an erotic and subversive subtext from W. H. Mallock's *A Human Document* (3 vols., 1892).

24 Leavis notoriously excluded Dickens from the novelists of *The Great Tradition* (1948), although he changed his position for *Dickens the Novelist* (1970).

25 See also D. M. Thomas's novel *Charlotte: The Final Journey of Jane Eyre* (2000).

26 John Fowles, *The French Lieutenant's Woman* (London: Vintage, 2004), 97.

27 See Gertrude Himmelfarb's *The Demoralization of Society: From Victorian Virtues to Modern Values* (London: Alfred A. Knopf, 1995).

28 'Neo-Victorian' is a recent and still contested coinage; 'retro-Victorian' and 'quasi-Victorian' are alternatives.

29 See Jules Vernes's *Twenty Thousand Leagues Under the Sea* (1870), Rider Haggard's *King Solomon's Mines* (1886), Bram Stoker's *Dracula* (1897), and H. G. Wells's *The Invisible Man* (1897).

30 *Tipping the Velvet* won the Somerset Maugham and *Sunday Times* Young Writer prizes in 2000. Andrew Davies adapted the novel for the BBC in 2002 and *Fingersmith* in 2005. The film of *Affinity* was released in 2008.

31 Christina Patterson, 'Sarah Waters: The Hot Tip', *Independent*, 16 Sept. 2006, www.independent.co.uk/news/people/sarah-waters-the-hot-tip-416255.html.

32 J. M. Mackenzie (ed.), *The Victorian Vision: Inventing New Britain* (London: Victoria and Albert Museum, 2001), 25.

33 Ibid., 7.

34 Cora Kaplan, '*Fingersmith*'s Coda: Feminism and Victorian Studies', *Journal of Victorian Culture*, 13 (2008), 52.

Further reading

1. Introduction

Kaplan, C., *Victoriana: Histories, Fictions, Criticisms*, Edinburgh: Edinburgh University Press, 2007

Sweet, M., *Inventing the Victorians*, London: Faber, 2001

O'Gorman, F. (ed.), Roundtable on 'Victorian "Afterlives"', *Journal of Victorian Culture* 13, 2 (2008), with essays by Carol Christ, Tracy Hargreaves, Peter McDonald and Sharon Aronofsky Weltman

O'Gorman, F. (ed.), 'Where Next in Victorian Literary Studies?', four essays by David Amigoni, John Bowen, Valerie Sanders and Joanne Shattock, *Literature Compass*, 4 (2007) (online journal)

O'Gorman, F. and Turner, K. (eds.), *The Victorians and the Eighteenth Century: Reassessing the Tradition*, Aldershot: Ashgate, 2004

Pulham, P., and Arias, R. (eds.), *Haunting and Spectrality in Neo-Victorian Fiction: Repossessing the Past*, Basingstoke: Palgrave Macmillan, 2010

Wilson, A. N., *The Victorians*, London: Arrow, 2003

After the Victorians, London: Hutchinson, 2005

2. Science and culture

Beer, G., *Darwin's Plots: Evolutionary Narrative in Darwin, George Eliot and Nineteenth-Century Fiction*, 2nd edn, Cambridge: Cambridge University Press, 2000

Cosslett, T., *The 'Scientific Movement' and Victorian Literature*, Sussex: Harvester Press; New York: St Martin's Place, 1982

Dawson, G., *Darwin, Literature and Victorian Respectability*, Cambridge: Cambridge University Press, 2005

Gossin, P., *Thomas Hardy's Novel Universe: Astronomy, Cosmology, and Gender in the Post-Darwinian World*, Aldershot and Burlington, VT: Ashgate, 2007

Levine, G., *Darwin and the Novelists: Patterns of Science in Victorian Fiction*, Chicago: University of Chicago Press, 1988

Dying to Know: Scientific Epistemology and Narrative in Victorian England, Chicago: University of Chicago Press, 2002

Lightman, B. *The Origins of Agnosticism: Victorian Unbelief and the Limits of Knowledge*, Baltimore: Johns Hopkins University Press, 1987

Lightman, B. (ed.), *Victorian Science in Context*, Chicago: University of Chicago Press, 1997

Rylance, R., *Victorian Psychology and British Culture 1850–1880*, Oxford: Oxford University Press, 2000

Shuttleworth, S., *George Eliot and Nineteenth-Century Science: The Make-Believe of a Beginning*, Cambridge: Cambridge University Press, 1984

Smith, J., *Charles Darwin and Victorian Visual Culture*, Cambridge: Cambridge University Press, 2006

Turner, F., *Between Science and Religion: The Reaction to Scientific Naturalism in Late Victorian England*, New Haven and London: Yale University Press, 1974

White, P., *Thomas Huxley: Making the 'Man of Science'*, Cambridge: Cambridge University Press, 2003

Willis, M., *Mesmerists, Monsters, and Machines: Science Fiction and the Cultures of Science in the Nineteenth Century*, Kent, OH: Kent State University Press, 2006

3. Technology

Asendorf, C., *Batteries of Life: On the History of Things and Their Perception in Modernity*, Berkeley: University of California Press, 1993

Bailey, P., *Popular Culture and Performance in the Victorian City*, Cambridge: Cambridge University Press, 1998

Benjamin, W., *The Arcades Project*, trans. Howard Eiland and Kevin McLaughlin, Cambridge, MA: Belknap Press, 1999

Crary, J., *Techniques of the Observer: On Vision and Modernity in the Nineteenth Century*, Cambridge, MA and London: MIT Press, 1992

Suspensions of Perception: Attention, Spectacle, and Modern Culture, Cambridge, MA., MIT Press, 1999

Giedion, S., *Mechanization Takes Command: A Contribution to Anonymous History*, New York: Norton, 1969

Mannoni, L., *The Great Art of Light and Shadow, Archaeology of the Cinema*, trans. Richard Crangle, Exeter: University of Exeter Press, 2000

Miller, A. H., *Novels behind Glass: Commodity Culture and Victorian Narrative*, Cambridge: Cambridge University Press, 1995

Picker, J. M., *Victorian Soundscapes*, Oxford: Oxford University Press, 2003

'Atlantic Cable', *Victorian Review*, 34, 1 (2008), 34–8

Seltzer, M., *Bodies and Machines*, New York and London: Routledge, 1992

Sternberger, D., *Panorama of the Nineteenth Century*, trans. Joachim Neugroschel, Oxford: Blackwell, 1977

Thurschwell, P., *Literature, Technology, and Magical Thinking, 1880–1920*, Cambridge: Cambridge University Press, 2001

4. Economics and business

Alborn, T., *Conceiving Companies: Joint-Stock Politics in Victorian England*, London: Routledge, 1998

Berg, M., *The Machinery Question and the Making of Political Economy 1815–1848*, Cambridge: Cambridge University Press, 1982

Gallagher, C., *The Industrial Reformation of English Fiction: Social Discourse and Narrative Form, 1832–1867*, Chicago: University of Chicago Press, 1985

Hilton, B., *The Age of Atonement: The Influence of Evangelicalism on Social and Economic Thought, 1785–1865*, Oxford: Oxford University Press, 1988

Maloney, J., *Marshall, Orthodoxy, and the Professionalisation of Economics*, Cambridge: Cambridge University Press, 1985

O'Gorman, F. (ed.), *Victorian Literature and Finance*, Oxford: Oxford University Press, 2007

Parsons, W., *The Power of the Financial Press: Journalism and Economic Opinion in Britain and America*, New Brunswick: Rutgers University Press, 1990

Pollard, S., *Britain's Prime and Britain's Decline: The British Economy 1870–1914*, London: Edward Arnold, 1989

Poovey, M., *Genres of the Credit Economy: Mediating Value in Eighteenth- and Nineteenth-Century Britain*, Chicago: University of Chicago Press, 2008

Searle, G. R., *Morality and the Market in Victorian Britain*, Oxford: Clarendon, 1998

5. War

Anderson, O. A., 'The Growth of Christian Militarism in Mid-Victorian Britain', *English Historical Review*, 86 (1971), 46–72

Bond, B. (ed.), *Victorian Military Campaigns*, London: Hutchinson, 1967

Bradby, D., James, L. and Sharratt, B. (eds.), *Performance and Politics in Popular Drama*, Cambridge: Cambridge University Press, 1980

Brantlinger, P., *Rule of Darkness: British Literature and Imperialism, 1830–1914*, Ithaca: Cornell University Press, 1988

Clarke, I. F., *Voices Prophesying War 1763–1984*, 2nd edn, Oxford: Oxford University Press, 1992

Cookson, J. E., 'The Edinburgh and Glasgow Duke of Wellington Statues: Early Nineteenth-Century Unionist Nationalism as a Tory Project', *Scottish Historical Review*, 83 (2004), 23–40

Cunningham, H., *The Volunteer Force: A Social and Political History, 1859–1908*, London: Croom Helm, 1975

Dawson, G., *Soldier Heroes: British Adventure, Empire and the Imagining of Masculinities*, London: Routledge, 1994

Erickson, C., *Her Little Majesty: The Life of Queen Victoria*, London: Robson, 2004

Girouard, M., *The Return to Camelot: Chivalry and the English Gentleman*, New Haven: Yale University Press, 1981

Harrington, P., *British Artists and War: The Face of Battle in Paintings and Prints, 1700–1914*, London: Greenhill Books, 1993

Hichberger, J. W. M., *Images of the Army: The Military in British Art, 1815–1914*, Manchester: Manchester University Press, 1988

Hill, R., 'The Gordon Literature', *Durham University Journal*, 47 (1955), 97–103.

Howard, M. E., *War and the Liberal Conscience*, London: Temple Smith, 1978

Johnson, D., 'The Death of Gordon: A Victorian Myth', *Journal of Imperial and Commonwealth History*, 10 (1982), 285–310

MacKenzie, J. M. (ed.), *Popular Imperialism and the Military, 1850–1950*, Manchester: Manchester University Press, 1992

Mangan, J. A. and Walvin, J. (eds.), *Manliness and Morality: Middle-Class Masculinity in Britain and America 1800–1940*, Manchester: Manchester University Press, 1987

Paris, M., *Warrior Nation: Images of War in British Popular Culture, 1850–2000*, London: Reaktion Books, 2000

Porter, R. (ed.), *Myths of the English*, Cambridge: Polity Press, 1992

Reader, W. J., *At Duty's Call: A Study in Obsolete Patriotism*, Manchester: Manchester University Press, 1988

Richards, J., *Imperialism and music: Britain 1876–1953*, Manchester: Manchester University Press, 2001

Richards, J. (ed.), *Imperialism and Juvenile Literature*, Manchester: Manchester University Press, 1989

Simon, B., and Bradley, I. (eds.), *The Victorian Public School*, London: Gill and Macmillan, 1975

Spiers, E. M., *The Scottish Soldier and Empire, 1854–1902*, Edinburgh: Edinburgh University Press, 2006

Streets, H., *Martial Races: The Military, Race and Masculinity in British Imperial Culture, 1857–1914*, Manchester: Manchester University Press, 2004

Summers, A., 'Militarism in Britain before the Great War', *History Workshop*, 2 (1976), 104–23

6. Music

Bashford, C., *The Pursuit of High Culture: John Ella and Chamber Music in Victorian London*, Cambridge: Boydell, 2007

Burgan, M., 'Heroines at the Piano: Women and Music in Nineteenth-Century Fiction', *Victorian Studies*, 30 (1986), 51–76

Ehrlich, C., *The Music Profession in Britain since the Eighteenth Century*, Oxford: Clarendon, 1985

Mackerness, E. D., *A Social History of English Music*, London: Routledge and Kegan Paul, 1966

Musgrave, M. *The Musical Life of the Crystal Palace*, Cambridge: Cambridge University Press, 1995

Musgrave, M. (ed.), *George Grove, Music and Victorian Culture*, Basingstoke: Palgrave Macmillan, 2003

Richards, J., *Imperialism and Music: Britain 1876–1953* (Studies in Imperialism), Manchester: Manchester University Press, 2001

Russell, D., *Popular Music in England, 1840–1914: A Social History*, 2nd edn, Manchester: Manchester University Press, 1997

Shaw, G. B., *Shaw's Music*, ed. Dan H. Laurence, 3 vols., New York: Dodd, Mead, 1981

Solie, R. A., *Music in Other Words: Victorian Conversations*, Berkeley: University of California Press, 2004

Weber, W., *Music and the Middle Class: The Social Structure of Concert Life in London, Paris and Vienna*, New York: Holmes and Meier, 1975
Young, P. M., *George Grove, 1820–1900: A Biography*, London: Macmillan, 1980

7. Theatre

Bibliographical note

One of the difficulties faced by scholars of Victorian drama, in comparison with the study of poetry or the novel, is the inaccessibility of primary materials. There are several well-edited volumes of plays in the Oxford World's Classics series, as well as collections published by Cambridge University Press and Broadview Press. Increasingly, the web is hosting digitized collections of plays and other theatrical source materials, such as drawings and photographs, playbills, set designs and other visual ephemera. The following websites offer useful and scholarly starting points for exploring this material (the list is not exhaustive):
The Adelphi Calendar: www.emich.edu/public/english/adelphi—calendar/m33d.htm
The Victorian Plays Project: http://victorian.worc.ac.uk/modx/
Victoria and Albert Museum, PeoplePlay: www.peopleplayuk.org.uk/
Buried Treasures: the Lord Chamberlain's Plays Project: www.rhul.ac.uk/Drama/Research/chamberlains-plays/index.html

Booth, M. R., *English Melodrama*, London: Jenkins, 1965
    Theatre in the Victorian Age, Cambridge: Cambridge University Press, 1991
    Victorian Spectacular Theatre, 1850–1910, London: Routledge and Kegan Paul, 1981
Bratton, J., *New Readings in Theatre History*, Cambridge: Cambridge University Press, 2003
Brooks, P., *The Melodramatic Imagination: Balzac, James, and the Mode of Excess*, New Haven: Yale University Press, 1976
Davis, J., and Emeljanow, V., *Reflecting the Audience, London Theatregoing, 1840–1880*, Iowa City: University of Iowa Press, 2001
Davis, T. C., *The Economics of the British Stage, 1800–1914*, Cambridge: Cambridge University Press, 2002
Donkin, E., and Davis, T. C. (eds.), *Nineteenth-Century British Women Playwrights*, Cambridge: Cambridge University Press, 1999
Hadley, E., *Melodramatic Tactics: Theatricalized Dissent in the English Marketplace, 1800–1885*, Stanford: Stanford University Press, 1995
Meisel, M., *Realizations: Narrative, Pictorial, and Theatrical Arts in the Nineteenth Century*, Princeton: Princeton University Press, 1983
Moody, J., *Illegitimate Theatre in London, 1770–1840*, Cambridge: Cambridge University Press, 2000
Moody, J., and O'Quinn, D. (eds.), *The Cambridge Companion to British Theatre, 1730–1830*, Cambridge: Cambridge University Press, 2007
Nicoll, A., *A History of English Drama, 1660–1900*, vol. IV: *Early Nineteenth Century Drama, 1850-1900*, 2nd edn, Cambridge: Cambridge University Press, 1955
    A History of English Drama, 1660–1900, vol. V: *Late Nineteenth Century Drama, 1850- 1900*, 2nd edn, Cambridge: Cambridge University Press, 1959

Powell, K. (ed.), *The Cambridge Companion to Victorian and Edwardian Theatre*, Cambridge: Cambridge University Press, 2004

8. Popular culture

Bailey, P., *Popular Culture and Performance in the Victorian City*, Cambridge: Cambridge University Press, 2003
Boardman, K., *Popular Victorian Women Writers*, Manchester: Manchester University Press, 2004
Donaldson, W. (ed.), *Popular Literature in Victorian Scotland*, London: Pergamon, 1986
Faulk, B. J., *Music Hall and Modernity: The Late Victorian Discovery of Popular Culture*, Athens: Ohio University Press, 2004
Ferguson, C., *Language, Science and Popular Fiction in the Victorian Fin-de-Siècle: The Brutal Tongue*, Burlington, VT: Ashgate, 2006
Haywood, I., *The Revolution in Popular Literature: Print, Politics, and the People, 1790–1860*, Cambridge: Cambridge University Press, 2004
Kember, J., *Marketing Modernity: Victorian Popular Shows and Early Cinema*, Exeter: University of Exeter Press, 2009
Mitch, D. F., *The Rise of Popular Literacy in Victorian England: The Influence of Private Choice and Public Policy*, Philadelphia: University of Pennsylvania Press, 1992
Victorian Popular Culture: A Portal. Adam Matthew Digital, 2008.
Waters, C., *British Socialists and the Politics of Popular Culture: 1884–1914*, Palo Alto: Stanford University Press, 1990
Wright, S. M., *The Decorative Arts in the Victorian Period*, London: Society of Antiquaries of London, 1989

9. Satirical print culture

Boyce, G., Curran, J., and Wingate, P., *Newspaper History from the Seventeenth Century to the Present Day*, London: Sage Publications, 1970
Collins, P., *Dickens and Crime*, 3rd edn, New York: St Martin's Press, 1994
Cronin, R., *Romantic Victorians: English Literature, 1824–1840*, Basingstoke and New York: Palgrave Macmillan, 2002
Hollis, P., *The Pauper Press: A Study in Working-Class Radicalism of the 1830s*, Oxford: Oxford University Press, 1970
Ledger, S., *Dickens and the Popular Radical Imagination*, Cambridge: Cambridge University Press, 2007
Kunzle, D., 'The First Ally Sloper: The Earliest Popular Cartoon Character as a Satire on the Victorian Work Ethic', *Oxford Art Journal*, 8 (1985), 40–8
Lodge, S., *Thomas Hood and Nineteenth-Century Poetry: Work, Play and Politics*, Manchester and New York: Manchester University Press, 2007
Rose, J., *The Intellectual Life of the British Working Classes*, New Haven and London: Yale University Press, 2001
Strachan, J., *Advertising and Satirical Culture in the Romantic Period*, Cambridge: Cambridge University Press, 2007

10. Journalism

Altick, R., *The English Common Reader: A Social History of the Mass Reading Public, 1800–1900*, 2nd edn, Columbus: Ohio State University Press, 1998

Anderson, B., *Imagined Communities: Reflections on the Origin and Spread of Nationalism*, rev. edn, London: Verso, 2006

Anderson, P., *The Printed Image and the Transformation of Popular Culture 1790–1860*, Oxford: Clarendon, 1991

Brake, L., *Print in Transition, 1850–1910: Studies in Media and Book History*, Basingstoke: Palgrave, 2001

  Subjugated Knowledges: Journalism, Gender and Literature in the Nineteenth Century, Basingstoke: Macmillan, 1994

Brake, L., Bell, B., and Finkelstein, D. (eds.), *Nineteenth-Century Media and the Construction of Identities*, Basingstoke: Palgrave, 2000

Brake, L., Jones, A. and Madden, L. (eds.), *Investigating Victorian Journalism*, Basingstoke: Macmillan, 1990

Brown, L., *Victorian News and Newspapers*, Oxford: Clarendon, 1985

Conboy, M., *Journalism: A Critical History*, London: Sage, 2004

Fraser, H., Green, S., and Johnston, J., *Gender and the Victorian Periodical*, Cambridge: Cambridge University Press, 2003

Hampton, M., *Visions of the Press in Britain, 1850–1950*, Urbana: University of Illinois Press, 2004

Hughes, L. K., and Lund, M., *The Victorian Serial*, Charlottesville: University of Virginia Press, 1991

Jackson, K., *George Newnes and the New Journalism in Britain, 1880–1910: Culture and Profit*, Aldershot: Ashgate, 2001

Jones, A., *Powers of the Press: Newspapers, Power and the Public in Nineteenth-Century England*, Aldershot: Ashgate, 1996

King, A., and Plunkett, J., *Popular Print Media, 1820–1900*, 3 vols., London: Routledge, 2004

Law, G., *Serializing Fiction in the Victorian Press*, Basingstoke: Macmillan, 2000

Leckie, B., *Culture and Adultery: The Novel, the Newspaper, and the Law, 1857–1914*, Philadelphia: University of Pennsylvania Press, 1999

Liddle, D., 'Salesmen, Sportsmen, Mentors: Anonymity and Mid-Victorian Theories of Journalism', *Victorian Studies*, 41 (1997), 31–68.

Onslow, B., *Women of the Press in Nineteenth-Century Britain*, Basingstoke: Macmillan, 2000

Potter, S. J., *News and the British World: The Emergence of an Imperial Press System 1876–1922*, Oxford: Clarendon, 2003

Shattock, J., *Politics and Reviewers: The Edinburgh and the Quarterly in the Early Victorian Age*, London: Leicester University Press, 1989

Shattock, J., and Wolff, M. (eds.), *The Victorian Periodical Press: Samplings and Soundings*, Leicester: Leicester University Press; Toronto: University of Toronto Press, 1982

Wiener, J. H. (ed.), *Papers for the Millions: The New Journalism in Britain, 1850s to 1914*, Westport: Greenwood, 1988

11. Art

Barlow, P., *Time Present and Time Past: The Art of John Everett Millais*, Aldershot and Burlington, VT, Ashgate, 2005

Barringer, T., *Men at Work: Art and Labour in Victorian Britain*, New Haven and London: Yale University Press, 2005

Cherry, D., *Painting Women: Victorian Women Artists*, London and New York: Routledge, 1993

Corbett, D. P., *The World in Paint: Modern Art and Visuality in England, 1848–1914*, Manchester: Manchester University Press, 2004

McConkey, K., *Memory and Desire: Painting in Britain and Ireland at the Turn of the Twentieth Century*, Aldershot and Burlington, VT, Ashgate, 2002

Mainardi, P., *Art and Politics of the Second Empire: The Universal Expositions of 1855 and 1867*, New Haven: Yale University Press, 1987

Pater, W., *The Renaissance: Studies in Art and Poetry: The 1893 Text*, ed. by D. L. Hill Berkeley: University of California Press, 1980

Prettejohn, E., *Art for Art's Sake: Aestheticism in Victorian Painting*, New Haven: Yale University Press, 2007

The Art of the Pre-Raphaelites, 2nd edn, London: Tate Publishing, 2007

Robins, A. G., *A Fragile Modernism: Whistler and his Impressionist Followers*, New Haven: Yale University Press, 2007

Ruskin, J., *The Works of John Ruskin (Library Edition)*, ed. E. T. Cook and A. Wedderburn, 39 vols., London: Allen, 1903–12

Sherman, C. R., with Holcomb, A. M., *Women as Interpreters of the Visual Arts, 1820–1979*, Westport and London: Greenwood, 1981

Smith, A., *The Victorian Nude: Sexuality, Morality and Art*, Manchester: Manchester University Press, 1996

Waterfield, G. (ed.), *Palaces of Art: Art Galleries in Britain 1790–1990*, exhibition catalogue, London: Dulwich Picture Gallery, 1991

12. Domestic arts

Primary texts

Acton, E., *Modern Cookery for Private Families*, new edn, Lewes: Southover Press, 1993

Alford, Lady M., *Needlework as Art*, London: Sapson Low, Marston, Searle and Rivington, 1886

Beeton, I., *Book of Household Management*, London: S. O. Beeton, 1861

Mrs Beeton's Book of Household Management, ed. Nicola Humble, new edn, Oxford: Oxford World's Classics, 2000

Caddy, F., *Household Organization*, London: Chapman and Hall, 1877

Cassell's Household Guide: Being a Complete Encyclopaedia of Domestic and Social Economy, and Forming a Guide to Every Department of Practical Life, 4 vols., London: Cassell, Peter and Galpin, 1869–71

Caulfield, S. F. A., and Saward, B. C., *The Dictionary of Needlework: An Encyclopaedia of Artistic, Plain, and Fancy Needlework*, 2nd edn, 6 vols., London: A. W. Cowan, 1884–7

Eastlake, C., *Hints on Household Taste in Furniture, Upholstery and Other Details*, 2nd edn, London: Longmans, Green and Co., 1869

Ellis, S., *The Daughters of England: Their Position in Society, Character and Responsibilities*, London: Jackson, 1842

The Mothers of England: Their Influence and Responsibility, London: Fisher, 1844

The Wives of England: Their Relative Duties, Domestic Influence, & Social Obligations, London: Fisher, 1843

The Women of England: Their Social Duties and Domestic Habits, London: Fisher, 1845

Haweis, Mrs [Mary], *The Art of Decoration*, London: Chatto and Windus, 1881

The Art of Housekeeping: A Bridal Garland, London: Sampson Low, Marston, Sewarle and Rivington, 1889

Marshall, A., *Mrs A. B. Marshall's Cookery Book*, London: Simpkin, Marshall, Hamilton, Kent, 1888

Orrinsmith, Mrs [Lucy], *The Drawing-Room, Its Decoration and Furniture*, London: Macmillan, 1877

Ruskin, John, 'Of Queens' Gardens', *Sesame and Lilies: Two Lectures*, London: Smith, Elder, 1865

Soyer, Alexis, *The Gastronomic Regenerator*, London: Simpkin, Marshall, 1846

The Modern Housewife, London: Simpkin, Marshall, 1850

A Shilling Cookery for the People, London: Routledge, 1855

Secondary texts

Alexander, L. M., *Women, Work, and Representation: Needlewomen in Victorian Art and Literature*, Columbus: Ohio University Press, 2003

Altick, R. D., *The Presence of the Present: Topics of the Day in the Victorian Novel*, Columbus: Ohio State University Press, 1991

Armstrong, I., *Victorian Glassworlds: Glass Culture and the Imagination 1830–1880*, Oxford: Oxford University Press, 2008

Attar, D., *Bibliography of Household Books Published in Britain 1800–1914*, London: Prospect Books, 1987

Banham, J., Macdonald, S., and Porter, J., *Victorian Interior Design*, London: Cassell, 1991

Beetham, M., *A Magazine of her Own? Domesticity and Desire in the Woman's Magazine, 1800–1914*, London: Routledge, 1996

Behlmer, G. K., *Friends of the Family: The English Home and its Guardians, 1850–1940*, Stanford: Stanford University Press, 1998

Brett, D., *On Decoration*, Cambridge: Lutterworth, 1992

Briggs, A., *Victorian Things*, London: Batsford, 1988

Bryden, I., and Flood, J. (eds.), *Domestic Space: Reading the Nineteenth-Century Interior*, Manchester: Manchester University Press, 1999

Casteras, S., *Images of Victorian Womanhood in English Art*, London: Associated University Presses, 1987

Chase, K., and Levenson, M., *The Spectacle of Intimacy: A Public Life for the Victorian Family*, Princeton: Princeton University Press, 2000

Cohen, M. F., *Professional Domesticity in the Victorian Novel: Women, Work and Home*, Cambridge: Cambridge University Press, 1998

Dillon, Steve, 'Victorian Interior', *Modern Language Quarterly* 62 (2001), 83–115

Flanders, J., *The Victorian House: Domestic Life from Childbirth to Deathbed*, London: Harper, 2004

Harris, B. (ed.), *Famine and Fashion: Needlewomen in the Nineteenth Century*, Aldershot: Ashgate, 2005

Humble, N., *Culinary Pleasures: Cookbooks and the Transformation of British Food*, London: Faber, 2005

Langland, E., *Nobody's Angels: Middle Class Women and Domestic Ideology in Victorian Culture*, Ithaca: Cornell University Press, 1995

Logan, T., *The Victorian Parlour*, Cambridge: Cambridge University Press, 2001

Miller, A. H., *Novels behind Glass: Commodity Culture and Victorian Narrative*, Cambridge: Cambridge University Press, 1995

Parker, R., *The Subversive Stitch: Embroidery and the Making of the Feminine*, London: The Women's Press, 1984

Schor, N., *Reading in Detail: Aesthetics and the Feminine*, New York: Methuen, 1987

Shaffer, T., 'Book Review: Women and Domestic Culture', *Victorian Literature and Culture*, 35 (2007), 23–46

Stewart, S., *On Longing: Narratives of the Miniature, the Gigantic, the Souvenir and the Collection*, Durham, NC, Duke University Press, 1993

Vickery, A., 'Historiographical Review: Golden Age to Separate Spheres? A Review of the Categories and Chronology of English Women's History', *Historical Journal*, 36 (1993), 383–414

13. Victorian literary theory

Anderson, A., *The Powers of Distance: Cosmopolitanism and the Cultivation of Detachment*, Princeton: Princeton University Press, 2001

Anger, S. (ed.), *Knowing the Past: Victorian Literature and Culture*, Ithaca: Cornell University Press, 2001

  Victorian Interpretation, Ithaca: Cornell University Press, 2005

Baldick, C., *The Social Mission of English Criticism, 1848–1932*, Oxford: Clarendon, 1983

Birch, D., and O'Gorman, F. (eds.), *Ruskin and Gender*, Basingstoke: Palgrave, 2002

Brake, L., *Subjugated Knowledges: Journalism, Gender and Literature in the Nineteenth Century*, New York: New York University Press, 1994

Collins, T. J., and Rundle, V. J., (eds.), *The Broadview Anthology of Poetry and Poetic Theory*, Peterborough, Ont.: Broadview, 1999

Eigner, E. M., and Worth, G. J. (eds.), *Victorian Criticism of the Novel*, New York: Cambridge University Press, 1985

Graff, G., *Professing Literature: An Institutional History*, Chicago: University of Chicago Press, 1987

Helsinger, E., 'Authority, Desire, and the Pleasures of Reading', in John Ruskin, *Sesame and Lilies*, ed. Deborah Epstein Nord, Rethinking the Western Tradition Series, New Haven: Yale University Press, 2002, 113–41

Jones, A. M., *Problem Novels: Victorian Fiction Theorizes the Sensational Self*, Columbus: Ohio State University Press, 2007

Koven, S., 'How the Victorians Read *Sesame and Lilies*', in *Ruskin, Sesame and Lilies*, ed. Nord, 165–204

Levine, C., *The Serious Pleasures of Suspense: Victorian Realism and Narrative Doubt*, Charlottesville: University of Virginia Press, 2003

Nadel, I. B. (ed.), *Victorian Fiction, A Collection of Essays from the Period*, New York: Garland, 1986

Olmstead, J. C. (ed.), *A Victorian Art of Fiction: Essays on the Novel in British Periodicals, 1870–1900*, New York: Garland, 1979

Orel, H., *Victorian Literary Critics: George Henry Lewes, Walter Bagehot, Richard Holt Hutton, Leslie Stephen, Andrew Lang, George Saintsbury, and Edmund Gosse*, New York: St Martin's, 1984

Psomiades, K. A., ' "The Lady of Shalott" and the Critical Fortunes of Victorian Poetry', in Joseph Bristow (ed.), *The Cambridge Companion to Victorian Poetry*, Cambridge: Cambridge University Press, 2000, 25–45

Robbins, B., 'Cosmopolitanism: New and Newer', *boundary*, 2, 34.3 (2007), 47–60

Robinson, S. C. (ed.), *A Serious Occupation: Literary Criticism by Victorian Women Writers*, Peterborough, Ont.: Broadview, 2003

Thomas, D. W., *Cultivating Victorians: Liberal Culture and the Aesthetic*, Philadelphia: University of Pennsylvania Press, 2004

Tucker, H., 'James's Browning Inside Out', *Henry James Review*, 26 (2005), 210–17

Turner, M. W., 'Time, Periodicals, and Literary Studies', *Victorian Periodicals Review*, 39, 4 (2006), 309–16

VanArsdel, R., 'The *Wellesley Index* Forty Years Later (1966–2006)', *Victorian Periodicals Review*, 39, 3 (2006), 257–65

14. The dead

Birch, D., *Our Victorian Education*, Oxford: Blackwell, 2007

Bown, N., *Fairies in Nineteenth-Century Art and Literature*, Cambridge: Cambridge University Press, 2001

Bown, N., Burdett, C., and Thurschwell, P. (eds.), *The Victorian Supernatural*, Cambridge: Cambridge University Press, 2004

Briggs, J., *Night Visitors: The Rise and the Fall of the English Ghost Story*, London: Faber, 1977

Curl, J. S., *The Victorian Celebration of Death*, Newton Abbot: David and Charles, 1972

Dames, N., *Amnesiac Selves: Nostalgia, Forgetting, and British Fiction, 1810–1870*, Oxford: Oxford University Press, 2001

Douglas-Fairhurst, R., *Victorian Afterlives: The Shaping of Influence in Nineteenth-Century Literature*, Oxford: Oxford University Press, 2002

Matthews, S., *Poetical Remains: Poets' Graves, Bodies, and Books in the Nineteenth Century*, Oxford: Oxford University Press, 2004

O'Gorman, F., 'Victorian Literature and Bringing the Body Back from the Dead', in Jane Macnaughton, Ulrike Maude and Corinne Saunders (eds.), *The Body and the Arts*, Basingstoke: Palgrave Macmillan, 2009

'Swinburne's Returns: The Endurance of Writing in *Poems and Ballads, Second Series* (1878)', *The Cambridge Quarterly*, 33 (2004), 197–216.

Owen, A., *The Darkened Room: Women, Power, and Spiritualism in Late Victorian England*, Chicago: University Press of Chicago, 1989

Place of Enchantment: British Occultism and the Culture of the Modern, Chicago: University of Chicago Press, 2004

Rowell, G., *Hell and the Victorians: A Study of the Nineteenth-Century Theological Controversies concerning Eternal Punishment and the Future Life*, Oxford: Clarendon, 1974

Silver, C. G., *Strange and Secret Peoples: Fairies and Victorian Consciousness*, Oxford: Oxford University Press, 1999

Thurschwell, P., *Literature, Technology and Magical Thinking, 1880–1920*, Cambridge: Cambridge University Press, 2001

Wheeler, M., *Death and the Future Life in Victorian Literature and Theology*, Cambridge: Cambridge University Press, 1990

Wolfreys, J., *Victorian Hauntings: Spectrality, Haunting, the Gothic, and the Uncanny in Literature*, Basingstoke: Palgrave, 2001

15. Remembering the Victorians

Anger, S. (ed.), *Knowing the Past: Victorian Literature and Culture*, Ithaca and New York: Cornell University Press, 2001

Clayton, J., *Charles Dickens in Cyberspace: The Afterlife of the Nineteenth Century in Postmodern Culture*, Oxford: Oxford University Press, 2003

Day, G. (ed.), *Varieties of Victorianism: The Uses of a Past*, Basingstoke: Palgrave Macmillan, 1998

Ellis, S., *Virginia Woolf and the Victorians*, Cambridge: Cambridge University Press, 2007

Flint, K., 'Plotting the Victorians: Narrative, Post-Modernism and Contemporary Fiction', in J. B. Bullen (ed.), *Writing and Victorianism*, Harlow: Longman, 1997, 286–305

Gardiner, J., *The Victorians: An Age in Retrospect*, London: Continuum, 2003

Gay, P., Johnston, J., and Waters, C. (eds.), *Victorian Turns, NeoVictorian Returns: Essays on Fiction and Culture*, Newcastle: Cambridge Scholars Publishing, 2008

Gilmour, R., 'Using the Victorians: The Victorian Age in Contemporary Fiction', in A. Jenkins and J. John (eds.), *Re-reading Victorian Fiction*, Basingstoke: Macmillan, 2000

Glavin, J. (ed.), *Dickens on Screen*, Cambridge: Cambridge University Press, 2003

Gutleben, C., *Nostalgic Postmodernism: The Victorian Tradition and the Contemporary British Novel*, Amsterdam: Rodopi, 2002

Hutcheon, L., 'Historiographic Metafiction', in Mark Currie (ed.), *Metafiction*, Harlow: Longman, 1995, 71–91

Joyce, S., *Victorians in the Rearview Mirror*, Athens: Ohio University Press, 2007

Kiely, R., *Reverse Traditions: Postmodern Fictions and the Nineteenth Century Novel*, Cambridge, MA: Harvard University Press, 1993

Kaplan, C., '*Fingersmith*'s Coda: Feminism and Victorian Studies', *Journal of Victorian Culture*, 13 (Spring 2008), 42–55

   Victoriana: Histories, Fictions, Criticism, Edinburgh: Edinburgh University Press, 2007

Krueger, C. L. (ed.), *Functions of Victorian Culture at the Present Time*, Athens: Ohio University Press, 2002

Kucich, J., and Sadoff, D. F. (eds.), *Victorian Afterlife: Postmodern Culture Rewrites the Nineteenth Century*, London: University of Minnesota Press, 2000

Lyotard, J., *The Postmodern Condition; A Report on Knowledge*, Manchester: Manchester University Press, 1992

Mackenzie, J. M. (ed.), *The Victorian Vision: Inventing New Britain*, London, V. & A. Publications, 2001.

Robbins, R., 'Hidden Lives and Ladies' Maids: Margaret Forster's Elizabeth Barrett Brownings', *Women: Cultural Review*, 15, 2 (July 2004), 217–29

Samuel, R., *Theatres of Memory*, vol. I:. *Past and Present in Contemporary Culture*, London: Verso, 1994

Schiller, D., 'The Redemptive Past in the Neo-Victorian Novel', *Studies in the Novel*, 29, 4 (Jan. 1997), 538–60

Stewart, G., 'Film's Victorian Retrofit', *Victorian Studies*, 38, 2 (1995), 153–98

Sweet, M., *Inventing the Victorians*, London: Faber, 2001

Taylor, M., and Wolff, M. (eds.), *The Victorians since 1901: Histories, Representations and Revisions*, Manchester: Manchester University Press, 2004

Yelin, L., 'Cultural Cartography: A. S. Byatt's *Possession* and the Politics of Victorian Studies', *Victorian Newsletter*, 81 (1992), 38–41

Index